Foreign Policy
in Perspective

Foreign Policy in Perspective

Strategy
Adaptation
Decision Making

JOHN P. LOVELL

Indiana University

HOLT, RINEHART AND WINSTON, INC.

*New York · Chicago · San Francisco · Atlanta
Dallas · Montreal · Toronto · London · Sydney*

For Nyla Metcalf Lovell

Preface

The last few years have seen the growth, especially among the young, of a new mood of refusing to entrust the future blindly either to fate or to government. New challenges to the "conventional wisdom" about important policy issues are being expressed. New demands are being made for candor in public discussion of policy. An increasing number of persons are demonstrating a passionate commitment to personal involvement in public affairs. I find these characteristics of the current era tremendously encouraging.

But the risks of the new mood should not be overlooked. At a time when each of us is being called upon to stand up and be counted on issues that are intensely controversial, there is a temptation for us to make such a great emotional investment in particular policy positions with which we agree that we close our minds defensively to contrary opinions and evidence.

There is also a temptation to embrace simplistic slogans as surrogates for thoughtful analysis of the troublesome complexities of political reality.

This is a book for those who are willing to make an intellectual as well as an emotional commitment to involvement in foreign affairs. It is a book for those who are concerned about where American foreign-policy decisions may lead us, but who also have the intellectual tenacity to commit themselves to rigorous analysis in order to gain a sound understanding of foreign policy and a firm foundation for policy assessment. It is a book devoted not only to the difficult empirical questions of how and why various foreign policies have been pursued, but also to the compelling normative questions about what is "good" or "bad" about various policies or about the way the policy process itself operates and how criteria for such a moral judgment are determined.

This is not a book of answers but of how answers are found. It is distinguished from most other foreign-policy texts in its emphasis on the logical requisites of systematic explanation and on the development and utilization of hypotheses and "narrow-gauge" or "middle-gauge" theory as a framework within which the "facts" at one's command can be ordered and interpreted. However, the book is not an abstract exercise in theory building. Rather, theoretical concepts and propositions are consistently related to the concrete reality of the American foreign-policy experience. Pertinent and, hopefully, vivid examples are employed to highlight the drama and the significance that foreign policy plays in all our lives.

The book is designed not only to assist the reader to achieve clarity and independence in his own assessment of foreign-policy phenomena, but also to provide guideposts that will enable him to utilize effectively other writings about foreign policy. The more advanced a field of study becomes, the more difficult it is for laymen to comprehend analyses by specialists in that field. Because the study of foreign policy remains relatively underdeveloped, nonspecialists are likely to find the literature of the field far less forbidding than the body of specialized writings found, for instance, in the physical sciences. However, the relatively nontechnical and nonmathematical terminology characteristic of foreign-policy analyses can be deceptive in its familiarity. Analysts approach their investigations from a variety of perspectives; but theoretical reference points that determine which questions will be asked in the gathering of data and underlying assumptions that are central to the interpretation of data often are not articulated. Thus, the nonspecialist can be lulled into uncritical acceptance of conclusions that he would question if he recognized the underlying framework of analysis; or conversely, the nonspecialist can miss significant insights in an analysis through ignorance of the theoretical context from which the analysis emerged.

I have not attempted to provide an exhaustive survey of the theoretical foundations or pretensions of professional studies of foreign policy. Instead, I have organized the book around three analytical perspectives that are especially prominent in the study of foreign policy: the perspective of strategy; the perspective of adaptation, or historical dynamics; and the perspective of decision making. The sequence in which the perspectives are introduced should acquaint the reader at the outset with some of the analytically important features of the nation-state system. The semianarchic quality of this system is a prime working assumption underlying most strategic analyses. Moving to the perspective of adaptation, the reader explores the evolution of the general orientation of the United States toward its world environment across broad spans of time. The transition to the third perspective, that of decision making, is one in which the scope of analysis is greatly reduced, allowing the reader to focus on the structure and process of foreign policy on a day-to-day level. The potential advantages of each of the three perspectives, as well as their limitations, are also discussed.

If the book in its finished form comes close to realizing the objectives that I have established, credit is due first of all to several hundred college students whose interest and concern in foreign policy over the past five years have sustained my own interest and commitment, and whose questioning and criticism have tested and sharpened my ideas. Those who have played a part include students from the University of Wisconsin-Milwaukee at a summer session in 1964, students from Indiana University in Bloomington over a period of several years, and a number of lively young women from Vassar College during 1968–1969. Graduate teaching assistants at Indiana University have also provided "feedback" from their students and comments of their own that have been valuable to me. These include Susan Stoudinger, Dick Boris, Fariborz Fatemi, Bob Gage, Robin Hunter, Arnold Leder, Slava Lubomudrov, David Perry, Boris Severenko, James T. Thomson, Tom Trout, and Marco Walshok.

At an early stage, I received encouragement to develop the book, as well as useful comments on a prospectus for it, from James L. McCamy, Bernard C. Cohen, Sven Groennings, Leroy N. Rieselbach, and Philip S. Kronenberg. Robert W. Hattery made the suggestion, which I have tried to follow, that I design a book that would be of interest and use not only to college students but also to other adults who are concerned about foreign affairs and who would like to organize more systematically their own thinking about foreign policy.

The entire manuscript in draft was reviewed by Jackson A. Giddens,

Roger Hilsman, J. David Singer, and Pio Uliassi, each of whom made perceptive and detailed criticisms and suggestions that I have found invaluable.

I was exceptionally fortunate to have the help of two persons who were unusually competent typists and also possessed knowledge and judgment upon which I drew in modifying or revising various passages in the manuscript. Lois Payne, a former Peace Corps volunteer in Brazil, and Martha Kenerson, Vassar College '71, did the typing. Jane Mullen, Vassar '71, served as a skillful and diligent research assistant. Karen Tkach helped with the proofreading, and Judy Granbois with the preparation of the index.

In addition to those who have been specifically identified, those who have contributed to the evolution and refinement of my ideas over the years cannot be fully documented. The footnotes provide some indication of my intellectual debt to others. In addition, I must single out Harry M. Scoble, Jr., who, more than anyone else, opened the door to modern political science for me.

Finally, I want to acknowledge the contribution of my wife, Joanne, my daughter, Sara, and my son, David, whose diversionary tactics may in some sense have prolonged the writing schedule, but certainly made it a more enjoyable one.

J. P. L.

Bloomington, Indiana
March 1970

Contents

Part I

Foundations
for Analysis

The demands upon American foreign-policy makers in the 1970s are awesome, in spite of the impressive human and material resources that the United States is able to devote to foreign affairs. Policy makers now have at their disposal more information about more parts of the world than ever before; but the world has become increasingly complex and difficult to understand. In the "computer age," the ability of policy makers to process information and to react to world events swiftly is vastly superior to that in any prior period; yet the pace of change has accelerated, confounding the perpetual problem of accurately identifying the pattern of events while demanding still more rapid reaction time. Furthermore, the computer age is also the age of nuclear weapons and missiles; thus, not only is there less time now for making important decisions but also the possible costs of misjudgment are greater.

1

Unprecedented demands are being made not only upon the practitioners of foreign policy, but also upon concerned observers. Given the deep involvement of the United States in international affairs in recent decades and the sizeable portion of the budget committed to foreign and defense policy support, every American is affected by important foreign-policy decisions in a personal way (for instance, through military service or through taxes). Greater numbers of Americans than ever before are receiving the education, the travel, and the exposure to news commentary that instill an awareness of world events. However, the pace of change coupled with the complexity of events impose a challenge that overwhelms many concerned observers of foreign policy. In response, they address issues posed in misleading or incomplete terms; they accept simplistic theories about why events occurred; they embrace illusory panaceas for problems confronting the nation.

The challenge of seeking accurate answers and sound solutions to meaningful foreign-policy problems is one that can be met successfully, however, even in the face of complexity and change. In Part I, we identify more explicitly the nature of the challenge and the requisites of sound foreign-policy analysis (Chapter 1). We also introduce three distinctive perspectives that can be fruitfully employed in the analysis of foreign-policy phenomena (Chapter 2). The discussion in Part I provides a foundation upon which we shall build in subsequent chapters.

1

Foreign-Policy Analysis

The Nature of the Task

The Challenge
of Foreign-Policy Analysis

Many persons would contend that if the practitioners find foreign-policy phenomena difficult to cope with, then the laymen must admit total inability to gain an understanding of, or to make sound independent judgments about, foreign policy. Not only are foreign-policy phenomena complex and constantly in flux, but also, many important decisions are veiled in secrecy. The layman, according to the skeptic's view of his analytical ability, suffers from an irremediable liability in foreign affairs—he cannot know what goes on behind closed doors in many key policy conferences, and he is unable to study classified papers, reports, and documents. In regard to the intricacies of foreign policy, some say, in short, "leave it to the experts."

Leaving it to the experts, however, in the

sense of invariably deferring to the judgment of those in positions of official responsibility, is a kind of intellectual abdication that few persons of democratic temperament can make. Complex as foreign-policy issues in fact are, only the timorous observer is likely to conclude that he cannot ultimately become well-informed about foreign policy. And only the naïve person will conclude that if he left it to the experts, he could trust in the infallibility of their judgment. As suggested later in the chapter, in the discussion of the interplay of values and beliefs, policy maker and layman alike are fallible in gathering and interpreting foreign-policy data. Rather than abandoning the task altogether, however, the layman should recognize not only his limitations but also his potential for compensating for these limitations.

Problems of Access to Data

The layman is obviously limited, for example, in his access to (and often in his ability to utilize) relevant technical data. Details of the construction and the capability of American and foreign weapons systems, aircraft, missiles, and the like are of this sort. Many of these details are made public in popular magazines or professional journals, but other details are classified and therefore generally not available. One might also properly regard as technical such details as the number of Chinese technicians and military advisers serving in Vietnam or, for that matter, the numbers of American technicians and military advisers working in Thailand. Although sometimes figures of this sort escape from independent sources or become available from official sources, often they remain secret.

Because of his limitations in this area, therefore, the layman needs to be cautious about making foreign-policy judgments that are heavily dependent upon technical questions. Furthermore, he can be rightly skeptical of those whose attempts to persuade him to accept a certain point of view rest heavily on the "intellectual terrorism" of a barrage of technical facts and figures to which he himself has no direct access. But quantitative details are often less important than qualitative information, and on questions of the latter sort, the attentive layman is frequently able to make well-informed judgments. For example, in the case of the war in Vietnam, although the layman may have been at a loss to know with any confidence the number of North Vietnamese who infiltrated south of the 17th parallel during any given month, he has certainly had adequate information at his disposal to judge whether the conflict in Vietnam was properly conceived of as "aggression" by one nation-state against another, as a civil war, or as something else. Again, although he may lack information about the disposition of nuclear weapons to American military units in various parts of the world, he has access to sufficient information to hold an informed opinion whether the employment of nuclear weapons in a particular conflict would be desirable or not.

With regard to the short-range plans and intentions of various foreign governments, political parties, and other political cliques and factions, the layman is also often at a disadvantage in comparison to the government official. Major news media abroad may speculate about such matters, but clearly those in government who have access to paid informants and other secret sources abroad, to their own embassy and military personnel, as well as to public news media, are normally in a better position than the layman to know whether the Hanoi regime really sent an emissary to a foreign nation in an effort to begin peace negotiations, whether Soviet leaders really refused to meet with President Johnson to discuss the Middle East crisis in 1967, and so forth. Perhaps it would be more accurate to say, in relation to examples such as those just given, that official policy makers are usually in a position to make an educated guess based on more of the relevant information than is available to the average layman. One should not suppose, however, that policy makers are dealing with questions that normally can be answered with great certainty.

Indeed, the importance of classified information in revealing short-term trends in world events should not be overemphasized. If short-range plans of a foreign government or political faction remain hidden from the view of public news media and the unofficial sources upon which an educated layman must rely, then such plans will often remain unknown to American government intelligence sources too. In fact, American government intelligence about day-to-day activities in most political systems derives heavily from sources that are available to enterprising and attentive laymen. Moreover, a comparison of the respective assets of the layman and the policy maker shows that the layman has resources available to him that compare very favorably with those of the policy maker in making informed judgments about long-range goals of nation-states and about general trends in world affairs. If he consults a sufficient number of available sources, he can become well-informed, for example, about the roots of the Sino-Soviet dispute and the general directions of relations between these two communist powers; he can have informed opinions about the future of NATO, now that SHAPE headquarters has been "evicted" from France; and he can analyze the probable consequences of future population projections for world affairs in relation to the pattern of resource depletion. In other words, although the layman can seldom be confident that the sources available to him, such as the daily newscast, reveal more than a small fraction of the information essential for correctly interpreting a contemporary event, if he is an intelligent and diligent student of foreign affairs, he can interpret *patterns* by which interrelated events acquire particular significance, and he can identify historical, political, economic, and social *roots* from which contemporary problems have grown.

Access to data dealing with American plans and intentions presents a third problem for the layman. The experienced lay analyst may speculate that a particular American military exercise involving the airlift of an entire division from the United States to Germany and back again within a few days has been designed as a "trial balloon" for the eventual substantial withdrawal of American forces from Europe. Or he may speculate that a seemingly "tough" address on public policy by the President was supplemented by undisclosed overtures to the Hanoi regime offering a compromise peace settlement in Vietnam. He may also speculate that the CIA had a major hand in political developments in a *coup* or attempted *coup* in a particular Latin American country. Over a period of time, the ability of the layman in making accurate interpretations of events such as those just described may become pretty good. With few exceptions, however (among which one would cite the Bay of Pigs invasion by the CIA, where originally secret planning became widely known and discussed in public news media), the layman, no matter how experienced and astute, cannot know with certainty (at the time, at least) how correct his speculation is. Only those responsible for making policy decisions and implementing them will know the exact plans and intentions of the government, and then, not even all of the policy makers may know. For example, military personnel participating in an airlift such as that described earlier might not be informed of the political rationale for the exercise.

Once again, however, as with the categories of data discussed previously, although the layman needs to recognize his limitations in dealing with questions of American plans and intentions, he need by no means be at a total loss about such questions. If he understands the broad outlines of American foreign-policy strategy in various parts of the world and has a good working knowledge of the general structure and process of American foreign-policy decisions, he is likely to be able to fill the gaps in his knowledge of particular plans and intentions with considerable reliability. Moreover, given a solid foundation of knowledge in American foreign-policy strategies and decision making, the layman can, over time, assess the credibility of various sources of information. By comparing what has been predicted or promised by government officials or other observers of foreign policy with what has actually happened, and by comparing different sources of information or interpretations of a given event, the layman can learn to discount certain sources or accounts and to utilize others more heavily.

Perception and Interpretation of Foreign-Policy Phenomena: Interplay of Values and Beliefs

Although problems of access to relevant data can be overcome by the concerned observer in his efforts to comprehend and to assess foreign-policy phenomena, other obstacles remain. Gaining access to relevant data often is a less formidable barrier to understanding than are various preconceived biases and beliefs that blur or distort one's images of reality; we all have areas of concern in which preexisting values and beliefs prevent us from being as objective as possible in our investigations.

The belief (cognitive) and evaluative (affective) components of the perception and interpretation of reality are closely intertwined. In the first place, our beliefs influence our likes and dislikes. Advertisers of course rely on such influences when they market products, and governments employ analogous techniques to promote their policies. Especially in wartime, adversaries are depicted as immoral, but allies as virtuous and courageous; government officials are portrayed as wise, selfless, and tireless on behalf of the societal welfare.

Of course, attempts to persuade may be factual as well as fabricated. The point to be made, however, is that our beliefs, whether well-founded or not, influence our value preferences. In Chapter 2 we shall describe events from the Korean War. Whether names such as Harry Truman, Dean Acheson, Douglas MacArthur, George C. Marshall, or Joseph R. McCarthy evoke enthusiasm, disgust, or some other emotion is likely to depend heavily upon beliefs that we maintain about what each of these men did or failed to do. Whether the Korean War or the more recent war in Vietnam arouses in us anger, sorrow, or pride depends largely upon our beliefs about the events that have occurred and about decisions that have been made during the war.

Perhaps more interesting and significant than the influence of beliefs upon value preferences, however, is the influence that value preferences have upon beliefs. The average individual's level of information about most issues of American foreign policy is low rather than high, yet he often formulates opinions even in the absence of factual information. Although it is true, of course, that in virtually every national opinion poll on foreign-policy issues a rather sizable group of those polled has expressed no opinion on one or more issues. It is also true, however, that on most issues, most people polled have expressed opinions; moreover, in those cases when polling has been accompanied by more extensive interviewing, it has been apparent that opinions are often based on minimal amounts of information. For instance, individuals took sides on the issue whether President Truman or General MacArthur was right during the Korean War controversy without knowing in any detail the policy positions of the two men. Individuals express opinions about whether or not the United States government should encourage or permit trade with eastern European countries without knowing the current legislative restrictions on trade and without any idea of what the economic effects of broadened trade would be. They shout agreement or disagreement with a political candidate who argues that foreign aid to Latin American nations should be reduced, although they lack knowledge of how much aid Latin American nations receive, how the aid is used, and what consequences could be anticipated if aid were reduced or eliminated.

In the absence of factual information, preexisting values and beliefs about other phenomena provide cues to which individuals respond in filling out their belief system. Stereotyping is one familiar device to which people resort in constructing belief images in conformity to existing values and biases. A pertinent example is the research findings of a social psychologist who has compared the views that Americans have of citizens of the Soviet Union with those that Soviet citizens have of Americans. Speaking both Russian and English fluently, he was able to interview a large number of Soviet citizens and a large number of Americans, and his interviews revealed a fascinating pattern of beliefs. The views that citizens of the Soviet Union had of Americans were essentially a mirror image of the views that Americans had of the Soviets. The pattern was one of mutual suspicion and distrust, generating a series of similar beliefs, such as the following: the Soviets (Americans) are aggressors; the Soviet (American) government exploits and deceives its people; the Soviet (American) people have no real emotional commitment to their government; the Soviets (Americans) cannot be trusted; Soviet (American) policies are unrealistic and irresponsible.[1]

Granted that the average person falls into a variety of intellectual traps, such as stereotyping and other practices that reveal that his values are distorting his beliefs, what about the person who is above average in various ways? For instance, what about the individual who is involved more deeply than the average person in foreign affairs or has an above-

[1] Urie Bronfenbrenner, "The Mirror Image in Soviet-American Relations: A Social Psychologist's Report," *Journal of Social Issues,* 17 (1961), 45–46.

average education? What about the individual who has traveled more than the average person? Do such individuals possess a capacity for objectivity in the perception and interpretation of foreign policy that the average person lacks? Are their opinions based solidly on the facts, uncontaminated by bias or preconceived images of reality?

In the first place, we know that the probability that one will have any opinion on a foreign-policy issue is higher among those with a college education than it is among those with only a high-school education. Among those with only a grammar-school education, still fewer are likely to have opinions on foreign-policy issues. We know also that the more formal education one has received, the more likely he is to express his opinions in ways that have an impact on the policy process—writing letters to his congressman, organizing citizens groups on behalf of a particular candidate, writing letters to the local newspaper, and so forth.[2] More pertinent to the point at hand, both formal education and informal experiences that increase exposure to and familiarity with foreign-policy issues are important bases for reducing one's susceptibility to error.

Nevertheless, it is interesting and significant to note that even with more education and more experience relevant to foreign affairs, individuals tend to perceive and to interpret issues and events selectively. Even those with relatively extensive education and experience tend to look at the world through a lens colored by their value preferences and prior beliefs. American business executives, for example, display an interest in foreign-policy issues and a level of information that exceed those of the average citizen. Moreover, they consult news sources with greater regularity than the average citizen; almost all the executives included in a study a few years ago indicated that they read at least one daily newspaper regularly, and in most cases, two or three newspapers regularly. (Nearly half read the *Wall Street Journal* daily, and roughly a third read *The New York Times* regularly.) Yet, authors of the study found that even among executives, with exposure to reading, discussion, and foreign travel much more frequent than is characteristic of the population at large, ". . . exposure to rebutting evidence was much less than one might expect and . . . systematic forces worked to favor exposure to reinforcing information."[3]

This conclusion highlights a general human inclination to expose oneself to viewpoints that are comfortably familiar and to avoid or repress

[2] The relationship between education and public opinion is discussed in V. O. Key, Jr., *Public Opinion and American Democracy* (New York: Knopf, 1961), pp. 315–343.

[3] Raymond A. Bauer, Ithiel de Sola Pool, and Lewis A. Dexter, *American Business and Public Policy* (New York: Atherton, 1963), p. 241.

those that challenge one's values and beliefs. The person of conservative disposition, for instance, might well turn regularly to the editorial pages of the *Chicago Tribune* or the *Indianapolis Star* for commentary on current issues of foreign policy, but it is unlikely that he would also regularly consult the foreign-affairs coverage in *The New Republic*. Conversely, the self-proclaimed radical might well be a devotee of the writings of Herbert Marcuse; it would be rare, however, if he were also to follow closely the writings of William Buckley, Jr.

It is not only laymen whose vision is limited and who perceive and interpret phenomena selectively on the basis of their values and beliefs. Policy makers, too, are susceptible to intellectual blindness and to distortions of view; historical and contemporary examples of the judgments of policy makers being distorted through the interplay of their values and beliefs are abundant. Perhaps the classic case is the multitude of conflicting images of reality held by various European powers leading to the outbreak of World War I, although similar examples from the American experience also are numerous.[4] A number of examples of the dynamic relationship between values and beliefs in the actions of American policy makers will be given in later chapters.

It is appropriate at this point to summarize the discussion of the past several pages. We have identified two major obstacles to objective and accurate analysis of foreign policy by the layman: the difficulty in gaining access to relevant data and the interplay of values and beliefs that can lead to misperception and distorted judgments. Emphasis has been placed on the observable fact that none of us, from the most uneducated layman to the most knowledgeable policy maker, is able to cope with the overwhelming maze of detail in the world around us with complete thoroughness and objectivity. Each of us is attentive to some aspects of the dynamic reality of world events and not to others. Our perception of phenomena is the result of a filtering process. Some aspects of the phenomena within the range of our observation are admitted without

[4] The conflicting images of reality held by leaders of the various European powers at the time are vividly depicted in Barbara Tuchman, *The Guns of August* (New York: Crowell-Collier-Macmillan, 1962). Professor Robert North and associates at Stanford University have been engaged for a number of years in rigorous analyses of the perceptions and attitudes of the leaders during this critical period. A brief recent article by Professor North that summarizes some of his findings is "Perception and Action in the 1914 Crisis," *Journal of International Affairs*, 21 (1967), 103–122. The same issue of the journal contains a number of other pertinent articles; of particular contemporary interest is the analysis by Ralph K. White, "Misperception of Aggression in Viet Nam," pp. 123–140. For a more recent extension of the analysis, see White's *Nobody Wanted War—Misperception in Vietnam and Other Wars* (New York: Doubleday, 1968).

distortion through the "filter" to be recorded, classified, or otherwise utilized in the cumulative process of learning. Other aspects are admitted but distorted as the filtering process twists information to make it accord with our emotional and intellectual predispositions. Still other aspects, which are too threatening to our egos to be emotionally tolerable, are rejected completely and omitted in our picture of reality as if they did not exist at all.[5]

Meeting the Challenge

The formidable obstacles to analysis that have been described will discourage the fainthearted; however, this book is directed to those who wish to meet the challenge of gaining an ability to explain the events of American foreign policy accurately and to assess foreign policy objectively. To the individual who would meet the challenge, recognition of obstacles to analysis will serve as a useful first step toward analytical competence. The continuing journey, although by no means effortless, is one that persons sensitive to the drama of foreign policy will find exciting and one that those who value intellectual accomplishment will find rewarding. The primary objective of the remainder of the book is to provide guidelines to help the reader (1) to distinguish meaningful questions from trivial ones, (2) to recognize the logical and empirical requisities of adequate explanation and of sound evaluation of foreign-policy phenomena, and (3) to move from the assessment of particular facts to the formulation of generalizations of a higher order about foreign policy. The book is not designed as a set of answers; rather, it is designed to assist the reader in formulating answers of his own to meaningful questions.

A secondary, closely related objective of the book is to assist the reader in utilizing effectively other writings about American foreign

[5] For the reader who wishes to pursue further topics that relate to the processes described here, a small sampler of a vast body of relevant literature can be suggested. An excellent description and analysis of leading theories of attitude change is provided in Roger Brown, "Models of Attitude Change," *New Directions in Psychology* (New York: Holt, Rinehart and Winston, Inc., 1962), pp. 1–85. A useful and reasonably brief discussion of the psychological functions of attitudes is provided by Daniel Katz, "The Functional Approach to the Study of Attitudes," *Public Opinion Quarterly*, 2 (1960), 163–204. There are several helpful analyses of attitudes as they relate specifically to American politics; two recent examples are Robert E. Lane and David O. Sears, *Public Opinion* (Englewood Cliffs, N.J.: Prentice-Hall, Inc., 1964) and Lewis A. Froman, Jr., *People and Politics* (Englewood Cliffs, N.J.: Prentice-Hall, Inc., 1962). As applied to the foreign-policy process, see Herbert C. Kelman, ed., *International Behavior* (New York: Holt, Rinehart and Winston, Inc., 1965), especially the essays in pt. I.

policy. Although the study of foreign policy is still in its youth in terms of theoretical development, a vast body of descriptive and interpretive accounts of various facets of American foreign policy already exists; if used with discrimination, such accounts can greatly enrich one's understanding of foreign policy. No attempt will be made in subsequent chapters to provide the reader with a comprehensive survey of writings on foreign policy, but as the reader becomes familiar on his own with other writings about various facets of foreign policy, the analytical framework developed here can help him (1) to recognize the kinds of questions and issues that are being explored in a given article or book and those that are being ignored, (2) to appraise critically the adequacy of conclusions that are drawn in a given investigation, and (3) to relate the isolated findings of a given study to a broader body of knowledge about foreign policy.

Moreover, if the framework developed here is a solid one, it should have utility not only for analysis of American foreign policy, but also for analysis of the foreign policies of other nation-states and for comparative foreign-policy analysis. Throughout the book, however, the process of developing this framework is closely tied to the American foreign-policy experience, because it is that experience with which the author and most readers are most familiar. Although no attempt is made to be comprehensive in describing interesting and important episodes in American foreign policy, nor to proceed chronologically, at every stage in the development of the analytical framework abundant examples from the American experience will be used to illuminate the particular analytical points that are made.

In the remainder of Chapter 1, we shall lay the foundation for the framework by identifying the interrelated tasks of such analysis, by distinguishing among various kinds of questions that might be posed in analysis in fulfillment of the analytical tasks, and by describing in a preliminary way the stages by which systematic analysis proceeds. In Chapter 2, we shall introduce and illustrate three alternative perspectives for analysis of foreign policy. The format of the remainder of the book is designed to emphasize (in Parts II, III, and IV) these three distinctive analytical perspectives and also (especially in Part V) the interrelationships between empirical and normative inquiry.

Interrelated Tasks of Analysis

As concerned observers of American foreign policy, we may be interested in trying to explain events that have already occurred or with predicting what is likely to occur in the future. We are likely to compare foreign-policy decisions made in the past with our notions of what should have been done and to speculate not only on what might occur in the future, but also on what actions ought to be taken. For sound analysis, it is useful to have an understanding of how these analytical tasks—explanation, prediction, evaluation, and prescription—are related to one another.

Explanation and Prediction

Sometimes one is able to make fairly accurate predictions without being able to explain the phenomenon that was predicted. For instance, one might predict accurately that the suicide rate in New York City would be higher in the summer months than in the winter without being able to explain *why* suicide rates increase in the summer. Or one might predict accurately that at least one military *coup* would occur in Latin America within the next year without understanding why military *coups d'état* occur. However, in both of the examples cited and in others that come to mind, although prediction does not presuppose an ability to explain, it is based upon a projection from past trends. Statistics from prior years reveal that suicide rates increase in the summer; therefore, it seems reasonable to suppose that suicide rates will increase during the next summer. Military *coups* have occurred with great frequency in Latin America in the past; therefore, it seems reasonable to predict that they will continue to occur in the immediate future.

Although projections from past trends provide some basis for predicting, even without being able to explain the trends, obviously an accurate understanding of the trends increases the probability that one will project accurately from a given set of data. One who simply seized upon interesting data about the length of names of presidential candidates in the twentieth century would have concluded in 1964 that Goldwater would defeat Johnson; since in every previous election in the twentieth century with only one exception (Taft's defeat of Bryan in 1908), of the candidates from the two major political parties, the one with the longest surname had won. However, nearly everyone who had some understanding of the nature of the American political process and of the state of the electorate in 1964 was able to predict accurately that the outcome of the 1964 election would bring Johnson, not Goldwater, to office. Prediction invariably involves making inferences about the future based upon observations of patterns and trends in the past. However, if one is able not only to observe what has occurred in the past, but also to explain past occurrences, he increases his ability to avoid drawing spurious inferences.

One might be able to explain, nevertheless, without being able to predict. For instance, from a thorough examination of available data, one might arrive at a reasonably accurate explanation of why the Korean War occurred, yet such an explanation would not necessarily enable one to predict accurately when and where future wars would occur. Prediction is difficult in human affairs, even when extensive study provides explanation about a fund of past events and decisions. Change is the most evident characteristic of international politics in the twentieth century; consequently, the observer as well as the practitioner of contemporary foreign policy must admit to a high degree of unpredictability in world affairs.

Nonetheless, although it is true that "the unexpected is to be expected" in many aspects of foreign policy, it is by no means true that foreign-policy phenomena are totally unpredictable. Those who are particularly awed by chance and unpredictability in world affairs are likely to emphasize that every historical event is unique, since the precise circumstances and factors that combined to produce the event are likely never to be exactly replicated. It is also true, however, that every event and every decision in foreign policy are likely to have certain characteristics in common with past events and decisions. There are patterns among events and regularities of human behavior that occur in foreign policy as in other areas of human endeavor. The search for such patterns and regularities is central to systematic analysis in the social sciences.

Explanation and Evaluation; Prediction and Prescription

The interplay of values and beliefs in one's thought processes was stressed earlier in the chapter. It is also true that analytically the processes of seeking to evaluate a particular foreign-policy phenomenon and of seeking to establish the facts about it are closely related.

Whether value questions or explanatory questions come first in one's analysis is a moot problem. Sometimes one begins with a set of value concerns that in turn make one curious about explaining various phenomena that relate to the values. At the onset of the Korean War, for instance, thousands of American men who had already served in the armed forces during World War II were recalled to active duty from the inactive reserves. A typical and understandable reaction of these men was, "Now, why in hell am *I* being called to serve again?" The value judgment implicit in this question in turn raises another that requires explanation; a feeling of personal grievance leads to curiosity about the policy that produced it.

On the other hand, often explanatory questions are the beginning of an investigation and lead to evaluative questions. The question of why the Truman administration sent troops to Korea leads the concerned observer almost inescapably to ask whether the decision was a good or bad one. The desirability of a decision or action, however, is determined from an assessment of the consequences; thus, one is led from evaluation back to explanation, in order to determine what the consequences were of a given decision or action.

It is possible to explain without making value judgments, although, as suggested above, explanatory questions usually lead naturally to evaluative ones. However, knowledgeable evaluation is invariably dependent upon adequate explanation. To decide whether the decision of the Truman administration to send troops to Korea was good or bad, it is essential to investigate its consequences. To make a judgment about whether CIA influence on American foreign policy has been beneficial or detrimental, it is imperative to determine how much influence the CIA has wielded and what kinds of consequences have stemmed from it. Actually, assessment of a decision or act requires not only a determination of the consequences, but also a comparison of the actual consequences with the probable ones if an alternative course of action had been selected. Assessment of the performance or influence of a given agency or institution requires not only the identification of how it is organized and how it relates to the overall foreign-policy process, but also a consideration of the probable consequences of relevant alternative forms of structuring foreign policy. In short, what is required in the evaluation of past decisions, programs, and organizations is a comparison of what was with what might have been.

The relationship between prediction and prescription is analogous to that between explanation and evaluation. Curiosity about the present and future leads us to attempt to predict the consequences of present events and the decisions to be made in the future. Our value preferences lead us naturally from the question of what will be to our preference about what should be. But in order to prescribe future courses of action, we must ponder their probable consequences. Thus, sound prescription rests upon accurate prediction, just as knowledgeable evaluation rests upon accurate explanation. Moreover, just as assessment of a past decision requires a comparison of what was with what might have been, assessment of future decisions and actions requires one to compare the consequences of a prescribed course of action with the probable consequences of alternative courses.

Most of the following text will be concerned with the explanation of American foreign policy. We shall save consideration of the normative dimension of the study of foreign policy—evaluation and prescription—until Part V because the importance of the topic requires a solid groundwork of a discussion of explanation to be laid first. In this way, the reader will have an opportunity to consider knowledgeably what the important value questions are in relation to the American foreign-policy experience and what norms for evaluation are appropriate.

The Kinds of Questions Posed in Analysis[6]

In pursuit of any of the various interrelated analytical tasks already described, one might pose various kinds of questions. It is useful to clarify distinctions between the kinds of questions posed, because the requisites of adequate analysis vary according to the questions one chooses to investigate.

Analysis of Purpose

First of all, as concerned observers of foreign policy, we are sometimes interested in knowing the purpose of a given foreign-policy program, the mission of an organization, or the motivation of a certain foreign-policy actor. In attempting to answer questions such as these, we are essentially trying to adopt the position of a policy maker, to see things as he does, to view an organization or program from the vantage point of its official doctrine. This kind of analysis is *analysis of purpose*, or, more technically, teleological explanation.

Although each of the questions just suggested requires explanation, obviously only a slight change of phraseology would change the analytical task involved from explanation to any of the other analytical tasks discussed above: evaluation, prediction, or prescription. A question, for instance could be phrased, "Have the purposes of the foreign-aid program been appropriate ones?" to focus on evaluation of the program rather than on explanation of it. Or the question could be phrased, "What will be the purposes of the foreign-aid program in the coming decade?" to change the task to prediction. A prescriptive task would be required by the question, "What should be the purpose of the foreign-aid program in the future?" In other words, analysis of purpose may include explanation, evaluation, prediction, and prescription.

[6] The discussion that follows is intended only to suggest some rough distinctions between various kinds of analytical questions. For a more complete and exacting discussion than the one provided here, see Ernest Nagel, *The Structure of Science* (New York: Harcourt, 1961), esp. pp. 23–25. See also Eugene J. Meehan, *The Theory and Method of Political Analysis* (Homewood, Illinois: Dorsey, 1965), chap. 4.

Analysis of Cause and Effect

Often, however, we are interested not in what a given program is supposed to achieve according to official doctrine, but what the observable accomplishments, failures, and consequences of the program have been. In addition, we may be interested not in the mission of a certain organization, but rather in the observable effects of its actual activities, extracurricular as well as prescribed. We may also be interested not in trying to probe the inner thoughts of a given foreign-policy actor to ascertain the goals he sought in a specific action, but to identify factors that brought about the action. Answers to this second category of questions require analysis of *cause and effect*.

Although each of the illustrative questions again requires explanation, we may note without further elaboration that analysis of cause and effect may include any or all of the analytical tasks previously mentioned: explanation, evaluation, prediction, prescription.

The term "cause" has fallen into disrepute among some social scientists in recent years because of the difficulty in establishing definite causality for complex social phenomena. If one recognizes this difficulty, however, and the dangers of attributing a spurious causal interpretation to associations between observed phenomena, one need not shy away completely from thinking in terms of cause and effect. Indeed, the concept of causality is useful if one thinks of it as a search for *preconditions* and *precipitants*, and if one recognizes that we are much more likely to have success in specifying the preconditions for the occurrence of various foreign-policy phenomena than we are in specifying the factors or events that precipitate the phenomena. The distinction between preconditions and precipitants can be made briefly in relation to an illustrative analytical problem: explaining the outbreak of World War I. Factors such as the rigidity of the alliance structure in Europe at the time, a naval and arms race between Germany and Great Britain especially, and the existence in several of the major powers of war plans, the success of which was predicated on rapid implementation at the first sign of an outbreak of war, might be viewed as conditions that made war probable in 1914. The assassination of Austrian Archduke Franz Ferdinand in Sarajevo, on the other hand, was one of those quirks of history that, given the existing preconditions, had repercussions far beyond those that might have prevailed in any other circumstances. In a highly volatile situation, the assassination was a precipitant that brought about a war the magnitude and duration of which none of the parties to the war had anticipated. The distinction between preconditions and precipitants allows us to avoid the confusion of treating the assassination of Archduke Ferdinand as a cause of World War I in the same sense that the rigidity of the alliance structure in Europe at the time was a cause. Because it is the nature of precipitants to be unusual events or even chance occurrences, one can rarely predict exactly when a particular foreign-policy phenomenon, such as a war, will occur. However, social scientists have had more success in identifying the preconditions that make a particular phenomenon probable; it may be possible, moreover, to identify the range of possible precipitants that, given a set of preconditions, will bring about a particular event, act, or decision.

Analysis of Structure and Process

Sometimes we are interested neither in the formal purpose of a given program nor in its consequences, but rather in the way the program relates to other programs or fits into a broad context ("How is economic aid to South Vietnam related to military aid?"). Or we are interested neither in the mission of an organization nor in its observable activities per se, but in the functions that the organization performs in the foreign-policy process ("To what extent does the Peace Corps serve as a symbol of youthful commitment to foreign policy, thereby enlisting the support of other youth to American foreign policies?"). At other times we are interested neither in the motivation of a given foreign-policy actor nor in a causal explanation of his behavior, but in identifying how or where he fits into the total policy process or in describing the function that a given act or series of acts serves within the foreign-policy process ("How have the press conferences of President Nixon compared with those of President Johnson as vehicles for mobilizing mass support for foreign policies?"). The end product of this third category of questions is *functional analysis*, that is, seeing the relationships among parts.

Once again, questions used to illustrate this kind of analysis are phrased to elicit explanation. As with analysis of purpose and analysis of cause and effect, however, analysis of function may include any or all of the analytical tasks mentioned previously: explanation, evaluation, prediction, prescription.

Kinds of Questions Posed: The Relevance of Distinctions

After these distinctions between various kinds of questions that one might pose in foreign-policy analysis have been made, it is worthwhile to emphasize the purposes of making the distinctions. The purpose of describing three kinds of analytical questions has not been to suggest the superiority of any one type to another; indeed, it is often appropriate in a given foreign-policy analysis to pursue questions from each of the three types of analysis or in some combination of two of the types. What is to be avoided is not any one type of question, but rather the confusion of one type of analysis with another. The point of making the distinctions between various kinds of analytical questions has been to help the reader to avoid confusion in appraising the works of others and in his own analyses.

For example, it would be appropriate in an analysis of United States involvement in Vietnam for one to seek to determine (1) what goals Presidents Eisenhower, Kennedy, Johnson, and Nixon, respectively, had in mind in committing American resources to the support of the South Vietnamese government; (2) what combination of factors served as the preconditions and precipitants to a given policy decision, such as the decision in 1954 to support Ngo Dinh Diem; and (3) what function an anticommunist ideology has served in the United States in the maintenance of public support for government policies in Vietnam. Questions of purpose, of cause and effect, and of function all would be investigated in such an analysis. To be avoided, however, is the confusion of one type of question with another. To say, for instance, that "the United States involvement in Vietnam is designed to prevent the imposition of rule by force," whether accurate or not as a statement of a fundamental *purpose* of the American commitment (and we need not decide that question at this point), is inadequate as an analysis of the preconditions and precipitants of American involvement in Vietnam. Let us take another hypothetical assertion: "General MacArthur's address to Congress after being relieved of his commands by President Truman in 1951 was nonpartisan in nature." Obviously, even as an analysis of the purpose that General MacArthur intended by the speech, the assertion is highly debatable. Whether or not the purpose was nonpartisan, however, the function that the speech performed in the American political system at the time clearly was a partisan one.

The point is not that statements by government officials of foreign-policy objectives or by public leaders of their motives are necessarily misleading or hypocritical (although they occasionally are, of course); rather, the point is that the evidence relevant to and adequate for one's analysis will vary according to the kinds of questions one chooses to investigate. It is important, therefore, to keep in mind the distinctions between questions of purpose, those of cause and effect, and those of function.

In subsequent chapters, when the occasion arises, we shall identify the kinds of questions that we are examining. Questions of purpose will concern us especially in Chapters 3 and 4, in which we shall view foreign policy from a strategic perspective. Questions of cause and effect will be emphasized starting with Chapter 5, when we shall begin analysis from the perspective of historical change, and will continue to the end of the book. Functional analysis will be of some concern, although less than causal analysis, beginning with Chapter 7, when we employ a decision-making perspective for analysis of foreign policy.

Stages of Analysis: A Preliminary Sketch

Supposing that one has posed questions such as some of those already formulated about particular foreign-policy phenomena or particular facets of the foreign-policy process. How does one go about answering the questions and what does the process of analysis involve? In this final section of the chapter, we shall sketch a series of steps characteristic of systematic analysis. The main theme here will be the importance of theoretical reference points in guiding one's investigation of particular phenomena and the usefulness in turn of relating particularistic findings to a broader body of theory. As we shall emphasize, systematic analysis moves from a body of general observations to particular ones and again to the body of generalizations.

We shall suggest here that theory has relevance to anyone interested in systematic analysis of foreign policy, even if one's interest in foreign policy stems from a highly personal concern for the practical consequences of day-to-day events, with little interest in academic research. Such a suggestion will run against the grain of those who like to believe that common sense or native instinct are the prime requisites for arriving at the truth about foreign-policy phenomena and that theorizing is a pastime that bears little or no relation to reality. The limits of common sense as a guide to analysis in the social sciences have been pointed out elsewhere.[7] Moreover, the general case for theory as a guide to understanding reality has been stated many times in other places more elaborately than we shall do here.[8] There are, of course, silly theories about

[7] Karl W. Deutsch, "The Limits of Common Sense," *Psychiatry*, 22 (1959), 105–112; reprinted in Nelson W. Polsby, Robert A. Dentler, and Paul A. Smith, eds., *Politics and Social Life* (Boston: Houghton Mifflin, 1963), pp. 51–58.

[8] As applied to the study of international politics and foreign policy, see, for example, the following articles in James N. Rosenau, ed., *International Politics and Foreign Policy* (New York: Free Press, 1961): Anatole Rapoport, "Various Meanings of 'Theory,'" pp. 44–52; Harold Guetzkow, "Long-Range Research in International Relations," pp. 53–59; Harold and Margaret Sprout, "Explanation and Prediction in International Politics," pp. 60–72.

various facets of foreign policy, as there are about most objects of human investigation, and some of the theoretical constructs of social scientists and others bear little relation to the real world. It is as erroneous, however, to conclude that because some theories are absurd all theory should be avoided, as it would be to conclude that because some newspapers are bad, all newspapers are to be ignored; in both cases, a more admirable position intellectually would be acquiring sufficient knowledge to distinguish between superior products and inferior ones. The place of theory in foreign-policy analysis is less esoteric than the apprehensive novice might assume or the cynical practitioner might admit.

Identifying Relevant Variables

Like the unraveling of the mystery in a detective novel, foreign-policy analysis begins simply with the compilation of clues. The elements of which clues are comprised are variables, that is, quantities or qualities that are subject to change. Among the countless examples of such variables are the number of policy makers involved in a decision, the political composition of Congress, the amount of the federal budget, the state of the President's health, the political stability of the South Vietnamese government, the size of the American nuclear arsenal, and the monthly draft call. A cluster or class of variables may be termed an explanatory "factor." Each factor—such as environment, situation, capability, personality, and organization factors—includes a number of variables.

The kinds of clues that we collect as armchair analysts of detective novels or as foreign-policy analysts of course depend on what we are trying to explain and also on the prior knowledge we can draw upon to help us. As we shall indicate in Chapter 2, this is where an analytical perspective comes in; it is also where theory first comes in. An analytical perspective is developed from an existing body of theoretical formulations (or from formulations so tentative as to be described as pretheoretical) to which we can turn in deciding which variables are likely to be relevant to our investigation and which irrelevant. Specifically, we begin piecing the puzzle together through the application of hypotheses, generalizations, and theories or models to the clues (variables) that we have identified in our investigation.

Formulating Hypotheses

A hypothesis is an unproved proposition that is accepted or offered tentatively to provide the basis for subsequent investigation; the hypothesis takes the form of a declarative sentence stipulating the relationship between two or more variables. The detective in the early chapters of a mystery novel begins to formulate hypotheses on the basis of preliminary inquiry into the crime. These hypotheses help him to begin to fit together the clues he has uncovered and also give direction to his subsequent investigation, which consists primarily of checking the hypotheses and following up additional clues as they are uncovered.

The formulation of interesting and fruitful hypotheses requires imagination, but fruitful hypotheses are seldom if ever pure acts of imagination. Rather, the detective's attention in a mystery novel to the factual details surrounding the crime, his experience with investigations in the past, and his theories about human behavior enable him to distinguish meaningful details from trivia and to provide a solid frame of reference that guides his imagination in the formulation of hypotheses. When we turn from the fictional world to the real world and try to explain such aspects of human behavior as foreign-policy phenomena, the need for supporting creative imagination with a solid grounding of careful empirical observation and general theory is still more crucial.

Fruitful hypotheses about particular foreign-policy actions and decisions are invariably drawn from one's sense of general patterns of behavior and events that the particular actions and decisions share to a greater or lesser degree. In some instances, one may be unable to articulate clearly a body of generalizations or a theory from which he has drawn a particular hypothesis. One may, in fact, be unconscious of having relied at all on general knowledge or a body of theory in developing the hypothesis and attribute the hypothesis to intuition, but intuitive hypotheses about the complex and rapidly changing phenomena of foreign policy are likely to lead nowhere unless they are rooted in a foundation of relevant theory and experience. In other words, a fruitful hypothesis is unlikely to be generated by pure guesswork; rather, it is likely to be the product of creative imagination guided by a study of particular events and decisions in the light of a general body of knowledge and theory. Just as the successes of heroes of mystery novels are attributable to a solid grounding in facts and theory that guide the imagination, the important contributions of Max Weber, Sigmund Freud, Harold Lasswell, and other notable figures in the social sciences are attributable to developing a broad base of empirical theory about human behavior as well as to imagination in the development of fruitful hypotheses.

The sources of theory from which foreign policy analysts draw, using three distinct analytical perspectives, will be identified in Chapter 2. It should be noted here that the body of theory associated with each category illustrates the kinds of theory that have had demonstrated relevance as applied from that particular perspective. Obviously, not all analysts draw from the same sources of theory. Some individuals, whose work would fall generally within one of the three categories, might draw only on one of the several sources of theory identified with a given category; others might draw not only from sources of theory most characteristic of the analytical perspective they employ, but also from other sources of theory. The point is that the broader the bases of theory with which each of us can become familiar, the more extensive will be the range of insights and sources of fruitful hypotheses in our analyses.

Developing Generalizations

The investigation of particularistic hypotheses—that is, those formulated to explain or to predict a particular occurrence—often suggests hypotheses about generic categories of phenomena of which the particular occurrence is one instance. In other words, one often moves from particularistic hypotheses to generalizations. In order to have confidence in the validity of a generalization, however, one needs to test it in the light of other particular occurrences. When numerous particular instances supporting a generalization have been found, it is often termed an *empirical generalization.* Such a term lends no infallibility to a generalization but merely indicates that repeated empirical testing has not disproved the generalization.

As noted earlier in the chapter, generalization is possible because regularities occur in human behavior. To assert that regularities occur is not to belittle that which is unique in human experience nor to deny that history never repeats itself exactly. Precisely because of the capacity of individuals to deviate from patterns of behavior characteristic of their society or to deviate from their own customary behavior, and because of the complex and dynamic course of human events, generalizations in the social sciences seldom, if ever, take the form of universal laws.

There is no universal law of human nature that guaranteed that President Truman would relieve General MacArthur of his commands in 1951, nor is there any universal law of presidential behavior that has dictated that Richard Nixon, Lyndon Johnson, John Kennedy, Dwight Eisenhower, Harry Truman, and their predecessors all perform the duties of the office in the same way; indeed, we know that no two Presidents have been exactly alike in the execution of their responsibilities. Yet, we also know that there are detectable patterns in the way various individuals have performed their roles in the foreign-policy process; for example, the approach of the President to Congress in time of war or severe external threat has tended to differ from his approach in time of peace. In other words, although human behavior is not reducible to universal laws, the regularities in human behavior mean that in the study of foreign policy, as in other areas of investigation of the social sciences, we may fruitfully seek to develop generalizations that take the form of statements of tendency or of probability.

Constructing Theories

Intellectual curiosity leads the concerned observer of foreign policy, as well as the clever sleuth of the mystery novel, not only to develop a series of working hypotheses or generalizations about what he observes, but also to attempt to explain the generalizations.

For example, the statement "Men more than women tend to support the use of armed force as an instrument of foreign policy" might serve as a general working hypothesis to explain a particular opinion poll in the United States in 1967 that showed a higher proportion of men than women favoring American bombing of North Vietnam. However, if we assume empirical support from historical and contemporary data for the general hypothesis, there remains the problem of explaining the generalization. If men are more apt than women to support the use of force in foreign policy, why is this so? Are such differences in attitudes rooted in biological differences between men and women? Do differences in the early childhood experiences and training explain such differences in attitude later in life? Is the fact that a large proportion of men serve in the armed forces, whereas women do not, related to the views that men and women, respectively, have about the use of armed force? Our purpose in the present discussion is not to offer our own favorite explanation of the generalization, but rather to point out that the task of analysis carries us beyond the formulation of empirical generalizations to attempts to explain the generalizations. Such explanations, which are of a higher order, are called *theories*.

Theories may be narrow in scope—focusing, for example, only on the problem of explaining differences in the attitudes of American men and American women toward the use of armed force as an instrument of foreign policy. On the other hand, theories might be very broad in scope —attempting to explain the process of attitude formation and change, for example, or the conditions under which nations will resort to the use of armed force as an instrument of foreign policy. The terms "narrow-gauge," "middle-gauge," and "broad-gauge" are sometimes used to suggest differences in scope among various theories.[9]

[9] For a detailed discussion of the terms, see David Easton, *The Political System* (New York: Knopf, 1959), pp. 52–63.

Ideally, we who wish to understand the foreign-policy process would like to be able to construct or to have at our disposal a broad-gauge theory of foreign policy that not only explained a whole series of empirical generalizations about the process, but also linked the generalizations together *deductively* into a coherent whole. However, theories currently available to the foreign-policy analyst, such as those to be identified in Chapter 2 as being associated with various analytical perspectives, are characteristically narrow- and middle-gauge theories, nondeductive rather than deductive in form. (Game theory is deductive, but the limits of deductive theorizing about complex foreign-policy behavior in a "multiplayer" environment mean that this is not an important exception to the generalization just cited.)

Although no comprehensive, deductive theory of foreign policy is likely to be developed in the foreseeable future, some success is evident, and more can be anticipated in the future in the construction of "factor theories" and "quasi theories" about various facets of foreign policy. A factor theory identifies a factor (group of variables) or factors that are associated with the occurrence of a given phenomenon and indicates (optimally) how and under what conditions the interaction of the factors relates to the phenomenon to be explained. Theories about voting behavior, for example, are generally of the factor variety. Factors such as educational attainment of voters, socioeconomic level, party affiliation, urban or rural home environment, and ethnic origins have been shown to correlate to some degree with voting patterns. Prediction of voting behavior in the United States by well-qualified political analysts has become impressively accurate in recent years because analysis has led from empirical generalizations about the relationship of each of several factors to voting outcome beyond to the development of middle-gauge theory suggesting how the various factors are related to one another. Thus, theories of voting behavior have proved to be extremely useful, although they are not, in a rigorous sense, deductive in form.

One might also include as part of the theoretical foundation that is being currently developed in the study of foreign policy the intellectual constructs termed "quasi theories." The term is not intended to suggest derogatory connotations, but merely to distinguish a particular kind of theoretical construct from one that is deductive in form and from factor theories. Broad schemes for conceptualizing phenomena or for classifying data that are nondeductive and are not factor theories may be termed quasi theories. Examples of quasi theory are the use of "models" to depict a particular set of relationships or a particular process and purely speculative theories about how various working hypotheses are related to one another.[10] The concept of a political system is another example of a quasi theory, which we shall develop at length in later chapters.

The process that we have described above—gathering clues, formulating hypotheses, and developing theories—moves from the general to the particular and again to the general. One's investigation of particular events is guided by his knowledge of a body of relevant theory; the particularistic investigation enables him to generate more general hypotheses, which in turn contribute to the cumulative development of theory.

Although a full cycle of analysis has been described here, the book as a whole focuses primarily upon the first stages in the analytical process. Our concern is to help the layman acquire a familiarity with the logic of systematic inquiry into foreign-policy phenomena and to encourage him to formulate his ideas rigorously in a format that facilitates checking the ideas through empirical observation. Because the formulation of hypotheses lies at the heart of the analytical process that we hope to cultivate, a number of hypotheses are developed in each of the subsequent parts of the book. The careful reader will recognize that expressing ideas about foreign-policy phenomena in the form of hypotheses, far from representing a false claim to having achieved precision in the explanation of human events, makes explicit the tentative nature of our knowledge; yet, hypotheses also provide a systematic format for expanding existing knowledge through empirical observation.

The hypotheses presented here are not to be accepted on faith; indeed, the reader should be warned that we have included some hypotheses primarily to provoke thought, even in instances where alternative explanations of events are equally persuasive to us. We hope that this technique will stimulate the reader to formulate two or three alternative hypotheses of his own for every hypothesis stated in the book. In each instance he should then consider the kinds of evidence that would be necessary and sufficient for him to accept either the original hypothesis or one of the alternatives and to reject the others. There are important questions of measurement and inference that arise when one moves to the stage of testing hypotheses, but in order to keep the book to manageable size, we must assume that the reader will search for answers to such questions elsewhere as they become pertinent to his own subsequent needs in analysis.

[10] For a discussion of factor theories and quasi theories, see Meehan, *The Theory and Method of Political Analysis*, pp. 150–167.

2

Perspectives for Analysis

We observed in Chapter 1 that no one can cope fully with the maze of complex and rapidly changing phenomena of foreign policy; for this reason, one must be selective. In part, as suggested earlier, one cannot fully control the filtering process—one's preexisting beliefs and values may repress or distort information despite a desire for objectivity. To the extent that one is able to attain objectivity, however, criteria for selectivity may be established according to his analytical interests and purposes. By establishing a precise focus for analysis and by identifying some theoretical points of reference in the selection and organization of data, one may avoid the mental daze that would occur if he tried to focus on every aspect of a situation at once, and one may go beyond the hodgepodge of conclusions that would result if he merely grasped at random for data.

In short, it is useful to begin analysis of

foreign policy by determining what analytical perspective to employ. We shall use the term "analytical perspective" to refer to the focus of an analytical inquiry and to the theoretical or pretheoretical foundations that guide the gathering and organization of data in the inquiry. Parts II, III, and IV of the book are devoted to extended discussion and illustration of the rationale of three distinct perspectives for analysis of foreign policy; various pertinent theoretical reference points will be identified in that discussion. The present chapter is devoted simply to introducing these three analytical perspectives. An extended case study will be used to illustrate variations that occur in one's findings and interpretations of events when one varies the analytical perspective.

A Case for Analysis: The Korean War

If, as Shakespeare observed, all the world's a stage, in few areas of human endeavor is the drama of life revealed so vividly, continuously, and significantly as in the foreign-policy process. In order to highlight the dramatic nature of foreign policy and its human import, throughout the book we shall regularly supplement the conceptualization and exposition by which an analytical framework is developed with discussion of specific, illustrative actions and events from the American foreign-policy experience; the actions and events selected will range from excerpts from historical experience, as in Part III, to much more recent situations, such as the war in Vietnam.

In the present chapter, the portion of American foreign-policy experience that has been selected to introduce and to illustrate the application of three distinct analytical perspectives is the Korean War. Despite the *Pueblo* incident of 1968, the North Korean downing of a United States' aircraft in 1969, and recurring border incidents along the 38th parallel that have reminded us that Korea is still a trouble spot, events from the period of the Korean War are by now as remote and unfamiliar to many Americans as the debate over the League of Nations or the sinking of the battleship *Maine*. Yet, as those readers who do recall the early 1950s will attest, events of the Korean War years have a continuing relevance to the concerned observer of American foreign policy. This relevance is attributable not simply to the fact that the division of Korea into two mutually hostile states continues to threaten world peace, but also to the fact that a number of the central policy issues that had to be faced by the American government during that period have recurred. Indeed, much of the dialogue from the drama of the early fifties is still familiar, especially from the recent debate of American foreign policies in Vietnam.

Thus, events from the Korean War period will serve as an extremely pertinent example for our present analytical purposes. We shall describe events from the period in brief outline form first; then we shall indicate how the events might be interpreted, depending upon one's analytical perspective.

Outline of Events

The Attack   The international atmosphere in early 1950 was turbulent and highly volatile. The Soviet delegate to the United Nations Security Council began a boycott in January to protest the continued representation of China in the United Nations by a Nationalist representative rather than a representative of the Communist government of Mao Tse-tung. In February, the Soviet Union and Communist China signed a thirty-year Treaty of Friendship, Alliance, and Mutual Assistance. Later in the spring, reports from Indochina indicated that the forces of the Viet Minh, which were fighting to free Vietnam from French control, were receiving assistance from the Communist Chinese. Thus in May, noting the urgency of the situation and describing the threat as "Soviet imperialism," Secretary of State Acheson announced the initiation of a program of economic and military assistance to the French in Indochina.[1]

One of the most tempestuous trouble spots in Asia was Korea, where, until mid-1948, American and Soviet forces had confronted one another along the 38th parallel. Except for advisers, forces of the two Cold War superpowers had been withdrawn in 1948; thus by 1950 they confronted one another in Korea only by proxy. American military government south of the 38th parallel and Soviet military government north of it were to have given way to a unified, independent, Korean government, but the occupying powers could not agree upon plans to effect such a transition. The United States had taken the matter to the United Nations in 1947; that organization, unable to arrange for elections throughout Korea, had agreed to supervise elections in South Korea alone. In 1948, elections supervised by the United Nations were held in South Korea, with Syngman Rhee, a Korean nationalist who had spent most of his adult years in the United States (B.A., George Washington University; M.A., Harvard; Ph.D., Princeton), becoming the first president. Neither the South Korean government of Syngman Rhee, nor the North Korean government

---

[1] *Department of State Bulletin* (May 22, 1950), p. 821. American aid to the French was increased during the Korean War; by the time of the French defeat at Dien Bien Phu in 1954 the United States was bearing approximately 80 percent of the financial cost of the French military effort in Vietnam.

led by Kim Il Song, however, regarded division of the peninsula into two separate states as permanent; each regarded his own government as the legitimate heir to the unified Korea which must be achieved, if necessary by force.

Consequently, from mid-1948 until June 1950, the situation along the 38th parallel had been one of mounting tension, punctuated by frequent incidents in which shots were exchanged between forces of the communist Democratic People's Republic of Korea (North Korea) and those of the anticommunist Republic of Korea (South Korea). In fact, during the last six months of 1949, more than 400 such incidents along the border had been reported, not including hundreds of additional skirmishes with guerrilla forces within South Korea.[2]

Although invasion rumors had been rife for months, when the attack finally came on Sunday, June 25 (Korean time), both the South Korean government and its American advisers were caught by surprise. The attack by North Korean forces began before dawn and proceeded rapidly southward against largely ineffective resistance. By 9 A.M., the ancient capital of Kaesong, north of Seoul, had fallen to the North Koreans. The U.S. Military Advisory Group to the Republic of Korea (KMAG) sent a message to the headquarters in Japan of General Douglas MacArthur, Commander of United States forces in the Far East with an urgent request for an emergency ten-day supply of ammunition for howitzers, mortars, and carbines. There was a real danger that the South Korean forces might run out of ammunition early in their efforts to withstand the North Korean attack. Seoul was being bombed and strafed by North Korean planes. A cable to Washington from the American Ambassador to South Korea gave the news of the desperate situation.[3]

The Response   At American request, the United Nations Security Council began an emergency meeting Sunday morning, June 25 (New York time), and continued in session throughout the day to consider the crisis in Korea. Happily for American policy makers, the Soviet delegate to the Security Council was continuing his boycott and therefore was not in a position to veto any action upon which the Council might decide. (If the Soviet delegate had decided to end his boycott and return to cast a veto, the American delegation's plan was to appeal for an emergency meeting of the General Assembly, in which there is no veto.) By Sunday evening,

[2] Robert K. Sawyer, with Walter G. Hermes, *Military Advisors in Korea: KMAG in Peace and War* (Washington: Office of the Chief of Military History, Department of the Army, 1962), pp. 73–74.

[3] Sawyer, pp. 114–139.

an initial Security Council resolution had been passed, calling for an immediate cease-fire in Korea and a withdrawal of North Korean forces to positions north of the 38th parallel. The exact nature of the United Nations response was not yet determined, but the resolution termed the North Korean attack a "breach of the peace," in the language of the United Nations Charter, and called upon members "to render every assistance . . . in the execution of this resolution. . . ." [4]

President Truman met with his advisers in Washington Sunday evening, just after the United Nations Security Council in Lake Success, New York, had adjourned for two days to give delegates an opportunity to consult with their governments and to prepare policy positions for the next meeting. The decision was made to send arms and supplies immediately to aid the South Koreans, to provide sufficient air support for the evacuation of American dependents from Korea, and to send the U.S. Seventh Fleet to the Formosa Strait to seal off Formosa from conflict. General MacArthur was to be instructed to send a party to Korea to survey needs and determine how American military forces might be employed if needed. [5]

It became increasingly apparent to the President and his advisers, as news of a worsening situation in Korea reached them, that if the total seizure of the Korean peninsula by the North Korean forces could be prevented at all, it could be done only by the substantial commitment of American armed force. On Monday, June 26 (Washington time), General MacArthur was authorized to make a limited commitment of American forces to support the South Koreans. On Tuesday, a resolution was obtained from the Security Council by a vote of seven to one (Yugoslavia opposing) recommending that all member nations furnish "such assistance to the Republic of Korea as may be necessary to repel the armed attack and to restore international peace and security in the area." [6] On Friday, June 30, with receipt of an on-the-spot report from General MacArthur, President Truman authorized MacArthur to use as many of the combat troops in his command as he felt the situation required, relying upon

[4] American activity in the United Nations during the Korean conflict has been analyzed in detail by Edwin C. Hoyt, "The United States Reaction to the Korean Attack: A Study of the Principles of the United Nations Charter as a Factor in American Policy-Making," *American Journal of International Law*, 55 (Jan. 1961), 45–76; reprinted in the Bobbs-Merrill reprint series in the social sciences, PS-132.

[5] Edwin C. Hoyt, *American Journal of International Law*, 55:45–76. See also Harry Truman, *Memoirs*, 2 vols. (New York: Doubleday, 1956), 2, *Years of Trial and Hope*, 380–382.

[6] United Nations, Dept. of Public Information, *Korea and the United Nations* (UN Bulletin Reprint, Oct. 1950), p. 12.

MacArthur's discretion to maintain sufficient force in Japan for the protection of that nation from attack.[7]

Crossing the 38th Parallel   In spite of American commitment of troops to the conflict, North Korean forces continued their advance; they were finally stopped only by deceptive tactics in deployment of forces and a successful rearguard action along what became known as the "Pusan perimeter." Having staved off defeat, however, MacArthur's forces moved from the defensive to the offensive by making a daring amphibious attack behind the enemy lines at Inchon in September 1950. North Korean forces now began a rapid retreat northward, many of them caught in a pincers movement by United Nations forces.

By early October, the first American forces were moving north of the 38th parallel. Authorization for the crossing of the parallel had been given by President Truman, subject to the conditions that neither China nor the Soviet Union entered the war, and providing United Nations approval was obtained; this authorization was given by a vote in the General Assembly, redefining United Nations goals in Korea as attaining the reunification of Korea and providing nationwide elections under United Nations supervision.

At the end of November, however, as United Nations forces began a final drive that was "to complete the compression and close the vise" on enemy forces, a Chinese force of some 200,000 troops counterattacked, inflicting upon the forces a series of defeats that produced the longest retreat in American military history.[8]

Truman's Dismissal of MacArthur   By the end of December 1950, United Nations forces had suffered thousands of casualties and were retreating southward on the Korean peninsula. General MacArthur had made an urgent request for reinforcements, but he was informed that they were not available. Discussions between the Joint Chiefs of Staff and MacArthur had begun from the possible necessity of evacuating United Nations forces entirely from the Korean peninsula. The situation had reached desperate proportions, and MacArthur believed that desperate measures were called for in an effort to stave off defeat. Thus, he

---

[7] A detailed description and analysis of this week of decision making is provided by Glenn D. Paige, *The Korean Decision* (New York: Free Press, 1968).

[8] S. L. A. Marshall, *The River and the Gauntlet* (New York: Morrow, 1953), chaps. 1–2. This book is probably the most famous of those written by "Slam" Marshall, a retired general and well-known journalist. The book depicts, in graphic detail, the trials of a small unit and the agonies of the individual foot soldier during the defeat of the U.S. Eighth Army by the Chinese in the battle at Chongchon River, North Korea, in November 1950.

made his most far-reaching proposal yet to commit the nation and the United Nations forces to an all-out effort against the enemy. In a message to the Joint Chiefs of Staff, he proposed that four steps be taken to exploit the vulnerability of the Chinese: (1) institute a blockade of the coast of China, (2) launch an air and naval bombardment of Chinese industry, (3) use Chinese Nationalist reinforcements in Korea, and (4) use the Nationalist troops to launch diversionary attacks on the mainland of China.[9]

After discussing General MacArthur's recommendations with key military and civilian advisers in Washington, however, President Truman concluded that the conflict in Korea must remain a limited one, rather than be expanded in the directions indicated by MacArthur. The policy objectives set forth by the President, therefore, in a message to MacArthur early in January, called for achieving a peace settlement as quickly as possible, rather than seeking the total defeat of the Chinese. MacArthur in turn replied that unless he was permitted to follow the steps that he had recommended, he would have to evacuate his troops to Japan.

In his memoirs, President Truman has reported that he found MacArthur's reply and his talk of the need for evacuation "deeply disturbing." After calling another special meeting of the National Security Council to discuss what should be done, the President decided to send a long letter to MacArthur, attempting to have him see the problem from the Washington perspective by elaborating more completely than previously the political considerations that provided the context within which military decisions had to be made.[10] Not the letter, but changing conditions in the war itself temporarily alleviated the mounting crisis of policy differences between Truman and MacArthur. The same week in which the letter to General MacArthur was dispatched, United Nations forces had begun to hold. The evacuation issue had become a moot point, and temporarily the issues seemed less desperate both to MacArthur and to Truman.

The situation continued to improve to the point that, by March 1951, United Nations forces had again reached the 38th parallel. It was in this context that the Truman administration decided that the situation was ripe to attempt to negotiate with the Chinese. The reasoning was that the communists had again been substantially ejected from South Korea, and heavy losses were being inflicted on them. Thus, they would be inclined to negotiate on the assumption that prolonging the war would only work in the favor of the United Nations forces.

[9] Douglas MacArthur, *Reminiscences* (New York: McGraw-Hill, 1964), pp. 378–380.

[10] Truman, 2:493–495.

The Department of State drew up a statement that was to be made by the President, announcing the willingness of the United Nations forces to enter into negotiations and outlining basic terms. General MacArthur was alerted to the impending announcement and was asked for recommendations; he replied only that he hoped no further restrictions would be placed on his forces. Upon receipt of MacArthur's comments, this major policy statement to be made by President Truman was cleared with other governments that had forces in Korea under United Nations command.[11]

Truman's probe for negotiations never reached the form of a public statement, however. On the eve of what was to have been a major policy address by the President, MacArthur released a statement of his own to the press, which took the form of a declaration to the enemy commander in chief that MacArthur, as the United Nations commander, stood ready at any time to confer about bringing hostilities to a close. Passages in the communiqué called attention to the weaknesses that had been revealed in the military and industrial capability of Communist China. This being the case, MacArthur ominously noted that the enemy "must by now be painfully aware that a decision of the United Nations to depart from its tolerant effort to contain the war to the area of Korea, through an expansion of our military operations to his coastal areas and interior bases, could doom Red China to the risk of imminent military collapse." Having made an implicit threat, MacArthur suggested that "there should be no insuperable difficulty at arriving at decisions on the Korean problem if the issues are resolved on their own merits, without being burdened by extraneous matters such as Formosa or China's seat in the United Nations." [12]

Although General MacArthur may have regarded the firm appeal to the enemy to negotiate with him as a response to the call of duty, President Truman saw the statement as a flagrant instance of insubordination. MacArthur's statement had been made in spite of directives to clear important policy statements in Washington first. More importantly, the policy thrust of the statement, consistent with the approach that MacArthur had repeatedly recommended but that Truman had repeatedly rejected, was, as Truman put it, "open defiance" of the President.[13] According to his memoirs, it was at this point that Truman began to consider seriously relieving General MacArthur of his command. By early April, when the Republican minority leader in the House of Representatives, Joe Martin, read into the record a letter from General Mac-

[11] Truman, 2:497–499.
[12] MacArthur, pp. 387–388.
[13] Truman, 2:499–501.

Arthur repeating his views of appropriate policies in Korea, Truman became certain that MacArthur must be dismissed. On April 5, 1951, newspapers throughout the country ran front-page stories of the letter from MacArthur to Martin, closing with the general's favorite phrase, "There is no substitute for victory." [14] On April 11, the headlines carried the news of MacArthur's dismissal from his commands by President Truman.

Stalemate and Truce General MacArthur returned to the United States to a hero's welcome. On April 19, he received a standing ovation from members of Congress as he appeared to express his views before a joint session of the legislative body. In the meantime, Lieutenant General Matthew B. Ridgway, who as the Eighth Army commander had been MacArthur's immediate subordinate, had assumed MacArthur's commands in East Asia.[15] By June, the front in Korea had again stabilized, roughly along the 38th parallel. In this context, peace negotiations were begun at Kaesong, the first important town overrun by the North Korean attack a year earlier. During the long months of negotiations that followed, the fighting dragged on, with mounting casualties on the battlefield, mounting friction among the United Nations allies, and mounting disillusionment on the American home front.

General Douglas MacArthur gave the keynote address at the Republican National Convention in Chicago in July 1952. As their presidential candidate, the convention selected another general, Dwight D. Eisenhower, who campaigned on the slogan, "I will go to Korea." In November, Eisenhower was elected by a substantial margin over the Democratic candidate, Adlai Stevenson.

Finally, on July 27, 1953, an armistice agreement in Korea was signed.

The Korean War in Strategic Perspective

What are the pertinent analytical questions about United States foreign policy during the Korean War? What kinds of data are relevant to answering the questions? The questions and data deemed relevant will vary according to the focus of one's inquiry and theoretical reference points. The discussion in this chapter is designed simply to identify distinguishing features of three alternative analytical perspectives by

[14] MacArthur, p. 386.

[15] For Ridgway's account of these events, including extended commentary on the Truman-MacArthur controversy, see his book, *The Korean War* (New York: Doubleday, 1967).

suggesting some pertinent questions and data regarding the Korean War experience; the rationale and theoretical foundations of each perspective will be made more explicit in subsequent parts of the book.

One way of viewing and interpreting the American foreign-policy experience during the Korean War would be in terms of the intentions of American policy makers. A focus that set the Korean War in the context of the Cold War struggle between the United States and the Soviet Union would provide a basis for relating particular policy decisions to broader strategic plans. From such a strategic perspective, a number of questions about American policies prior to and during the Korean War come to mind. For instance, why was the United States government so unprepared for the attack that started the war? Why was it that the American response took the form of a commitment of American combat forces? What was the rationale of the policies actually pursued by the Truman administration toward the Chinese, once they entered the war in Korea, as compared with the rationale of MacArthur's proposal for expanding the war? Clues to answering these questions may be seen in the European emphasis of the containment strategy as it existed in 1950 prior to the North Korean attack, in the reinterpretation of Soviet strategy by the Truman administration as a result of the North Korean attack, and in the differing assessments by President Truman and his advisers and by General MacArthur, respectively, of American priorities and capabilities and of Soviet and Chinese capabilities and intentions.

American Unpreparedness for the Attack   As we shall indicate in greater detail in Chapter 3, the evolution of the containment strategy in the early years after World War II had a European emphasis. Landmarks in the evolution included the Greek-Turkish aid program, initiated with the Truman Doctrine; the European recovery program, established with the Marshall Plan; and the military alliance with the nation-states of Western Europe concluded with the NATO pact.

The fall of China to Communist rule in 1949, followed by the Sino-Soviet pact of January 1950, became the occasion for a reassessment of American strategic interests and posture in Asia. It was the contention of the Truman administration that the fall of China to communism, although unfortunate, was the consequence of a vast civil war over which the United States could have exerted no determining influence. Commenting in January 1950 on the plight of the forces of the Nationalist Chinese leader, Chiang Kai-shek, which were by then regrouping on the island of Formosa (Taiwan) in anticipation of an invasion by the Communist forces of Mao Tse-tung, President Truman observed that the United States would not become further involved in a Chinese civil war and would "not provide military aid or advice to Chinese forces on Formosa." [16] Secretary of State Acheson, in a major policy speech the same month, elaborated the administration's position by describing the defense perimeter of the United States in the Far East as running from the Aleutian Islands through Japan to the Philippines. Notably excluded from this description were Formosa and South Korea, where the United States had carried out military government responsibilities in the early postwar liberation of the area from Japanese rule and had helped to establish an independent government, to which it had committed military assistance. Speaking in generalities, but clearly referring to Korea by implication, the Secretary of State said that in the event of an attack, ". . . the initial reliance must be on the people attacked to resist it and then upon the commitments of the entire civilized world under the Charter of the United Nations. . . ." [17]

In short, there was a hope within the Truman administration that South Korea could be kept out of the Communist orbit. But regarding the priority of policy concerns and the estimates of the major focus of a Soviet threat, the allocation of American resources continued to be concentrated on Europe. Thus, until June 1950, American aid to South Korea had been minimal. Fewer than 500 American military advisers, many of them having had little military experience, assisted in the training of a South Korea army of approximately 100,000 men. The equipment provided was adequate for a force of only 65,000 men, and the supply of ammunition, spare parts, and maintenance materials was diminishing rapidly. In March 1950, Congress had approved appropriations of about $10 million in military aid for South Korea for the fiscal year 1950, but by June 1950, with the fiscal year nearly ended, less than $1000 of aid had arrived in Korea.[18]

American Response to the Attack   Once the attack came, however, in the calculations of President Truman and his advisers, it became essential that a forcible American response to the attack be made. Such a response seemed essential not only for preventing the loss of Korea, which in turn would endanger Japan, but also for avoiding a precedent in which the use of armed force by Communists to achieve their objectives would be successful. In strategic perspective, the commitment of American combat forces to Korea, coupled with the dispatch of the Seventh Fleet to the

[16] *China and U.S. Far East Policy, 1945–1966* (Washington: Congressional Quarterly Service, April 1967), p. 48.

[17] The full text of Secretary Acheson's speech to the National Press Club on Jan. 12, 1950, is contained in *China and U.S. Far East Policy*, pp. 257–261.

[18] Sawyer, pp. 96–113.

Formosa Strait, also represents an important shift in foreign-policy priorities—an evolution of the containment strategy with heavier emphasis on Asia than previously.

Truman's and MacArthur's Differences on Strategy   It was assumed from the first days of the war by President Truman and his advisers in Washington that the major responsibility for the attack lay in Moscow. It seemed probable that the attack had been planned there; as a minimum, the Soviet Union had approved and supported it. It became urgent, therefore, to reassess Soviet strategic intentions in the light of the Korean invasion. The reassessment included the belief that the Soviets wished to avoid an all-out war with the United States, but that the Korean attack, by proxy, might have been designed to divert American attention and resources to Korea in order to make some other area more vulnerable to a Soviet move. It therefore seemed desirable to key members of the Truman administration to respond forcibly to the Communist attack in Korea without making an all-out commitment there. Keeping the conflict and the American commitment limited would both reduce the danger of an all-out war with the Soviet Union and keep a portion of American military and economic resources in reserve for commitment quickly elsewhere if needed.

The reasoning of the Truman administration with regard to the appropriate strategy in Korea remained basically the same even after the Chinese entered the war in late November 1950. In a briefing for key congressional leaders in mid-December, the President informed them that serious consideration was being given to the possibility that the Soviets might find some excuse to intervene in a number of other places if the United States were to become overcommitted in Korea. Berlin, Western Germany, Yugoslavia, Iran, and Indochina were among the locations specifically mentioned by the President as likely areas for trouble. Thus, because of the great concern with avoiding an all-out war and the belief that scarce resources had to be utilized prudently in Korea in order to be prepared elsewhere, President Truman and his advisers placed great emphasis on keeping the war in Korea limited.[19] In the light of this reasoning, Truman's rejection of MacArthur's suggestions for expanding the war becomes understandable.

From MacArthur's viewpoint, however, once the Chinese entered the war in Korea in force, the war became "an entirely new war." [20] To

[19] Truman, 2:491–492.

[20] U.S. Congress, Senate Committees on Foreign Relations and Armed Services, *Joint Hearings, Military Situation in the Far East*, 82d Cong., 1st sess., 1951, Pt. 5, app., p. 3495.

MacArthur, the rules of conducting the war and the strategic considerations that had prevailed prior to the Chinese entry into the war had become outmoded. In his opinion, the restrictions that had been imposed on him for fear of provoking the Chinese were now irrelevant and would increase the handicaps under which the United Nations forces suffered, being numerically inferior to the enemy and tactically off balance because of the unexpected Chinese move.

The item of highest priority had to be finding sufficient arms and men to counter the Communist Chinese attack. A logical source of reinforcements, MacArthur believed, was Formosa, where Chiang Kai-shek was eager to commit his sizable Nationalist Chinese army to avenge the humiliating defeats suffered while being driven from the mainland of China. MacArthur had visited Chiang on Formosa in July and had been impressed by his observations of the Nationalist army. However, although the previously stated policy of noninterference in the civil war in China had been reversed in June, to the extent of using the Seventh Fleet to protect Formosa from attack by the Communist Chinese, neither President Truman nor the United Nations allies had been prepared to permit Chiang Kai-shek to send forces to fight in Korea or to launch an invasion of the Chinese mainland. The first of several policy restrictions imposed on the United Nations effort in Korea that MacArthur wanted removed after the Chinese Communist troops entered the war, therefore, was the restriction on Chiang Kai-shek. MacArthur wired Washington, urgently recommending that he be permitted to make direct contact with Chiang Kai-shek to work out arrangements for utilization of the Nationalist troops. To some of the United Nations member governments, however—the British, for example—Chiang Kai-shek was a has-been, a leader who had once been the dominant figure in China, but who had lost popular support through the corruption and ineptitude of his government. Reviving the hopes of Chiang-Kai-shek for the restoration of his control in China, many felt, would be a serious mistake; moreover, the United Nations cause would be tarnished by having Chiang's forces included in its contingent. President Truman and his advisers were convinced that the maintenance of unity among the United Nations allies outweighed whatever advantage might be gained by the employment of Chinese Nationalist troops. Thus, General MacArthur's urgent request was denied.[21]

MacArthur was becoming increasingly impatient with what he felt was the shortsightedness, or perversity, of the various United Nations member nations and with President Truman and his advisers for succumbing to

[21] MacArthur, pp. 339–344, 375–376.

pressures from other United Nations governments, to the serious detriment of the war effort.

In this context MacArthur made the four-step proposal described previously for expanding the war by bombing and blockading the Chinese mainland. In MacArthur's opinion, the actions that he recommended presented no additional risks of retaliation by the Chinese, since it was clear that China was already committing her entire military resources to the Korean conflict. The actions would involve the risk of Soviet intervention, but in MacArthur's judgment, the Soviets would base their decision entirely on pragmatic considerations of their own relative capability, not simply responding in anger at the attack on an ally, or out of a commitment to an alliance. As for the concern of policy makers in Washington and of United States allies that deeper involvement in the war in Asia would lead the United States to neglect Europe, MacArthur expressed his concern also with European security; he added however, that if the United States accepted defeat in Asia, such acceptance would "insure later defeat in Europe itself." [22]

Once again, MacArthur's advice was rejected in Washington. In strategic perspective, the events that culminated in Truman's dismissal of MacArthur were rooted in important differences of opinion about strategy. The proposals that MacArthur deemed imperative were repeatedly rejected. Truman viewed the same proposals as reckless, and MacArthur's continued public expression of these views after they had been rejected in Washington eventually became, in Truman's view, insubordination.

The Korean War in the Perspective of Historical Dynamics

Instead of seeking to explain the intentions of American policy makers during the Korean War by viewing events in the context of the broader Cold War struggle, one might attempt to interpret American policies in the Korean War in terms of historical preconditions for the policies. What questions would then become pertinent? What kinds of data would be relevant to answering them?

From the perspective of historical dynamics, the fact that the United States made a combat commitment in Korea and the strategic limitations assumed in this commitment are of less interest analytically than are the following: the United States' assumption of a major role in the affairs of East Asia; the broad goal-values and beliefs that defined that role; and the instrumentalities, such as the United Nations, that were selected as

22 MacArthur, pp. 378–380.

appropriate means to perform the role. Relevant to the analysis of such topics are several broad explanatory factors: patterns of distribution of resources and technology and patterns of authority, which, since the 1890s, and especially since World War II, left the United States in a favorable competitive position in international politics in general, and in East Asian politics in particular; the redefinition of "the American destiny" that was made by American leaders over half a century and was hastened by World War II; and changes that had occurred in estimates by American leaders of the capability of the United States to exercise a powerful role in international politics.

Emergence of a Major American Role in East Asia   In Part III, we shall describe and discuss in some detail the significant changes in the evolution of American foreign policy during the 1890s; here we may simply note that the 1890s were also a significant period of change in East Asia (China, Japan, Korea). It is interesting to consider interrelationships between the changes in the American orientation toward world affairs during this period and the concurrent changes in East Asia. From a historical perspective, such interrelationships help to define the roots of the major role in East Asia that the United States played by the 1940s and 1950s.

The "opening" of Asia to the West is usually identified with a series of treaties negotiated in the middle of the nineteenth century, although missionary activity and limited trade by Europeans and Americans in Asia had already taken place for many decades. By the final decades of the nineteenth century, however, a period of greatly intensified contact between East and West had begun, which generated far-reaching social and political changes in East Asia and greatly altered its system of international relations. The intensification of contacts characteristic of the period is especially attributable to industrialization in Europe and the United States, since it stimulated a competitive search for new markets and sources of raw materials, which led to East Asia, among other areas. Industrialization also meant technological advances—such as the steamship and the engineering feat represented by the Suez Canal—that facilitated contacts between Europe and Asia.

The enfeeblement and decadence of the Manchu dynasty brought China by the 1890s to the brink of total collapse and conquest by imperialist powers; its plight was partly analogous to that of Turkey throughout much of the nineteenth century. In contrast, since the Meiji Restoration of 1868, Japan had made a remarkable transformation from a feudal to an industrial society, able to engage in imperialistic competition with the western powers on their own terms. Korea, which had existed as a nominally independent kingdom for over a thousand years, although in tributary status to China, now became the victim of Japanese imperialistic desires and increased strength. The Sino-Japanese War of 1895, which was fought in Korea, marked the end of dominant Chinese influence in Korea; Japan, now assuming a controlling position, formally annexed Korea in 1910.

The emergence of the United States as an important power in Asia paralleled in some respects, and eventually conflicted with, the expansion of Japanese influence there. Like Japan, by the 1890s the United States had emerged as a nation-state with the capability and the desire to compete with the major European powers. The rationale that had sustained the traditional American posture of nonentanglement in international politics had been eroded by time and changing circumstances; new capabilities combined with new images of the American destiny to produce a surge of interest by American leaders in establishing an important American presence in Asia. A series of actions around the turn of the century manifested this interest in Asia and established the foundation for subsequent American influence. Such actions included the annexation of Hawaii, a way station to Asia, in 1898; the acquisition of the Philippines and Guam as a result of war with Spain; the Open Door notes of the McKinley administration, registering an American desire to prevent any European powers from achieving hegemony in China; and the seizure of Panama and the digging of the Panama Canal, providing access to the Pacific from the American east coast.

Thus, by the early twentieth century, the United States posed a major potential threat to new Japanese goals in Asia; conversely, especially after her surprising victory over Russia in 1904–1905, Japan represented the major potential threat to American interests in Asia and the Pacific. By mutual observance of a series of agreements that outlined the respective spheres of interest of the two parties, armed conflict between the United States and Japan was avoided for several decades.[23] However, the expansion of Japan with the conquest of Manchuria in 1931, followed by the invasion of China in 1937, and the expansion of Japanese control to Indochina in 1940 represented a redistribution of authority and influence in East Asia that seriously threatened American interests, as they were perceived by American leaders at the time. The American response was a freezing of Japanese assets in the United States and an embargo on

---

[23] The mutual agreements included, most notably, the Taft-Katsura memorandum of 1905, the Root-Takahira agreement of 1908, and multiparty agreements reached in regard to the Pacific and to naval strengths at the Washington Conference in 1921–1922.

the shipment of petroleum products to Japan. The Japanese rejoinder was the attack on Pearl Harbor.

The devastation and defeat of Japan in World War II produced the most significant single change in the pattern of distribution of authority and resources in East Asia that occurred during that period. Moreover, China at the end of the war was weak and torn by civil war. Given the prior interests of the United States in Asia and in the Pacific, therefore, plus the dominant role that the United States played in defeating the Japanese, it was natural that the strength of the United States in East Asia in the postwar period should increase roughly in proportion to the decrease in Japanese influence and control since 1940.

There was, however, a notable failure by American policy makers (most notably by President Roosevelt, in whom so much authority was invested during the war) to anticipate the momentous social and political changes that characterized East Asia after World War II and to make systematic preparations for a major American role there. The failure in planning and the general ambiguity of American policies in East Asia at the end of World War II may be accurately described as having contributed directly to the division of Korea in the first place and as having generated conditions conducive to the North Korean attack in June 1950.[24] In this perspective, the Korean War represented a test of the limits of authority and responsibility of the United States in its major role in East Asian affairs after World War II.

The United Nations as an Instrument of American Policy   That the United States should play a major role in East Asia in the post-World War II period was dictated, as suggested above, by previous historical circumstances and by the outcome of the war. There was considerable controversy within the United States, however, especially with the fall of China to Communist rule in 1949, over American goal-values in Asia and over the appropriate instrumentalities of American policy there.

The watchword of American foreign policy from the time of Washington and Jefferson until the 1890s had been to "avoid entangling alliances." From the 1890s until World War II, as we shall suggest in greater detail in Part III, the American orientation toward its world environment vacillated between a new involvement and the traditional posture of nonentanglement. World War II substantially closed the debate. The responsibilities and needs of a superpower were such that

[24] A carefully documented elaboration of this general thesis is made by Soon Sung Cho, *Korea in World Politics 1940–1950* (Berkeley: University of California Press, 1967).

a broad consensus emerged among American leaders regarding the legitimacy of American participation in the United Nations and in NATO —the nation's first participation in a military alliance except in wartime. Nevertheless, the extent to which the United States should compromise its own flexibility and prerogatives on behalf of harmony among members of an alliance or organization to which it had made a commitment remained a matter of debate.

For instance, the President's proposal in the Truman Doctrine speech to Congress in March 1947 called for strict reliance on American government channels in funneling extensive aid to Greece and Turkey; the urgency of the situation was said to preclude a multilateral response through the United Nations. Numerous critics, however, expressed dismay that, less than two years after America's commitment of membership to the United Nations, the institutional mechanisms of the organization were to be ignored. Criticisms ranged from those by prominent columnists, such as Walter Lippmann, to key members of Congress, such as Senator Arthur Vandenberg. A makeshift amendment to the bill was necessary in order to salvage sufficient support to put the Greek-Turkish aid program into operation.

When the Korean attack came, however, the mistake of neglecting the United Nations as the appropriate channel through which to direct the American response was not repeated by the Truman administration. Indeed, beyond the desirability of working through the United Nations to legitimize actions in response to the attack, it is clear from memoirs and interviews of key American policy makers at the time that most of them saw the North Korean attack as representing a crucial test of the fundamental *raison d'être* of the United Nations. In the view of the President and his top advisers, the United Nations faced the oblivion that had been the fate of the League of Nations if its members responded to the blatant armed attack in Korea with nothing more than feeble, perfunctory gestures of disapproval of the sort that members of the League had made in response to the Japanese aggression in Manchuria, to the German remilitarization of the Rhineland, and to the Italian invasion of Ethiopia.

The domestic consensus that supported the decision to work through the United Nations depended, however, upon an additional consensus among the member nations; once the latter consensus disintegrated following Chinese entry into the war, the former did also. The old rationale for a foreign-policy posture that allowed freedom from entanglements of international commitments gained a renewed appeal.

Alliances and other commitments to international organization were essential concomitants of the vast responsibilities of one of the two superpowers in the post-World War II world. It was axiomatic that the success of an international organization depended upon the willingness of member nations to compromise and adjust their national goals to meet the collective interests of the organization. Yet, as Washington, Jefferson, and other architects of early American foreign policy had correctly observed, alliances were entangling; compromises by American policy makers would invariably be regarded by some domestic critics as the sacrifice of fundamental principles and essential national interests. Thus, from the perspective of historical dynamics, the Korean War provides interest, among other reasons, as a case study of the tensions between the continuing appeal of the traditional rationale for nonentanglement of the United States in international politics and the practical exigencies of the role of a superpower in international affairs.

The Korean War in Decision-Making Perspective

Finally, one might analyze the events of the Korean War by focusing on specific decisions made during the conflict, seeking to explain them as aspects of the structure and process of foreign-policy decisions prevalent at the time. Although analysis from a strategic perspective is also concerned with explaining specific decisions, a decision-making perspective, as the term is used here and explained further in Part IV, differs in seeking to identify the calculations that policy makers have made in selecting a given alternative; in identifying the kinds and sources of influence that led them to select a given alternative; and in specifying the functions that various foreign-policy actions and institutions perform in relation to the political system as a whole.

For instance, the decision to respond forcibly to the North Korean attack was explained from a strategic perspective in terms of the felt necessity to avoid a precedent in which Communist use of armed force could be successful in attaining political objectives and in terms of assigning a higher priority than before to Asia in the evolution of the containment strategy. From a decision-making perspective, however, other variables might be considered. For instance, one might focus on such variables as the persons who were involved in making key decisions, the institutional structures within which they operated, the pressure of time under which they made decisions, and the adequacy and nature of information available to them in considering alternative courses of action. The last one, for instance, would be important in explaining the delay of almost a week from the receipt of news of the North Korean attack to the actual decision to commit American ground forces. It was impossible for policy makers in Washington to keep fully abreast of the rapidly changing situation in Korea. During the second day of the war, the South Korean army headquarters abruptly moved out of Seoul to retreat southward, severing communications with their own front-line units defending the city and giving American military advisers no notice of their departure or their destination. The radio station of the American embassy in Seoul was destroyed early the same day; by that time large numbers of Americans in Korea were out of contact not only with Washington, but also with one another. Given the chaotic situation in Korea and the fragmentary reports, it was not until General MacArthur had flown to Korea from Tokyo to make a personal reconnaissance and report, that President Truman and his advisers felt they had sufficient information for considering a large-scale commitment of American troops.[25]

Domestic Politics and the Decision to Commit Troops From a decision-making perspective, one might also focus on the effects of domestic politics on foreign-policy decisions. It is instructive, for instance, to consider the response of the Truman administration to the North Korean attack in the light of preceding and concurrent domestic politics.

Many Americans had found the Truman administration's disclaimer of responsibility for the fall of China to communism in 1949 unacceptable and had viewed with anxiety and doubt the administration's commitment in the ensuing months to the containment of communism in the Far East. Members of the Republican opposition in Congress were especially vocal in their criticism of the policies of the Democratic administration. Among those who led the sharpest attacks upon the Truman administration in 1950 was a young Senator from Wisconsin named Joseph R. McCarthy, who, in the first year after the Second World War, had scored a surprising victory in the primary election, defeating the younger Bob LaFollette and going on to take his place in the United States Senate. The speech that launched the era that was to bear McCarthy's name was made by the Senator in Wheeling, West Virginia, in February 1950, to the Ohio County Women's Republican Club. Contrary to the thesis of the Truman administration that the American government had been helpless to prevent the fall of China to the Communists, Senator McCarthy argued that the American government had been consistently playing into the hands of Communists. The State Department, he charged, was "thoroughly infested with Communists." At

[25] For details of the chaos of the early days of the war, see Sawyer, pp. 114–139; Marguerite Higgins (who covered the early stages of the Korean War as a correspondent for the New York *Herald-Tribune*), *War in Korea* (New York: Doubleday, 1951), pp. 157–166; and T. R. Fehrenbach, *This Kind of War* (New York: Crowell-Collier-Macmillan, 1963), pp. 65–76.

various times in subsequent months, McCarthy was to claim that he had firm evidence to support such charges. The gist of Senator McCarthy's appeal in West Virginia, however, and to thousands of other Americans who learned from the mass media of his allegations that day, was not to documented evidence, but rather to the widespread anxiety and malaise that made the charges emotionally plausible. "How else can we account for our present situation," Joe McCarthy asked his audience rhetorically, "*unless we believe* that men high in the government are concerting to deliver us to disaster? This *must be* the product of a *great conspiracy* on a scale so immense as to dwarf any previous venture in the history of man." [26]

McCarthy repeated his accusations on the floor of the Senate on February 20 and 22. In response, as a means of countering McCarthy's charges by demonstrating that they were unfounded, the leader of the Democratic party in the Senate introduced a resolution that provided for hearings on the charges, to be conducted by a subcommittee of the Senate Committee on Foreign Relations. In March, with Joseph R. McCarthy testifying as the first witness, the widely publicized hearings of the Tydings committee began.[27]

The hearings continued their widely publicized course for several months, and Senator McCarthy repeated and expanded his charges of communist activity and communist sympathy in high places in the government. Secretary of State Acheson called the McCarthy attacks "mad" and "vicious," and President Truman denounced McCarthy by clear implication in a speech to the Federal Bar Association; in turn, McCarthy denounced Truman. Such was the highly charged atmosphere in which the congressional campaigns were developing in June 1950.[28] The salient point is that the allegations of McCarthy and others that the Truman administration was "soft" on communism created pressures upon the administration to demonstrate that these allegations were unfounded. One may hypothesize, therefore, that a concern for this aspect of the domestic political climate contributed to the decision to take a "tough" line in response to the North Korean attack.

[26] Quoted in Norman A. Graebner, "Dean G. Acheson," in Graebner, ed., *An Uncertain Tradition: American Secretaries of State in the Twentieth Century* (New York: McGraw-Hill paperback ed., 1961), p. 282. Italics are added.

[27] The Tydings committee hearings and other related phenomena during, and in the years immediately preceding, the McCarthy era are discussed in scholarly detail by Earl Latham, *The Communist Controversy in Washington* (Cambridge, Mass.: Harvard University Press, 1966).

[28] For a brief chronology of these events and others especially relevant to the Korean War and American policies in Asia, see *China and U.S. Far East Policy*, pp. 35–219.

The distinction between a strategic perspective and a decision-making perspective in analysis can be illustrated also in relation to the Truman-MacArthur controversy. From a strategic perspective, the controversy was produced by intense differences of opinion between the President and the military commander in the field regarding matters of military strategy. From a decision-making perspective, however, one might seek further clues about the controversy in terms of the personalities of the key individuals in the controversy, the roles that they occupied, and the interpersonal relationships that may have influenced their interpretation of events.[29]

Differences in Personality and Experience of Truman and MacArthur

In the first place, it is interesting to note that in many respects Truman and MacArthur were antithetical not only in their views of what was strategically desirable during the Korean War, but also in personality and style. Truman was earthy, close to the people, and humble about the momentous role in history that he had been called upon to perform. MacArthur was aristocratic in temperament, with a sharply defined conception of his rights and obligations as a commander of men and with a profound sense of personal destiny.

Moreover, MacArthur had been a prominent national figure years before Harry Truman's name became known to the public. While still in his twenties, he served as personal military aide to President Theodore Roosevelt. A colorful hero of World War I, MacArthur used to stride through the trenches wearing an overseas cap rather than a helmet and carrying no weapon other than a riding crop. After the war, while still in his thirties, he became superintendent at West Point, pursuing his duties with a vigor that startled the older professors and that effected profound changes throughout the Academy.[30] A few years later, MacArthur was appointed to the top of the army hierarchy as Chief of Staff, where he dealt with the "bonus marchers" and other difficult problems of the Great Depression era. Then, on the eve of World War II, he was called out of retirement by Franklin Roosevelt to assume command of all United States forces in the Far East. MacArthur became an almost

---

[29] The most detailed published account of the controversy focuses primarily upon issues of strategy and tactics, but incorporates abundant description of the political climate of the times; John W. Spanier, *The Truman-MacArthur Controversy and the Korean War* (New York: Norton, paperback ed., 1965).

[30] For the period of his superintendency, see William A. Ganoe, *MacArthur Close-Up* (New York: Vantage, 1962). Ganoe was adjutant to General MacArthur during this period.

legendary leader of American battle with the Japanese in the Pacific, fulfilling his promise in the first months of the war, as he left the embattled Philippines, "I shall return." By the war's end, as Supreme Commander of Allied Powers in Japan, General MacArthur had become the symbol of the authority of the conqueror, held in awe even by the conquered. These were the impressive credentials of General Douglas MacArthur when, at the age of seventy, he became commander in chief of the United Nations forces in Korea.

In contrast, except to those who followed politics closely, Harry Truman was little known nationally even at the time Franklin Roosevelt designated him as his running mate in 1944. Thrust suddenly into the presidency with Roosevelt's death in 1945, Truman had no illusions that he had been destined to serve in the presidency or that he was uniquely qualified to make presidential decisions. On the contrary, as he said at the end of his presidency, Truman guessed that there might be a million people in the country who could have done a better job as President than he. However, as he added on that occasion, "I had the job and I had to do it." [31] Both the relative obscurity of Truman's national record prior to becoming President and his determination to live up to his responsibilities, whatever the gaps in his preparation, would be relevant in explaining the conflict that arose between MacArthur and Truman.

The Web of Interpersonal Relationships   In addition to analyzing the personalities of Truman and MacArthur, it is interesting to explore the interpersonal relationships that existed among other top leaders and between them and Truman or MacArthur. Such interrelationships helped to define the patterns of authority and communications during the months leading up to the dismissal of MacArthur, and they also defined the patterns of confidence and trust among some figures and the lack of confidence among others that contributed to the alignments finally taken when the break between Truman and MacArthur occurred.

For instance, President Truman's top advisers in Washington during the period of mounting friction with MacArthur included General Omar Bradley, as Chairman of the Joint Chiefs of Staff; George C. Marshall, as secretary of defense; and Dean Acheson, as secretary of state. Although each was hesitant, when the occasion arose, to advise Truman to relieve

---

[31] Transcript of presidential press conference for the American Society of Newspaper Editors, April 17, 1952, on file in the Truman Library at Independence, Missouri, as cited in Richard Neustadt, *Presidential Power* (New York: Wiley, 1960), p. 175.

MacArthur, each had been identified previously with policy positions antithetical to those advocated by MacArthur. At least from MacArthur's perspective, therefore, Truman had surrounded himself with advisers unlikely to give MacArthur's views a sympathetic hearing.

Omar Bradley had been a West Point classmate of General Dwight Eisenhower; he had intended to retire from military service in 1950, but with the outbreak of the Korean War, he knew that his retirement plans would have to be delayed.[32] General Bradley was among the group of senior military officers who had fought in Europe during World War II and who had ardently subscribed to the philosophy of the Army Chief of Staff at that time, General George C. Marshall, that the war in Europe merited first priority in the American war effort. Openly critical of this philosophy had been the American commander in the Pacific, General Douglas MacArthur; animosities between those advocating Europe's priority, of whom General Marshall was the symbolic leader, and those advocating Asia, rallying around General MacArthur, lingered in the postwar period.[33]

Omar Bradley was close to George Marshall not only in professional outlook and philosophy; the two had had long years of close personal association. Bradley, as a young major, had served as a faculty member at the Infantry School at Fort Benning under Marshall, who had been Assistant Commandant in charge of training. On the eve of World War II, when Marshall was appointed Chief of Staff of the Army, Bradley served as one of three members of a secretariat under Marshall on the General Staff.[34]

George C. Marshall was born in 1880, as was MacArthur. Marshall graduated from the Virginia Military Institute (VMI), whereas MacArthur graduated from West Point. The two knew one another casually as young lieutenants, when both were stationed at Fort Leavenworth prior to World War I. Like MacArthur, Marshall served with distinction during the First World War, although MacArthur emerged from the war

[32] Omar Bradley, *A Soldier's Story* (New York: Holt, Rinehart and Winston, Inc., 1961), p. ix.

[33] An interesting analysis of these and other factional rivalries within the American military establishment has been made by Morris Janowitz, *The Professional Soldier* (New York: Free Press, 1960), esp. chap. 14.

[34] In 1959, Bradley became president of the George C. Marshall Research Foundation, at Lexington, Virginia, where most of General Marshall's papers and memorabilia are kept. General Bradley has written the foreword to both of the two volumes completed to date of the three-volume biography by Forrest C. Pogue, *George C. Marshall*, 1, *Education of a General, 1880–1939* (New York: Viking, 1963), ix–xi; 2, *Ordeal and Hope, 1939–1942* (New York: Viking, 1966), ix–xii.

as a brigadier general, and Marshall, as a colonel. Ironically, although Marshall's efficiency reports continued to note his exceptional performance, he did not become a brigadier general until late in 1936. For several years previous to the promotion, the Army Chief of Staff, to whom numerous appeals were made on behalf of the promotion of George Marshall, was four-star General Douglas MacArthur. Marshall's biographer notes that "the often repeated story that Marshall's promotion was held up by General MacArthur because of differences between them dating back to World War I is not borne out by the record at any point";[35] nevertheless, the fact that the rumor of MacArthur's hindrance of Marshall's career was repeated contributed to the acerbic relations between the two officers. The reversed relationship during World War II, with Marshall as Army Chief of Staff and thus the man to whom MacArthur was directly responsible in the military chain of command, had only made the relationship more awkward.[36]

After World War II, General Marshall had been sent by President Truman to China, to seek to achieve a reconciliation between the Nationalists and the Communists. Marshall had spent most of 1946 in China in a futile effort to bring the opposing groups to a harmonious agreement; in December, he had been called back to Washington to become Secretary of State. But although President Truman's confidence in Marshall's character and judgment had obviously remained high, those who subsequently saw in the fall of China to communism the contrivance or stupidity of American officialdom linked the name of George Marshall with those of Franklin Roosevelt, Harry Truman, and others considered responsible for failure in the Far East. Among the critics was Douglas MacArthur.[37]

[35] Pogue, 1:294.

[36] See Pogue, 2: esp. 184–185.

[37] In his memoirs, MacArthur has referred to Marshall as having "made the tragic mistake of using American prestige as a lever for attempting to force a coalition government on Chiang Kai-shek." Referring to American policy toward China during the early postwar period, MacArthur observed, "Instead of pushing on to the victory that was within the Generalissimo's grasp, an armistice was arranged, and General Marshall was sent to amalgamate the two opponents. . . . Mentally, he had aged immeasurably. . . . The former incisiveness and virility were gone. . . . After months of fruitless negotiation, he withdrew without tangible results, and the war for China resumed. But in this interval of seven months a decisive change had taken place." The result of the Marshall mission, according to MacArthur, was that American aid to Chiang Kai-shek had been suspended, while the Chinese Communists had gained a decisive advantage through aid from the Soviet Union. This was "the beginning of the crumbling of our power in continental Asia, . . ." the results of which "will be felt for centuries. . . ." MacArthur, pp. 343, 320.

In September 1950, immediately after MacArthur had engineered the masterful landing at Inchon, Marshall came out of semiretirement to become secretary of defense. Thus, the man whom Bradley regarded as his "ideal of the best type of officer" had become his civilian chief.[38] Bradley and Marshall, together with the Army Chief of Staff, General J. Lawton Collins, and the President, Harry Truman, comprised the "higher authority" about which MacArthur, according to his memoirs, had begun to have misgivings even in the moment of victory at Inchon.[39]

Although not a part of the chain of command to whom MacArthur was formally responsible, Secretary of State Dean Acheson was also part of the *de facto* group higher authority and also among those who was suspect for his role in shaping postwar American policy in the Far East. The most conspicuous aspect of Acheson's policy role, subject to repeated attacks by critics as having been the lure that brought on the initial North Korean attack, was his speech in January 1950, in which he effectually declared Korea and Formosa to be outside of the American defense perimeter in the Far East. That occasion, MacArthur was later to recall, convinced the general that "the Secretary of State was badly advised about the Far East"; thus, MacArthur invited Acheson to Tokyo to give him an opportunity to improve his knowledge. Acheson declined; but he did, however, MacArthur pointedly noted, visit Europe eleven times during his tenure as secretary of state.[40] Actually, Acheson had been linked to the controversial policies of the Roosevelt and Truman administrations in the Far East through much earlier activity, having served in the State Department since 1941. Throughout George Marshall's futile, or, from MacArthur's perspective, disastrous, mission to China in 1946, Dean Acheson, then under secretary of state, had served as Marshall's personal representative, relaying messages from Marshall to the President and getting information back to Marshall promptly.[41] Consequently, Acheson was not only among those prominently identified with postwar American policies in the Far East, but, like Bradley, also with serving Marshall. In fact, upon Marshall's return from China to become secretary of state, Acheson, as under secretary of state, had become Marshall's immediate subordinate, and like Bradley, he had developed a tremendous admiration and respect for Marshall.[42] More-

[38] Bradley's praise for Marshall is from his foreword to Pogue, 1:ix.
[39] MacArthur, p. 357.
[40] MacArthur, p. 322.
[41] This role is described by Acheson in his chapter on General Marshall in *Sketches from Life of Men I Have Known* (New York: Harper & Row, 1959), pp. 147–166.
[42] Acheson's high regard for Marshall is revealed in the former's *Sketches from Life.*

over, he had a high regard for President Truman, a feeling that was reciprocated.[43]

Joe Martin's Political Acumen In addition to noting the background of interpersonal relationships that characterized Truman's advisers in Washington, we can also analyze the pattern of interaction between MacArthur and Congressman Joe Martin, which culminated in a widely publicized letter, triggering Truman's final decision to dismiss MacArthur.

By early 1951, the policies that General MacArthur had recommended for an all-out effort against China, but which President Truman and his advisers in Washington had rejected, were widely known and debated in the United States and elsewhere. Joe Martin, the Republican minority leader in the House of Representatives, was among those who joined the debate in the winter of 1950–1951. Fully named Joseph W. Martin, Jr., by 1951 he had been in Congress for nearly thirty years as a representative from Massachusetts; he had acquired not only seniority, but plenty of political savvy. As a man who prided himself in being a practical politician rather than a theorist or an ideologist, Martin had always had a sense of mutual understanding with Franklin Roosevelt, although they had battled over many political issues. Martin's relationship with Truman was similar. Joe Martin and Harry Truman regarded each other as friends and as colleagues. But in Martin's mind, the issues in early 1951 transcended personal friendship. The policies of the Truman administration in Korea, he thought, had become policies of defeatism and appeasement of communism. Thus, he saw in Douglas MacArthur an attitude that he felt should be widely spread.[44]

At a Lincoln Day dinner in Brooklyn in February 1951, Martin took up the cry. "What kind of logic is it that lets our soldiers die in Korea when, by shipping the proper supplies to the Generalissimo [Chiang Kai-shek], a second front could be opened in China without a single GI being forced to place a foot on the soil of the Chinese mainland?" he asked his audience of the Kings County Republican Committee. "What are we in Korea for—" he demanded, "to win or to lose? . . . If we are not in Korea to win, then this administration should be indicted for the murder of thousands of American boys." [45]

[43] Joseph Jones, who worked in the State Department under both Marshall and Acheson, notes that even as early as 1947, when Acheson was still under secretary of state, he had established an extremely close and effective relationship with the President and enjoyed his complete confidence. Jones, *The Fifteen Weeks* (New York: Harbinger, 1964; first ed., New York: Viking, 1955), pp. 110–113.

[44] Joe Martin, as told to Robert J. Donovan, *My First Fifty Years in Politics* (New York: McGraw-Hill, 1960).

[45] Martin, pp. 202–203.

Although his convictions were firm, Martin recalls in his memoirs that he recognized that it might be desirable to temper his opinions by getting facts from someone more knowledgeable about "the true state of affairs in the Far East. . . ." What better source of information was there than General MacArthur, who "was on the scene and knew what was happening"? Thus, because he felt that "Republicans were entitled to the truth if we were effectively to defend our side of the argument," Martin wrote a letter to MacArthur, enclosing a copy of his Lincoln Day speech calling for enlargement of the war in Korea in order to secure victory. The letter told MacArthur that Martin would deem it "a great help" if he could have MacArthur's views on the issue, either on a confidential or other basis.[46]

MacArthur notes in his memoirs that he had "always felt duty-bound to reply frankly to every congressional inquiry into matters connected with [his] official responsibility." Therefore, in a letter dated March 20, MacArthur replied to Martin, stating his strong agreement with his views, including those on the wisdom of using Chinese Nationalist troops from Formosa. "As you point out," MacArthur wrote in closing, "we must win. There is no substitute for victory."[47]

Martin reveals in his memoirs a few days of anguish after his receipt of the letter. MacArthur had not indicated whether or not the letter was to be kept confidential, and Martin knew that its contents would bring a sharp outcry from the Truman administration because of its provocative contents, which were directly contradictory to the policies of the Truman administration. He revealed the contents only to a few persons, Martin notes, such as the public relations director for the Republican National Campaign Committee. In early April, listening to debate in Congress that seemed to Martin to reflect the confused thinking that had become so rampant, suddenly all his doubts about what to do with the letter disappeared; he reasoned, "If ever there was a time when a voice of authority needed to be heard it was now." Therefore, the following day, on the floor of Congress, Martin made the letter public.[48]

Martin's disclosure of the letter from MacArthur was the final act, according to Truman, that convinced the President that "the time had come to draw the line" with General MacArthur. As a footnote on Martin's role in the aftermath of Truman's dismissal of MacArthur, it is interesting to note that it was Martin who, within hours of learning of Truman's action, called Tokyo and heard from MacArthur's senior aide that MacArthur would agree to address a joint session of Congress upon

---

[46] Martin, pp. 203–204.
[47] MacArthur, p. 386.
[48] Martin, pp. 205–207.

his return to the United States. Martin quickly called a political strategy meeting of top Republican leaders in Congress and engineered the invitation to MacArthur from the Speaker of the House, Sam Rayburn, a Democrat from Texas.

MacArthur returned to the United States after fifteen consecutive years in Asia and half a century of service in uniform as a legendary figure. It is unnecessary to recall here the tumultuous welcome that he received upon his return or to recite details of his famous speech to Congress. The close interrelationship of the foreign-policy process and domestic politics can be underlined, however, by noting the impact of MacArthur's speech. Although the issues with which he dealt in his speech were those of foreign policy, which, in his words, "reach beyond the realm of partisan consideration," the domestic political significance of this widely publicized attack on the policies of the Truman administration by a military hero, with a presidential election campaign only a year away, was obvious to everyone. The reaction of Congress was therefore one of sentiment mixed with glee or anxiety, depending upon one's political persuasion. As Joe Martin observed of the reaction on both sides of the aisle of Congress as MacArthur spoke his final words, "there wasn't . . . a dry eye on the Republican side nor a dry seat on the Democratic." [49]

Perspectives for Analysis: Significance of the Distinctions

The events and decisions made during the Korean War, like most important foreign-policy phenomena, are composed of the interplay of numerous variables. We do not purport to have explained fully American foreign policies during the Korean War; rather, our objective thus far has been to use the foreign-policy experience of the Korean War as a frame of reference from which to make the simple point that as one applies varying perspectives for analysis of foreign policy, the questions that one explores will vary, and the kinds of data that are pertinent will vary.

In Parts II, III, and IV of the book, we shall identify more precisely the underlying rationale of each of the three analytical perspectives that have been introduced. Many terms and ideas mentioned only briefly in discussing the Korean War experience will be expanded and clarified: for example, the concept of strategy and the doctrine of containment; the historical evolution from a posture of nonentanglement in interna-

[49] "The theatrical effect was superb," Martin added. Martin, p. 212.

tional politics to deep involvement; and the concept of a political system and the variables that relate to its structure and functioning. Subsequent discussion will allow us to build further a framework for analysis through a more systematic identification of relevant variables, from each analytical perspective, to explanation of foreign-policy phenomena, and through the formulation of hypotheses that postulate interrelationships between variables.

In a conclusion of the introductory section of the book, it is appropriate to explain further how the distinctions between various analytical perspectives relate to the two major objectives of the book—developing guidelines that will be useful to the reader in his own analysis of foreign policy and assisting him in utilizing effectively other writings about American foreign policy.

We have suggested above how a strategic perspective, a perspective of historical dynamics, and a decision-making perspective, respectively, might be applied to the analysis of a particular set of foreign-policy phenomena. Of course, the number of ways in which it is possible to view foreign-policy phenomena is, as a matter of abstract logic, infinite. Grouping all possibilities into three broad categories is, therefore, an arbitrary judgment that is defensible only in terms of their utility. In practice, the number of perspectives utilized by modern observers of foreign policy in their writings about foreign policy is limited; rather, distinct similarities among perspectives are apparent. In spite of the great variety that exists in research methods, stylistic idiosyncracies, and political values among analysts of foreign policy, classification of foreign-policy analyses into a handful of categories is feasible in terms of the kinds of data that authors consider relevant and in terms of the theories to which they are especially attentive. In the author's judgment, one can usefully describe much of the extant writing on foreign policy in terms of the three analytical perspectives that have been identified; the categories are especially applicable if one limits his review to studies that are clearly analytical rather than merely descriptive or polemical.

We use the term "analytical perspective" to refer to the focus of an analytical inquiry and to the theoretical or pretheoretical foundations that guide the gathering and organization of data in the inquiry. Distinguishing features of the three key analytical perspectives are summarized in Table 1 and described in the remainder of the chapter. No extensive classification of specific studies will be made in the book, although a few particular works are cited below to provide further illustration of the application of distinctive perspectives to analysis of the Korean War experience. As the reader becomes more familiar with each of the perspectives, he will see not only features that distinguish

TABLE 1
Key Perspectives for the Analysis of American Foreign Policy

Analytical Perspective	Focus of Analysis	Characteristic Form of Analysis	Theoretical Reference Points
Strategic	Broad pattern of continuity and change *or* Decision or series of decisions	Purposes of policy makers (strategic and tactical)	Theories of military strategy Economic theory Theory of games
Historical dynamics	Broad pattern of continuity and change	Preconditions for and precipitants of events	Theories of history Theories of social change Theories of development Systems theory
Decision making	Decision or series of decisions	Structure and process of decision making	Theories of political process Systems theory Organization theory Social-psychological theory Economic theory

some important writings on foreign policy from others, but also advantages and limitations in the employment of each of the perspectives for his own analytical purposes.

Strategic Perspectives

From a strategic perspective, broad patterns of continuity and change in foreign policy are explained in terms of the strategic purposes of policy makers. Specific decisions or series of decisions are interpreted in terms of tactical considerations. An instructive example of an analysis of foreign policy from a strategic perspective is Morton H. Halperin's *Limited War in the Nuclear Age*, of which Chapter 3 focuses on the Korean War.[50]

[50] Morton H. Halperin, *Limited War in the Nuclear Age* (New York: Wiley, 1963). See also Robert Osgood, *Limited War* (Chicago: University of Chicago Press, 1957), chap. 8; and Martin Lichterman, "Korea: Problems in Limited War," in Gordon B. Turner and Richard D. Challener, eds., *National Security in the Nuclear Age* (New York: Praeger, paperback ed., 1960), pp. 31–56.

Foreign-policy analysts who employ a strategic perspective have drawn especially on three bodies of theory. The first of these comprises theories of military strategy, including those of Julius Caesar, Frederick the Great, Napoleon, Clausewitz, and such twentieth-century theorists as Douhet, Ché Guevara, and Mao Tse-tung. Aspects of economic theory that relate to maximal utility, bargaining, and the use of resources constitute a second body of theory. Closely related to economic theory is the third body of theory, which is the most recent and perhaps the most important current source of theoretical guidance for the strategic perspective; this is the theory of games, which will be discussed further in Chapter 3.

Perspectives of Historical Dynamics

A second alternative in analysis of foreign policy is to focus upon a particular facet of the American experience, such as the Korean War, in the context of historical continuity and change. The object of analysis from the second perspective is the general orientation or stand of the nation-state to its world environment or to a major portion of it over a broad span of time. Analysis focuses on explaining how and why particular orientations are developed and why change occurs, in terms of preconditions and precipitants. John Lukacs' *History of the Cold War* is an imaginative example of foreign-policy analysis from this perspective; for Lukacs' interpretation of the Korean War, see his fourth chapter.[51]

Theories of history, such as those associated with Arnold Toynbee, are an important part of the theoretical heritage upon which this second perspective draws. So closely related to theories of history as to be often indistinguishable are theories of social change, such as that of Karl Marx. In the modern era, concern with the processes of economic, social, and political change in developing areas has generated another body of theory that contributes to the historical-dynamics perspective. Finally, the treatment of relations between nation-states in terms of the concept of a system reflects still another body of relevant theory, which is systems theory.

Decision-Making Perspectives

A third important perspective from which many analyses of American foreign policy have been made is a decision-making perspective. The key

---

[51] John Lukacs, *A History of the Cold War* (New York: Doubleday, Anchor paperback ed., 1962).

object of analysis in this case is a particular foreign-policy decision or series of decisions. Analysis relates the structure and process of foreign-policy making to the outcome of particular decisions. Glenn Paige has done an exacting study of the American foreign-policy process during the first week of the Korean War in *The Korean Decision*, which provides an excellent illustration of analysis from this perspective.[52]

The decision-making perspective is rooted in various theories. Much of the work of twentieth-century political theorists has been concerned with the process of political decision making, and their formulations constitute one important source of the decision-making perspective. A second source is systems theory, as applied to the concept of a political system; more will be said about this concept in Chapter 7. Third, especially from sociological analysis, a body of organization theory has developed, which too has provided insights for the decision-making perspective. Fourth, many analyses from a decision-making perspective have drawn upon social-psychological theories of human behavior. Finally, as in the case of the strategic perspective, the decision-making perspective is indebted to economic theory.

Although specific books, articles, or monographs will be occasionally cited in subsequent chapters to illustrate or to provide a further source of information on particular points, no individual foreign-policy analysts or works will be singled out for extended critical appraisal; commenting adequately on the vast array of works that might be included in each category would transform this book into a bibliographical essay, which is not our intention. Our method will be to articulate a rationale for using each of the three analytical perspectives that have been identified above; when the distinctive characteristics of each perspective have been clarified, each perspective will be applied to the analysis of particular aspects of the American foreign-policy experience in order to illustrate the utility as well as the limitations of each approach.

[52] Glenn Paige, *The Korean Decision* (New York: Free Press, 1968).

Part II

Strategic Perspectives

Our first analytical view of American foreign
policy will be from a strategic perspective; other
important aspects of foreign policy will receive
emphasis in later chapters. Many of the important American foreign-policy decisions in the
post-World War II period have stemmed from
strategic considerations, however, and much of
the recent writing about foreign policy employs
a distinct strategic perspective and language.
In the contemporary period of "think tanks,"
war games, and strategic scenarios, therefore,
one who seeks to understand and assess American foreign policy knowledgeably and to utilize
available studies of foreign policy with maximum insight should master the vocabulary and
identify the rationale of strategy.

Theories of military strategy, economic theories, and especially the modern theory of games
constitute the key theoretical reference points
in analysis from a strategic perspective. How-

61

ever, not all studies that one might classify as analyses from a strategic perspective would explicitly refer to any or all of these bodies of theory; some authors draw upon a body of theory explicitly and rigorously in their analyses, others do not. Irrespective of such differences, however, we would describe analyses as utilizing a strategic perspective when they interpret foreign-policy phenomena primarily in terms of a conscious design by policy makers to attain goals in competition with other nation-states. Attentiveness to a body of theory that has been developed in relation to, or with relevance for, such a situation can help the reader to apply a strategic perspective in his own analyses more systematically or to interpret more critically other analyses in which a strategic perspective is employed.

Detailed knowledge by the reader of the body of theory that is most relevant to analysis from a strategic perspective would help him to identify the distinguishing features of this perspective and to apply it with rigor. However, such detailed knowledge is not assumed here. Moreover, it is not our intention to provide a disquisition on game theory or on other relevant bodies of theory that would be sufficient to provide such detailed knowledge.[1] Rather, a few key concepts and assumptions from game theory, deterrence theory, and other relevant bodies of theory will be introduced simply as means of suggesting how foreign-policy phenomena tend to be viewed and what kinds of actions and events tend to be emphasized when a strategic perspective for analysis is employed.

Analysis from a strategic perspective can provide useful insights in the study of foreign policy, many of which we shall try to convey in Chapter 3 and 4; it is also an approach with limitations and potential pitfalls, however. The reader is invited to consider what the limitations and potential pitfalls may be; some of the important ones will be identified in the concluding section of Chapter 4.

---

[1] The exposition of game theory that stands as the classic in the field is that of John von Neumann and Oskar Morgenstern, *Theory of Games and Economic Behavior* (Princeton: Princeton University Press, 1944). The relationship between game theory and foreign-policy strategy is described and illustrated extensively by Thomas C. Schelling, *The Strategy of Conflict* (New York: Oxford University Press, paperback ed., 1963). An entertaining and useful popular treatment of some of the key ideas of game theory is available in paperback form in John McDonald, *Strategy in Poker, Business and War* (New York: Norton, Norton Library ed., 1963).

3

Playing the Game of International Politics

The Game of International Politics

The Claim of Sovereignty

The most basic institutional fact about the world environment is that the international system, as distinguished from the domestic political system, lacks a single, commonly recognized locus of higher authority. Of course, no nation-state in the modern world can operate completely as a law unto itself, and to a greater or lesser degree the leaders of every nation-state accept limitations upon the authority of their state— through alliances and agreements with other states, through informal habits and practices, through commitments to the United Nations or to others of the more than two hundred formal international organizations that exist today, and through moral restraints. The crucial point, however, is the overriding claim of national sovereignty on the emotions and commitments of leaders when the interests of their nation-states are at stake. As George Kennan, long in the diplomatic service of the United States, has aptly observed, "the sovereign national state, this child of the modern age, notwithstanding the mantle of nebulous moral obligation in which it likes to wrap itself still recognizes in the crucial moments of its own destiny no law but that of its own egoism—no higher focus of obligation, no overriding ethical code." [1]

One may deplore, as many do, the semianarchic quality of the international system. The experience of the twentieth century is ample testimony to the conduciveness of the system to violent conflict when the interests of nation-states, each committed to the perpetuation of its own sovereignty, collide. Yet, the transformation of the international system into a more unified, tranquil whole is not a likely prospect in the foreseeable future.

Kennan has described the predicament with pathos as well as humor:

> I am often accused of approving this state of affairs (that is, the egoism of nations) because I insist on the recognition of its reality. Actually, I think, no one could be more sadly conscious than is the professional diplomatist of the primitiveness, the anarchism, the intrinsic absurdity of the modern concept of sovereignty. Could anything be more absurd than a world divided into several dozens of large secular societies, each devoted to the cultivation of its own myth of its own overriding importance and virtue, of the sacrosanctity of its own unlimited independence? A thousand times right are the enthusiasts of world government in their protest against the philosophic childishness of this concept, however many times wrong they may be in their ideas as to how it might be corrected.
>
> But the diplomatist, as people frequently forget, is the servant of this system of nation-states; it is precisely to the working of this imperfect mechanism that his efforts are dedicated. He is professionally condemned to tinker with a badly built and decrepit car, aware that his function is not to question the design or to grumble over the decrepitude, but to keep the confounded contraption running, some way or other. [2]

The predicament of the policy maker is that, however absurd he may personally regard the concept of absolute sovereignty of the nation-state, under existing conditions of the international system, he is virtually compelled by his role to view his primary responsibility as that of ad-

---

[1] George Kennan, "History and Diplomacy as Viewed by a Diplomatist," *The Review of Politics,* 18 (Apr., 1956), 170–177, 171.

[2] Kennan, p. 171.

vancing the interests of his own nation-state in competition with the interests of more than one hundred other nation-states. The prime task of foreign-policy making from his perspective, in other words, is that of designing strategies for competing effectively in the complex and sometimes deadly game of international politics.

One means by which the concerned observer can increase his understanding of foreign policy is to try to emulate the perspective of the policy maker and to view events and decisions in terms of his responsibility for designing effective strategies. Analysis from a strategic perspective, in other words, involves putting oneself in the position of the policy maker in order to discern the rationale for his actions. In treating international politics or a particular encounter in foreign policy as a game, the consequences of the decisions and actions of policy makers are seen in relation to an implicit (and sometimes explicit) scoreboard or tally sheet, by which the progress of the game is assessed. Thus, more so than in other perspectives for analysis, a normative dimension is an integral part of analysis from a strategic perspective. Observers who employ this perspective often tend to be "Monday-morning quarterbacks" about the game of international politics—and sometimes "Monday-morning Napoleons."

The remainder of Chapter 3 is devoted to introducing concepts characteristically important to analysis from a strategic perspective and to identifying particulary salient variables.

Foreign-Policy Strategy

Although the term "strategy" has been used primarily in reference to the design of military operations for war, it has a much broader applicability. It can be used to refer to any predesigned set of moves, or series of decisions, in a competitive situation where the outcome is not governed purely by chance.[3] The concept of employing a strategy, in fact, is a familiar one in most games, whether the game is an explicit one with formal rules, such as chess or football, or an implicit game with largely informal rules, such as courtship or politics.[4]

In international politics, over one hundred nation-states each pursues interests that conflict with those of other nation-states in a game where rules are largely unwritten and informal, evolving mainly through the wishes of the stronger players. In a broad sense, a foreign-policy strategy

[3] Obviously in a game of pure chance, such as "Russian roulette," the concept of a strategy is irrelevant.

[4] Other examples of implicit games are discussed by Eric Berne, *Games People Play* (New York: Grove, 1964).

is a plan for advancing one's own national interests (as one defines those interests) while preventing other players from impinging on them. However, since strategy is a concept adaptable to broad or narrow usage and to a variety of situations, two points should be kept in mind.

The first is that a series of moves that might be regarded as strategic in relationship to an immediate objective might be regarded as tactical in longer-range terms. The second is that, whereas for some purposes a given series of interactions might be regarded as a game in itself, for other purposes the interactions might be regarded simply as a phase of a larger game. A hypothetical but familiar example will illustrate these points. Imagine the process in a college student's mind as he discusses with his date what they should do after attending the movies. In a sense, this discussion between a boy and a girl is a game in itself, and the boy's plan to persuade his date to do what he wants might be termed a strategy. From a longer-range perspective, however, the discussion might be viewed as part of a game of longer duration and as a tactical move to develop a longer-range strategy.

Likewise, in foreign policy, we frequently hear the observation that various crises during the post-World War II period—for example, the events in Greece and Turkey that led to the Truman Doctrine in 1947, the Korean War, or the Cuban missile crisis of 1962—were but individual battles in the Cold War. In one sense, the Cold War is the game, and each of the various crises are only stages in this game. Moreover, from that perspective, the plans that the United States government designed in order to cope with the various crises were but tactical elements of the broader Cold War strategy of containment. From another perspective, however, one could term each crisis a game; and in that case, the plans for dealing with each one would be termed strategy.

Although there is no single correct scope of applicability of the concepts of game, strategy, and tactics, as applied to international politics, we shall largely be using the terms "game" and "strategy" broadly, in reference to international politics generally or to a conflict such as the Cold War that extends over a period of years. We shall view specific decisions or series of decisions as tactical maneuvers within a broader context of strategy.

The Rationale of Strategy: Cost–Gain Estimates

Strategy, as indicated above, is basically a plan for achieving success in a contest; in foreign policy, strategy is a plan by which policy makers seek to advance the interests of their nation-state while preventing other nation-states from impinging on such interests. There are, analytically, two components of strategy: an offensive component—the design for making gains—and a defensive component—the design for preventing losses.

The offensive component must take into account not only the possible rewards to be derived from particular actions, but also the chances of success and the estimated cost of the actions. To take a hypothetical example, suppose that the American government were to decide to support actively insurgent groups in various parts of Africa, in hopes of bringing the apartheid policy of South Africa to an end and of freeing Angola from Portuguese rule. The questions that would confront American policy makers in the design of such a strategy would be the desirability of the goal, the likelihood of accomplishing it, and the cost (in human lives, money, other material resources, or prestige) to pursue such a strategy. Presumably, questions similar to these were asked by the administrations from Franklin Roosevelt's time to the present regarding Communist control of Eastern Europe. From the perspective of American policy makers, the issue has never been whether or not it would be desirable for the peoples of Poland, Czechoslovakia, Hungary, Albania, Bulgaria, and Rumania to exercise a free choice in the selection of their governments; every American administration since the closing months of World War II has gone on record as favoring such a goal. Rather, the issue has been what the United States could do about the situation and the costliness (for example, an all-out war with the Soviet Union) of an effort to rectify the situation. In practice, even the call of John Foster Dulles during the election campaign of 1952 for a policy of "rollback" rather than mere containment of communism turned out to be but an amplified statement of desiderata rather than a revision of strategic intentions, as American passivity in response to the Soviet suppression of an uprising in Hungary in 1956 vividly revealed.

Defensive strategy includes a plan for preventing actions by others that would threaten one's interests, as well as a plan for responding to threats in the event that prevention fails. Much of the speculation by American policy makers as well as armchair strategists in the past twenty years has been devoted to the design of means and techniques for preventing international threats or attacks. "Deterrence" is the term usually applied to such preventive design in foreign policy, and the means or instruments to be employed are termed "deterrents." Whereas offensive strategy is based on at least a crude estimate of probable gains versus risks of loss from various courses of action, defensive strategy is designed in relationship to the cost–gain estimates that underly the strategies of other nation-states. Deterrence involves an effort to influence the strategies of others by increasing their cost-gain estimates in considering a course of action that those designing deterrence wish to prevent or by making alternative courses of action more attractive. In simple terms, successful deterrence is a matter of finding the right "sticks and carrots" to influence the actions of others. (It should be noted that in most of the writings about deterrence theory, deterrents have been described exclusively as "sticks"—that is, as threats. Experienced policy makers and diplomats know, however, that "carrots" as well as "sticks" are needed in successful strategy.)

What makes the design of effective deterrence especially complicated for policy makers is that cost–gain estimates are subjective judgments. Successful deterrence is therefore a matter of correctly appraising the strategic perspective of the party to be deterred and of communicating effectively to influence his judgment. Specifically, successful deterrence imposes the following requirements: (1) The deterrent must be based upon an accurate assessment of the courses of action available to the party to be deterred and of the relative risks and probable gains, from his perspective, of various courses of action. (2) The deterrent must impose potential costs for the course of action that policy makers hope to prevent that are greater than the adversary's gains would be from the action; alternately the deterrent must make an alternative course of action more attractive. (3) The intention to impose costs or to provide rewards for various courses of action must be communicated to the party. (4) The intention to carry out the deterrent threat (or reward) must be credible; that is, the party to be deterred must believe the threat or the promise. What makes the game interesting is that a shrewd policy maker will not always intend to make good the threat or the reward that he has communicated to another player in order to deter him from a particular course of action. For reasons to be indicated later in the chapter, occasional bluffing is a desirable tactic in supporting effective strategy.

Having distinguished between offensive and defensive strategy, we must emphasize that in practice the distinction is rarely neat. In international politics, as in a fast-moving game of basketball or hockey, a successful team must remain continually attentive both to advancing its interests and to preventing an opponent from impinging on them. Moreover, in international politics, determination of which strategic elements or instruments are offensive and which defensive depends to some extent on who is in a losing position. From the viewpoint of the American government, NATO was created as an instrument of defense against an ominous threat of attack on Western Europe by Soviet armies; the later Warsaw Pact, on the other hand, from the American perspective, was further evidence of the offensive threat of Soviet strategy. To the Soviets, however, NATO was an offensive threat aimed at them, whereas the Warsaw

Pact, created after NATO had come into existence, was merely a defensive response. The tyranny of euphemisms that exterminates "War Departments" and replaces them with "Departments of Defense" obscures the distinction between offensive and defensive components of foreign-policy strategy still further. Thus, although the strategy used for illustration in Chapter 4 is that termed "containment," which by definition would seem to be defensive, one should recognize that offensive as well as defensive calculations were inextricably involved in this strategy. Such a mixture of offensive and defensive considerations is typical of foreign-policy strategy.

Analysis of the Design of Strategy: Key Variables

As indicated above, we are using the concepts "game" and "strategy" broadly in our discussion of international politics, to refer to selected facets of the foreign-policy experience of a nation-state (especially of the United States) over a considerable span of time—often a period of years. Foreign-policy analysis from a strategic perspective seeks to explain discernible patterns in terms of the calculations that policy makers have made about certain goals. Even in instances where abundant data exist about what policy makers said or did at the time of particular decisions and actions, obviously the analyst cannot be certain that the data reflect completely accurately the thought processes of policy makers. Indeed, the policy makers themselves may not be able to identify the underlying motivations for their decisions. However, to the extent that a series of foreign-policy actions over a period of time creates identifiable patterns, the policy analyst may assume that the moves reflect a design rather than merely random action. His retrospective judgment about the design can be guided by knowledge of the logical requisites of successful competition in various kinds of circumstances.

Having identified a pattern of decisions, the analyst of foreign policy who employs a strategic perspective deduces a rationale for the decisions, basing it upon his retrospective assessment of the key variables at the time decisions were made. Assuming the position of the policy maker, he asks the following questions. What parties were involved in the game that was being played, as American policy makers defined the game, and what alignments were formed among the parties? What were the stakes in the game, as perceived by American policy makers? What were the perceived capabilities of the United States to compete in the game, at the time a strategy was designed? What estimates did American policy makers make of the strategies that other parties would pursue? What rules were accepted by the United States in the course of the game? The relevance of each of the questions to the explanation of the design of strategy will be indicated below, with a suggestion of the kinds of evidence that one might use to answer each of the questions in a particular context.

Parties and Alignments

Chess, football, tennis, bridge, and most other familiar games that are played for recreation or professional sport are characterized by competition between two single opponents or two opposing teams, each of which seeks to score points at the other's expense. Some athletic contests, such as track meets, may involve competition among several teams concurrently, although the rules forbid conspiracy or alliances among teams. In many other forms of competition, however, not only are there multiple parties, but the parties may bargain and negotiate among themselves, forming coalitions or conspiracies to compete more successfully. Such a situation prevails, for instance, in economic competition among firms and in competition among interest groups to realize their objectives in politics. The situation also prevails in competition among nation-states in international politics; the analysis of foreign-policy strategy is thereby complicated, for reasons that can be specified briefly.

From a strategic perspective, a coalition is a means whereby a party may achieve an increase in the benefits derived ("payoffs," in the language of game theory) or at least a reduction in the risks to its interests. (In game theory, the reduction of risks is expressed as an increase in one's "security level.") In a game where coalitions among parties are possible, the design of effective strategy necessarily includes decisions about what kinds of coalitions to form (for example, military alliances, economic cartels); what parties to include in a coalition; and what costs ("side-payments," in the language of game theory) one should be willing to incur in order to form a coalition.

The complexity that distinguishes a game where coalitions are possible from one where there are merely two opponents can hardly be overstated. In international politics, even conflicts that appear on the surface to be struggles between two parties characteristically involve efforts by one or both of the parties to strengthen their position in the conflict through coalitions with other nation-states. For instance, the Cold War has been the central focus of American foreign-policy strategy since the end of World War II. As discussion in Chapter 4 will suggest, in some respects the Cold War has resembled a two-party game, a struggle between the world's two superpowers. It is also true that American policy makers have often been inclined to view each Soviet gain in the international arena as a setback for American interests and to view each American gain as a defeat for the Soviet Union. Even within the context of the Cold War, however, it is clear that the formulation of American strategy has not been based exclusively on calculations regarding the Soviets. Rather, alliances as well as less formal working agreements with other nation-states have constituted an integral part of the design of American strategy. Furthermore, it is instructive to observe that American-Soviet relations have included some elements of cooperation, designed to further mutual interests, however dominated the relationship has been by conflict.

In short, like most important conflicts in international politics, however much the Cold War may have resembled a "two-person, zero-sum" game—as students of formal game theory would put it—close analysis reveals that it has been an "N-person, nonzero" game. That is, more than two parties have been involved, with the number of parties and alignments among them fluctuating. Moreover, the gains of one party have not always been made at the expense of another. Rather, in some instances, cooperation has led to outcomes beneficial in varying degrees to all parties (a "positive-sum" outcome—cultural exchange programs, for instance). In other instances, competition has led to a net deficit of costs versus gains for all parties concerned (a "negative-sum" outcome— as in the competition between the United States and the Soviet Union to develop and stockpile H-bombs).

Analysis of foreign-policy strategy is thus tremendously complex. A starting point for the concerned observer lies in identifying the parties that are involved in the contest for which the strategy is designed, in observing alignments that occur among and between parties, and in determining the kinds of bargains that have been struck in forming coalitions.

Stakes of the Game[5]

A poker player is likely to alter his strategy depending upon whether the pot is large or small, just as a football quarterback is likely to employ a somewhat different strategy for the league-championship game from the one for the preseason warm-up game with the junior varsity. Likewise, it is clear that variations in the stakes of a game of international politics lead to variations in the strategies. The stakes are calculated in

[5] Conceived of in the terminology of game theory as the "payoff matrix" for the game.

terms of priorities that policy makers assign to various national interests and objectives and in terms of their estimates of the extent to which particular interests are threatened or made secure by the contest at hand.

The difficulties of making an accurate retrospective analysis of what were once considered the stakes of a game lie not only in the fact that the policy makers' judgments might have been implicit rather than explicit, but also in the fact that the stakes may have changed over time. Moreover, the stakes may not be the same for all players. Many times a poker game that started out as nothing more than a friendly game of penny ante has eventually developed into a game in which one or more players were staking a month's wages on the outcome. Likewise, Vietnam is a vivid instance in international politics where the stakes, for American policy makers at least, changed dramatically over a period of years. At the outset of the American involvement in Vietnam in the early 1950s, it seems clear that, in the judgment of the Truman administration, the stakes were relatively low. As a series of setbacks threatened the initial investment of men and resources that the United States had made in the game, the investment was increased; from the standpoint of American policy makers, the stakes of the game thereby rose. As the subsequent investment was threatened, the investment was supplemented still further, and the stakes went higher. This process was repeated several times until by the mid-1960s, Vietnam represented a deadly game with extremely high stakes. It may be that the series of setbacks that led American policy makers to push their investment progressively higher resulted in part from an underestimate by American leaders of the stakes of the game from the viewpoint of their adversaries. Whether such speculation is accurate or not, the point is that not all parties to a given contest in international politics will have equal stakes in the outcome. Variations in strategy and in the intensity with which a game is played by various players often reflect differences in their calculations of what is at stake.

Capability Estimates

By determining the estimates a given player has made about his relative capabilities, one can identify a third clue to the rationale for the player's strategy. Policy makers have no totally reliable formula for estimating the capabilities of their own nation-state to compete successfully in a given situation; the analyst can only surmise which factors the policy maker may have considered in appraising capabilities. In a later chapter, the complexity of foreign-policy capability estimates will be discussed in greater detail; here it will be sufficient to note the relevance of such estimates to explanations of strategy.

A football quarterback or a coach will vary his strategy depending upon his resources and his estimate of the resources of the other team. Likewise, foreign-policy strategies reflect estimates by policy makers of the capabilities of their own nation-state in comparison with the capabilities of probable adversaries. A few military examples of foreign-policy strategy can illustrate this. As an island power with a great stake in foreign trade, Britain relied heavily at the peak of her power in the nineteenth century on retaining the world's foremost navy and on controlling the seas. As an enormous land power, Russia in the past and in the twentieth century has based her military strategy on a large army and the concept of defense in depth. And the foremost technological power in the world today, the United States since World War II has devoted considerable emphasis in its military strategy to retaining supremacy in air power. These examples refer to gross and obvious indexes of the capability of a nation-state to compete internationally; in particular situations, however, the judgments that policy makers must make about the capabilities of their nation-state are often rooted in more intricate and less obvious calculations. For the observer, therefore, discerning the capability estimates that policy makers have made is likely to be difficult and inexact; nevertheless, such estimates provide one further clue about the foreign-policy strategy that policy makers have formulated.

Estimates of the Strategies of Other Parties

In any contest involving two or more parties, one's chances of success rest not only on his own actions, but also on those of the other parties. The design of a successful strategy, therefore, must rest partly on an attempt to anticipate the strategies of others. Especially in international politics, where coalitions are possible, strategies are interdependent in that each party is attempting to incorporate into his own strategy an estimate of the strategies of others; at the same time, adversaries are attempting to elude the predictions that are made by others.

Foreign-policy analysis from a strategic perspective seeks to identify the estimates that policy makers of a given nation-state have made of the strategies of other nation-states; the analyst uses these estimates as a clue in unraveling the rationale for the foreign-policy strategy that he is seeking to explain. In the Cold War, as we shall indicate in Chapter 4, a major factor in an explanation of American strategy consists of the estimates that American policy makers have made of the strategy of the Soviet Union, and to a lesser extent, of the strategies of other adversaries, of allies, and of neutrals.

Rules of the Game

Checkers players compete within the framework of a mutual agreement that precludes strategy involving moves on the red squares of the board; basketball players are forbidden to take more than two steps without dribbling the ball. Likewise, in international politics, foreign-policy strategy is formed within the framework of a set of rules. As indicated earlier in the chapter, the rules of conduct in international politics are largely unwritten and informal, and often vary according to the wishes of the more powerful participants. However, it is important to recognize the existence of any rules at all, because particular facets of a given strategy may be inexplicable except in terms of the rules of a contest.

Policy makers may be inclined to alter their strategy if they perceive that the rules of the game have been changed or violated by others, or they may try to persuade others to accept a particular set of rules. During the Korean War, the Truman-MacArthur controversy, from a strategic perspective, was rooted in differences of opinion as to the rules of the game for the United States in its conduct of the war. From MacArthur's viewpoint, as indicated in Chapter 2, the massive Chinese entry into the war represented a blatant violation of preexisting rules of the game. Consequently, continuing adherence to the old restraints was, in his view, foolhardy. From Truman's standpoint, restraint from expanding the battleground to include China, constraint of Chiang Kai-shek's forces, and abstention from the use of nuclear weapons were desirable in order to prevent still further escalation of the war by China or the Soviet Union. The concept of limited war, as applied in this instance by Truman and as subsequently developed by policy makers and by military and civilian theoreticians into an important American strategic doctrine, rests heavily on the supposition that the acceptance of self-imposed restraints in the conduct of war may induce other participants to act with similar restraint, thereby keeping the costs of engaging in the contest from growing out of proportion to the interests at stake.

Analysis of the Implementation of Strategy: Tactics and Techniques

Over a period of time, the interaction of the United States with other nation-states defines patterns that help the observer identify goals that policy makers have been seeking and interests they have been attempting to protect. Clues to the calculations that policy makers have made lie in the key variables described above: the parties involved in a particular contest and their alignments; the stakes of the game; estimates of American capabilities relative to those of other nation-states; estimates of the strategies that other nation-states will pursue; and the rules of the game.

From a strategic perspective, however, the observer is often interested not only in the broad patterns of a strategic design, but also in the specific decisions involved. The focus on specific decisions is essentially the same as that employed in foreign-policy analysis from a decision-making perspective. However, the theoretical reference points, and thus the kinds of questions deemed important, are different in the two perspectives. From a decision-making perspective, to be discussed in Part IV, the emphasis is on the structure within which, and the process by which, decisions are made. *How* a decision was made is treated as an important component in explaining *why* it was made. From a strategic perspective, however, explanation of why a decision was made is formulated basically in terms of the conscious intentions of policy makers in relation to the particular situation and its context.

In relation to theoretical reference points such as those of game theory and of military strategy, particular kinds of situations can be seen from a strategic perspective as imposing special tactical requirements. Decisions are seen as tactical maneuvers, some of which deviate from the overall pattern of ongoing strategy. The frequently quoted advice of Lenin to fellow Communists always to be ready ". . . to make all necessary practical compromises, to 'tack,' to make agreements, zigzags, retreats and so on in order to accelerate the coming into political power . . ." simply gives expression to a rule of tactical maneuver endorsed by strategists generally in games ranging from poker to revolution or war.[6] A review of some familiar tactical objectives and techniques will help to clarify the kinds of questions and data that are important from a strategic perspective.

Tactical Objectives

From a strategic perspective, specific decisions are viewed in relation to overall strategic purposes. Tactically, however, particular actions may serve one or more of several short-range objectives. For example, a tactical action may be designed to legitimize prior moves or impending

[6] V. I. Lenin, *"Left-Wing" Communism: An Infantile Disorder* (New York: International Publishers, revised trans., 1934), p. 74. First ed. in Russian, 1920.

actions; to exploit tactical advantages; to cover or to reduce tactical disadvantages; to improve one's bargaining position; and to strengthen deterrence.

Legitimation   Foreign-policy analysis from a strategic perspective tends to place far less emphasis than analysis from a decision-making perspective on the political process and on such institutions as public opinion, the press, interest groups and Congress in shaping or limiting policy decisions. In analysis from a strategic perspective, however, there tends to be at least an acknowledgement of the necessity for policy makers to justify their actions at home as well as to allies and foreign clients and onlookers. Legitimation may be sought of prior moves or of actions anticipated in the future. Tactical actions designed to seek legitimation for other actions, completed or anticipated, characteristically are staged for the benefit of those most likely to criticize these acts. For instance, acts of escalation have been used in military situations in order to placate domestic "hawks," legitimating a more moderate strategy by convincing them that a tougher approach would yield no higher ratio of gains to losses. Conversely, acts of deescalation have been used in an effort to placate domestic "doves" by convincing them of the futility of unilateral concessions, thereby paving the way for further escalation of the conflict. The war in Vietnam has provided illustrations of actions undertaken for purposes of legitimation. Theodore Draper is among the critics who have argued that the primary purpose of the American government for the 37-day bombing pause that began in December 1965 and for the 4-day cease-fire during the lunar year in February 1967, was to legitimate subsequent American escalation of the war.[7]

Exploitation of Tactical Advantage   A professional boxer who stuns his opponent with a left hook in an early round is likely to move in swiftly to try to score a knockout, whatever pace he may have set for himself as an overall strategy at the beginning of the fight; a hockey team that receives a one-man numerical advantage as a result of the temporary suspension of a member of the opposition for having committed a foul will attempt to score quickly while the opposition is at a disadvantage. Likewise, in international politics, alert policy makers are quick to exploit a tactical advantage. The actions of the Johnson administration and

---

[7] "Vietnam: How Not to Negotiate," *New York Review of Books* (May 4, 1967, special supp.), pp. 17–29. A more extensive presentation of Draper's views on Vietnam is his book, *Abuse of Power* (New York: Viking, 1967). See also Franz Schurmann, Peter D. Scott, and Reginald Zelnik, *The Politics of Escalation in Vietnam* (New York: Fawcett, paperback ed., 1966).

subsequently of the Nixon administration to rejuvenate the NATO alliance in the wake of the 1968 Soviet invasion of Czechoslovakia, for instance, may be interpreted in this light. Whereas European members of NATO had increasingly minimized the threat that was the *raison d'être* of NATO, the harsh Soviet response to signs of liberalization in one of their satellite states stimulated anxieties in Western Europe about the continued reality of a threat of Soviet attack. Discussions of NATO cooperation took on a renewed relevance.

Reduction of Tactical Disadvantage　Just as exploitation of a tactical advantage can be instrumental to success in a contest, so one must be alert to situations of tactical disadvantage in order to avoid major losses in such situations. A whole series of decisions by the American government, in fields such as space research and technology, education, and defense, following the spectacular Soviet achievement of launching an orbital satellite (Sputnik I), can be interpreted as efforts to reduce the tactical advantage that the Soviets had thereby attained.

Various actions of the American government during the war in Vietnam, including especially the change of policy emphasis by the Kennedy administration and the subsequent major escalation of the war by the Johnson administration in 1965, can also be viewed as efforts to compensate for tactical disadvantages, in this case those presented by the difficulties for the United States of guerrilla warfare. When the Kennedy administration took over in 1961, the President personally urged a major emphasis throughout those government agencies with responsibilities for foreign affairs on developing a strong counterinsurgency capability. He urged others in the government to read the writings on guerrilla warfare by Mao Tse-tung and Ché Guevara, as he had done. The Special Forces received more funds and greater emphasis. Throughout the Army, officers and men received compulsory lectures and training in guerrilla tactics. A counterinsurgency task force was established to coordinate policies among various key departments; General Maxwell Taylor headed the task force and Robert Kennedy served as the President's representative. The problem for which the major effort in counterinsurgency was to be made was, of course, Vietnam. The assumption was that by mastering the techniques of guerrilla warfare, Americans could beat the guerrillas (that is, the forces of the National Liberation Front) at their own game.

However, the general ineptness of the South Vietnamese forces at the time, the chronic instability in Saigon that followed the assassination of Diem in late 1963, and the successes of the National Liberation Front, called the assumption into serious question and increasingly placed the United States at a tactical disadvantage. By the winter of 1964–1965, there was a serious possibility that the peninsula of South Vietnam would be cut in two, that the South Vietnamese forces would collapse completely, and that the American investment in Vietnam would be totally lost. Thus, although the doctrine of counterinsurgency was not abandoned, the attempt to win the war in Vietnam by beating the guerrillas at their own game gave way to a major effort to change the rules of the game from those determined by the NLF, in favor of rules that matched American technological superiority. The shift to massive bombing, the use of American combat troops transported by helicopter, the defoliation of extensive areas of jungle, and other aspects of American major escalation of the war from 1965 on may be seen as techniques designed to change the rules in Vietnam, thereby reducing or eliminating the tactical disadvantage that the American government had experienced.

Improvement of Bargaining Position   Even in situations that occasion no particular advantage or disadvantage tactically, policy makers will often consider it desirable to prepare for the future with acts that strengthen their bargaining position. The position of the Nixon administration at the outset of the debate regarding deployment of the Sentinel antimissile-missile system, for instance, revealed a concern not only for the significance of such a system in defending the United States against attack, but also for the utility of such deployment to strengthen the American position in arms-control negotiations with the Soviet Union. Under pressure from various critics in Congress, Secretary of Defense Melvin Laird ordered a freeze early in February 1969 on the deployment of the Sentinel system to various sites throughout the United States, pending review of the system. A week earlier, however, he had been quoted as favoring continuation of the system because, he said, in relation to possible arms-control discussions with the Soviet Union, "I do not want to be in a position when we go into these talks, if we do, with one hand tied behind our back." [8]

Strengthening Deterrence   A final, familiar purpose for various tactical actions is to strengthen deterrence. Arguments favoring deployment of the Sentinel anti–ballistic-missile (ABM) system included that of strengthening deterrence, as well as the bargaining rationale cited above. As suggested earlier in the chapter, there are several requisites for successful deterrence, including especially the credibility of one's capa-

[8] William Beecher, "Laird Supports Antimissile Net," *New York Times*, Jan. 31, 1969, p. 1. Many critics argued to the contrary. For example, Senator George McGovern contended that "in reality, as a bargaining counter the ABM would be of no value or of negative value." Letter to the *New York Times*, Feb. 26, 1969, p. 16.

bility and willingness to carry out the threats that comprise the deterrent. A given tactical move designed to strengthen deterrence may be simple (dispatching a battalion of marines to an area) or complex (signing a multiparty alliance treaty). It may be mild (sending a cautious diplomatic note), or it may be strong (threatening the use of military force). The techniques utilized by policy makers to strengthen deterrence or to accomplish other tactical objectives will vary according to the particular interests at stake, the resources at hand, the history of relationships with parties to the contest, and the context of the situation. Various techniques will be discussed below, any of which might serve one or more of the tactical purposes that have been identified. The concerned observer of foreign policy cannot enjoy absolute certainty in his efforts to determine which purposes motivated a particular decision or action. For instance, the variety of motives attributed to President Johnson by newspaper columnists, television commentators, political candidates, college professors, barber-shop pundits, and others who attempted to explain the underlying reasons for his announcement at the end of March 1968 that he would not seek reelection provides a vivid illustration of how elusive motivation can be as the object of investigation. Nonetheless, the observer can use discrimination in weighing the statements that policy makers make to justify their actions against conflicting interpretations of them and arriving at his own educated guesses about the tactical purposes of particular moves.[9]

Tactical Techniques

Techniques employed to serve tactical purposes are as varied as the instruments of warfare and diplomacy and as varied as the nuances of situations in which they might be employed. The more familiar species, however, includes declarations and commitments, demonstrations of capabilities, promises and threats, bluffs and challenges to bluffs, and rewards and punishments.

Declarations and Commitments, Promises and Threats As we shall suggest below in a discussion of bluffing, ambiguity may be a desirable attribute of foreign policy under some circumstances, although not in all. Ambiguity regarding the American commitment to Korea on the eve of the Korean War, for instance, may have been an important inducement to the North Koreans to risk an armed attack. Thus, often it is

[9] An example of a carefully researched, thorough analysis of an intrinsically elusive topic is a report by Hedrick Smith, William Beecher, and assistants, "The Vietnam Policy Reversal of 1968," *New York Times*, Mar. 6 and 7, 1969, pp. 1 and following.

desirable for policy makers to clarify both the importance that they attach to various interests and their intentions.

Issuing official policy statements declaring the importance that the government attaches to particular areas or interests is one technique that can be employed to clarify policy goals, and various devices can make such statements more convincing. For example, if policy makers not only declare their intentions but also support the declaration with formal commitments like alliances, budgetary allocations, or written or publicly declared pledges, they have effectually increased the costs in the currency of prestige and diplomatic reliability that would be incurred by departing from their expressed intentions. The act of commitment therefore serves to strengthen the credibility of their declared intentions.

A military alliance is not only an indication of the kinds of interests to which policy makers attach salience, but also is a promise and a threat. It is a promise to those with whom the alliance has been formed; it is a threat to any who would launch an armed attack against a member of the alliance. The wording of Article 5 of the NATO treaty that was signed in April 1949 is similar to the activating provision of other multilateral and bilateral defense agreements that the United States government has made over the past two decades. The article provides that an armed attack against any one member would be deemed an attack against all members; in response, "each of them . . . will assist the Party or Parties so attacked by taking forthwith . . . such action as it deems necessary, including the use of armed force. . . ."[10] The willingness of the United States government to live up to such agreements is not 100 percent certifiable and will not be unless the deterrent effect of the alliance fails, and an attack on a member of the alliance occurs. The credibility of the commitment, however, is strengthened by its status as a treaty, rather than as a mere declaration of intent.

The more specific a promise or threat is, and the more authoritative its source, the greater the credibility of the intentions it expresses. At the time of the Cuban missile crisis of October 1962, a specific and widely publicized pledge was made by President Kennedy that the United States would not invade Cuba, providing the Soviets removed their missiles from Cuba. In making this pledge, the President in effect made his stand irreversible by ruling out invasion as a policy option for dealing with Castro in the future. However, the pledge was a concession convincing enough to evoke from the Soviets the reciprocal concession of a humiliating withdrawal of their missiles from Cuba. As Iklé has put it, "If someone says that he will not retreat, he may be making a true

---

[10] U.S., *Statutes at Large*, 62:2241–2253.

prediction or only be boasting, but after he has burned his bridges, his intention has turned into necessity—at least until the bridges have been rebuilt." [11]

The diplomatic value of a declaration or a commitment may diminish over time, unless evidence is provided of its continuing validity. A technique commonly employed to provide such evidence is a high-level policy statement reaffirming the nation's commitment to the alliance, defense agreement, or whatever other institutionalized relationship is at stake. Every American President since the days of the Berlin blockade of 1948–1949, for example, has declared the willingness of the United States to risk war in defense of West Berlin. President Nixon's visit to Berlin in early 1969, at a time of renewed East-West frictions over rights of access to the city, was a dramatic reaffirmation of the American commitment in Berlin, much as President Kennedy's "Ich bin ein Berliner" speech at Rudolf Wilde Platz had been six years earlier.

The dispatch of a high-level diplomatic mission to India in November 1962, headed by Ambassador Averell Harriman and scheduled several days after a major Chinese attack along the Indian border, is an illustration of the clarification of a commitment that had become ambiguous due to complex political circumstances. The widely publicized mission served as evidence, especially for Chinese consideration, that despite the complications for American policy makers presented by the American alliance to Pakistan and the frictions between Pakistan and India, the United States was determined to help India resist Chinese attack.

Demonstration of Capabilities   Even unaccompanied by any statement of intent or indication of a particular policy for utilization of resources, the demonstration that one has the capabilities to undertake particular kinds of actions and programs is a technique that is sometimes used to strengthen one's bargaining position in a contest or to legitimize one's general policy posture domestically. Used in conjunction with implicit or explicit indications of intent, however, a demonstration of tactical capabilities can serve as a show of strength to increase the credibility of a promise or threat. The call-up of units of the Army Reserve and the National Guard and the tripling of draft calls during the Berlin crisis of 1961 illustrate this technique. It seems clear that the hope of the Kennedy administration was that such actions would be a highly visible demonstration of the ability and the willingness of the United States to go to war rather than yield to Soviet demands over Berlin.

[11] Fred Charles Iklé, *How Nations Negotiate* (New York: Harper & Row, 1964), p. 66. Much of the book is highly relevant to the present discussion of techniques used to serve tactical purposes in foreign policy.

It is entirely possible, however (and in the author's view, probable), that in this instance the Kennedy administration was bluffing. From a strategic perspective at least, bluffing is not necessarily undesirable; although truth and candor are virtues in some circumstances of international politics, deception is a requisite for success under other circumstances, as it is in many forms of competition.

Bluffs and Challenges to Bluffs   Feinting and bluffing are familiar tactics used in many contests to utilize more effectively the available resources by eluding the predictions of the opponents; successful foreign policy, like successful poker or football, for example, must include enough bluffing to keep opponents guessing and enough willingness to risk calling the occasional bluff of an adversary to keep from being the prisoner of his deception. Bluffing is a delicate art, and policy makers, like poker players, tend to develop reputations over time for the way they play the game—reputations for being shrewd or foolish, tough or weak, decisive or vacillating, and fulfilling their stated intentions most of the time or bluffing. Although, as indicated, a certain amount of bluffing is essential to skillful maneuvering in foreign policy or in poker, obviously one's reputation as a bluffer can jeopardize the successful utilization of the bluff.

There are other problems that can develop from excessive bluffing in foreign policy. One of these is the alienation of foreign allies and the domestic public. Half-truths employed by a policy maker in a series of speeches delivered to domestic audiences may be rationalized by him as useful in bluffing a foreign adversary into a more conciliatory posture than he would otherwise assume, but from the viewpoint of most of the domestic public, these half-truths are likely to be regarded as a violation of the responsibilities of a public servant to keep his constituents accurately informed. The term "credibility gap" is often used to describe the measure of disbelief accorded by the public to statements by government officials, especially in foreign policy, as a result of such deception. Although the term has been in vogue only recently, the phenomenon of a credibility gap between government officials and the public has been present, in varying degrees, in all American administrations. Indeed, it can be persuasively argued that the popular tradition of regarding government explanations of foreign policy with some skepticism is a healthy one. Excessive bluffing, however, can turn healthy skepticism into alienation, not only on the part of the domestic public, but also on the part of allies and other international observers.

Perhaps graver than the alienation of friends and supporters, however, is that, in crucial situations where one's threats reflect accurately one's intentions, an adversary exposed to excessive prior bluffing may disregard them, with disastrous consequences for all concerned. The legend about the boy who cried, "Wolf!" once too often is a pertinent analogy here. Successful deterrence of acts by an adversary that would be detrimental to one's interests, including acts of war, depends heavily on the credibility of one's deterrent threat; excessive bluffing can destroy one's credibility, thereby undermining the deterrent and leaving him vulnerable to the acts he had hoped to prevent.

Rewards and Punishments   If one's threats and promises are not to be treated consistently as bluffs and thereby devalued, occasionally he must make good his stated intentions. The failure of Soviet Premier Khrushchev to carry out threats, uttered in 1958 and again in 1961, that the Soviets would conclude a separate peace treaty with the East German regime unless the Western allies agreed within six months to conclude a peace treaty with Germany on the terms prescribed by the Soviet Union, called into serious question the credibility of subsequent Soviet threats. In contrast, the forcible response by the United States in conjunction with United Nations allies to the attack by North Korean forces in June 1950 represented the fulfillment of the threat, indicated in the United Nations Charter and endorsed by the United States, to employ force to counter armed aggression. The credibility of American willingness to respond in a like manner to similar violations of the Charter was thereby enhanced.

The fulfillment of a threat that was largely implicit is illustrated by the Gulf of Tonkin incident of 1964. By the summer of 1964, the United States had constructed a large air base at Danang, 350 miles north of Saigon, and American ships were employed in prominent roles off the Vietnamese coast. Although American forces had not yet been employed in direct combat, the highly visible presence of a substantial combat force that could be utilized if the occasion warranted it represented an implicit threat to the North Vietnamese and to the National Liberation Front that, if they took action injurious to American bases or personnel, severe retaliation would follow. According to official reports released by United States government officials, three North Vietnamese patrol torpedo boats fired torpedoes and 37-millimeter shells at an American destroyer in the Gulf of Tonkin on August 2, 1964. Two days later, according to the official report, the North Vietnamese PT boats had attacked again. In response, the report indicated, American forces had sunk two of the boats and had launched air strikes against PT-boat bases in North Vietnam and against certain other targets, including an oil storage depot. The air raids on targets in North Vietnam may be viewed as a means of strengthening the credibility of American threats while simultaneously posing another threat by demonstrating American willingness to escalate the war in response to North Vietnamese actions.

Rewards and punishments are techniques that can be used to strengthen deterrence by enhancing one's credibility, to increase one's legitimacy through demonstrating the reliability of one's statements, and to exploit a tactical advantage or compensate for a tactical disadvantage by making rewards in accord with one's interests or punishment of acts detrimental to one's interests. Within weeks of the dramatic break between Tito and Stalin in 1953, the first rift in the so-called Communist bloc, the American government released some $57 million in Yugoslav gold and assets that had been frozen since World War II. In return, the Tito government agreed to pay about $17 million to the United States as a settlement for various American claims ranging from lend-lease to indemnity for the downing of two airplanes over Yugoslavia two years earlier. The American action can be regarded as a reward, designed to strengthen Tito's hand in maintaining a position of independence from Moscow, while also serving to suggest to other Communist-bloc nations of the possible advantages of seeking an independent course.

Foreign-Policy Strategy and Tactics: Conclusions

Foreign-policy strategy and tactics have a distinctive logic, highlights of which we have given in the present chapter. From a strategic perspective, the concerned observer of foreign policy attempts to understand both broad patterns of continuity and change in foreign policy and specific policy decisions and actions by imagining himself in the position of the policy maker. Since he is *not* the policy maker, however, he must rely on what actual policy makers have said or done and on other accounts of events. In some instances, therefore, he himself will be bluffed, especially if the policy maker whose actions he is attempting to explain is skillful at bluffing. Analysis of past events is facilitated, however, by the hindsight that allows one to see if threats and promises were carried out or not and to relate particular actions to a broader pattern of moves in a strategic design.

In the following chapter, we shall apply the framework developed in the present one to analysis of American strategy and tactics in the Cold War. Such application will help to highlight further the characteristics of analysis from a strategic perspective; a balance sheet suggesting the key advantages and limitations of analysis from a strategic perspective will be presented at the conclusion of the chapter.

4

American Cold-War Strategy and Tactics

American Strategy in the Cold War

The evolution of American foreign policy during the decade and a half after the end of World War II has special interest and relevance to the concerned observer for understanding the key issues confronting American policy makers today, because the lingering effects of World War II and the struggle that developed between the two superpowers after the war have forged many of the most troublesome of the current world problems and have defined the limits within which solutions might be reached. From a strategic perspective, the overriding feature of the post-World War II period is the Cold War; it can be seen as a game played for high stakes, but with means short of all-out combat, by two powerful parties, the United States and the Soviet Union, and their respective allies and clients.

Most serious students of the subject have identified the onset of the Cold War with the growing friction in the months immediately following World War II.[1] There are differences of opinion, however, about the duration of the Cold War. Whether or not it is accurate to describe the Cold War as a phenomenon that has continued into the late 1960s and early 1970s is a question that need not concern us here,[2] and which raises problems of definition as much as substantive problems. It is clear, however, that the bipolarity that distinguished international politics in the early years of the Cold War has given way to a more complex system of interrelationships, with looser and partially defunct alliance structures dividing East and West, and with the proliferation of new nation-states that decline allegiance to either camp. Consequently, whereas most important American foreign-policy decisions in the late 1940s and in the 1950s could be analyzed meaningfully in terms of their consequences for the conflict with the Soviet Union, in many decisions in recent years such analysis is no longer very relevant.

It is convenient, therefore, to limit discussion of the Cold War to a period of roughly a decade and a half after the end of World War II. American foreign-policy decisions during this period include such prominent ones as the Truman Doctrine of 1947; the Marshall Plan, which was announced the same year; the Berlin airlift of 1948–1949; the organization of the NATO alliance in 1949; the initiation of the Military Defense Assistance Program in 1949; the commitment of American troops to Korea in 1950; the conclusion of defense pacts with the Philippines, Japan, South Korea, Nationalist China, and the SEATO nations in the period 1951–1954; the decisions leading to the Geneva Summit Conference of 1955; the Eisenhower Doctrine of 1957; the dispatch of troops to Lebanon in 1958; the response to the downing of an American U-2 plane over the Soviet Union in 1960; the support of the Bay of Pigs

[1] How much of the responsibility for the onset of the Cold War must be borne by American leaders is a question that has generated much debate. A useful review of scholarly studies of the Cold War, with special attention to revisionist interpretations, is by Christopher Lasch, "The Cold War, Revisited and Re-visioned," *New York Times Magazine*, Jan. 14, 1968, pp. 26 and following.

[2] To describe a pattern of interaction between nation-states as a "cold war" is, after all, a question of terminology. It is difficult to fault observers for some ambiguity, therefore, about when such a conflict starts or ends. Some reflections that point to a definite change in United States-Soviet relations, without declaring definitely that the Cold War has ended, are as follows. David S. McLellan, *The Cold War in Transition* (New York: Crowell-Collier-Macmillan, 1966). Charles O. Lerche, Jr., *The Cold War . . . and After* (Englewood Cliffs, N.J.: Prentice-Hall, 1965). Eleanor Lansing Dulles and Robert Dickson Crane, eds., *Détente: Cold War Strategies in Transition* (New York: Praeger, 1965).

invasion in 1961; and the confrontation with the Soviet Union in the Cuban missile crisis of 1962.

The pattern of these decisions reflects a strategy of containment—essentially a species of deterrence, designed primarily to prevent moves by the Soviet Union that would extend Communist influence or control, or that would damage or threaten important American interests. Analysis of the rationale for a containment strategy is made in terms of variables introduced in Chapter 3, the first portion of the present chapter is devoted to analysis of the design of the containment strategy.

Foreign-policy decisions such as those identified above may be analyzed from a strategic perspective not merely as elements of broad patterns of policy, but also as independent objects; with the latter focus, explanation is made in terms of tactical objectives and techniques such as those described in the last half of Chapter 3. Much of the last part of the present chapter is devoted to analysis of American tactics in the Cold War. In the final section of the chapter, some concluding observations are made about the distinctive insights that analysis of foreign policy from a strategic perspective can provide, but also about some important limitations of this perspective.

Containment: The Rationale

The main lines of what was eventually termed the containment strategy were already emerging in 1945 and 1946. Because pursuit of a containment strategy meant a drastic reversal of the strategy of working with and aiding the Soviet Union as a wartime ally, the reversal puzzled and troubled many Americans at the time. With the benefit of hindsight, however, the shift in strategy by American policy makers becomes comprehensible in terms of the five key variables identified in Chapter 3.

Shifting Coalitions From a strategic perspective, alliances and other forms of coalition exist merely for the advancement of the self-interest of the parties to the coalition; a party will not join a coalition unless he perceives that his self-interest will be advanced by joining. Conversely (according to game theory, on which analysis from a strategic perspective usually relies heavily), at the moment that it appears that a coalition no longer serves his self-interest, a party will leave it or form a new one that does serve his interests. The rationale of expediency for forming a coalition was vividly expressed by Winston Churchill, whose staunch anticommunist views did not stand in the way of his decision to seek an alliance with the Soviet Union in the desperate early stages of the war against Germany. As he put it, "I have only one purpose, the destruction of Hitler, and my life is much simplified thereby. If Hitler invaded Hell I would make at least a favourable reference to the Devil in the House of Commons." [3] For similarly pragmatic reasons, Churchill sought to maneuver American and British forces into a strong bargaining position with the Soviets as the war drew to a close, thereby anticipating and somewhat aggravating the conflict between allies that was developing.

It was the United States and the Soviet Union, however, as superpowers in relation to all other nation-states at the end of the war, that played the strongest roles in creating the postwar international political alignments. Why did these two superpowers not use their enormous influence in collaboration with one another for the creation of a lasting peace and stability? There were, of course, plans for such collaboration, most notably through the creation of a United Nations Organization. American policy makers had devoted considerable time and energy during the war to plans for the postward period, rooting them in the assumption, or at least the hope, that the United States and her wartime allies would continue to work together for common purposes. But, from a strategic analytical perspective, one can see that such an assumption was frail. Once the defeat of Germany was assured, the mutual self-interest that formed the basis of the alliance, which lay primarily in neutralizing the threat of Germany, was eliminated. Thus, with the vast range of interests of the two superpowers at the war's end, the threat that each could pose to the self-interests of the other now exceeded the probable gain to be derived from working as partners, unless each could be certain that the other was perfectly truthworthy. But it is precisely the absence of such trust that characterizes the system of sovereign nation-states, as we suggested at the outset of Chapter 3. Modern students of game theory as well as classical political philosophers have explored some of the consequences of mistrust in a highly competitive situation. From the perspective of game theory, the breakup of the wartime alliance and the polarization of international politics into new coalitions led by the United States and the Soviet Union, respectively, might be explained largely in terms of what Riker calls the "size principle." This principle states that parties to a contest will ". . . create coalitions just as large as they believe will ensure winning and no larger." [4] Winning in international politics can be described as the success that policy

---

[3] Winston S. Churchill, *The Second World War*, 6 vols. (Boston: Houghton Mifflin, 1950), 3, *The Grand Alliance*, 370.

[4] William H. Riker, *The Theory of Political Coalitions* (New Haven: Yale University Press, paperback ed., 1962), p. 47. The size principle is explained by Riker, and evidence in support of it produced in chaps. 2–4.

makers realize in advancing the interests of their nation-state, as they define those interests. After the victory of the Allies in World War II, leaders of the nation-states participating in the alliance formulated new interests and reordered the priorities of existing interests. Therefore, according to the size principle, the coalition that had won the war was too big (too expensive, in terms of resources expended and compromise required) to be retained in the pursuit of new goals. A coalition of the United States and the Soviet Union, as the only two superpowers, would have violated the size principle; thus, new alignments were in the self-interest of each of the two superpowers. As Riker has observed, the breakup of the victorious alliance of World War II is not a historically unique phenomenon; on the contrary, it is typical of the fate of coalitions at the end of a war, as illustrated, for instance, by the nation-states that defeated Napoleon and by the victorious alliance in World War I.[5]

If the probability of conflict (that is, activity intended to damage or to threaten one another's interests) between the United States and the Soviet Union was inherent in their very existence as two superpowers in a world of sovereign nation-states, explanation of the content of American strategy for competing with the Soviet Union requires reference to other variables.

Estimates of Soviet Intentions   One of the variables that is particularly useful in explaining American strategy for the emerging conflict with the Soviet Union lies in the estimates that American policy makers made of Soviet intentions. Elsewhere in the book, especially in Chapter 7, we will discuss the distortions in the images that policy makers (and all of us) formulate of various facets of reality, including the reality of the intentions of other nations. For instance, it is clear in retrospect that the image that American policy makers had of international communism as a monolith totally responsive to Moscow, was initially accurate for the Soviet-controlled areas of Eastern Europe, but was a misrepresentation of the situation in Western Europe, in China, and in many other parts of the world, where indigenous Communists maintained a degree of independence from their ideological comrades in Moscow. Nonetheless, our analytical concern at this point is with the estimates that were made by American policy makers, whether they were accurate or not, because these estimates affected American policies.

Abundant evidence of the estimates made by American leaders is

---

[5] These and other examples from domestic and international politics are discussed by Riker, chap. 3.

available from documents, memoirs, and interviews of those who participated in the policy-making process at the time. Many American policy
makers experienced a profound change in their estimates of Soviet intentions during 1945. At the Yalta Conference early that year, cooperation with the Soviets in the postwar period still seemed to many key
leaders, including President Roosevelt, both possible and desirable. As
the President's close adviser, Harry Hopkins, described the prevailing
sentiment, "The Russians had proved that they could be reasonable and
farseeing and there wasn't any doubt in the minds of the President or
any of us that we could live with them and get along with them peace-
fully for as far into the future as any of us could imagine."[6] However,
during the few climactic months of the war after Yalta, American-Soviet
relations had deteriorated so far that Acting Secretary of State Joseph
Grew could predict that "a future war with Soviet Russia is as certain
as anything in the world can be certain." [7]

An emerging pattern of Soviet actions seemed evident. It was a pattern,
as most top American leaders saw it, of increasing belligerency, of
willingness to ignore wartime agreements, and of an intention to expand
Communist control by any means, including the use of force. The tactics
of the Soviets in installing a government in Poland that would staunchly
support Moscow and in subverting, through the arrest of key leaders and
through other means, the efforts of the Polish government-in-exile to
regain control became a symbol to Western leaders of Soviet intentions
to dominate Eastern and Central Europe. A series of bitter Communist-
led strikes in France and Italy suggested a possible plan of extending
Soviet control to Western Europe as well. Efforts to work out an amicable
agreement with the Soviets for areas previously designated to be ad-
ministered jointly seemed increasingly futile in Germany, in Korea, and,
at the time, in Austria. Turkey was being subjected to intense Soviet
pressure to sign a new treaty with the Soviets regarding access to the
Straits, ceding territory along the Black Sea to the Soviet Union, and
leasing military bases to the Soviets. In Iran, Soviet armed forces that
had occupied the northern provinces during the war remained after the
war, providing protection for indigenous Communists to attempt to
establish an autonomous province of Azerbaijan, sympathetic to Moscow.

Soviet intentions seemed evident in their speech as well as in their
action. In February 1946, in an address reported publicly in the party
newspaper *Pravda*, Stalin spoke of the inevitability of conflict with the
capitalist powers. He urged the Soviet people not to be deluded that the

---

[6] Quoted in Robert E. Sherwood, *Roosevelt and Hopkins* (New York: Harper &
Row, 1948), p. 870.

[7] Grew, *Turbulent Era*, 2 vols. (Boston: Houghton Mifflin, 1952), 2:1446.

end of the war meant that the nation could relax. Rather, intensified efforts were needed to strengthen and defend the homeland.[8]

Roughly a week after the speech of Stalin cited above, George F. Kennan, the second-ranking civilian diplomat in the American embassy in Moscow, sent to the State Department an 8000-word cable assessing the motivations of Soviet leadership. The cable was widely circulated among policy makers in Washington and became important in crystallizing the views of many persons regarding Soviet intentions and actions. After exploring at some length the roots of the views of Soviet leaders and the implications of these views, Kennan noted, "In summary, we have here a political force committed fanatically to the belief that with [the] U.S. there can be no permanent modus vivendi, that it is desirable and necessary that the internal harmony of our society be disrupted, our traditional way of life be destroyed, the international authority of our state be broken, if Soviet power is to be secure."[9]

A few weeks later, Winston Churchill spoke at Westminster College in Fulton, Missouri, with President Truman beside him on the platform. "From Stettin in the Baltic to Trieste in the Adriatic," Churchill observed, "an iron curtain has descended across the continent."[10] Warning of the threat of Communist expansion and subversion, Churchill nevertheless assured his audience that he did not believe that the Soviet Union desired war. But the pattern of Soviet expansion and subversion, he contended, could only be met by strength and determined resistance on the part of the United States and Britain.[11] A consensus was growing among American policy makers in support of the position that Churchill advocated.

Stakes and Rules of the Game   The determination of American policy makers to adopt a tougher strategy in dealing with the Soviet Union seems to have been reinforced by the perceptions of American policy makers as to what was at stake in the contest with the Soviets and what rules of the game were appropriate.

Although American foreign policy had become global by the end of World War II, with the acceptance of unprecedented responsibilities for

[8] *Pravda*, Feb. 9 and 10, 1946, as cited in Marshall D. Shulman, *Stalin's Foreign Policy Reappraised* (New York: Atheneum, paperback ed., 1965), pp. 14–26.

[9] Long excerpts from the cable, including the passage quoted, are contained in George F. Kennan, *Memoirs 1925–1950* (Boston: Little, Brown, 1967), app. C, pp. 547–559.

[10] Excerpts from the speech of March 5, 1946, are contained in William A. Williams, ed., *The Shaping of American Diplomacy* (Chicago: Rand McNally, 1956), pp. 992–994.

[11] Churchill speech of March 5, 1946, as excerpted in Williams, pp. 992–994.

involvement in the affairs and destinies of other nation-states and peoples, the major zone of confrontation and friction between the United States and the Soviet Union was Europe. Europe, especially the portion that bordered directly on the Soviet Union, was of vital interest and concern to Soviet leadership. However, Europe was also an area to which the United States had deep if ambivalent cultural ties and important economic links, and it was an area for which, however belatedly, American policy makers had twice in the twentieth century demonstrated a willingness to go to war. It is clear, therefore, that American policy makers regarded the contest with the Soviet Union as one with extremely high stakes, especially in Europe. The European emphasis, as we shall see, was reflected in the initial formulation of the containment strategy.

Although a tough line with the Soviets seemed to American policy makers to be called for, the devastation of the two previous wars and the awesome prospect of a war involving atomic weapons were compelling arguments for building a strategy around the threat of armed force rather than employing such force in all-out combat with the Soviets. In turn, an objective of strategy was to persuade the Soviets to refrain from armed aggression in support of their diplomatic objectives. In other words, the rules of the game that seemed appropriate to American policy makers and that defined the framework of the strategy called for avoiding war except as a last resort, but for meeting force with force as necessary to contain Communist expansion. That such rules involved great risk for all parties to the contest was as evident to policy makers at the time (some of whom believed that war with the Soviets was imminent) as it is apparent to us in restrospect. Given the prior experiences of the twentieth century, it is amazing that the rules were maintained, at least to the point of avoiding a third world war.

Comparisons of American and Soviet Capabilities   The comparisons that American policy makers made of American strategic capabilities with those of the Soviet Union at the end of World War II provide a further clue to explaining the containment strategy. Capability estimates especially help to explain the nature and magnitude of a Soviet threat for which American policy makers thought a strategy must be devised and the kinds of "carrots and sticks" among American resources that seemed particularly important in persuading Soviet leaders (primarily Stalin) to be reasonable in American terms.

Of the two superpowers that emerged from World War II, the United States had a number of important advantages over the Soviet Union. These included first the fact that the United States had suffered no damage to its homeland, in contrast to vast devastation in the Soviet

Union, which represented an enormous task of reconstruction. Moreover, approximately one-tenth of the prewar Soviet population had been killed in the war. The magnitude of the loss can perhaps be appreciated by the fact that the ratio of Soviet to American war deaths was about seventy to one. Nearly 300,000 Americans had been killed in the war; the number of Soviet soldiers and civilians killed has been estimated at twenty million.

Closely related to the differences between the two powers in the amount of physical punishment from the war were the differences in economic productivity. In spite of problems of conversion from a peacetime to a wartime economy, manpower relocation, shortages of certain commodities, and disruption by a number of highly publicized strikes, the war had been a tremendous boon to the economy of the United States. In constant dollars (1953 base), the gross national product of the United States had risen from $239.2 billion in 1941 to $329.3 billion in 1944. Agricultural production had increased nearly 25 percent during the war. Between 1939 and 1944, civilian consumption of goods and services, as one index of trends in the standard of living, had risen by 20 percent.[12]

In contrast, the economy of the Soviet Union had been seriously impaired by the war. Vast industrial areas had been laid waste, transportation and communication networks had been destroyed or damaged, and industrial production had been cut almost in half. Millions of Russians and Ukrainians returned to the Soviet Union at the end of the war as refugees, having spent months or years in concentration camps or work camps in Germany, where their health had deteriorated. The system of Soviet agriculture, which had been maintained during the war almost entirely by women, had suffered severely and food was scarce. The number of livestock in 1945 was far below that at the beginning of the war.[13]

By the end of the war, the Soviet Union had gained control of substantial territory and resources in Central and Eastern Europe that the Soviets exploited to bolster their own economy. On the other hand, maintaining control in these areas required an enormous investment of personnel and equipment that offset to a large extent the economic gain. Moreover, the Soviets had been unsuccessful in attempting to persuade the United States and Great Britain that the wealthy industrial area of the Ruhr should be under international control, with Soviet participation. Instead, the Ruhr remained in the British zone of occupation, and

[12] Figures are from Walter Johnson, *1600 Pennsylvania Avenue* (Boston: Little, Brown, paperback ed., 1960), pp. 156–164, and notes, p. 342.

[13] Data are from Alexander Werth, *Russia at War, 1941–1945* (New York: Avon, 1965), pp. 904–907.

its resources were utilized for the postwar reconstruction of West Germany.

In short, the United States had vast economic advantages over the Soviet Union at the end of World War II. Moreover, the Soviets expected and needed American help in their reconstruction effort. As the American Ambassador to the Soviet Union, Averell Harriman, explained in a conference with President Truman only a week after the death of Franklin Roosevelt, the desire of the Soviets to retain American economic assistance would enable the United States to take a firm line on important issues "without running serious risks"; Truman assured Harriman that he intended to stand firm and agreed, as he has recorded in his memoirs, that "the Russians needed us more than we needed them." [14]

In addition to the substantial lead that the United States had over the Soviet Union in general economic health and productivity, it also led in capital investment and research innovation, which enhance further productivity. A substantial investment had been made by the American government during the war in basic and applied scientific research, which, although undertaken for military purposes, led to major breakthroughs with potential applicability to civilian needs, in areas such as atomic energy, electronics, jet propulsion, aircraft design, and the development of synthetic fabrics. Beyond the $2 billion that the government had spent in the development and production of atomic weapons, another half a billion had been invested in scientific research.[15]

In military force, the key Soviet asset as the war drew to a close was an awesome land army. In the final drive westward in the winter and spring of 1945, the Soviets had been able to mass nearly 250 divisions against the Germans.[16] At the end of the war, these units were deployed along a line from the Elbe River in Germany south to the Czech-German border and along a line west of Vienna, which defined the Soviet zone of occupation in Austria. On the other hand, the Soviets had a relatively small navy and a small air force.

The United States Army was also of impressive strength in the final months of the war, but of the approximately 60 American divisions that had fought in the final European campaign, great numbers were trans-

---

[14] Both the Harriman and the Truman quotations are from Harry S Truman, *Memoirs*, 2 vols. (New York: New American Library, Signet paperback ed., 1965), 1, *Years of Decisions*, 86.

[15] I. Stewart, *Organizing Scientific Research for the War: The Administrative History of the Office of Scientific Research and Development* (Boston: Little, Brown, 1948), p. 322.

[16] T. D. Stamps, Vincent J. Esposito, and associates, *A Military History of World War II*, 2 vols. (West Point: U.S. Military Academy, 1953), 1:276.

ferred to the Pacific theater as soon as the war with Germany ended. Moreover, as soon as the surrender of Japan was announced, the American armed forces began a rapid demobilization. Churchill questioned President Truman on the consequences of rapid demobilization for the United States and Great Britain *vis-à-vis* the Soviets in a letter to the President in May 1945, when he asked, "What will be the position in a year or two, when the British and American Armies have melted and the French has not yet been formed on any major scale, when we may have a handful of divisions, mostly French, and when Russia may choose to keep two or three hundred on active service?" [17] Nevertheless, at the war's end, President Truman responded to what he felt was massive public pressure for rapid demobilization. Within a month after the Japanese surrender, the United States Army was discharging over 15,000 soldiers per day; the President pledged that the number would be increased to 25,000 discharges per day by January 1946.[18] Thus, from a wartime peak strength of roughly 6 million men, the Army had been reduced to fewer than 1.5 million by mid-1946 and to fewer than 700,000 men by mid-1947. A 2-million-man air force and 3-million-man navy had been reduced by mid-1947 to approximately 300,000 and 500,000, respectively. Moreover, because the massive exodus from the services had included trained personnel in key positions, many of the Army, Navy, and Air Force units that remained were in a poor state of combat readiness.[19]

In spite of the massive demobilization, the United States possessed at least one fearsome military advantage over all other powers—atomic weapons. A single bomb had virtually destroyed the city of Hiroshima in August 1945; another had obliterated Nagasaki a few days later. At the war's end, the United States had a monopoly on atomic weaponry and the knowledge that had produced such unprecedented destruction. Even before the explosive potential of the atom bomb had been proved, some officials sensed that it could effect a radical change in the game of international politics. Secretary of War Stimson, for instance, urged that vital negotiations with the Soviets be postponed until the United States held "the master card";[20] the United States, he believed, would then be bar-

---

[17] Churchill, 6, *Triumph and Tragedy*, 573. In the same letter, using phraseology that became famous in a speech the following year in Fulton, Missouri, Churchill observed of the Soviets, "An iron curtain is drawn down upon their front."

[18] Truman, 1:558.

[19] W. W. Rostow, *The United States in the World Arena* (New York: Harper & Row, 1960), p. 172 and notes, p. 265.

[20] H. L. Stimson, Diary, May 15, 1945, cited in Gar Alperovitz, *Atomic Diplomacy: Hiroshima and Potsdam* (New York: Simon and Schuster, 1965), p. 57.

gaining with "a royal straight flush and we mustn't be a fool about the way we play it. . . ." [21]

Containment: The Strategy Enunciated

President Truman's speech to Congress in March 1947, in which he set forth the principles that became known as the Truman Doctrine, provided an occasion for enunciating the basic features of the American strategy at that time. Details of the Truman Doctrine and of the specific events that led to the response described in the speech will be discussed later in the chapter. One might note, however, that further actions indicating the strategy that the American government had adopted followed in rapid succession after the Truman Doctrine was enunciated.

"Carrot and Stick"   The Marshall Plan for providing large-scale American economic assistance to the war-torn countries of Europe was announced by Secretary of State George Marshall in a commencement address at Harvard University in June 1947. The Marshall Plan may be viewed as the "carrot" of the American deterrence strategy; the major deterring "stick," NATO, followed in a few months. The Marshall Plan was intended to help deter belligerent Soviet moves by making other options more attractive. A member of the State Department who helped to draft the Marshall Plan noted that the rationale was "that the primary objective of United States policy toward Europe should be to bring about conditions in Europe and in our relations with the USSR which would cause Soviet leaders to decide that their interests were better served by negotiating a political and economic settlement and collaborating with the United States on European matters rather than continuing a policy of unilateral expansion. . . ." [22] Realistically, it was not expected that the Soviets would participate in the European Recovery Program (the formal designation of the Marshall Plan), but the lure was held out to them. Moreover, if the Soviets refused to participate, they would have the onus both of refusing to aid in the reconstruction of Europe and of declining benefits that they themselves might enjoy.

Further clarification of the emerging American strategy was provided during the same month that Secretary Marshall spoke at Harvard by an article titled "The Sources of Soviet Conduct" in the July issue (published in June) of *Foreign Affairs*, a quarterly publication of the Council on Foreign Relations. The author was listed as "X," although it soon became

[21] Stimson, Diary, May 14, 1945, cited in Alperovitz, p. 61.
[22] Joseph M. Jones, *The Fifteen Weeks* (New York: Harcourt, paperback ed., 1955), p. 243.

widely known (especially through a column by Arthur Krock) that the article had been written by George F. Kennan, then chairman of the State Department Policy Planning Staff, along the lines of his cable from Moscow a year earlier. Kennan has recently revealed that the article did not, as was supposed at the time, have official sanction; moreover, some ambiguity in phraseology led to subsequent misrepresentation of Kennan's views about how containment should be implemented.[23] The salient point, however, is that the article expounded an explanation of Soviet actions and intentions that key American policy makers had found persuasive and that had become a basic element in the rationale for an American Cold War strategy. In capsule form, the advice by Kennan that other policy makers had found particularly persuasive was ". . . that the main element of any United States policy toward the Soviet Union must be that of a long-term, patient but firm and vigilant containment of Russian expansive tendencies." [24]

Containment, as defined not simply in Kennan's article but also in actions and policies of the American government, represented the basic strategy that American policy makers would continue for at least a decade and a half.[25] It is not essential for our analytical purposes to describe in detail the subsequent evolution of containment, with such modifications as the "massive retaliation" emphasis of the Eisenhower-Dulles years and the subsequent shift to "flexible and controlled deterrence" under Kennedy and McNamara. Our purpose thus far in the chapter has simply been to suggest the basic form of the strategy of containment and to identify the bases for its design.

Rationale for Containment: Summary Events of the Cold War are, of course, subject to various interpretations, even from a strategic per-

[23] The background of the "X" article, as Kennan relates it, plus a fascinating critique by Kennan of his own piece in retrospect, is contained in his *Memoirs: 1925–1950*, pp. 354–367. The article has been reproduced in full in Kennan's *American Diplomacy: 1900–1950* (New York: New American Library, Mentor paperback ed., 1952), pp. 89–106.

[24] Kennan, *American Diplomacy*, p. 99.

[25] Some critics of government policies in recent years have argued that the containment strategy has lingered on, long after the rationale for it had become outmoded by events. For example, see Senator J. W. Fulbright's discussion, *Old Myths and New Realities* (New York: Random House, paperback ed., 1964); see also two provocative essays by Carl Oglesby and Richard Shaull, *Containment and Change* (New York: Crowell-Collier-Macmillan, paperback ed., 1967). As indicated earlier in the chapter, for our purposes we may describe American strategy for the first decade and a half after World War II without joining the debate over whether or not the Cold War has ended, and whether containment continues to provide a guiding rationale for action by policy makers.

spective. However, the rationale for a containment strategy identified through application of the key variables indicated above illustrates analysis from a strategic perspective. The breakdown of the wartime alliance between the United States and the Soviet Union and the transformation of the relationship from partnership to conflict are interpreted primarily as the logical pursuit of self-interest of each party, which, after the defeat of Germany, made continued partnership more costly than desirable. A growing belief on the part of American policy makers that the Soviets would not, in any event, adhere to the pacts of postwar cooperation that had been signed in the waning months of the war contributed to a feeling that the United States must pursue a vigorous policy of containment of Communist expansion. The strategy of the Soviets seems to most American policy makers to be based upon the assumption that conflict between the two systems was inevitable and that continual probing and exploitation of weak spots in the West was a fruitful means of expanding the domain of communism. The appropriate response to such a strategy seemed to be meet pressure with counter-pressure—to yield nowhere, thereby convincing the Soviets that they must adopt a more moderate position. The high stakes, especially in Europe, seemed to make a tough line desirable; economic advantages and a monopoly of atomic weapons made such a posture feasible. But the awesome prospect of a third world war, coupled with the debilitation of the American armed forces that occurred during the demobilization period, were arguments for avoiding a violent showdown with the Soviets.

Some General Propositions

For some analytical purposes, it would be useful to move beyond interpretation of particular series of events to generalizations about foreign-policy strategy. One might, for instance, attempt to develop a typology of foreign-policy strategies and to formulate some general propositions about the variables that are associated with various types of strategy. Viewing strategy broadly as the overall orientation of the nation-state toward its geopolitical environment, a nation-state might be termed "*status quo*" or "revisionist" according to its commitment to preservation or to change, respectively, of existing institutions and international relationships. Such a typology will be expanded in Part III of the book, together with the identification of the distinctive preconditions of each type.

However, viewing strategy more narrowly here as a series of moves for a particular contest or encounter, we may attempt to generalize about patterns of interaction. With the Cold War as a particular frame of reference, a couple of hypotheses at a rather high level of abstraction will be developed. Only two of the variables identified above will be employed in the hypotheses, but they will suffice to illustrate the move from particularistic analysis to generalization.

The Cold War was a contest involving a number of parties, not just two. In a sense, therefore, the American strategy for the Cold War was the composite of the several strategies needed to define the relations of the United States to each of the other parties involved. The general style of interaction with another nation-state will be determined, we hypothesize, by two of the variables identified earlier: the policy makers' estimate of the strategy that the other nation-state is pursuing and their estimate of their own relative national capabilities. The relationship is depicted graphically in Figure 1; it is made more explicit verbally in Hypotheses 1 and 2.

HYPOTHESIS 1 *When policy makers believe that the strategy of another nation-state supports their own nation's interests—*

HYPOTHESIS 1(a) *They will pursue a leadership strategy if their own national capabilities are deemed superior to those of the other nation-state.*

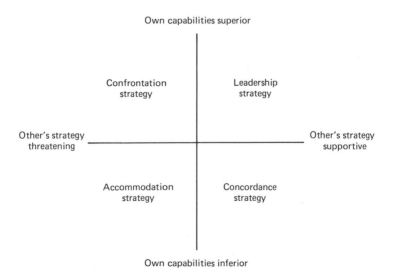

Figure 1 Policy Makers' Estimates of the Strategy of Another Nation-State and Estimates of Their Own Relative Capabilities as Determinants of the Style of Interaction

The term "leadership" is used here to mean control by persuasion and bargaining, rather than by pure coercion (although coercion in some instances may be combined with other forms of persuasion). Nation-state *A* may be said to be successfully pursuing a leadership strategy in respect to nation-state *B* to the extent that *B* follows *A*'s initiative and policy guidelines. Since the situation postulated in the hypothesis is one of mutuality of interests, *A*'s strategy is one of providing reinforcement to incentives that already exist for *B* to follow a course of action supporting *A*'s interests.

> HYPOTHESIS 1(b)   *They will pursue a concordance strategy if their own national capabilities are deemed inferior to those of the other nation-state.*

Again, mutuality of interests is postulated. However, recognizing the inferiority relative to nation-state *A*, the policy makers of nation-state *B* will seek to maintain harmonious relations with *A* by avoiding extreme deviations from the policy preferences of *A* and by acting in concord with *A*'s initiatives. In some instances, *B*'s strategy may be to seek a "junior-partnership" strategy relative to *A*, in which *B* is regularly consulted by *A* and is thus in a position to exert some influence over joint actions.

> HYPOTHESIS 2   *When policy makers believe that the strategy of another nation-state threatens their own nation's interests—*

> HYPOTHESIS 2(a)   *They will pursue a confrontation strategy if they believe their own national capabilities to be superior to those of the other nation-state.*

In pursuing a confrontation strategy, nation-state *C* will seek to sharpen the issues in which its interests conflict with those of nation-state *D*, forcing *D* to modify its position through recognition of the superior capabilities of *C*.

> HYPOTHESIS 2(b)   *They will pursue an accommodation strategy if they believe their own national capabilities to be inferior to those of the other nation-state.*

Recognizing the superior capabilities of nation-state *C*, it is postulated that nation-state *D* will attempt to make adjustments in order to avoid conflict, although in the long run *D* may envisage a confrontation strategy vis-à-vis *C* as its own capabilities improve.

The hypotheses can be illustrated briefly through reference to previous discussion. As indicated in the discussion above, estimates by American policy makers that the capabilities of the United States were superior in most respects to those of the Soviet Union and that the Soviets were embarked on a strategy that threatened important American interests were important determinants of an American containment strategy. The strategy was essentially one of confrontation with the Soviet Union, which was mitigated, as indicated earlier, by a desire to avoid a showdown that would result in all-out combat. In contrast, the strategy of the United States in relation to most European allies in the early postwar years might be accurately described as a leadership strategy. The strategies of the West European governments generally supported American interests, but American capabilities were so vastly superior to those of European nation-states that the American government was largely able to design policy guidelines to which the Western alliance as a whole was expected to adhere. (This is not to say that allies were denied a voice in policy discussions, but relatively speaking, the relationship of the United States to its allies was definitely that of leader to follower.) Conversely, the European allies in the early postwar years pursued what may be termed a "concordance strategy," adhering to policy guidelines set forth by the United States, but generally approving the guidelines, since American strategy supported the interests of Western European nation-states.

Of course, the style of interaction between nation-states was not as clear-cut, and seldom is, as suggested by the four strategies described in Hypotheses 1 and 2. American policy makers adopted a general strategy of confrontation with the Soviet Union, but accommodated themselves to Soviet dominance in Eastern Europe, where Soviet armies and the proximity of the territory to the Soviet Union gave the Soviets a substantial strategic advantage over the United States. Likewise, in some instances, American policies such as the termination of lend-lease were threatening to rather than supportive of interests of European states such as Great Britain. British strategy in this instance might therefore be described as accommodation to American policies, rather than concordance. The nuances of the relations between any two nation-states, plus the vast complications that enter when one moves from a single pattern of interaction to a consideration of relationships to large numbers of other nation-states, mean that the design of strategy is far more complex than Hypotheses 1 and 2 might suggest. A complex strategy is likely to include plans for accommodation on some issues, confrontation on others, leadership in some situations, and concordance in others. Some appreciation of variations that occur within the broad outlines of a given strategy can be attained through consideration of foreign-policy tactics; this subject will be dealt with in the following section of the chapter.

Cold-War Tactics

American Cold-War strategy has been identified and explained on the basis of inferences from observations of the pattern of foreign-policy decisions over a period of years. Particular decisions and events have concerned us only insofar as they have helped to define the broad outlines of strategy. We now turn, however, to an explicit focus on specific foreign-policy decisions, interpreting them in terms of tactical objectives and techniques. Because the decisions to be discussed will be presented in chronological sequence, some sense of the pattern of continuity and change in American Cold-War policies from one administration to another will be conveyed. However, no effort is made to trace fully the evolution of American foreign policy in the post-World War II period; rather, a small sample of policy decisions during the period will be discussed merely to illustrate a variety of tactical objectives and techniques.

Several hypotheses will be introduced, which, like Hypotheses 1 and 2, are designed to serve limited objectives. First, in formulating hypotheses, we illustrate how analysis may move from the identification of relevant variables to a second stage, in which some interrelationships between variables are postulated, thus making more explicit one's hunches about the reasons for certain foreign-policy decisions. Second, the hypotheses, which are cast in general language rather than in terms of specific events, are designed to encourage or provoke the reader to relate observations about particular occurrences both to other particular occurrences and to broader generalizations about foreign policy. As we suggested in Chapter 1, the process of analysis moves from some general theoretical reference points to particular observations and back to generalizations again.

The small handful of hypotheses that follows merely suggests the analytical process. It must also be emphasized that discussion of particular foreign-policy decisions only illustrates the hypotheses and is not a test of the validity of the hypotheses. We encourage the reader to test, to modify, and to supplement the hypotheses.

Legitimizing a Nuclear Arsenal

The "Quick and the Dead": An American Proposal   The first decision to be discussed is the so-called Baruch Plan of 1946. Presiding over the first meeting of the United Nations Atomic Energy Commission in

June 1946, the American representative to the commission, Bernard Baruch, described the urgency of the task before the group as follows:

> We are here to make a choice between the quick and the dead. . . . We must provide the mechanism to assure that atomic energy is used for peaceful purposes and preclude its use in war. . . . We must remember that the peoples do not belong to the governments but that the governments belong to the peoples. We must answer their demands; we must answer the world's longing for peace and security.
>
> In that desire the United States shares ardently and hopefully. The search of science for the absolute weapon has reached fruition in this country. But she stands ready to proscribe and destroy this instrument, to lift its use from death to life, if the world will join in a pact to that end.[26]

Having indicated the strong desire of the American government to achieve a system of international control of atomic energy, Mr. Baruch introduced a plan for such control, representing a modification of a design prepared under the supervision of Under Secretary of State Dean Acheson and scientific consultant David Lilienthal. The plan called for the creation of an International Atomic Development Authority (IADA), the composition of which was unspecified except that its members were to be highly knowledgeable in atomic energy and recruited on an international basis. Key aspects of the authority to be entrusted to the IADA were "managerial control or ownership of all atomic energy activities potentially dangerous to world security"; "power to control, inspect, and license all other atomic activities"; and primacy in engaging in research and development in atomic energy.[27] The body was to have power to impose penalties upon any violator; IADA investigations or the imposition of sanctions by the IADA were not be prevented by the veto of any nation-state (in contrast to procedures in the UN Security Council).

The Baruch Plan provided assurances of the willingness of the American government to stop the manufacture of atomic bombs, to dispose of its existing stockpiles, and to provide the IADA with full information essential to the development of atomic weapons, "when an adequate system of control of atomic energy, including the renunciation of the bomb as a weapon, has been agreed upon and put into effective operation and condign punishments set up for the violations of the rules of control which are to be stigmatized as international crimes. . . ."[28]

---

[26] United Nations, Atomic Energy Commission, *Official Records* (New York: Hunter College, June 14, 1946), no. 1, pp. 4–5. Cited hereafter as UN, AEC *Records*.

[27] UN, AEC *Records*, no. 1, p. 7.

[28] UN, AEC *Records*, no. 1, p. 8.

At the second meeting of the UN Atomic Energy Commission, Soviet representative Gromyko proposed an alternative to the Baruch Plan. Agreeing with Baruch that the issue was urgent, he added his view that inherent in the existing atomic-weapons situation were ". . . reasons that can only increase the suspicion of some countries in regard to others and give rise to political instability. . . ." [29] He therefore recommended that an international convention take place as soon as possible to sign a treaty prohibiting the production and employment of atomic weapons, with all existing stockpiles of atomic weapons, completed or uncompleted, to be destroyed within three months from the day the treaty became active. He further recommended that an international committee for the free exchange of scientific information be established immediately, with the task of working out details of the treaty, including provisions for control of atomic energy, policing, and sanctions.

Details of subsequent debate of the American and Soviet proposals need not concern us here. It is sufficient to note that the two positions proved to be irreconcilable; thus the United States continued its production and testing of atomic weapons, and the Soviets their research and development, which led to the successful test of an atomic device in 1949. The surprisingly rapid acquisition by the Soviets of an atomic capability in turn stimulated the American government, by a process that one observer has described as "how to decide without actually choosing," to push ahead to an even more "super" weapon (in the terminology of officials)—the H-bomb.[30]

The Policy Dilemma   The Baruch Plan has often been depicted as a major effort on the part of the United States government to help mankind to remove the threat of an atomic holocaust, by assigning the devastating weapons and technology over which the United States held a monopoly to international control. Only when American efforts were thwarted by lack of Soviet support was there a reversal of American policy objectives, according to a common interpretation of events. Soviet rejection of the American initiative paved the way for the onset of the Cold War, stimulating American development of a nuclear arsenal for deterring Soviet aggression.

Such is one interpretation that might be made of the Baruch Plan, even from a strategic perspective. However, a strategic perspective also lends itself to a quite different interpretation, especially if the range of

[29] UN, AEC *Records* (June 19, 1946), no. 2, pp. 23–30.

[30] Warner R. Schilling, "The H-Bomb Decision: How to Decide without Actually Choosing," *Political Science Quarterly*, 76 (March 1961), 24–46; reprinted in Davis B. Bobrow, ed., *Components of Defense Policy* (Chicago: Rand McNally, 1965), pp. 390–409.

tactical objectives and techniques described in Chapter 3 is considered. American policy makers in 1945–1946 faced a dilemma. On the one hand, in the aftermath of the devastation at Hiroshima and Nagasaki, there was worldwide concern that means be found for eliminating the future use of atomic weapons. Pressures on the American government for taking the initiative in devising such means can be described as a particular instance of the following general hypothesis.

> HYPOTHESIS 3 *The greater the opprobrium attached to a given weapon or weapons system, the greater the demand on a government to demonstrate that it shares popular repugnance of the possible consequences of using the weapons.*

On the other hand, although there is no doubt that American officials shared the general concern about preventing a future atomic holocaust, American officials were also becoming increasingly concerned with the felt necessity for designing a strategy to contain Communist expansion; the unpleasant prospect that they might be drawn into a war with the Soviet Union was being faced. As indicated earlier in the chapter, the Soviets far surpassed the United States in the conventional forces available, but the United States retained an awesome strategic advantage in possessing a monopoly of atomic weapons. It is clearly plausible that key American policy makers felt that they must not abandon that advantage. If atomic weapons were to be retained and developed further as a major component of American strategic capabilities, however, how could foreign and domestic pressures for abolition, or at least control, of atomic weapons be satisfied? One may suggest the following hypothesis.

> HYPOTHESIS 4 *If a government decides that it is desirable to develop a weapons system that is opposed by public sentiment, then such a decision can be legitimated in only one of two ways.*

>> HYPOTHESIS 4(a) *If the public can be convinced that the initial opprobrium attached to the weapons system was misplaced, the decision to develop or to utilize the weapons system will be legitimated, providing a threat sufficient to justify its maintenance or use can be demonstrated.*

For instance, the Johnson administration seems to have sought to legitimate the use of napalm by American forces in Vietnam in this manner, arguing that stories of burns inflicted on women and children had been exaggerated and that napalm was no more horrible a means of inflicting death than conventional weapons of war.

> HYPOTHESIS 4(b)   *If the public can be convinced that serious efforts to control or abolish a weapons system failed in spite of the government's desire to attain such control or abolition, the government's decision to develop or to utilize the weapons system will be legitimated, providing a threat sufficient to justify its maintenance or use can be demonstrated.*

The Baruch Plan Interpreted: Legitimizing Bluff   The Baruch Plan may be viewed as an instance of the application of the technique outlined in Hypothesis 4(b). That is, it may be interpreted as a tactical bluff used to convince domestic and foreign leaders and the public of American reasonableness about the control of atomic weapons, without in fact risking the loss of atomic weapons as a major element of bargaining and threat in the emerging containment strategy.

Quite apart from the inspection provision of the Baruch Plan for granting the IADA authority to make inspections within the territory of any state to ensure that no atomic weapons were being produced—provisions that no doubt were abhorrent to the Stalin regime—the provision that allowed the United States to retain a monopoly of atomic weapons until it was assured that the IADA could reliably assume control was virtually certain to prevent the Soviet government from accepting the Baruch Plan. Acceptance of such an agreement by the Soviets could be based only on their faith in the American government until such time as the IADA had supervised destruction of the American atomic stockpile. It is true, of course, that acceptance of the Soviet proposal would conversely have required an act of faith by the American government that the Soviets would not take advantage of American abandonment of its atomic capability by launching a conventional attack or by secretly developing a Soviet atomic capability before a control system became operational. The pertinent point is that leaders of sovereign nation-states are not inclined to entrust their nation's security to faith. The mutual distrust between American and Soviet leaders in 1946 made the probability that the Baruch Plan (or the Soviet alternative) would be accepted all the more infinitesimal.

One may suppose that, had the shoe been on the other foot, with the Soviets in sole possession of atomic weapons and offering the United States a control plan along the lines of the Baruch Plan, American government leaders would have found it impossible to agree to such a proposal. Indeed, even in the circumstances that actually existed, with the United States in possession of an atomic monopoly, it is difficult to imagine Congress ratifying a treaty based on the Baruch Plan even if the

Soviets had agreed to it. At least it is fair to say that it would have been an unprecedented departure from characteristic behavior for Congress to agree to a plan that allocated authority in such a vital field to an international body and that presented the possibility of severe competition with domestic power companies by an internationally owned and operated system of atomic energy.

Nevertheless, however improbable the translation of the Baruch Plan into operational reality may have been, it is clear that the plan was widely regarded at the time as an imaginative and magnanimous act on the part of the United States government. Many persons in the United States and abroad, who had been at the forefront of public discussion about the dangers of atomic war, enthusiastically supported the Baruch Plan. Scientists who had worked on the Manhattan Project, for instance, and who had experienced agonizing cleavages in their ranks over the issue of dropping the bomb on Japan, were temporarily unified by the Baruch Plan. It seemed to offer a rational design for transforming the awesome scientific developments from a threat to mankind into a positive contribution to its betterment.[31]

In short, having proposed a seemingly reasonable and generous plan for the international control of atomic energy, the American government was able to depict Soviet intransigence on the issue as the only obstacle to a world freed from the threat of atomic war. If we assume that the Truman administration recognized in advance that the Baruch Plan would be rejected and that conflict with the Soviets would continue, the Baruch Plan may be interpreted as a means of legitimizing American retention of an atomic arsenal as a major deterrent threat to be used in bargaining with the Soviets and in deterring further Soviet expansion. In this light, the Baruch Plan is an initiative that *succeeded* rather than failed, in terms of the objectives of American policy makers.[32]

Strengthening Deterrence through Commitments

A second decision, or series of decisions, to be considered is that of commitments by the United States to military assistance or defense of

---

[31] Attitudes of the American scientific community toward the Baruch Plan are described by Robert Gilpin, *American Scientists and Nuclear Weapons Policy* (Princeton: Princeton University Press, paperback ed., 1965), pp. 39–63.

[32] Not only the Baruch Plan, but also subsequent United States-Soviet negotiations regarding arms control and disarmament illustrate Cold War tactics. Such an interpretation is provided by John W. Spanier and Joseph L. Nogee, *The Politics of Disarmament: A Study in Soviet-American Gamesmanship* (New York: Praeger, 1962).

other nation-states. Commitments of this sort during the post-World War II period raise some fascinating questions. Why did the United States, which on the eve of World War II still adhered to a long tradition of abstaining from military alliances and other forms of "political entanglement," become involved in the post-World War II period in defense agreements with over forty other nation-states and in military assistance programs to still more nation-states? Why did the United States seek to incorporate Germany and Japan into an American military defense system within a few years after fighting a bloody war to defeat them and to thwart their military ambitions? Why did the United States commit itself to the defense of a number of nation-states in which freedom was severely curtailed by the regimes in power and yet justify the commitments on the grounds of defending "the free world" against communism?

In part, answers to the questions require explanation in terms of historical dynamics, which must be postponed until Part III of the book. From a strategic perspective, however, the military assistance and the alliance commitments of the United States during the post-World War II period represent the selective application of apparent lessons from history (especially recent history) by American policy makers to the exploitation of tactical advantages in some situations and to the reduction of tactical disadvantages in others. We shall advance three hypotheses regarding the tactical judgments that policy makers employ as the bases for military commitments. The first two of these, Hypotheses 5 and 6, suggest conditions under which policy makers are willing to discount historical experience and to disregard other factors that might otherwise make close relations with a given regime undesirable. The third of the hypotheses, Hypothesis 7, suggests conditions under which policy makers will attempt to replicate previous experience in making a commitment. Thus, the hypotheses provide a tentative framework for answering the questions posed above, in terms of tactical purposes and techniques.

> HYPOTHESIS 5 *The greater and more immediate the risks to prominent interests of withholding or denying military assistance or an alliance commitment, the greater will be the willingness of American policy makers to discount other factors (for example, experience in previous relations with the nation-state or political characteristics of the regime in power) in estimating whether the commitment should be made.*

> HYPOTHESIS 6 *The greater the dependence that a potential ally or recipient of aid has—or will have if a commitment to the nation-state is made—the greater will be the willingness of policy*

makers to discount other factors (for example, experience in previous relations with the nation-state or political characteristics of the regime in power) in estimating whether a military assistance or alliance commitment to the nation-state should be made.

Hypotheses 5 and 6 can be illustrated by the Greek-Turkish aid program that was enunciated in the Truman Doctrine of 1947 and by the assimilation of Germany and Japan into the American defense system during the Truman administration.

Aid to Greece   The Truman Doctrine refers to a set of principles set forth by President Truman in a speech before a joint session of Congress in March 1947, the crux of which was embodied in the assertion that "it must be the policy of the United States to support free peoples who are resisting attempted subjugation by armed minorities or by outside pressures." [33] The Truman Doctrine thus enunciated principles seemingly global in applicability. The far-reaching implications of the potential commitment of the United States to oppose Communist expansion gave the speech immense significance as a statement of American policy, although it was precisely these implications and the crusading language in which they were shrouded that led some persons to criticize the Truman Doctrine.[34]

The immediate occasion for Truman's speech before Congress, however, had been provided by events in Greece and in Turkey—especially the former—and by an urgent request from the British government that the United States come to the assistance of Greece and Turkey. The circumstances in Greece, especially, made the foreign-policy problem for the American government particularly complex; the way in which the American government coped with these complexities is illustrative of Hypotheses 5 and 6.

[33] Background of events leading to the Truman Doctrine and the Marshall Plan and a detailed description of the process by which each decision was made are provided in highly readable form by Joseph Marion Jones, *The Fifteen Weeks* (New York: Harcourt, paperback ed., 1964). The full text of the President's speech to Congress of March 12, 1947, is contained as an appendix to Jones, pp. 269–274.

[34] For instance, Walter Lippmann criticized Truman's speech on these grounds, in a column entitled, "Policy or Crusade." On roughly the twentieth anniversary of Truman's speech, President Johnson singled out Lippmann as opposing aid to Greece and Turkey in 1947. In reply, Lippmann reprinted his 1947 criticism of the Truman Doctrine. In fact, Lippmann had supported aid to Greece and Turkey, but had argued that "since the reasons are sufficient why Congress should vote the authority to intervene in the Middle East, it does not necessarily follow that it should indorse the idea that our intentions are henceforth to become general and global." *World Journal Tribune* (New York), April 6, 1967, p. 26.

In brief, the central fact of the complex choice confronting American policy makers in Greece was that the situation presented no simple choice between good and bad. Rather, the choice was either to acquiesce, through inaction, in the probable take-over of Greece by indigenous Communists or to make a substantial commitment of economic aid and military assistance to bolster a regime that lacked broad support and that engaged in various autocratic practices. The bitterness of the strife among competing political factions in Greece since the last months of World War II made it improbable, by the time American policy makers were confronted with a decision whether or not aid to Greece was warranted, that any really moderate government or a coalition representing all major factions could be developed in the near future.

By the final months of World War II, Greek politicians had begun a struggle to secure control of the government that would take over in Greece when the German occupying forces had been finally evicted. The principal contending groups had been the Greek government-in-exile, committed to the restoration of King George II to the throne, and various groups that had established a reputation in Greece during the war as courageous patriots by engaging in guerrilla activity against the Germans. Among the guerrilla groups, the Communist-led Popular Army of Liberation (ELAS), the military arm of the National Liberation Front (EAM), was by far the largest.[35] The EAM appears to have been in a relatively strong position also in terms of its political support at the end of the war. As one analyst of the events of the period described the group,

> EAM furnished a fighting gospel when average Greeks wanted a fighting gospel and when the old-line political gospeleers sat mute in their Athenian homes . . . . After the liberation of Greece, amidst the bankruptcy and bickering of the old-line parties, EAM offered so many fresh and dynamic possibilities that it still continued to attract what many observers believe to have been the largest and most enthusiastic following ever gained by a Greek political group.[36]

The British, however, who had primary responsibility among the allied powers for affairs in Greece in the final months of the war, had been committed to the support of the government-in-exile. Churchill, in particular, had been convinced that restoration of the monarch to his throne

[35] The ELAS was estimated to have an army of 30,000 during the war. The commanding officer, Colonel Sarafis, was said to be non-Communist. Likewise, the ELAS and EAM attracted a sizable non-Communist following, but the organizational core of the group was clearly Communist. *Keesing's Contemporary Archives*, 5 (1943–46), 6091.

[36] Floyd A. Spencer, *War and Postwar Greece* (Washington: U.S. Library of Congress, 1952), pp. 49–50.

was essential in Greece, and had thus pursued policies relentlessly to that end, against the advice of British advisers closer to political developments in Greece. His advisers had tried unsuccessfully to convince Churchill that insistence on backing the royalist cause would strengthen rather than weaken Greek Communists, for they were using opposition to the King as a rallying cry among non-Communists.[37] Consequently, when fighting had broken out in Greece shortly after the departure of German forces between the pro-loyalist government and dissident elements led by the EAM, Churchill had favored vigorous action by the government, with the assistance of British troops, to suppress the insurgency. Having worked out his famous "percentages" agreement with Stalin, Churchill had been confident that Greek Communist insurgents could be suppressed with no interference from Stalin.[38] Indeed, in the early stages of the conflict, it appears that Stalin had adhered to his agreement with Churchill, leaving the Greek Communists to their own devices. Thus a cease-fire had been arranged in 1945 on terms favorable to the Greek government.

However, fighting had resumed in Greece late in 1946. It gradually became apparent that Greek Communist guerrilla forces were now being provided with sanctuary and supplies from bases in Yugoslavia, Bulgaria, and Albania.[39] Moreover, the British were now facing up to the alarming state of their own postwar economic difficulties, and support of the

[37] See Reginald Leeper, *When Greek Meets Greek* (London: Chatto & Windus, Ltd., 1950), pp. 31–35. Also C. M. Woodhouse, *Apple of Discord* (London: Hutchinson, 1948), p. 54. Leeper and Woodhouse were, respectively, Ambassador to the Greek government-in-exile in Cairo and head of the British Military Mission with guerrilla forces in Greece.

[38] The agreement was worked out informally between Churchill and Stalin at a meeting in Moscow, Oct. 9, 1944, on the basis of figures Churchill had jotted down on half a sheet of paper. Britain was to have 90 percent predominance in allied responsibilities for Greece, with 10 percent for the Soviets. In Rumania, the reverse arrangement was to apply. In Bulgaria, the Soviets were to have 75 percent responsibility, and the British 25 percent. In Yugoslavia and in Hungary, the British and the Soviets would share responsibilities on a fifty-fifty basis. After quickly getting Stalin's assent to the agreement, Churchill suggested, " 'Might it not be thought rather cynical if it seemed we had disposed of these issues, so fateful to millions of people, in such an offhand manner? Let us burn the paper.' 'No, you keep it,' said Stalin." Churchill, 6, *Triumph and Tragedy*, 227–228.

[39] A UN Inquiry Commission, with representatives from the USA, USSR, Great Britain, France, China, Poland, Australia, Belgium, Syria, Brazil, Colombia, and Norway was in Greece, investigating charges by the Greek government that insurgents were being supported externally, at the time of the Truman Doctrine decision. The Commission's report, adopted by the Security Council in April over the protests of Soviet and Polish delegates, indicted Yugoslavia, Albania, and Bulgaria for interfering in internal Greek affairs.

Greek government represented a drain on an already overburdened economy. It was in this context that the British ambassador to the United States informed the American government in February 1947 that the British would be unable to provide further aid to Greece or to Turkey; although the needs of Greece exceeded those of Turkey, the British could maintain neither obligation. The British government indicated its hope that the United States government shared the concern that neither Greece nor Turkey should fall under Communist control. Thus, the United States government was being asked, in effect, to take over traditional British responsibilities in the eastern Mediterranean in order to bolster the area against Communist pressures.

The immediate purpose of President Truman's speech to Congress in March 1947 was to get authorization for an American commitment in response to the British (and Greek and Turkish) request.[40] Retaining our exclusive focus on the Greek situation, we can suggest that the decision made by the Truman administration is illustrative of Hypotheses 5 and 6 in the following respects. It is clear from the President's speech at the time, as well as from other reports of policy-making discussions that occurred, that the Truman administration was aware of the corruption, repression, and incompetence that had characterized the succession of governments in Greece. The President noted,

> The Greek Government has been operating in an atmosphere of chaos and extremism. It has made mistakes. The extension of aid by this country does not mean that the United States condones everything that the Greek Government has done or will do. We have condemned in the past, and we condemn now, extremist measures of the right or the left.[41]

The Truman administration and its supporters on the issue in Congress were also sensitive to charges that American aid was serving merely to bolster monarchy in Greece and to maintain the last vestiges of British imperialism. Attempting to reassure skeptics, Arthur Vandenberg, chairman of the Senate Foreign Relations Committee, insisted, "We are not 'bailing out the British Empire.' We are not 'perpetuating the Greek monarchy.' We are making it possible for the Greek people to survive in

[40] Specifically, the request called for a commitment of $300 million in financial aid, plus the dispatch of American civil and military advisers to Greece and Turkey, and training of Greek and Turkish personnel in the United States.

[41] U.S., *Recommendations on Greece and Turkey*, The President's Message to Congress, March 12, 1947, Dept. of State Pub. 2785, Near Eastern Series, 6 (Washington: Government Printing Office, 1947), p. 5. As indicated previously, the speech also appears in Jones, appendix.

stability and self-determination. We are doing the same thing for the world." [42]

In short, the American commitment to Greece was made in spite of, not because of, the most visible attributes of the regime in power. From a strategic perspective, the decision confronting the Truman administration is seen in the context of other calculations made during 1945 and 1946 defining a rationale for a strategy for the emerging conflict with the Soviet Union. The question of whether or not to aid the Greek government can be viewed as one that involved weighing the probable costs of inaction against the probable utility that a tangible commitment would serve in strengthening the credibility of the American deterrent threat generally. The apparent inability of the Greek government to cope with the guerrilla threat without substantial external aid made it probable that American inaction would result in a Communist take-over in Greece. If Greece should fall, the Truman administration feared a "dominoes effect" elsewhere. In seeking congressional support for an American commitment to the Greek government, President Truman warned,

> If Greece should fall under the control of an armed minority, the effect upon its neighbor, Turkey, would be immediate and serious. Confusion and disorder might well spread throughout the entire Middle East. Moreover, the disappearance of Greece as an independent state would have a profound effect upon those countries of Europe whose peoples are struggling against great difficulties to maintain their freedoms and their independence while they repair the damages of war.[43]

Thus, the Truman administration saw vital interests at stake in Greece. Moreover, the economic and political weakness of the Greek government meant that if American aid were rendered, the dependence of the Greek government on the aid would put the United States in a relatively strong position to influence Greek policy. The above calculations, we suggest, led the Truman administration to discount the autocratic characteristics of the Greek regime and the possible stigma of pursuing policies identified with British imperialism and to make an economic and military commitment to Greece.

It is interesting that the rationale that the American government applied in moving to fill a vacuum left by the partial withdrawal of the British from the Mediterranean was strikingly similar to the rationale

[42] Arthur H. Vandenberg, "Soviet Pressure, A World Peril," *Vital Speeches*, 13 (April 15, 1947), 391.

[43] *Recommendations on Greece and Turkey*, p. 8.

that the British themselves had employed throughout much of the nineteenth century in making commitments to nondemocratic governments in the Mediterranean area and elsewhere. For instance, nearly seventy years before the promulgation of the Truman Doctrine, the British Foreign Minister Lord Salisbury had argued as follows in favor of a British commitment to the autocratic regime in Turkey:

> . . . however important it is that Turkey should be reformed, and though [we] will rightly require of their Government that every exertion should be made in order to carry out these reforms, yet the question of a reformed or unreformed Turkey does not affect the necessity of keeping Russia from Constantinople and from the Aegean. In past times we have not inquired what the government of a country was in deciding to protect great strategic positions which it was necessary for the interests of England and Europe should be kept from an overwhelming power.[44]

The decision that the British faced many times in the nineteenth century and that the Truman administration faced in Greece in 1947—whether or not one's own liberal principles should preclude assistance to a regime whose practices were antithetical to those principles—was one that the American government would confront numerous times in the post-World War II period. The choice that the American government seems to have made consistently in rendering aid to regimes in such nations as Korea, Taiwan, Guatemala, Vietnam, Lebanon, and the Dominican Republic lends further support to Hypotheses 5 and 6.

Remilitarization of Germany and Japan   Hypotheses 5 and 6 also can be illustrated by the reversal of American postwar policies toward Germany and Japan. Whereas early postwar policies had been designed to prevent either of the two states from ever again wielding military power, as concern about communism increased in the United States,

[44] Lord Salisbury went on to observe, "The constitution of Poland was about as detestable as any constitution could be, yet Poland was followed by the sympathy and exertions of liberal Europe for half a century, not for her own merits, but because she was a bulwark against the advance of a power that was feared. Spain again—when Napoleon invaded Spain, the Government of Spain was the most detestable of governments which the corruption of the last century left to us; yet we never hesitated for a moment to spend the blood and treasure of this country in defending Spain against Napoleon, and we were never hindered by the thought that her Government was bad." Speech in Manchester, England, Oct. 2, 1879, printed in F. S. Pulling, *The Life and Speeches of the Marquis of Salisbury, K.G.* (London: Sampson, Low, Marston, Searle and Livingston, 1885), 2: 36–37; quoted in *Principles and Problems of International Politics: Selected Readings*, Hans Morgenthau and Kenneth Thompson, eds. (New York: Knopf, 1952), pp. 57–58.

there were more of those who argued that Germany and Japan must be integrated into the system of defense against communism. The outbreak of the Korean War proved to be decisive in promoting the latter point of view.

The new postwar Japanese Constitution, drafted by General MacArthur's headquarters and accepted by the Japanese Diet in 1946, had proclaimed that ". . . land, sea, and air forces, as well as other war potential, will never be maintained. The right of belligerency of the state will not be recognized." [45] Within weeks following the outbreak of the Korean War, however, the United States promoted the organization of a "National Police Reserve" in Japan. The following year, a change of policy made it possible for officers who had served in the Japanese armed forces before and during World War II to join the organization. In September 1951, representatives of the United States and the Japanese governments concluded a peace treaty, formally terminating the state of war between the two nation-states, in which Japan's "inherent right of individual or collective self-defense" was specifically recognized.[46] The same day on which the peace treaty was signed, the United States concluded a security treaty with Japan, providing for the retention of U.S. troops in and around Japan, "in the expectation, however, that Japan will itself increasingly assume responsibility for its own defense. . . ." [47]

Although Germany was not close to Korea geographically, which had made the North Korean attack especially pertinent in the decision to include Japan in the network of defense and deterrence against Communist expansion, the parallel between the German and the Korean situation was a cause for alarm. Both nations had been divided between Communist and Western rule. The Communists had been willing to risk all-out war in order to reunify Korea by force. Thus, perhaps an attack on Germany, where NATO forces were feeble in comparison to the Soviet armies, was imminent.

Several prominent persons, including John J. McCloy, American High Commissioner in Germany; General Lucius Clay, who had been Military Governor in Germany; and British Field Marshal Viscount Montgomery, had proposed even before the Korean War that Germany be rearmed as part of the Western defense against Communist expansion. The American

---

[45] Constitution of Japan, Art. 9. Official English translation in U.S., Dept. of State Pub. 2836, Far Eastern Series, 22 (Washington: Government Printing Office, 1947).

[46] U.S., Dept. of State, *Conference for the Conclusion of the Treaty of Peace with Japan: Record of Proceedings* (Washington: 1951), Dept. of State Pub. 4392, International and Conference Series, 2; Far Eastern Series, 3:102–119.

[47] U.S., Dept. of State, *U.S. Treaties and Other International Agreements* (Washington: 1952), TIAS 2491, TIAS 2492, vol. 3, Pt. 3, 3330–3419.

Joint Chiefs of Staff had tentatively approved German rearmament early in 1950. With the Korean War, plans moved ahead much more quickly. In September, President Truman approved plans for rearming West Germany, within the context of creating an integrated European Defense Community. (Later, when EDC failed to win French parliamentary support, the West German forces were brought into the strategic formulation under the auspices of NATO.) The President announced that a substantial addition to the American troop commitment would be made. The United States would agree to a unified command structure for NATO; General Dwight D. Eisenhower was selected by President Truman as the new Supreme Commander of Allied Powers in Europe.[48]

Expansion of the Alliance Network   By the time that Eisenhower took office as President in 1953, NATO had established a growing reputation as a successful alliance. Since the inception of the alliance, not an inch of European territory had been yielded to the Soviet Union or its satellites. (The fall of Czechoslovakia to Communist rule in 1948 preceded the signing of the NATO treaty by several months and was in fact an important stimulus to the commitment of the North Atlantic nation-states to an alliance.)

Efforts by American policy makers, especially during the first years of the Eisenhower administration, to capitalize on the apparent success of the NATO idea, provide the basis for Hypothesis 7. Like Hypotheses 5 and 6, it describes tactical judgments on the basis of which military commitments are made.

> HYPOTHESIS 7   *The greater the conviction of policy makers that a relatively unprecedented military commitment has proved its worth as a tactical technique where the stakes are high, the greater the probability that they will replicate the commitment in other contexts.*

The first post-World War II commitment of the United States to a mutual defense treaty was not that of NATO, but the Rio Pact, signed in 1947. Many persons, however, regarded the Rio Pact (formally the Inter-American Treaty of Reciprocal Assistance) as a mere modern-day extension of the Monroe Doctrine and therefore a justifiable adaptation of traditional commitments in the Western Hemisphere. The NATO pact, however, signed in 1949, represented an unprecedented peacetime commitment by the United States to the defense of European nations; it was

[48] Laurence W. Martin, "The American Decision to Rearm Germany," *American Civil-Military Decisions*, Harold Stein, ed. (Birmingham, Alabama: University of Alabama Press, 1963), pp. 645–660.

the antithesis of the nonentanglement posture that Washington, Jefferson, and other founding fathers had advocated.

NATO not only won broad support at the outset, but also growing belief in its significance and success. The transition from the Truman to the Eisenhower administration marked an increase rather than a diminution in the belief in NATO. Enthusiasts in the new administration included not only Eisenhower, the former commander of the allied powers, but also the new secretary of state, John Foster Dulles, who had led the United States mission that had concluded the peace treaty with Japan and had negotiated a security treaty with the Japanese in the final year of the Truman administration. During the week prior to the signing of the two agreements with Japan, Dulles had participated in the initiation of a bilateral defense treaty with the Philippines and in signing a defense pact among Australia, New Zealand, and the United States (the ANZUS Pact).

Upon assuming the top post in the State Department, Dulles moved rapidly to build a whole series of interlocking defense arrangements, virtually around the entire periphery of the area under Communist control. In 1954, the military commitment that the United States had made to the Republic of Korea during the Korean War was extended for the period following the cease-fire by a mutual defense treaty. In September of 1954, the Southeast Asia Treaty Organization (SEATO) was formed, involving the United States, the United Kingdom, France, Australia, New Zealand, Pakistan, the Philippines, and Thailand. In December 1954, on behalf of the United States, Dulles signed a mutual defense pact with the Nationalist Chinese government of Chiang Kai-shek. During the same year, he had been promoting a series of mutual defense agreements in the Middle East that would fill the gap between NATO and SEATO in creating a network of alliances along the Sino-Soviet borders. By 1955, the Eisenhower administration had decided not to associate itself formally as a signatory member of the Baghdad Pact, as the agreements became known collectively. However, the United States agreed to send delegates to meetings of the organization and to cooperate in the defense of its member nations against attack.

Thus, within two years of assuming office as Secretary of State, Dulles had expanded the network of collective defense treaties with which the United States was affiliated to include over forty nations. Especially after the death of Stalin in 1953, some persons challenged the creation of a vast network of anti-Communist military alliances on the grounds that it would deepen Soviet mistrust of the United States at a time that might be ripe for improving relations with the Soviets. Other critics questioned the viability of alliances such as SEATO and the Baghdad Pact, given the instability and economic weakness of several of the governments to whom the United States was making a commitment and the absence of common traditions and institutions such as those linking the NATO members. Moreover, since the alliance network forged during the Eisenhower-Dulles years was closely tied to a strategy of massive retaliation, some critics questioned the credibility of the deterrent that had supposedly been broadened in scope through expansion of the alliance system. For instance, Chester Bowles, former American ambassador to India, noted that it was probably correct to assume that the Soviets would recognize that the American government would risk a nuclear war in defense of its NATO allies. "But would America be willing to accept these same terrible risks to meet local aggression in Asia—say, in Afghanistan, Burma, Iran or Indochina?" he asked. "Our deep-felt reaction to the war in Korea and to the bare prospect of an even more limited involvement in Indochina seems to say clearly that we would not." [49]

It seems apparent, however, that Eisenhower and Dulles drew a different lesson in deterrence from the Korean experience and from the success of NATO. If the Soviet Union had been convinced prior to June 1950 that an attack on South Korea would be met by American armed force, the attack would never have occurred; such was the reasoning of the Eisenhower-Dulles administration. Its expectation, therefore, was that the American willingness to respond forcibly in defense of Korea and other areas potentially or actually threatened by Communist attack would be made more credible by supplementing NATO with formal United States commitment to a broad network of mutual defense pacts. To span the Sino-Soviet border with the collective military forces of the United States and its allies would provide containment, it was hoped, in a literal sense.

Economic Aid as Reward and Punishment

The final tactical decision to be discussed in the chapter concerns a problem that has attained vastly increased importance in American foreign policy in recent decades: relations with developing nation-states; it also concerns the use of a familiar instrument for maintaining such relations: economic aid. The background of the specific decision, support for the construction of the Aswan High Dam, will be sketched briefly.

In 1952, a *coup d'état* in Egypt ousted King Farouk and brought a revolutionary military junta to power. By 1954, Colonel Gamal Abdel

[49] Chester Bowles, "A Plea for Another Great Debate," *New York Times Magazine,* Feb. 28, 1954, pp. 11 ff.

Nasser had emerged as the key figure of the new regime.[50] Nasser soon established a worldwide reputation as a charismatic leader aspiring to be the dominant voice for Pan-Arabic sentiments and to promote greater unity on the African continent. After an Afro-Asian conference at Bandung, Indonesia, in 1955, Nasser (along with Nehru and Sukarno) became identified as a leading spokesman for the assertion by developing nations of a "third force" in world affairs, independent of the control of either of the two Cold-War superpowers.

Dollars for a Dam at Aswan   However, the paramount declared objectives of the Nasser regime were domestic ones, including the elimination of the last vestiges of British colonial rule and vast improvement in the Egyptian standard of living through economic development. The most important stimulus to economic development was to be provided by the construction of a massive dam at Aswan, on the Nile River some 300 miles south of Cairo and four miles upstream from a smaller dam that had been completed in 1902. The so-called High Dam would be designed to provide greatly improved means of controlling the floods that had devastated the Nile valley annually; to provide a major source of hydroelectric power; and to increase by more than 25 percent the arable land in Egypt through land reclamation and irrigation. In proposing to construct the Aswan High Dam, however, the Nasser regime faced a dilemma characteristic of nation-states that have not yet reached a high level of economic development. The project was important as a long-term investment that, once completed, would improve immensely the prospects for sustained economic growth and for greater independence from more economically advanced nation-states. However, precisely because the existing economic situation was so desperate, external assistance by more economically advanced nation-states was essential for the project to be undertaken at all.

In December 1955, it was announced that the United States and Great Britain had agreed to make a joint grant of $70 million to finance the first phase of construction of the Aswan High Dam.[51] The following month, the American-British proposal was expanded. The World Bank would make a loan to the Egyptian government of half the $400 million that was needed in foreign exchange for construction of the dam ($900 million was to be provided by the Egyptians themselves). In addition to the $70 million-grant already committed, the United States and Great Britain agreed to provide another $130 million in grants or loans, thereby

[50] For analysis of various facets of Egyptian society since that time, see P. J. Vatikiotis, ed., *Egypt since the Revolution* (New York: Praeger, 1968).

[51] "British-U.S. Offer to Finance Nile Dam," London *Times*, Dec. 19, 1955, p. 6.

making up the difference in the amount of foreign exchange needed.[52] During the next several months, representatives of the Egyptian government discussed terms of the proposed loans and grants with representatives of the World Bank and with representatives of the governments of the United States and Great Britain. In July 1956, the Egyptian Ambassador to the United States Ahmed Hussein announced that the Egyptian government had definitely decided to accept the offer; he made an appointment with Secretary Dulles to confirm the agreement.[53] In a heated discussion with Hussein, however, Dulles withdrew the American offer.[54] Shortly thereafter the British government and officials of the World Bank announced that their offers of aid for the Aswan Dam project also were withdrawn.

The explosive aftermath of the withdrawal of Anglo-American aid for the Aswan Dam project is well known. One week after Dulles had abruptly canceled the American offer, Nasser announced that the Suez Canal Company was being nationalized and that proceeds from users of the canal would be used to finance construction of the Aswan Dam. Efforts throughout the remainder of the summer and the early autumn to negotiate a new treaty among interested nations for international use of the canal proved fruitless. On October 29, units from the Israeli armed forces suddenly struck across the Egyptian frontier, moving rapidly across the Sinai peninsula to the Suez Canal. The following day, the British and French governments issued an ultimatum to the Egyptian and Israeli governments, ordering them to withdraw troops ten miles on either side of the Suez Canal and to permit British and French forces to occupy crucial points along the canal. When the Egyptian government rejected the ultimatum, British and French forces bombed Egyptian airfields and then launched an airborne and seaborne assault near Port Said. After a week of fighting, a cease-fire was arranged under United Nations auspices, supported by strong statements from the American and Soviet governments. Under the supervision of a United Nations peacekeeping force, British and French troops were evacuated from the Suez area by the end of the year.[55]

---

[52] "New Offer to Egypt," London *Times*, Jan. 24, 1956, p. 8.

[53] "Cost of Building Aswan Dam," London *Times*, July 18, 1956, p. 10.

[54] One critic of Dulles's sudden withdrawal of the offer suggests that "on the spur of the moment, all the resentment of a man who had monumental self-righteousness, a reborn Calvinist who was a deeply committed lay pillar of the Christian church— all this boiled up and was visited on Nasser." Herman Finer, *Dulles over Suez* (Chicago: Quadrangle Books, 1964), p. 51.

[55] Ten years after the Suez crisis, Peter Calvocoressi conducted interviews in a series of documentary broadcasts on BBC with many of the principal figures from the Egyptian, Israeli, British, French, and American governments who had been

Analyzing the American Offer Complex and intriguing as are the events of the Suez crisis, our analytical concern here is limited to the American foreign-policy decision to make, and subsequently to withdraw, an offer of financial aid to the Egyptian government for construction of the Aswan High Dam. Why was the offer made? Why was it withdrawn? The official rationale of the Eisenhower administration for having made the offer in the first place was that the project made sense as a major investment in long-range economic development in Egypt. For instance, early in 1956, Under Secretary of State Herbert Hoover, Jr., expressed the views of the Eisenhower administration in assuring the Senate Appropriations Committee that the World Bank had judged the Aswan High Dam project to "be thoroughly feasible and basically sound, both from the engineering and economic points of view." [56] In announcing several months later, however, that the American offer of aid for the project had been withdrawn, the State Department indicated that aid was no longer "feasible under present conditions." [57]

From a strategic analytical perspective, however, considerations of the economic feasibility and significance of the Aswan High Dam are only incidentally relevant to the American decision. Rather, the decision can be seen as a tactical one, designed to further American objectives in the Cold War. The following general hypothesis stipulates conditions under which economic rewards will be used to further tactical purposes.

> HYPOTHESIS 8   *The greater the strategic significance attached to a given nation-state by American policy makers and the greater their belief that American influence on the policies of the nation-state is in jeopardy, the more dramatic will be the inducement offered by American policy makers to officials of the nation-state in an effort to preserve or to increase American influence.*

The strategic significance of the Middle East in general and of Egypt in particular had been apparent to American policy makers from the early days of the Cold War. When the Eisenhower administration took office, interest in the area was heightened. Secretary of State Dulles was convinced that the Soviets had begun a concerted effort to gain a dominant influence in the area; he "decided to increase American in-

---

involved in the crisis. The transcript of the broadcasts, which also includes comments by other persons with expertise in Middle Eastern affairs, is available in book form: Peter Calvocoressi, *Suez Ten Years After*, Anthony Moncrieff, ed. (New York: Pantheon, 1966).

[56] U.S. Congress, Senate Committee on Appropriations, *Hearings, Financing of Aswan High Dam in Egypt*, 84th Cong., 2d sess., Jan. 26, 1956, p. 3.

[57] "U.S. Rebuff to Egypt," London *Times*, July 20, 1956, p. 10.

fluence there at the earliest possible moment." [58] Thus, in the spring of his first year in office, Dulles made a tour of the Middle East. President Eisenhower had attached particular importance to Egypt, suggesting possible American aid, including support for construction of a high dam at Aswan, as an inducement to Egyptian leaders to pursue policies favorable to American interests. [59]

Efforts to make Egypt the keystone of a western military-alliance system in the Middle East met with Egyptian recalcitrance. Nevertheless, with only one Arab state (Iraq) in membership, an alliance was created. As suggested previously in the chapter, the Eisenhower administration decided against formal membership in the Baghdad Pact, which was formed early in 1955; however, the American government identified itself closely with the purposes and activities of the pact.

Nasser denounced the Baghdad Pact as an ingenious effort to preserve imperialist influence in the Middle East. Moreover, having been unable to reach agreement with the United States on the purchase of arms that Nasser claimed he needed to protect Egypt against increased Israeli raids, Nasser began discussions with the Soviet Union about securing arms. It is significant that it was only after the latter discussions materialized in September 1955 into an agreement by the Soviet satellite Czechoslovakia to provide arms to Egypt, and after Egyptian and Soviet officials had made public the possibility of Soviet aid for the construction of the Aswan High Dam, that also an Anglo-American offer of aid for the Aswan Dam materialized. [60] The stimulus that Nasser's overtures to the Soviet Union (and vice versa) had provided to American and British interest in the Aswan Dam project was aptly described by a correspondent for the London *Times*. As he put it, Nasser's ". . . strong Russian card has manifestly taken the Aswan negotiations out of the desultory course they have followed for several years and the project now appears to have reached the phase of practical realities." [61]

The tactical appeal to the Eisenhower administration for supporting the Aswan Dam project lay not only in the fact that such support represented a means "to buy Egypt away from the Russians," as Eisenhower

[58] Louis L. Gerson, *John Foster Dulles* (New York: Cooper Square Publishers, 1967), in Robert H. Ferrell, ed., The American Secretaries of State and Their Diplomacy Series, 17:241.

[59] Memoranda from Eisenhower to Dulles; various dates in April 1953, as cited in Gerson, p. 247.

[60] Details of the Egyptian-Czech arms deal and discussion of its broad political repercussions in the West were provided in front-page news coverage by the *New York Times* from Sept. 28, 1955 through the first week of October 1955.

[61] "British-U.S. Offer to Finance Nile Dam," London *Times*, Dec. 19, 1955, p. 6.

told Dulles,[62] but also in its potential representation of a gigantic feat of engineering. As Under Secretary of State Hoover cautioned the Senate Appropriations Committee, in urging their support of the Aswan Dam project, ". . . our help will largely fail in its appeal and effectiveness if it cannot be expressed in terms of major projects which can catch the imagination of the people." [63]

Nasser, however, proved to be more recalcitrant, rather than less, in the months after the American-British offer of aid. Actions such as granting recognition to the Communist regime in China and continued denunciation of "Western imperialism" and especially of the Baghdad Pact provoked growing anger among American and British officials. Moreover, there was increasing support in American and British policy circles for the thesis that in the arms agreement with Czechoslovakia, Nasser had mortgaged the Egyptian economy so far that the frugality required of Egyptians to sustain payments for the construction of the Aswan Dam would make the project unpopular. Thus, in the long run, American and British prestige would suffer rather than benefit from supporting the project.[64] In reply to a memorandum from Dulles in March 1956 on the Middle East, Eisenhower indicated that "the time to close the door on Nasser had not come, but it could appear at any moment." [65] When the Egyptian government forced the issue of the Aswan Dam in July by accepting the American-British offer, "the time to close the door" appeared, and the offer was withdrawn. In short, from a strategic perspective, the offer of aid for the construction of the Aswan Dam appears as a move designed to further tactical ends (under the conditions outlined in Hypothesis 8); it was withdrawn when it became apparent that the tactical objectives would not be accomplished.

Cold-War Tactics: Concluding Observations

From a strategic perspective, foreign-policy decisions are viewed in terms of the utilization of various techniques in an effort to attain one or

---

[62] Gerson, p. 272.

[63] *Hearings, Financing of Aswan High Dam,* p. 2.

[64] For instance, Dulles told Eisenhower in the spring of 1956 that "he was beginning to think that any nation associated with construction of the dam would eventually wind up very unpopular among the Egyptians." Dwight D. Eisenhower, *The White House Years, 2, Waging Peace* (New York: Doubleday, 1965), 32. British Prime Minister Eden also recalls being increasingly disturbed at Nasser's "mortgaging of the country's economy," as well as at his propaganda attacks on Western "imperialism." Anthony Eden, *Full Circle* (Boston: Houghton Mifflin, 1960), pp. 468–469.

[65] Gerson, p. 275.

more tactical objectives. Among the techniques commonly employed are declarations and commitments; promises and threats; demonstrations of capabilities; bluffs and acts of calling the bluffs; rewards and punishments. Tactical objectives may include legitimation of prior moves or of actions intended for the future; exploitation of a tactical advantage; reduction of a tactical disadvantage; improvement of the bargaining position; strengthening of deterrence.

The American foreign-policy decisions in the Cold War that have been discussed above illustrate some of the familiar techniques and objectives from a tactical standpoint. However, the decisions also illustrate the complexity of the problems with which policy makers must deal and the paradoxical quality of the results, even from a strategic perspective. The paradox is revealed in a comparison of the immediately apparent accomplishments in the decisions discussed above with circumstances that prevail today.

Except for the offer of aid for the Aswan Dam project, each of the decisions described above was successful in fulfilling immediate tactical objectives. The Baruch Plan temporarily legitimated continued American development of atomic weapons. The program of aid to Greece enunciated in the Truman Doctrine provided resources essential to preventing a Communist-led insurgency from succeeding. The shift of policy to provide for the rearming of Germany and Japan bolstered American deterrent capabilities. The expansion of the alliance network may have enhanced, for a time, the credibility of an American military commitment to distant areas along the Sino-Soviet borders.

Yet in each of these decisions, as well as in the Aswan Dam offer, some troublesome problems had emerged by the 1970s, if not earlier. The aftermath of the Baruch Plan had been an awesome spiraling of a nuclear-arms race between the United States and the Soviet Union, despite a nuclear-test-ban agreement (ratified in 1963) and a nuclear-nonproliferation treaty (1969).[66] The government of Greece, far from moving toward democracy after 1947, as envisaged in President Truman's speech, had become an authoritarian military-controlled regime.[67] Germany, although in its Western half prospering economically, remained a

[66] For a recent assessment, see J. P. Ruina, "The Nuclear Arms Race: Diagnosis and Treatment," *Bulletin of the Atomic Scientists,* 24 (Oct. 1968), 19–22.

[67] In January 1969, the Assembly of the Council of Europe voted to exclude Greece from the Council unless parliamentary democracy was restored within a year. "What That Military Junta We Arm is Doing to Liberty in Greece," *I. F. Stone's Weekly,* 16 (Feb. 19, 1968), 4. For an assessment describing the Greek regime as being essentially in the best interests of the Greek people, although dictatorial in form, see James Burnham, "What Are We Asking For?" *National Review,* 20 (Oct. 22, 1968), 1062–1064.

divided nation and a key impediment to a détente with the Soviet Union. Japan, although also prospering economically, had become increasingly dissatisfied with an American military presence and with the mutual-security treaty that had been negotiated in the early 1950s.[68] Other alliances also had become weakened or obsolete. SEATO, especially, had been put to the test in the years of the American commitment in Vietnam and had been found wanting. Even NATO, the model for most of the other American alliances, had experienced important centrifugal tendencies, most notably in the withdrawal of French military forces and in the shift of NATO headquarters from Paris to Brussels.[69] The Aswan Dam project, which in the mid-1950s had been seen as a vehicle for expanding American influence and for reducing Soviet influence in Egypt, had become sponsored and supervised by the Soviets. Indeed, throughout much of the Middle East, American influence had diminished rather than increased; while Soviet influence had grown enormously.[70] Moreover, the Arab-Israeli dispute, which had tormented American policy makers since the American recognition of Israel in 1948, remained one of the world's prime powder kegs more than twenty years later.

In short, success in foreign policy is not only difficult to attain, but also difficult to measure. Apparent tactical victories may contribute to strategic losses; in any event, determination of the gains and losses will vary according to the hierarchy of values of the scorekeeper.

Analysis From a Strategic Perspective: A Balance Sheet

The chief characteristics and insights of foreign-policy analysis from a strategic perspective have been indicated in some detail in Chapters 3 and 4. A few highlights can be summarized briefly. From a strategic perspective, the concerned observer essentially put himself in the position of the policy maker, explaining broad patterns of action in terms of

[68] See John K. Emmerson, "Japan: Eye on 1970," *Foreign Affairs*, 47 (Jan. 1969), 348–362.

[69] It should be noted, however, that the Soviet invasion of Czechoslovakia in August 1968 was an important stimulus to reinvigoration of NATO. See Harlan Cleveland, "NATO After the Invasion," *Foreign Affairs*, 47 (Jan. 1969), 251–265. For an assessment of continuing problems of attaining unity within the alliance, see John W. Holmes, "Fearful Symmetry: The Dilemmas of Consultation and Coordination in the North Atlantic Treaty Organization," *International Organization*, 22 (Autumn 1968), 821–840.

[70] See Walter Laquer, "Russia Enters the Middle East," *Foreign Affairs*, 47 (Jan. 1969), 296–308.

the policy maker's strategy for competing successfully in a "game" of international politics and explaining specific decisions in terms of particular tactical techniques. Analysis from a strategic perspective is useful for highlighting the logical requisites of action in various types of foreign-policy situations, ranging from an insurgency in a new nation-state to a direct confrontation between two superpowers. Propositions from game theory, historical and contemporary studies of military strategy, and economic theory provide useful reference points for ascertaining the logic of foreign-policy strategy. Once the logic of particular moves in various contexts is understood, otherwise disparate acts and policies become comprehensible in terms of a strategic or tactical rationale.

Inferences of the purposes of policy makers rest upon an assumption that they act rationally. Just as studies of the prices and wages established by business firms ordinarily rest on the assumption that businessmen seek to maximize profit, analysis of foreign policy from a strategic perspective assumes that policy makers seek to maximize gains and to minimize losses in international competition. Neither in the analysis of business firms nor in the strategic analysis of foreign policy is the analyst required to believe that in reality persons never engage in nonrational acts; the assumption of rationality is used as an analytical simplification to identify logical relationships.

Conceptualization of the task of foreign policy as that of successful competition in a game (or in various games being played concurrently) usefully highlights a basic fact of international politics: the claim to sovereignty by the more than one hundred nation-states that interact internationally. Moreover, the game image used in analysis from a strategic perspective calls attention to the interdependence of the actions of the nation-states. In analysis of American strategy in the Cold War, we have indicated how closely American strategic calculations were tied to an assessment of Soviet actions and intentions. The various games of international politics link the moves of each player to those of every other player, with each one attempting to predict the moves of his opponent while eluding prediction himself.

Limitations of Strategic Analysis

We have identified some distinct advantages of analysis from a strategic perspective; but analysis from this perspective also has limitations, some of the most important of which are the following: the inability to explain nonrational acts; the inattention to environmental and other factors outside the context of any particular "game"; and the neglect of the various structures that are involved in the process of making strategic and tactical decisions.

The rational policy maker, from a strategic perspective, will consistently select among the alternative courses of action the one that promises the optimum ratio of gain to cost in relation to the nation's interest. Upon reflection, however, it is clear that the circumstances that would have to prevail in order for policy makers to achieve rationality in decision making are never fully realized in practice. The contrast between an imaginary ideal world in which policy makers behave perfectly rationally and the "real world" in which they do not will be discussed in some detail in Chapter 7.[71] Here we may simply note that disagreement among policy makers as to goals, incompleteness of information, distrust and cultural differences that influence attitudes toward foreign leaders, pressures of time that preclude a careful consideration of all alternative courses of action, and the operation of the subconscious in individual thought are among the factors that condition the behavior of the actual policy makers. Thus, rather than analyzing United States-Soviet relations exclusively in terms of strategies and tactics, it would be useful to consider a number of other factors as well in explaining the behavior of American policy makers: the postwar American public opinion; the influence of domestic politics on foreign policy; the tensions and links that existed between the President and Congress; the sense of urgency that affected some of the key decisions, such as the Greek-Turkish aid program and the Marshall Plan; and the personalities of key decision makers, such as John Foster Dulles and Lyndon Baines Johnson. Such factors can explain many policies and acts that, purely from a strategic perspective, seem to be random acts of irrationality.

Beyond the Game Context   A second, related limitation of analysis from a strategic perspective is viewing the actions of policy makers exclusively in relation to given international "games." After all, the task of foreign policy is not merely competing with other nation-states; more broadly, it is adapting to and imposing a measure of control upon the geopolitical environment in order to achieve national goal-values. Therefore, the foreign policies of a nation-state over a period of years may be usefully analyzed not only in terms of specific contests, such as the Cold War, but also in terms of environmental demand and change and in terms of internal structural and value change that may produce a

[71] The term "real world" is placed in quotation marks to suggest the subjective nature of reality. The distinction between conditions subject to empirical investigation and those contrived in fantasy, however, remains a useful one, as we shall indicate in Chapter 7.

restructuring of goals. Since Part III of the book is concerned with analysis of foreign policy from this broader perspective, that discussion will serve as an extended commentary on the limitations of viewing broad patterns of continuity and change exclusively in terms of given "games."

From Purposes to Structure and Process   When analysis is focused on specific foreign-policy decisions rather than on patterns of actions over a period of years, the limitations of analysis purely in terms of strategic or tactical purposes are also apparent. The Baruch Plan, the Greek-Turkish aid program, the decision to make a commitment to NATO and subsequent military alliances, the decision to rearm Germany and Japan, and the offer and then the withdrawal of support for the construction of the Aswan High Dam were all decisions made in an intensely political process. Analysis of the process in which various individuals, groups, and institutions interacted and of the structural relationships between them, would provide important additional understanding of the decisions. The discussion in Part IV of analysis from a decision-making perspective will identify these additional dimensions of understanding in detail.

Two Caveats

Two caveats must be offered in concluding this brief critique of strategic analysis. First, we are not concerned with assessing the writings of particular scholars of foreign policy. Some of the qualities of the writings of various game theorists, military strategists, or others who view foreign policy essentially from a strategic perspective correspond to those identified here; yet, each individual work is likely to have its own peculiar insights and its own limitations. Thus, each specific work must be judged on its own merits and not prejudged on generalizations about works with which it happens to share a common focus.

Second, our concern has been with summarizing briefly some of the distinctive features and key limitations of a strategic perspective for *empirical* analysis of foreign policy; we have not been concerned with assessing a strategic perspective in evaluating past policy decisions or in prescribing future courses of action. As we suggested at the outset of Chapter 3, however, many persons who analyze foreign policy from a strategic perspective tend to interject value judgments and recommendations implicitly, if not explicitly, in their analyses. Some critics of deterrence theory, for instance, have contended that there are numerous characteristic biases in the writings of strategic analysts: acceptance of the national interest as an ultimate norm for determining the value of an action; commitment to the *status quo*; a preference for military solutions to problems; and an elitist bias in policy making.[72] We suggest, however, that it is possible for a person analyzing foreign policy from a strategic perspective to have an internationalist outlook rather than a nationalist one; to be committed to revolutionary change rather than to the *status quo*; to abhor military solutions to foreign-policy problems; to have a populist rather than elitist bias regarding the extent to which policy makers should defer to popular opinion. In short, we suggest that it is wise to avoid preconceptions about the probable biases of authors; as suggested above, each work should be judged on its own merits. The pertinent point is that, even in studies of foreign policy that purport to be purely empirical, underlying value assumptions and biases of some sort are often to be found. Therefore, intelligent use of such studies requires alertness to the value commitments of the authors and comparison with one's own values. Parts III and IV of the book provide additional perspectives for empirical analysis. In Part V, we shall consider in detail the problem of making value judgments in foreign-policy analysis, also exploring the close relationship between empirical and normative questions.

Summary of Hypotheses Developed in Part II

1. When policy makers believe that the strategy of another nation-state supports their own nation's interests—
   a. They will pursue a leadership strategy if their own national capabilities are deemed superior to those of the other nation-state.
   b. They will pursue a concordance strategy if their own national capabilities are deemed inferior to those of the other nation-state.
2. When policy makers believe that the strategy of another nation-state threatens their own nation's interests—
   a. They will pursue a confrontation strategy if they believe their

---

[72] A provocative example of such a contention is that of Philip Green, *Deadly Logic* (Columbus, Ohio: Ohio State University Press, 1966), pp. 213–276. Unlike many criticisms of strategic analysis in which strategic arguments are rejected merely on the basis of the critic's repugnance for military concepts, especially those that involve speculation about nuclear weapons, Green's book has the merit of critically examining various aspects of the theory of nuclear deterrence, not only in terms of the ethical implications of the theory, but also in terms of the methodology on which the arguments of prominent theorists have been based. See also Anatol Rapoport, *Strategy and Conscience* (New York: Harper & Row, 1964); and Robert Levine, *The Arms Debate* (Cambridge, Mass.: Harvard University Press, 1963).

own national capabilities to be superior to those of the other nation-state.

  b. They will pursue an accommodation strategy if they believe their own national capabilities to be inferior to those of the other nation-state.

3. The greater the opprobrium attached to a given weapon or weapons system, the greater the demand on a government to demonstrate that it shares popular repugnance of the possible consequences of using the weapons.

4. If a government decides that it is desirable to develop a weapons system that is opposed by public sentiment, then such a decision can be legitimated in only one of two ways.

  a. If the public can be convinced that the initial opprobrium attached to the weapons system was misplaced, the decision to develop or to utilize the weapons system will be legitimated, providing a threat sufficient to justify its maintenance or use can be demonstrated.

  b. If the public can be convinced that serious efforts to control or abolish a weapons system failed in spite of the government's desire to attain such control or abolition, the government's decision to develop or to utilize the weapons system will be legitimated, providing a threat sufficient to justify its maintenance or use can be demonstrated.

5. The greater and more immediate the risks to prominent interests of withholding or denying military assistance or an alliance commitment, the greater will be the willingness of American policy makers to discount other factors (for example, experience in previous relations with the nation-state or political characteristics of the regime in power) in estimating whether the commitment should be made.

6. The greater the dependence that a potential ally or recipient of aid has—or will have if commitment to the nation-state is made—the greater will be the willingness of policy makers to discount other factors (for example, experience in previous relations with the nation-state or political characteristics of the regime in power) in estimating whether a military assistance or alliance commitment to the nation-state should be made.

7. The greater the conviction of policy makers that a relatively unprecedented military commitment has proved its worth as a tactical technique where the stakes are high, the greater the probability that they will replicate the commitment in other contexts.

8. The greater the strategic significance attached to a given nation-state by American policy makers and the greater their belief that American

influence on the policies of the nation-state is in jeopardy, the more dramatic will be the inducement offered by American policy makers to officials of the nation-state in an effort to preserve or to increase American influence.

Part III

The Perspective of Historical Dynamics

In Part III, we turn from strategic perspectives to historical-dynamics perspectives. Such a transition involves a shift from interpretation of foreign policy in terms of strategies and tactics to interpretation in terms of historical dynamics. Although one may focus on patterns of events over a broad period of time with either a strategic perspective or a historical-dynamics perspective, in the former case, foreign policy is conceptualized in relation to specific international "games." In analysis from the perspective of historical dynamics, in contrast, foreign policy is viewed in relation to the overall efforts of the national political system to adapt to its geopolitical environment and to impose a measure of control upon it in order to satisfy the goal-values of the system.

In some periods of history, the orientation of a nation-state toward its world environment has been virtually indistinguishable from its engagement in a particular international contest or "game." During war, for instance, such a distinction is often of little importance in the analysis of foreign policy. Likewise, in the early years after World War II, the Cold War so fully consumed the energies and attention of American policy makers that the principal features of American strategy for the contest with the Soviet Union, on the one hand, and the overall orientation of the United States toward its world environment, on the other, were virtually synonymous. Even in such instances, however, one can usefully distinguish between analysis of foreign policy from a strategic and a historical-dynamics perspective. The analyst who employs a strategic perspective is typically concerned with explaining events in terms of the *purposes* of policy makers. The analyst who employs the perspective of historical dynamics, on the other hand, is typically engaged in searching for the factors—including those of which the policy makers themselves may have been only dimly aware—that provided the necessary and sufficient conditions for the emergence of a particular orientation toward the world environment at a particular historical period. Although the purposes of policy makers are important in the perspective of historical dynamics, explanation goes beyond—or beneath—purposes to the identification of preconditions and precipitants of continuity and change. Moreover, the analyst who employs a strategic perspective is particularly hampered in his efforts to explain foreign policy in periods where several concurrent foreign-policy contests generate conflicting demands and where no overall strategy for the integration of policies in the various games has been devised. From the perspective of historical dynamics, however, it is possible to examine factors associated with broad patterns of continuity and change in foreign policy irrespective of an overall strategy.

We must note that the perspective of historical dynamics, as we shall describe it, is not necessarily synonymous with the perspective of the historian. The foreign-policy analyses of many historians, especially studies that focus on isolated events, would not fit our characterization of analysis from the perspective of historical dynamics. On the other hand, some analyses of foreign policy by sociologists, anthropologists, economists, political scientists, and other historians would fit.[1] The dis-

---

[1] For example, see a collection of essays by scholars of various disciplines assembled by N. D. Houghton, ed., *Struggle against History: United States Foreign Policy in an Age of Revolution* (New York: Simon and Schuster, Clarion paperback ed., 1968). Much of Gabriel A. Almond, *The American People and Foreign Policy* (New York: Praeger, paperback ed., 1960), fits the historical-dynamics description. The same is true of Margaret Mead, *And Keep Your Powder Dry* (New York: Morrow, 1942). A commentary on United States policies since 1945 that emphasizes historical

tinguishing characteristics of analysis from a historical-dynamics perspective, as we shall use the term, are in the object of analysis and the theoretical reference points. The primary object of analysis is the general orientation of the nation-state toward its geopolitical environment over a broad period of time. Theories of history, social change, development, and systems provide the key reference points in an analysis of broad patterns of continuity and change.

The distinction between analysis of foreign policy from the perspective of historical dynamics and from a strategic perspective has been indicated; it is also useful to distinguish between analysis from a historical-dynamics perspective and from a decision-making perspective. The two perspectives correspond to viewing American foreign policy from two different levels. Looking at the panorama of American foreign policy from the mountaintop of historical dynamics, one can detect broad patterns of continuity and change that would be obscured if one were to descend to the level of day-to-day decisions. The nation-state as a whole is treated as the primary unit of action for analytical purposes from the former level, and the object of analysis is the overall relationship between the political system and its geopolitical environment. On the other hand, if we descend to the level of day-to-day decision making, where broad patterns of change become obscure, there is a compensating new awareness of detail and complexity.

The historical-dynamics perspective and the decision-making perspective are distinct from one another, but interrelated; these differences and relationships between the two will become clearer in Parts III and IV of the book. At this stage in our discussion, an analogy between analysis of constitutional interpretation and analysis of foreign policy will provide some initial clarification of this point.

To depart momentarily from our concern with foreign policy in order to employ a relevant analogy, let us suppose that we were interested in analyzing the interpretation of the Constitution by the United States Supreme Court. The American Constitution has survived as a significant and useful body of law partly because it was written in language sufficiently general to be adaptable over the years to changing circumstances and to problems that could not be anticipated by its framers. If one were to examine the Court's interpretation of the Constitution across a broad span of history, he would discern certain patterns in the evolution of the meaning that the Court has given to various key elements of consti-

---

dynamics is Edmund Stillman and William Pfaff, *The New Politics: America and the End of the Postwar World* (New York: Harper & Row, Colophon paperback ed., 1962).

tutional doctrine, which are rooted in, and reflect, hundreds of individual decisions. Major Court decisions often serve as convenient landmarks to describe continuity and change in constitutional doctrine, but change is seldom, if ever, fully recorded in a single decision. Rather, the factors that produce a change in constitutional interpretation by the Court—for example, change in the composition of the Court, change in the economic and social needs of the society and in the demands made by various groups in the political arena, and change in deep-rooted societal values—make their impact incrementally over a series of decisions. Thus, an intensive analysis of any single decision is likely to be inadequate as explanation of the broad pattern of change. Conversely, almost every case that comes before the Court has unique features; parties to the case vary from one case to the next; the briefs are presented in differing terms; and the political climate in which the case is argued is constantly changing. Thus, analysis of the broad pattern of change may not be adequate to an explanation of the Court's decision in a specific case, even though the decision in the case contributes to the broad pattern of change.

In short, analysis of broad patterns of continuity and change in constitutional interpretation by the Supreme Court has requirements that make it distinct from analysis of a single decision, although the two levels of analysis are complementary. That is, knowledge of broad patterns of constitutional interpretation by the Court helps one to understand why it has made a particular decision, and analysis of decisions in individual cases contributes to an understanding of broad patterns of constitutional interpretation.

Analysis of broad patterns of continuity and change in foreign policy, as in constitutional interpretation, is related to, but distinct from, analysis of specific decisions. In Part III, our analysis will focus on broad patterns in the orientation of the United States toward world affairs, such as the posture of nonentanglement that characterized American foreign policy throughout much of the nineteenth century. In Part II, we focused upon strategic doctrines adopted to cope with a generic category of problems, such as the problem of Communist expansion, for which the strategy of containment was adopted in the post-World War II period. Broad patterns in the orientation of foreign policy as well as foreign-policy strategies originate in a series of important specific decisions. As former Secretary of the Navy Paul Nitze has described "national strategy," the term that he has applied to the general orientation of the nation-state toward its geopolitical environment, ". . . this strategy must be recast from epoch to epoch. To do this requires encompassing judgments and broad decisions which set the tone and establish the general premises of our undertakings in world affairs."[2]

But as Nitze has also noted, although one can point to various great decisions of historical import in the nation's foreign-policy experience, it is ". . . most difficult to identify the moment when [a strategy became] resolved, or when multifarious forces converged to produce one clear stream of action, or to say that this or that was the procedure by which it was accomplished." [3] For example, Washington's farewell addess is a convenient landmark from which to identify the formal origins of the doctrine of nonentanglement that guided American foreign policy for roughly a hundred years. But the factors that converged to make the idea of nonentanglement powerful in American foreign policy are not reducible to the initiative of the first President, however important a reference point his farewell address came to be. Likewise, the Truman Doctrine provides a handy bench mark from which to describe the beginnings of the American foreign-policy strategy of containment; yet, as indicated in Chapter 4, the origins of containment are more complex than the decision embodied in Truman's message to Congress in March 1947, despite the significance of the speech for enlisting broad support for the policy position rapidly evolving in the executive branch.

In viewing foreign policy over time from the perspective of historical dynamics, certain general themes or patterns become visible that one might miss if his focus were restricted to the day-to-day decision-making process, or if he concentrated exclusively on the logical requirements of the strategic problem. It is the broad focus, with the American political system as the primary analytical unit, that we shall employ throughout Part III. However, unless at some point one also takes a more microcosmic analytical perspective, looking at the day-to-day activities of individual policy makers confronting specific problems, both routine and urgent, one's understanding of various patterns of American foreign policy and one's appreciation of the magnitude of the problems of foreign-policy making must remain limited. Thus, in Part IV we shall shift to the decision-making level of analysis.

---

[2] Statement of Paul H. Nitze before the Subcommittee on National Policy Machinery, U.S. Senate Committee on Government Operations, June 17, 1960, quoted in Andrew M. Scott and Raymond H. Dawson, eds., *Readings in the Making of American Foreign Policy* (New York: Crowell-Collier-Macmillan, 1965), p. 314.

[3] Nitze, in Scott and Dawson, p. 315.

5

The Nation-State and its World Environment

Analysis of Broad Patterns

Viewed over a period of years, the foreign policies and actions of a nation-state form patterns that describe the relationship that it has maintained toward its world environment during that period. Foreign-policy analysis from the perspective of historical dynamics focuses on such patterns. Terms such as "general foreign-policy orientation," "foreign-policy posture," and "patterns of continuity and change in the evolution of foreign policy" will be used interchangeably in this chapter and the next in reference to the broad patterns. If these patterns may be considered the dependent variable for investigation from a historical-dynamics perspective, then the analytical task is to identify relevant independent or intervening variables and to specify relationships among the variables. Chapter 5 is devoted to identifying some key variables relevant to the explanation of patterns of continuity and change in foreign policy, and in Chapter 6, a number of

139

hypotheses about interrelationships among variables will be formulated.

As implied in the introductory remarks to Part III, from the mountain-top where one views foreign policy with the perspective of historical dynamics, the key variables are unlikely to be, for example, the personality of a secretary of state, the timing of an election, the health of the President, or the rainfall during the monsoon season in Vietnam, which may be relevant from a closer, decision-making perspective. Instead, usually in a perspective of historical dynamics the focus is on broad explanatory factors (clusters of variables) that seem basic to the relationship of the nation-state as a whole to its geopolitical world environment. In the present chapter, we shall identify and suggest the relevance of three such factors: the structure of the geopolitical environment; estimates of adaptive capabilities of the nation-state; and general goal-values. The discussion in the chapter will be largely in the form of generalizations that could also be applied to political systems other than the American one. Such generalizations are designed to stimulate the reader to consider the American experience in comparison with the foreign-policy experience of other nation-states, reflecting on aspects of the American experience that are common to many other states as well and on others that may be unique. Chapter 6, however, will draw exclusively upon specific highlights from the historical evolution of American foreign policy in order to elaborate and illustrate various analytical points in a context familiar to most readers.

Structure of the Geopolitical Environment

It is useful to begin explanation of patterns of continuity and change in the evolution of foreign policy with a focus on the structure of the geopolitical environment. Environmental structure not only represents demands upon the political system to which foreign policies represent a response, but also broadly defines the limits of foreign-policy endeavors. In general, the structure of the geopolitical environment refers to the form of the world external to the national political system; it refers not only to physical and technological dimensions of the environment, but to social and political dimensions as well. Countless aspects of the environment have some significance in defining the necessities and the possibilities of foreign affairs—such as climate, transportation networks, and population density. At the risk of neglecting some important aspects, we may identify the following as being particularly crucial: (1)

spatial relationships; (2) the pattern of supply of, and demand upon, natural, material, and human resources; (3) authority patterns and trends; and (4) the "rules of the game" of international politics.

We are concerned with identifying and ideally measuring elements of the environmental structure at various periods. The reader alert to the gap that always exists to some extent between reality and the perception of reality by policy makers might appropriately ask, "Is it not the policy makers' *perceptions* of the environment that should concern us analytically, rather than the 'objective' environment?" There is no simple answer to the question. As Harold and Margaret Sprout, coauthors of one of the most thorough appraisals of the problem of analyzing "man-milieu relationships" have indicated, the distinction between the "psycho-milieu" (the environment as it is perceived) and the "operational milieu" (the environment as operationally identified, independent of the beliefs of those whose behavior is being studied) is important. However, properties of the operational milieu may affect behavioral outcomes even if they are not recognized by those whose behavior is affected.[1] A drunk man placed on a wild horse may get thrown off whether or not he recognizes his predicament. Likewise, governments—even sober ones—may be toppled by circumstances that they do not recognize. The argument is not deterministic, but a synthesis of reasoning about the possible and the probable. The operational milieu sets limits to what is possible and makes some kinds of behavior more probable than others.

We repeat that the problem of accounting for both the effects of the operational milieu and those of the psycho-milieu in analysis is not simple. We shall attempt to cope with the problem in this chapter and the next one in the following manner. References to environmental structure will denote the operational milieu—that is, elements of the environment as they are identified by us as analysts, without attempting to account for misperception of the environment by policy makers. However, the psycho-milieu of policy makers will be accommodated in our analysis by its incorporation into the other two key explanatory factors. That is, in focusing upon the estimates that are made by policy makers of adaptive capabilities of the nation-state and upon the goal-values of policy makers, we shall be emphasizing the perceptions that policy makers have of what can be done and what should be done in the orientation of the nation-state to its world environment.

---

[1] Harold and Margaret Sprout, *The Ecological Perspective on Human Affairs* (Princeton: Princeton University Press, 1965).

Spatial Relationships and Resource Patterns

The term "spatial relationships," as we shall use it, refers to the geographical pattern of nation-states and other political units on the globe, in terms of distances and topographical features that connect and divide them. Such relationships have been fundamental in determining the frequency of contact between various political units, as well as in facilitating some forms of contact and hampering others. For instance, the seas have been an insulating factor in the history of England and of Japan, just as relatively unprotected land frontiers have rendered Russia and Poland vulnerable to attack. In the rugged Himalayas, Tibet has had infrequent contact with the rest of the world. In her strategic location on the shore of the Mediterranean astride the isthmus of Suez, Egypt has been unable to avoid frequent contact with other powers. Throughout much of American history, the Atlantic Ocean has served as a vast moat, which, with the largely benign assistance of the British navy for several decades, protected the United States from the instrusion of European powers; by the 1820s, the absence of a strong power on any border provided the United States with added security.

It is a truism, although an important one, to observe that natural, material, and human resources are distributed unequally around the globe. Moreover, demand patterns vary geographically and change with developments in technology. Combined with the pattern of spatial relationships and with authority patterns, resource patterns form the bases from which communication and association among nation-states in a given era stem. Associational patterns include friendship (for example, trade agreements and military alliances) and conflict (for example, war, trade rivalries, and border disputes).

The distribution of natural, material, and human resources is also important because it helps to determine the outcome of associations among states—which nations will be dependent upon, or subordinate to, others, and which will dominate. Rich and poor nations can be identified at various eras of world history not only in economic terms, but also in skills, technology, weaponry, and other foreign-policy assets. The United States is unusual in the abundance of natural, material, and human resources that have characterized it from the early days of independence. In this respect, the experience of the United States as a new nation differs radically from that of many nations that have gained their independence in recent decades in Asia and Africa. As we shall see in subsequent discussion, abundant resources contributed not only to the establishment of patterns of successful trade and commerce and to the growth of the United States as a major world power by the end of the nineteenth century; the wealth of the land also had an important impact upon the values and perspectives of American national leadership and contributed to the distinctive outlook that they brought to world affairs.

Authority Patterns and Trends, and the "Rules of the Game"

As emphasized in Chapter 3, the most fundamental institutional fact in world affairs for several centuries has been that of the so-called sovereign nation-state. The nation-state, of which there are now well over one hundred, by claiming sovereignty, recognizes, at least in moments of threat, no authority higher than its own. But in fact, there have always been institutions claiming authority that to a greater or lesser extent has conflicted with that of the nation-states.[2] The Catholic Church is a prominent historical example of such a competing institution. The Communist party is an important current example. Furthermore, the mushrooming of international organizations such as the United Nations and its many specialized agencies or affiliated bodies presents further potential conflict with the claims of sovereignty by nation-states. Even though international organizations have generally made very limited claims of authority, their mere existence suggests the growing interdependence of nation-states and the failure of the sovereign nation-state to cope fully with man's needs. Moreover, although an international organization such as the United Nations may often be unable to back up decisions of the organization with physical sanctions, it has come to exert influence over many aspects of the foreign policies of nation-states by according or withholding legitimacy to actions that they take or propose. The dismantling of colonial empires since 1945, for example, has been hastened by a growing expression of consensus within the United Nations that colonialism has ceased to have legitimacy.[3] The point to be stressed here is simply that the nature and number of institutions claiming political authority have changed radically over time, as has the distribution of natural, material, and human resources in the world. In order to understand the environmental structure that exists at a given period, one must identify these basic patterns. Moreover, as the patterns change, they represent changes in the environmental demands or the restraints within which the foreign policies of nation-states are formulated. Thus, pressure is in turn exerted for change in foreign policy.

[2] This point is expounded with great insight and cogency by Edward H. Buehrig, "The Institutional Pattern of Authority," *World Politics*, 17 (Apr. 1965), 369–385.

[3] The "collective legitimization" function of the United Nations is discussed by Inis Claude, *The Changing United Nations* (New York: Random House, 1967), pp. 73–103.

Furthermore, one must look at the rules by which the game of international politics is played in order to understand fully the structure of the geopolitical environment and the relationship of this structure to patterns of continuity and change in foreign policy. In Part II, we introduced the metaphor of international politics as a game, played for high stakes. At this point we may note that the rules of the game take the form of implicit or explicit mores defining the expectations that international policy makers have of the behavior of one another. Such mores or rules may be codified as international law or diplomatic protocol, or they may be informal, such as the general understanding among delegates to the United Nations that they are to address one another with personal courtesy even if engaged in bitter debate on issues that divide the organization. The relevance of game rules to one interested in the analysis of foreign policy from a historical-dynamics perspective is that the rules of a given era and place condition the preferences of policy makers for certain courses of action rather than others, for certain instruments of foreign policy and for observing certain kinds of limits and restraints in the conduct of foreign policy.

The rules of the game, being largely informal and unwritten, seldom, if ever, have been observed universally among all states within a given historical era; moreover, the rules evolve from one era to another. For instance, at the time of Metternich and the Congress of Vienna in 1814–1815, certain rules were quite clear and pervasive throughout European diplomacy. But these rules were quite different from those in the early sixteenth century, which Machiavelli's cynical writings have described so well.[4] Similarly, by the time of World War I, the rules had again acquired a new tone, which was quite different from that at the Congress of Vienna. The pleas of Woodrow Wilson, on the one hand, for "open covenants openly arrived at," and of Lenin, on the other hand, for regarding traditional European diplomatic practices as ingenious devices by capitalist ruling classes to deceive the masses, ushered in a new pattern of expectations in international politics. Thus, the twentieth century has been one of democratization of the rules, in the sense of increasing the demands upon the diplomat to conduct diplomacy with a focus upon public desires. It has also been one of heterogeneity among

[4] Machiavelli's most celebrated work, *The Prince*, offers caustic advice to a ruler on manipulating the rules of the day to the best advantage. This work and another perhaps even more important treatise on politics, *The Discourses*, appear in paperback with an introduction by Max Lerner (New York: The Modern Library, 1950). A highly readable discussion of the historical evolution of the rules of the game of international politics is provided by Harold Nicolson, *Diplomacy* (New York: Oxford, 3rd ed., 1964).

the diplomats of the various nation-states (many more of which are now in existence than ever before) as to what the rules of the game actually are, relative to the homogeneous views among eighteenth- and nineteenth-century European diplomats. Again, the point is that the nature of the rules and the extent to which they are shared at a given period of time are part of the environmental structure that helps to shape the broad orientation of a nation's foreign policy.

Rules of the game and patterns of authority are closely related in the environmental structure. The rules of a given era are largely maintained and defended by those nation-states that enjoy the greatest international authority and by other key institutions of authority. Conversely, nation-states and groups that resent existing patterns of authority or that lack access to authority tend to be revisionist with regard to the existing rules. Therefore, it is not surprising that the China of Mao Tse-tung tends to be highly revisionist with regard to the rules of the game that generally govern international politics today, just as it is not surprising that the Chinese emperors of the Ming dynasty (1368–1644), for instance, tended to maintain staunchly the rules that governed diplomacy throughout East Asia at a time when Chinese authority in the region was pervasive. Nor is it surprising that many of the economically and politically poor nations of the world today have protested that various aspects of international law, such as the law of the seas, are biased in favor of the major powers.[5] One can also understand why the smaller nation-states, more than the major powers, have attempted to enhance the authority of the United Nations General Assembly, where the votes of all nations are equal, regardless of population or power, and where the smaller nation-states have the potential for altering some of the rules of the game in their favor.

The United States was largely liberated from the influence of European authority early after American independence by the fortunate circumstances of geographical distance and of the turmoil of the Napoleonic Wars, which occupied the attention of the major powers of Europe. By the post-Napoleonic era, America's borders had been largely secured, the Louisiana Territory had been acquired, and the American government was able to issue a brazen warning, in the form of the Monroe Doctrine, that European authority must no longer be extended to the Western Hemisphere. Yet, if the United States was secure enough for such a warning, European powers were still dominant enough to discount it, largely in terms of the rules of the game that influenced their

---

[5] For example, see Robert L. Friedheim, "The 'Satisfied' and 'Dissatisfied' States Negotiate International Law," *World Politics*, 18 (Oct. 1965), 20–41.

own foreign-policy calculations. It was not until the beginning of the twentieth century that the United States joined the major European power as a key rule-maker in international affairs; by the end of World War II, the United States had become the dominant rule maker on the world scene.

Estimates of Adaptive Capability

Several elements of the structure of the geopolitical environment have been described, with emphasis on their relevance to the general foreign-policy orientation of the nation-state. A second but closely related factor is that of the estimates made by national leaders of the adaptive capability of the nation-state in relation to the world environment. By adaptive capability, we mean those natural, material, human, and institutional resources of the nation-state that comprise its potential over an extended period of time for coping with present and foreseeable demands from the geopolitical environment and for exerting a measure of control over it. Adaptive capability is thus distinguished from strategic and from tactical capability. By strategic capability, we refer to those resources that define the capacity of the nation-state to compete successfully in a particular international contest over an extended period of time; we use tactical capability to refer to the resource potential of the nation-state in relation to a specific situation or in pursuit of a discreet objective over a limited period of time.

The complexity and probable imprecision of any capability estimates—adaptive, strategic, or tactical—must be noted. Generally speaking, capability is the potential to exercise power, but power involves complex relationships, which make the estimation of capability necessarily speculative. First, power is a dynamic, not a static, phenomenon. Second, it is relative to the situation. For instance, American armored units played an important role in determining the outcome of the war against Germany, but not in the war against Japan, where geographical considerations made armor impractical. Third, power is a reciprocal phenomenon. Capability estimates that predict that in a confrontation between the United States and Panama, the United States will be victorious obscure the important possibility (clearly revealed in the confrontation of 1964) that a nominally weaker power may also exert some influence over the stronger.

One may search for seemingly objective indexes in an effort to reduce capability estimates to a reliable formula—the geographic position of the nation-state and its relative vulnerability to attack; the economic productivity of the nation; the prestige that the nation-state enjoys among other peoples; the size and quality of its armed forces. Calculations from past experience may enable an individual or a group to identify fairly accurately the factors that are likely to be instrumental in influencing a given situation and therefore ought to comprise indexes of capability. But, in fact, the power of parties can only be ascertained at the time of or after the situation. The army with the most troops, the best training, and the best equipment is likely to win the battle, but the authoritative test of the power of opposing armies occurs only when the battle takes place. Moreover, as suggested in Chapter 4, apparent tactical successes may prove to be liabilities in the long run.

Thus, no totally reliable formula exists to which anyone could turn in attempting to estimate the nation's tactical capability in relation to specific problems; its strategic capability in relation to an extended contest with other nation-states; or its overall adaptive capability. Estimates of capability are necessarily speculative. Thus, estimates of capability that help guide policy may seem pretentious to critics (as President De Gaulle's estimate of French capabilities seemed to many persons), or they may seem unduly modest (as critics of the relatively passive role of the United States in world affairs during the 1920s and 1930s argued that the estimates by American policy makers had been).

The salient point, however, is that capability estimates, rigorous or careless, accurate or inaccurate, are nonetheless formulated from time to time by national leaders, as their writings and speeches reveal. It is clear that such estimates have been important in conditioning the actions of leaders in regard to tactical or strategic problems, and in regard to the broader task of adaptation to the demands of the world environment. Therefore, for our present purposes it is of interest analytically to attempt to determine the content of various estimates of adaptive capability that were formulated at various periods of history and the extent to which consensus prevailed among national leaders in the estimates that were made.

It is convenient to postpone until the section in which goal-values are discussed a definition of the term "national leaders," as well as an indication of why their views—their estimates of adaptive capability and their general goal-values—rather than the views of others are of particular concern analytically. However, the relevance of estimates of adaptive capability by national leaders to an explanation of continuity and change in foreign policy can be suggested by a brief reference to the American foreign-policy experience.

The perceived weakness of the United States relative to the major powers of Europe in the first decades after independence was a major factor that convinced national leaders from Washington on, through the next several Presidents, to avoid becoming embroiled in the political affairs of Europe. By the end of the nineteenth century, however, it was generally agreed among national leaders that American capabilities had increased dramatically. To many leaders, the gigantic increase in American capabilities made it both possible and desirable for the United States to abandon the foreign-policy posture it had traditionally maintained. Other leaders, however, resisted the abandonment of the traditional foreign policy; yet, their resistance was not attributable to a disagreement that American capabilities had changed—no prominent leader at that time disputed the fact that American capabilities had grown dramatically. Rather, those who resisted change based their resistance on an assessment of values that, in their minds, would be threatened if the traditional American foreign-policy posture were abandoned. Nearly half a century passed before the debate over this issue was resolved by the imperatives of World War II. The heavy responsibilities of World War II and its aftermath irreversibly altered the orientation of the United States toward a far broader and more binding pattern of relationships to the world environment. Those still dubious about the new foreign-policy course kept their skepticism largely to themselves during the war, and in the end, most of them revised their views to adjust to the new realities. By 1945, American capabilities not only surpassed those of any other nation-state in terms of virtually every estimate of capability made, but also, the United States had become the world's first nuclear power. Nuclear technology was an awesome and ambiguous new element of adaptive and strategic capability and a new dimension of the structure of the geopolitical environment. Some aspects of American strategic calculations during the nuclear era were discussed in Chapter 4; at this point it may be simply noted that the fantastic destructive possibilities of nuclear weapons seemed by the late 1960s and the early 1970s to have had the paradoxical effect of rendering a nuclear arsenal useless as an element of power in many kinds of foreign-policy situations. Yet, neither was the prospect in sight that the leaders of nations possessing nuclear weapons were ready to relinquish their possession of this form of threat.

General Goal-Values of Foreign Policy

The third and final factor that we shall cite as relevant to an explanation of broad patterns of continuity and change in the evolution of foreign policy is that of general goal-values of foreign policy. General goal-values are relatively abstract values that define goals to be attained within an unspecified period of time or values to be maintained over an indefinite period of time. Thus, they are distinguished from particular goal-values, which refer to specific foreign-policy objectives within a definite time context. For example, seeking to fulfill a "Manifest Destiny" in the Western Hemisphere was a general goal-value widely shared by American leaders in the nineteenth century. The desire to annex Canada, on the other hand, was a particular goal-value, less widely shared and obviously never attained. The desire to contain Communist expansion has been a general goal-value to which most American leaders in the post-World War II period have subscribed. The desire to see the Fidel Castro regime replaced by a government more sympathetic to the United States, on the other hand, was a particular goal-value that became embodied in a specific, but unsuccessful, action by the United States government in supporting an invasion at the Bay of Pigs in 1961. Our focus in the ensuing paragraphs is on general, and not particular, goal-values.

The Elements of General Goal-Values

The content of general goal-values varies from one individual to another, yet the common elements of such goal-values are images of the national identity and interests.

Images of National Identity   A sense of national identity, like a sense of personal identity, is established not only in relationship to others and to the environment, but also in relationship to the past, the present, and the future. An individual's self-image, for example, is built not only upon his perception of his present self, interacting with others in the contemporary environment; rather, it also is built upon images of a past self, including in many instances strong images of an ancestral heritage with which he identifies. Moreover, there is a more or less clearly defined future self, embodying expectations, hopes, and dreams. Similarly, images of a national self are composed of more than the contemporary image that a people have of their national identity. Rather, they include images of a real or mythical national heritage and visions—realistic or utopian—of the future destiny of the nation, like the sense of Manifest Destiny that prevailed among Americans throughout much of the nineteenth century.[6]

---

[6] For some purposes, one might wish to distinguish between the images that people have of what their nation really is like, was like, and will be like in the future, and their idealized notions about the past, present, and future of the nation. Such a distinction would roughly correspond to the analytical distinction made between the operation of the ego and the superego in individual personality. However, for our purposes, it is convenient to treat a sense of national identity as a composite that includes images of the real national self and images of an idealized national self.

To recall a national heritage, one often must recall extensive cultural borrowing from others or even a period of subordination to another authority. In images of national identity among those who have experienced colonial rule, therefore, one finds a fascinating mixture of emotional attraction to and repulsion from attributes that characterize the former "mother country." There is some parallel between the process by which new nations establish their identity and the process by which young individuals lay claim to their own personal identity.

On the one hand, the identities of authority figures often become important objects of emulation. Among individuals, parents especially are emulated by their offspring. Among nations, people who have experienced some extended period of subordination to others often partially incorporate into their national self-image, images of the nations with greater authority. The Chinese-like images of the national self of many of China's neighbors, after centuries of experiencing Chinese suzerainty, is one example. The intrusion of Western values and beliefs into the images of the national self that various peoples, especially the indigenous elites of Asia, the Middle East, and Africa, maintain are other examples. The intensive incorporation of English customs, values, and perspectives into the images of national identity among American leaders from the American Revolution on is still another example.

On the other hand, the relationship of the individual to parental authority, or of the peoples of a new nation to the former colonial power, is likely to be one of repulsion as well as of attraction. Therefore, although authority figures may be important objects of emulation in some respects, in others it is the assertion of distinctiveness from authority figures that provides the source of values and beliefs to be incorporated in individual self-images or in national self-images. As we shall see, for example, perception by Americans, especially in the early decades after independence, of Europe as decadent and corrupt became important to the assertion of uniqueness in the identity of the new nation.

It is interesting to observe that the distinctiveness of individual self-images as well as of images of the national self is often most intensely asserted at a period when independence of former authority has been achieved at least partially, but remains insecure or not fully recognized by others. The young person in late adolescence or early adulthood often feels an intense need to establish and to assert his own sense of identity, independent of the identity of his parents. At the same time, he may feel insecure, confused, and resentful because of the dependence that he in fact continues to experience. Whether these sentiments manifest themselves in brash, boisterous rebellion or in moody silence and introspection, they are likely to reveal an intensity of desire for self-expression not equaled again in life, except perhaps in the face of a traumatic event that threatens one's identity.

Within young nations, too, one frequently observes an intensity of expression of national identity rarely found in older, more established nations, except on occasions when an older nation experiences a profound internal crisis or a severe external threat to its existence. Nationalism is the term ordinarily used to describe a people's expression of their feeling of national identity; especially in an intense form, it is a phenomenon of profound and continuing importance in the history of international relations. Many historians and others have commented on the outbursts of nationalist sentiment in American history, which were particularly strong in the late nineteenth and the early twentieth centuries, at a time when America was coming of age, but still had not won recognition as a power of stature equal to the great European powers.

Images of the National Interest   Closely related to one's sense of national identity is his sense of the needs of the nation. Images of the national interest, in other words, are woven together with images of the national identity to constitute general goal-values. Images of the national interest may be highly idealistic, highly pragmatic, or a blend of idealism and pragmatism.[7] In American history, some national leaders, such as Woodrow Wilson, are remembered especially for having defined the interests of the nation in terms of moral purpose and the promotion in world affairs of the tenets of American democracy. Other leaders, such as Theodore Roosevelt, are remembered especially for having championed the advancement of American capabilities and prestige in a fierce but (to Roosevelt at least) invigorating competition with other nations; the national interest was defined in terms of power. Most leaders in American history, however—including Wilson and Roosevelt at various points in their leadership—have displayed a commitment to ideals rooted in their sense of the nation's identity, combined with a pragmatic assessment of its military, economic, and other needs.

It is important to recognize that definitions of the national interest that seem idealistic to some persons will seem perverse to others. (Controversy over the rationale for United States involvement in Vietnam is a case in point.) Likewise, images of the national interest that some persons describe as pragmatic realism will seem to others sheer folly. (Early debate among American leaders about Project Apollo, designed to

[7] See Robert Osgood, *Ideals and Self-Interest in America's Foreign Relations* (Chicago: University of Chicago Press, 1953).

put a man on the moon, reflected such differences of viewpoint.) Like estimates of capability, judgments about the interests of the nation are subjective and will differ from one individual to another.

But whatever the basis or the character of images of the national interests at a given time may be, they merge with images of the national identity to define general foreign-policy goal-values. That is, general goal-values reflect convictions about what direction the nation should take in order to remain true to its identity and in order to protect and advance its interests.

Goal-Values of Analytical Relevance

We have indicated that general goal-values constitute one of the three basic factors (sets of independent variables) revelant to explanation of broad patterns of continuity and change (the dependent variables) in foreign policy. However, a basic question of analytical procedure remains. Whose general goal-values are to be included in our analysis? Whose images of national identity and the national interest are relevant to our analytical purposes? Three alternatives will be considered.

First, one might focus on the general goal-values that have been articulated by key individuals, whose decisions and pronouncements seem to have been particularly prominent in defining the course in which foreign policy has evolved. In the history of American foreign policy, Washington, Jefferson, Monroe, Polk, Theodore Roosevelt, Wilson, and Franklin Roosevelt are among those important individuals in the period 1783–1941 whose views might be included, if this focus were adopted.

One might, however, decide that not only a few, but all members of a nation-state have views relevant to determining the pattern of evolution of the nation's foreign policy. Thus, a second alternative would be to focus on the general goal-values held by all members of the nation-state. In analysis of American foreign policy, such a focus would mean attempting to identify which national goal-values Americans, collectively, have sought at various periods.

A third option would be to adopt an intermediate focus larger than a few key decision makers but smaller than the total population. One might, for example, make a rough distinction between persons who are relatively influential in shaping foreign policy and persons who are relatively noninfluential, focusing on the images of national identity and interest held by the former group.

A sound decision as to which of the three focuses to adopt must be based upon an analytical assessment of the structure of influence upon the policy-making process, as well as upon pragmatic assessment of the kinds of data that are available about general goal-values. Whose views matter in determining policy outcomes, and what kinds and amounts of information are available about the views of various individuals and sectors of the society throughout American history?

Our answer to the question leads us to select the third among the focuses that were described. Specifically, in subsequent discussion, we shall be concerned with the general goal-values (and capability estimates) that have been held at various periods by those whom we shall identify below as comprising the national leadership. We must emphasize that the reasons for focusing, at this point, on the views of the leadership portion of the nation rather than on the nation as a whole are a pragmatic concern for available evidence as well as a recognition of the empirical reality of the disparity of influence between leaders and nonleaders in foreign policy. No normative commitment to elitist preferences is intended. Indeed, later in the book, in Part V especially, we shall explore in detail some of the important normative issues that arise in a political system such as the American one, which espouses democratic ideals, when many trends in foreign policy make the vital nerve centers of decision making less accessible, rather than more accessible, to the influence of the average citizen. In Part IV, the empirical justification for focusing on national leadership will be revealed in somewhat greater detail through an extended analysis of the structure and process of foreign-policy making. However, in our description below of the approximate boundaries for the identification of those to be included in the national leadership category, some of the conclusions from Part IV most salient to justifying the focus adopted here will be anticipated.

"National Leadership" Defined

The term "national leaders" will be used here (following a definition provided by Professor James Rosenau) to refer to "those members of the society who *occupy positions which enable them to transmit, with some regularity, opinions about foreign policy issues to unknown persons.*" [8] National leaders are distinguished from local leaders, the former having access "to unknown persons outside of the state in which they work or reside, whereas local leaders are those whose opinion-making capacities are confined to unknown audiences in their own city or state."[9] Persons included in the national-leadership category are many in absolute terms, but few relative to the total population. (Rosenau estimates that at the present time, between 50,000 and several hundred thousand persons, less than one-quarter of 1 percent of the total population, could be classi-

[8] James N. Rosenau, *National Leadership and Foreign Policy* (Princeton: Princeton University Press, 1963), p. 6. Italics in original text.

[9] Rosenau, p. 7.

fied as national leaders.) National leadership includes policy makers, that is, those in government with formal responsibilities for making policy decisions, but also nongovernmental opinion makers, such as newspaper columnists, directors of large corporations, leaders of national or international trade unions, prominent religious spokesmen, important and prestigious scientists and scholars, and others in positions that give them a potential for influencing opinion in the national community. Nongovernmental leaders can play important roles in supporting or opposing policy alternatives developed by governmental leaders or in alerting them to issues that demand attention or to policy options that merit consideration.

Focus in subsequent discussion on general goal-values and estimates of adaptive capability that have been formulated by national leaders is justified not only in terms of the realities of the distribution of influence within the political system, but also in terms of manageability of data. The views of national leaders, although difficult to describe with certainty, are more susceptible to investigation than the values of the society as a whole, precisely because of the prominence of national leaders, whose speeches, books, and correspondence frequently become a part of the public record. Thus, we have a more thorough record of what Thomas Jefferson thought about world affairs in the late eighteenth and early nineteenth centuries than we have about what the average American, or the average Virginian thought. Likewise, we have a multitude of recent speeches and writings that can be analyzed to describe the values of contemporary American leaders, whereas the views of the contemporary mass public are less susceptible to investigation for a variety of reasons. First, the mass public is a much larger group, representing a greater diversity of views. Second, the views of the average person are seldom recorded. Third, and related to the second point, despite the current plethora of nationwide opinion polls in the United States, general foreign-policy goal-values are less likely to be fully and clearly articulated by the average person than they are by national leaders. As V. O. Key has wisely noted in a study of American opinion, "The average American manages to get along very well without a burdensome equipment of sophisticated political attitudes; so, too, may the masses of people in almost any stable political system. Characteristics, beliefs, and attitudes attributed to the mass of the people are often only projections of the anxieties, the preferences, or the fantasies of the intellectual analyst." [10]

Our reluctance to attempt to describe the values and beliefs of the

[10] V. O. Key, Jr., *Public Opinion and American Democracy* (New York: Knopf, 1961), p. 49.

society as a whole because of the elusiveness of available data is reinforced by conclusions about the relative insignificance of mass opinion. As Rosenau, among others, has pointed out, "Most citizens delegate, knowingly or otherwise, their voice in foreign affairs to those leaders— both in and out of government—who can effectively claim to speak for them." [11] To be sure, policy makers are concerned with retaining public support for foreign policies, but "plainly the mobilization of public opinion in support of a foreign policy does not involve informing and activating the mass public so much as it requires the fashioning of a consensus within the leadership structure." [12]

Although consensus within the leadership structure is important, as the quotation from Rosenau suggests, if foreign policies are to have a base of domestic support requisite to their successful implementation, the maintenance of consensus among national leaders cannot be assumed *a priori*. That is, we cannot assume agreement among national leaders as to the national identity and interest any more than we can assume consensus among national leaders in the estimates they make of strategic capabilities. Rather, in each case the extent of their agreement is an empirical question. It is also a difficult question. As we trace the course of American history, we find not only that the views of individual leaders sometimes change over time, but also that there is mobility into and out of the national leadership structure. That is, persons formerly noninfluential become influential; persons formerly influential lose their influence. Thus, a change in the distribution of views—from consensus to dissension, for example—may be attributable to changing views among given individuals, to change in the composition of national leadership, or to both.

As difficult as the question is about what patterns of consensus in the views of national leaders have existed at various times, with the imprecision in available data, the question is important to our analysis. In the following chapter, we shall hypothesize about the relationship between consensus and stability in the orientation of the nation-state toward its world environment, examining the relationship in the context of the American experience.

Summary

Three key factors (comprising sets of independent or intervening variables) have been identified and described as the basis for explaining

---

[11] Rosenau, p. 28.
[12] Rosenau, p. 27.

broad patterns of continuity and change (the dependent variables) in American foreign policy. The factors are the structure of the geopolitical environment, estimates by national leaders of the adaptive capabilities of the nation-state, and the general goal-values of national leaders.

The structure of the geopolitical environment has been described in terms of four essential elements: (1) spatial relationships within the environment; (2) the pattern of supply of, and demand upon, natural, material, and human resources; (3) patterns of authority and trends in allegiance to various centers of authority; and (4) the prevailing rules of the game of international politics.

Adaptive capability has been distinguished from strategic capability and tactical capability; moreover, capability in general has been distinguished from power. Capability estimates, it has been emphasized, cannot reliably be reduced to an exact formula. Nonetheless, national leaders do make such estimates, and these estimates are important to us analytically.

General goal-values, as distinguished from particular ones, have been described as relatively abstract values that define goals to be attained within an unspecified period of time or values to be maintained over an indefinite period of time. General goal-values have been described as consisting of images of the national identity and images of the national interest. The reasons for focusing on the general goal-values of national leaders, rather than on those of only a few key decision makers or on those of the entire society, have been explained in terms of the structure of influence upon the policy-making process, as well as in terms of the availability of relevant data. The same reasoning applies to selecting national leadership as the focus in discussions of estimates of adaptive capability. Both in our analysis of general goal-values and in analysis of estimates of adaptive capability, we are interested not only in the content of the views of national leaders, but also in the extent to which consensus has prevailed among national leadership.

The following chapter provides us with an opportunity to develop more fully a framework for analysis of foreign policy from the perspective of historical dynamics, by postulating interrelationships among variables that have been identified in Chapter 5. By retracing the dynamics of specific highlights in the evolution of American foreign policy, we shall provide illustrative data for the hypotheses, thereby making more vivid and meaningful the ideas that we have developed thus far.

6

Continuity and Change in American Foreign Policy

To restate very loosely the thesis that was developed in the last chapter, the broad posture of a nation-state toward its world environment is determined by the environmental structure at a particular period of history; by the beliefs that leaders have about the ability of their nation-state to cope successfully with the environment (adaptive capability estimates); and by their images of the nation's needs and its destiny in world affairs (general goal-values). In the present chapter, we shall develop a typology of foreign-policy postures, clarifying the relationships between the variables identified above and variations in foreign-policy posture. We shall also propose that when there is consensus among national leadership about the nation's adaptive capability and about the general goal-values, the orientation of the nation-state to its world environment remains stable; where there is dissension, instability in orientation occurs.

157

These propositions do not constitute a definitive basis for the inter-pretation of broad patterns of foreign policy nor a novel theory. The point of the propositions and the major objective of the chapter as a whole is to illustrate the distinctive characteristics of analysis of foreign policy from the perspective of historical dynamics.

We shall combine discussion of concrete facets of the American foreign-policy experience with rather abstract theorizing in this chapter because formulations of a theoretical or pretheoretical nature are most useful if they enable one to pull together otherwise disparate threads from a relevant context of specific events. Accordingly, we shall focus especially on two important periods in the evolution of United States foreign policy: the period from 1783 to the 1820s and the period of the 1890s and the turn of the century.

The reader with a sensitivity to the perspective of historical dynamics will find that examination of American foreign policy during these periods can help him to understand better not only the past, but also the present, in at least two ways.

First, some of the problems that were confronted at an earlier time and the ideas and policies that were formulated then continue to affect American foreign policy. The period from 1783 to the 1820s, for instance, marks the origins of the foreign-policy orientation of the United States that was followed throughout most of the nineteenth century and that established a tradition that has lingered on in diluted form into the present. The period of the 1890s and the turn of the century marked the first major departures from the tradition, as dramatic assertions of full status as a great world power were made by the United States in world affairs. The resulting debate in the United States about the implications of worldwide involvement raised a number of normative and pragmatic issues that still have not been fully resolved to the satisfaction of all Americans.

Second, analysis of patterns of continuity and change in earlier periods provides an informed basis for reflecting on present-day trends in world affairs and on the implications of these trends for American foreign policy. In the final section of the chapter, we shall draw upon discussion of continuity and change in the past evolution of American foreign policy to raise some difficult but provocative questions about American foreign policy in the 1970s.

It is assumed in the following discussion that the reader has a general knowledge of American history and that his intellectual curiosity will lead him to review independently details of events or of particular periods with which he is unfamiliar, weighing the present analysis against his own interpretation of the facts.[1] In analysis from the perspective of historical dynamics, emphasis characteristically is on general patterns of evolution; fine detail, subtlety, and complexity are thereby sacrificed. What we shall describe as a pattern of continuity includes, at a more microcosmic level of analysis, elements of discontinuity as well. Periods that we characterize as having consensus would not appear free of important elements of disagreement if one were to examine in detail the actions and expressed opinions of national leaders.

Even in terms of broad patterns, we must emphasize that the data presented in the present chapter do not constitute proof of the validity of the explanatory framework developed here. Rather, such information is designed to illustrate concepts and hypotheses that might otherwise seem pure abstractions.

1783–1820s: Origins of a Foreign-Policy Tradition

The broad pattern of American foreign policy was so consistent throughout most of the nineteenth century, and the rationale for the pattern so deeply imbedded in the thoughts and writings of American policy makers, that it came to be regarded as the traditional American orientation. Indeed, although the pattern was altered sharply in the twentieth century, the appeal of the tradition lingered on, occasionally manifesting itself in the arguments of critics of policy if not in the views of policy makers themselves. We are first concerned with describing the traditional foreign-policy posture of the United States and with explaining its origins.

[1] A concise paperback description and interpretation of events is provided by Dexter Perkins, *The Evolution of American Foreign Policy* (New York: Oxford, Galaxy Books, 2d ed., 1966). Standard texts in American diplomatic history include Julius W. Pratt, *A History of United States Foreign Policy* (Englewood Cliffs, N.J.: Prentice-Hall, 1955); Thomas A. Bailey, *A Diplomatic History of the American People* (New York: Appleton, 7th ed., 1964); and Samuel F. Bemis, *A Diplomatic History of the United States* (New York: Holt, Rinehart and Winston, Inc., 5th ed., 1965). A text that covers the entire historical period, but is especially thorough in treatment of events since the 1890s, is Robert H. Ferrell, *American Diplomacy: A History* (New York: Norton, 1959). An extensive and provocative collection of readings and documents, with penetrating supplementary commentary by the editor, is William A. Williams, *The Shaping of American Diplomacy* (Chicago: Rand McNally, 1956). The Williams collection is also available in paperback in two volumes by the same publisher.

Describing the Traditional Posture

"Isolationism" is the term popularly used to describe the traditional posture of the United States toward its world environment. As Albert Weinberg and others have noted, however, the term is a misleading one.[2] Policies of the United States never cut it off from the rest of the world (as those of Japan had done, for example, in the years before the Perry expedition). On the contrary, Americans were establishing or maintaining trade and communication with most other parts of the world virtually from the day of independence. The commerce with Europe that the thirteen colonies had begun was continued and expanded. Immediately following the Treaty of Paris ending the Revolutionary War, American ships were fighting the Barbary pirates in an effort to protect their commerce in the Mediterranean. By 1800, dozens of American ships were engaged in trade with China; in ensuing years, the United States remained in the forefront of opening East Asia to the commercial and missionary activities of the West. Frictions between the young American nation and European powers in the early nineteenth century, including those that led to the War of 1812, resulted in part from the refusal of the United States to abide by the restrictions that European powers placed upon trade with their colonies in the Western Hemisphere and elsewhere. Such activities, begun with the founding of the nation and increasingly continued thereafter, can scarcely be regarded as isolationist either in intent or in effect.

Rather, the traditional posture of the United States can be described more accurately in terms of the two following components: the territorial expansion on the North American continent and the avoidance of entangling alliances with other nation-states.

The broad pattern of American foreign policy was clear at least by the 1820s. The period from the Treaty of Paris in 1783, in which Great Britain acceded to the independence of her American colonies, until approximately the 1820s has generally been regarded by historians as a period when the precarious base of American independence was being solidified and the continued independent existence of the new nation assured. At the beginning of this period, the territory of the United States was bounded to the south by Spanish-controlled Florida; to the west, by the Spanish-owned Louisiana territory, which included the crucial Mis-

---

[2] See Albert K. Weinberg, "The Historical Meaning of the American Doctrine of Isolation," *American Political Science Review*, 34 (June 1940), pp. 539–547. For a refutation of the thesis that isolationism is an apt description of American policies in the 1920s and 1930s, see William A. Williams, "The Legend of Isolationism," *Science and Society*, 18 (Winter 1954), pp. 1–20.

sissippi River port of New Orleans; and to the north, by the British colony of Canada. By the 1820s, the United States had gained control of all of Florida; American territory had doubled through the acquisition of Louisiana from France (which in the interim had acquired it from Spain); and, although Canada remained in British hands, through the Rush-Bagot agreement of 1817 the British were to keep naval armaments at a minimum on the waterways that separated the United States and Canada. Moreover, in 1823, the Monroe Doctrine gave notice to European powers that neither their colonization nor their interference in the affairs of the Western Hemisphere would be tolerated by the United States. Washington in his farewell address and Jefferson in his first inaugural address had advocated an American foreign-policy posture unencumbered by alliances or other binding commitments to European powers. The Monroe Doctrine simply appended this advice by describing an American sphere of interest from which European powers could properly be excluded.

The orientation of the United States toward its world environment that had been defined by the 1820s was substantially maintained until the 1890s, a period of change that we shall examine presently. First, however, let us attempt to explain the emergence of the traditional foreign-policy posture.

Explaining the Emergence of the Traditional Posture

It is convenient to begin consideration of the evolution of American foreign policy in 1783, with the Treaty of Paris, which formally ended the Revolutionary War; by the 1820s, a distinctive pattern of American foreign policy had emerged. As indicated, the two major components of the pattern were territorial expansion in the North American continent and the avoidance of entangling alliances with European nation-states.

Applying the analytical framework outlined at the beginning of the chapter to the period under consideration, we shall seek to explain the foreign-policy posture that had emerged by the 1820s within the structure of the geopolitical environment of the time, the capability estimates of American leaders, and their general goal-values. The environmental structure provided unusual opportunities for territorial expansion by the United States; moreover, it reinforced the conviction of those American national leaders who were unfavorably disposed toward political involvement with Europeans and convinced most of those who had favored such involvement that they were wrong. The goal-values of American leaders included a strong sense of national destiny that generated both a desire to expand the nation's borders and a desire to avoid "contamination" of the nation's ideals through political involvement with Europe. Estimates by national leaders of the capabilities of the United States convinced them that the desired course of action was also a realistic one. The explanatory factors will be discussed in greater detail below.

Opportunities and Cues in the Environmental Structure   In Chapter 5, we identified four particularly crucial elements of environmental structure: (1) spatial relationships; (2) the pattern of supply of and demand upon natural, material, and human resources; (3) authority patterns and trends; and (4) the rules of the game of international politics. During the period under consideration all of these elements underwent change; the important changes that were occurring in the world environment in turn provided significant opportunities and cues for American policy makers.

First, most of the governments of Europe experienced, directly or indirectly, profound social and political upheaval during the period. The great catalyst of change was of course the French Revolution, which, in its turn, had received impetus from the American Revolution. In fact, a prominent student of the circumstances that led to the French Revolution has called the American Revolutionary War ". . . the principal direct cause of the French Revolution, both because in invoking the rights of man it stirred up great excitement in France, and because Louis XVI in supporting it got his finances into very bad condition." [3]

The ideals of the French Revolution were widely disseminated throughout Europe. Revolutionary demands for the rights of man and for expansion of popular voice in government were threatening the autocratic regimes that were then so prevalent. Even with the period of Thermidor—the reaction that represented the abandonment of many of the goals of the revolution—the government of Napoleon could delay, but not erase or indefinitely suppress, popular demands for an expanded voice in government. The subsequent installment of Louis XVIII, after the Congress of Vienna, may have temporarily satisfied French aristocrats that they had achieved the Bourbon Restoration, but Louis XVIII could not be Louis XVI; the days of the latter were gone forever.

The same trend was occurring elsewhere in Europe, however assiduously Metternich and others worked to forestall it in the days after the Congress of Vienna. In current terminology, adopted to describe the changing outlook in recent decades of the peoples of "developing areas," the Europeans in the nineteenth century were experiencing a "revolution

---

[3] Georges Lefebvre, *The Coming of the French Revolution*, trans. R. R. Palmer (New York: Vintage Books, 1959), p. 19.

of rising expectations." Hegel, for one, recognized the profound transformation of attitudes and beliefs that was occurring when he wrote early in the nineteenth century of his fellow Germans: "The quiet contentment with what is, the despondency, the patient acceptance of an all-powerful fate has been transformed into expectancy, and into courage for something different." [4]

Changing expectations were not exclusively the product of ideology emanating from the French Revolution, of course. The economies of the nation-states of Europe were becoming altered, and consequently, changes in social structure were also occurring. Industrialization and its twin, urbanization, had begun to make their impact; thus, the agrarian base of social and political influence was shrinking. The industrial revolution was advanced the furthest in England. In England, too, the mercantile middle class had made the greatest strides socially and politically to displace the landed aristocracy. However, this process also was going on in France, where it had contributed to the Revolution, and in varying degrees in all other parts of Europe. In short, throughout much of Europe, the formerly dispossessed classes were gaining political influence or, where influence was denied, were making ever greater demands upon the ruling strata of society. The felt necessity to repress, to forestall, or to accommodate the demands of the dispossessed increasingly occupied the attention of the ruling classes of Europe.

War also occupied the attention of European rulers during much of the period under consideration. Prussia and Austria had gone to war with France shortly after the French Revolution had begun. Thus began the first in a series of conflicts that continued intermittently until the peace settlement at the Congress of Vienna in 1815, involving at one time or another every major power in Europe. It was war that provided the occasion for the rise of Napoleon; it was also war that became the key instrument of diplomacy under Napoleon.

In pursuing his diplomatic objectives through war, and armed with the most formidable weapons of his day, Napoleon effected important changes in the pattern of authority in Europe, through extension of French rule and through constitutional revision in the states that fell to French control. He also radically altered the rules by which international politics in Europe had been played for roughly two hundred years. For one thing, the grandiose territorial ambitions of Napoleon threatened to disrupt radically the balance of power that the rulers of the major

[4] "Concerning the Most Recent Internal Affairs in Württemberg, and More Especially the Shortcomings of the Constitution of City Magistrates," in Carl J. Friedrich, ed. and trans., *The Philosophy of Hegel* (New York: Modern Library, 1953), p. 523.

powers had implicitly agreed to maintain among themselves. Moreover, with this implicit agreement to pursue limited territorial and other diplomatic objectives in their competitions with one another, wars had previously been fought within certain rather well-defined limits. These limits Napoleon violated. During most of the eighteenth and seventeenth centuries, wars had consisted of limited engagements by small numbers of professional, mercenary troops, with results that were seldom conclusive. The emphasis in military doctrine had been on defense, fortifications, and the art of siege. With Napoleon came the *levée en masse*—the concept of a nation in arms—employed in daring offensive maneuvers designed to destroy the enemy.

A *levée en masse* was possible because the French Revolution had generated not only universal ideals of liberty but also particular ideals of French nationalism. Napoleon had mobilized the latter as well as the former on behalf of his own ambitions. It seems to be characteristic of revolutions to generate a paradoxical mixture of universal and exclusively national ideals, as Crane Brinton has noted in his comparative analysis of the English, American, French, and Russian revolutions. As Brinton said of nations experiencing revolution, "They end up with a God meant indeed for all mankind, but brought to mankind, usually a not altogether willing mankind, by a Chosen People." [5] In the aftermath of the French Revolution, it was the expansionist nationalism of Napoleonic France that carried the universal message of revolution to other parts of Europe. As this message spread, so also did nationalism—French nationalism among some people where French culture was already strong (for instance, Savoy), but more often nationalism of indigenous people banding together in opposition to French rule.

Those who assembled at the Congress of Vienna in 1814–1815 (most notably, Prince Metternich of Austria, Viscount Castlereagh of Great Britain, Tsar Alexander of Russia, Prince Hardenberg of Prussia, and Count Talleyrand of France) made efforts to restore those rules of the game that had governed international politics prior to the French Revolution and the Napoleonic rule.[6] These efforts were partially successful. That is, until Europe exploded into war a century later, diplomacy remained largely the art of compromise and accommodation, and large-scale conflict was avoided. As suggested earlier, however, the trend

[5] Brinton, *The Anatomy of Revolution* (New York: Vintage Books, revised ed., 1952), p. 206.

[6] An interesting case study of the Congress of Vienna that depicts classical diplomacy as it was performed by the masters of the art assembled at Vienna has been written by Henry A. Kissinger, "The Congress of Vienna," in John G. Stoessinger and Alan F. Westin, eds., *Power and Order* (New York: Harcourt, 1964), pp. 1–32.

toward expansion of the popular voice in government could not be reversed at Vienna; nor could the rising tide of nationalism.

The pertinence of the changes in Europe during the period 1783–1820s to the concurrent emergence of a distinctive American orientation toward its world environment can now be briefly suggested. First, the events and political circumstances that have been described generally distracted European rulers from affairs in the Western Hemisphere. Moreover, because their overseas commitments had lower priority than the heavy demands on the European continent, the European influence on events in the Western Hemisphere was reduced. This reduced European interest and influence facilitated America's effort to secure its borders and promoted the expansion of American influence into areas where European control had diminished.

For example, the Louisiana Territory was purchased from Napoleon at a time when such a transaction seemed expedient to him in the light of war commitments in Europe. Napoleon himself had acquired Louisiana only recently from the Spanish, who also subsequently yielded Florida to the United States, and whose colonies in Latin America in rapid succession asserted their independence from Spain.

Among European powers, Spain and Portugal in particular—both of which had had substantial holdings in the Western Hemisphere—were in a period of sharp decline as world powers. The vitality of each nation had diminished to the point that, as Ortega y Gasset said of Spain a century later, it was little more than ". . . a cloud of dust that was left hovering in the air when a great people went galloping down the high road of history." [7]

Although there were rumors circulating in America after the Congress of Vienna that the series of conferences that were held (1817–1822) among the great powers of Europe (the so-called Concert of Europe) might take action to restore the Latin American colonies to Spanish control, the opposition of the British to such an idea effectively squelched it. Great Britain represented an exception to the generalization made above about the declining European interest and influence in the Western Hemisphere during the period. After suffering a major loss to her own imperial holdings with the successful revolution of her thirteen American colonies, Great Britain exploited the ever weakening hold of Spain and Portugal on their Latin American colonies to increase British trade and influence. These policies of Great Britain in the Western

---

[7] José Ortega y Gasset, "Particularism and Disintegration," in Alexander Baltzly and A. William Salomone, eds., *Readings in Twentieth-Century European History* (New York: Appleton, 1950), p. 227. The selection is extracted from the author's work, *Invertebrate Spain* (New York: Norton, 1937).

Hemisphere put her in major competition with the United States, which also was nurturing contacts in Latin America.[8] In time, however, British sea power became, in effect, a useful buffer between continental Europe and the United States, thereby working primarily to the benefit rather than to the detriment of American interests.

In addition to the opportunities that the turbulence in Europe in the years following the French Revolution provided for an expansionist foreign policy by the United States, another facet of the European situation seems pertinent here. The turmoil, machinations, and bloodshed that characterized European politics during the period reinforced the preconceptions of American leaders that Europe was a decadent civilization— which provided all the more reason, therefore, for the United States to avoid becoming embroiled in the troubles of Europe. Moreover, the great ocean that separated the United States from Europe helped to make such a policy of avoidance feasible.

Capabilities and Goal-Values: The Emerging Consensus   While changes in the world environment (especially in Europe) of the kind described above were occurring, American foreign policy was devoted primarily to making independence secure. By the time that this objective had been accomplished, a strong consensus had emerged among national leaders regarding American adaptive capabilities and the identity and destiny that set the new nation apart from Europe.

The observation that the perceptive Frenchman, Alexis de Tocqueville, made after visiting the United States early in the nineteenth century identifies figuratively if not literally the beliefs that had been prevalent among Americans for generations regarding their identity and place in history. The discovery of America, Tocqueville suggested, which provided an asylum for persecuted peoples from Europe, was as if America "had been kept in reserve by the Deity and had just risen from beneath the waters of the Deluge." [9] Early American colonists, especially the Puritans, had expressed similar beliefs. Puritan leaders expressed the conviction that they and their followers had been delivered from persecution by God in order to fulfill a unique mission on earth. Although the aspirations of Puritan leaders for the establishment of a theocracy in America

---

[8] A penetrating analysis of British diplomacy in the period is provided by William W. Kaufman, *British Policy and the Independence of Latin America, 1804–1828* (New Haven, Conn.: Yale University Press, 1951). American policies are discussed by Arthur P. Whitaker, *The United States and the Independence of Latin America* (Baltimore: Johns Hopkins Press, 1941).

[9] Alexis de Tocqueville, *Democracy in America*, ed. Phillips Bradley, 2 vols. (New York: Vintage Books, paperback ed., 1957), 1:302. First English trans., 1835.

foundered, the sense of destiny did not. Rather, as initial hardship gave way to prosperity, the belief that initially had been drawn from passages in the Old Testament of a unique historical mission gave way to a less explicit sense of destiny that was supported by secular experience; this experience in its general characteristics was shared not only by New England Puritans, but by other American colonists as well.[10]

Leaders of the American revolution drew upon this sense of national destiny, in addition to the pragmatic as well as idealistic considerations of the benefits of independence from British colonial rule, in forming their images of the appropriate role that the nascent nation could and would play in world affairs. For example, Tom Paine, the most famous pamphleteer of the cause of revolution, reiterated the early Puritan theme of Americans as a "chosen people," and anticipated the later observations of Tocqueville, when he noted in his essay, "Common Sense," that the Protestant Reformation had been briefly preceded by the discovery of America, "as if the Almighty graciously meant to open a sanctuary to the persecuted in future years. . . ." His argument rested not only upon the idealistic claim that America was "the asylum for the persecuted lovers of civil and religious liberty from *every part* of Europe," but also upon a pragmatic assessment of the capabilities of the colonies to maintain their independence. Some leaders in the colonies argued that Americans could not survive without the protection afforded by the colonial connection to British mercantilism; Paine argued that independence would mean economic gain, not loss: "As Europe is our market for trade, we ought to form no partial connection with any part of it." To do so, he warned, "tends directly to involve this continent in European wars and quarrels, and set us at variance with nations who would otherwise seek our friendship, and against whom we have neither anger nor complaint." [11]

Avoidance of political entanglement with European nation-states was to become a central goal-value around which consensus among American national leaders would emerge. However, the consensus did not develop

[10] Thus, as Daniel J. Boorstin has said in an imaginative essay on the history of American political ideas and practices, key tenets of American political faith tended to be increasingly drawn from a sense of their "givenness" in the American historical experience, rather than from formal theological or ideological sources. Boorstin, *The Genius of American Politics* (Chicago: University of Chicago Press, 1953), especially chap. 2: "The Puritans: From Providence to Pride."

[11] H. H. Clark, ed., *Thomas Paine: Representative Selections* (New York: American Book, 1944), pp. 18–34; excerpted in Avery Craven, Walter Johnson, and F. Roger Dunn, eds., *A Documentary History of the American People* (Boston: Ginn, 1951), pp. 154–158. Emphasis in the source cited. "Common Sense" was first published, anonymously, in January 1776.

immediately. Washington, for example, as the nation's first President, was confronted during his two terms with continuing doubts and differences of views that to a large extent had troubled the nation since the beginning of the movement for independence. Some leaders, such as Washington's first secretary of the treasury, Alexander Hamilton, argued that the future of the new nation was inexorably linked to the former mother country, upon which continued dependence could be a blessing, not a curse. Other leaders urged, at least until the rise of Napoleon, that the alliance with the French that had helped to achieve American independence ought to be maintained. Washington, however, subscribed instead to the belief that the United States had an identity and a set of interests that were distinct from those of Europe; he had therefore urged his fellow countrymen that the United States must remain aloof from European politics and retain her freedom of action. His most famous statement of such advice came in his farewell address as President.

"Europe has a set of primary interests which to us have none or a very remote relation," President Washington observed. "Hence she must be engaged in frequent controversies, the causes of which are essentially foreign to our concerns." He pointed to geographic considerations favorable to the course which he recommended: "Our detached and distant situation invites and enables us to pursue a different course." And, combining a realistic assessment of national potential with an idealistic appeal to national pride, he urged, "If we remain one people, under an efficient government, the period is not far off when we may defy material injury from external annoyance; when we may take such an attitude as will cause the neutrality we may at any time resolve upon to be scrupulously respected; when belligerent nations, under the impossibility of making acquisitions upon us, will not lightly hazard the giving us provocation; when we may choose peace or war, as our interest, guided by justice, shall counsel." [12]

As Lipset has observed, Washington's contribution to the development of the new nation was particularly great because he combined immense charisma with considerable restraint in using it. Not only did the strength and the pervasiveness of his personal appeal to Americans of various political leanings and from all sections of the country promote national unity, but the fact that he voluntarily retired from office at the end of a

---

[12] Collections of documents on U.S. diplomatic history characteristically include Washington's farewell address. For example, the message is contained in its entirety or in part in Craven, Johnson, and Dunn, pp. 217–224; in Williams, pp. 42–43; and in Armin Rappaport, ed., *Sources in American Diplomacy* (New York: Crowell-Collier-Macmillan, 1966), pp. 27–29.

second term, rather than exploiting his popularity by remaining in office, paved the way for the institutionalization of a process of orderly succession in government and thereby furthered national harmony.[13] Thus, the image of the national self that Washington had promoted provided a rallying point around which, amidst external threats to destroy the union and internal threats to abandon it, consensus could eventually develop.

When the Democratic-Republicans, with Thomas Jefferson as their leader, replaced the Federalists as the dominant power in the federal government, a major early test was presented of whether the orientation to world affairs defined by Presidents Washington and Adams would be maintained. In his first inaugural address, President Jefferson suggested the continuity that would follow, when he argued for "peace, commerce, and honest friendship with all nations, entangling alliances with none. . . ."[14]

It was under Jefferson too that great impetus was given to the expansionist thrust in American foreign policy, with the purchase of Louisiana in 1803. The size and the cost of the territorial acquisition far exceeded Jefferson's expectations. When he sent James Monroe to assist Robert Livingston, the minister to France, to negotiate with Napoleon, their instructions were only to try to obtain New Orleans, or at least the land in the Mississippi delta that would guarantee Americans complete freedom of navigation from the Mississippi River to the gulf. Moreover, Jefferson had been committed to a strict interpretation of the Constitution, which precluded the purchase of additional territory for the Union. But as early as 1801, Jefferson had expressed a view that justified abandoning constitutional scruples in order to take advantage of the unexpected opportunity to acquire all of Louisiana. "However our present interests may restrain us within our own limits," he had written to Monroe, "it is impossible not to look forward to distant time, when our rapid multiplication will expand itself beyond those limits, and cover the whole northern if not the southern continent."[15]

How could a hemispheric conception of national interests such as the one Jefferson had articulated in his letter to Monroe be reconciled with avoidance of involvement in European politics, when several nation-states of Europe (notably Spain, France, England, Russia, and Portugal) continued to have political interests in the Western Hemisphere that

[13] Seymour M. Lipset, *The First New Nation* (New York: Basic Books, 1963), pp. 16–23.

[14] Williams, *The Shaping of American Diplomacy*, p. 44.

[15] Jefferson to Monroe, cited in Charles A. Beard, *The Idea of National Interests: An Analytical Study in American Foreign Policy* (New York: Crowell-Collier-Macmillan, 1934), pp. 53–54.

could conflict with the expansion of the United States' influence? An occasion for answering this question occurred during the presidency of James Monroe, two decades later.

This situation was the one mentioned previously, in which restoration of the former Spanish colonies in Latin America seemed threatened by the Concert of Europe. As indicated, however, the British revealed strong opposition to any such action by the Concert. In fact, in order to strengthen their own position, the British sought the collaboration of the American government in issuing a statement warning the continental powers to leave the Latin American nations alone.

It was in this context that the American Secretary of State John Quincy Adams suggested, in lieu of collaboration with the British, a unilateral declaration by the United States. Such a course would be "more candid, as well as more dignified . . . than to come in as a cockboat in the wake of the British man-of-war," Adams urged.[16] The Monroe Doctrine, which was drafted largely by Adams in implementation of his suggestion, provided the occasion for at once defining American interests in hemispheric terms while maintaining and attempting to bolster a course of action independent of European entanglements or interference.

The continuity between the self-confident assertion of an American sphere of interest, which the Monroe Doctrine represented, and the earlier territorial acquisitions, such as the Louisiana Purchase, which made self-confidence in an expanded notion of national interests possible, is apparent. In fact, as Frederick Jackson Turner noted on the centennial of the Louisiana Purchase, "The Monroe Doctrine would not have been possible except for the Louisiana Purchase. It was the logical outcome of that acquisition." [17]

In summary, by the time of Monroe, a consensus among national leaders had emerged regarding American capabilities and the goal-values to be pursued in foreign policy. Threats to the borders, and perhaps to the continued independence, of the United States had been all but eliminated. Moreover, the size of America had doubled. American adaptive capabilities were perceived as substantial if utilized to promote the future development of the nation in the Western Hemisphere, rather than pitted against the still superior forces of the major European powers. Paine, Washington, Jefferson, and other early leaders had all spoken of the pragmatic advantages of freedom of action that the avoidance of political entanglements in Europe would provide. They had also foreseen a period of future national greatness if their advice were followed.

---

[16] Adams Diary, quoted in Williams, 1:160.

[17] Frederick Jackson Turner, "The Significance of the Louisiana Purchase," *Review of Reviews,* 27 (May 1903), 578–584; reprinted in Williams, 1:71–81.

By the time of Monroe, the sense of national destiny had become articulated more explicitly in terms of American supremacy in the Western Hemisphere. Warning European nations against further encroachments in the hemisphere satisfied the sense of national identity, which was defined especially in contrast with the perceived tyranny of Europe; the warning was also congruent with pragmatic beliefs about the benefits to be derived from maintaining maximum freedom from the interference of European powers in the extension of American influence in the hemisphere.[18]

Dynamics of Foreign Policy: Some Tentative Generalizations

We have applied the analytical framework developed in Chapter 5 to explanation of the particular American foreign-policy posture that emerged in the period from 1783 to the 1820s. Yet, from the perspective of historical dynamics, events of this period have more than historical interest; they also provide clues about general interrelationships among variables. We may fruitfully speculate about such general interrelationships without discounting the distinctive aspects of the period that we have discussed.

Three factors have been introduced previously as central to explaining the orientation of the nation-state to its geopolitical environment: the structure of the environment; estimates of adaptive capabilities; and general goal-values of national leaders. If the full range of possible variation in each of these factors were explored, numerous possibilities would exist for hypotheses about various facets of the foreign-policy orientation of a nation-state. However, since our purpose here is merely to illustrate the development of hypotheses as an analytical tool, and not that of constructing a full theory or a pretheoretical foundation, we shall explore only a small sample of the possible relationships among variables.

Our efforts can be facilitated by developing a simple typology of the dependent variable—the foreign-policy posture, which is identified essentially by responses made by the nation-state to environmental demands and by the demands that it makes upon the environment. In starting to develop a typology, therefore, we might make a gross distinction between a pattern of foreign policies that basically conforms to or maintains the

[18] The continuing appeal in the twentieth century of definitions of the national interest that combine idealistic sentiments with pragmatic considerations is described by Robert E. Osgood, *Ideals and Self-Interest in America's Foreign Relations* (Chicago: University of Chicago Press, 1953).

existing environmental structure and a pattern that basically deviates from or challenges the existing environmental structure. In conventional terminology, the former pattern may be termed a *status quo* posture in world affairs, the latter pattern, a revisionist posture. A revisionist posture would be reflected, for instance, in decisions that threatened or altered territorial boundaries; in actions that defied treaties and other international agreements; in initiatives that created new trade patterns or reallocated existing world resources; and in challenges to existing international institutions and centers of authority. Conversely, a *status quo* posture would be reflected in actions to maintain existing boundaries; in policies supporting treaty arrangements; in the utilization of current trade patterns; and in the acknowledgment or defense of existing authority.

Revisionism and the Status Quo

The gross distinction between a *status quo* and a revisionist posture is refined slightly in the hypotheses that follow, with a typology that includes four categories of foreign-policy posture, as indicated in Figure 2. The categories are developed in relationship to two dimensions, or vari-

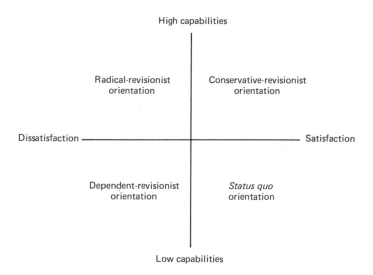

Figure 2   Extent of Leader Satisfaction with Existing Environmental Structure and Estimates of Adaptive Capabilities as Determinants of the Orientation of a Nation-State toward its World Environment

ables. The first, depicted by the vertical axis in Figure 2, is in the estimates by national leaders of the adaptive capabilities of the nation-state. The second, depicted by the horizontal axis in Figure 2, essentially corresponds to an affective component of the general goal-values of national leaders. The variable is the leaders' degree of satisfaction with the existing environmental structure. The postulated relationship between the two dimensions and the orientation of the nation-state toward its geopolitical environment is indicated in Hypotheses 9 and 10.

HYPOTHESIS 9 *When the leaders of a nation-state are generally dissatisfied with the existing environmental structure—*

HYPOTHESIS 9(a) *The nation-state will assume a radical-revisionist posture in relation to the world environment if policy makers estimate that the adaptive capabilities of the nation-state are high.*

HYPOTHESIS 9(b) *The nation-state will assume a dependent-revisionist posture in relation to the world environment if policy makers estimate that the adaptive capabilities of the nation-state are low.*

The distinction suggested here between a radical-revisionist and a dependent-revisionist posture is essentially one between a nation-state in which policies are an accurate reflection of the aspirations of its national leaders and a nation-state in which a wide gap exists between aspirations and policies. In both instances, it is postulated that national leaders are dissatisfied with important facets of the environmental structure—territorial boundaries, perhaps, or the provisions of treaties or rules of international law. The leaders will therefore aspire to change or to defy the existing structure. In a nation-state where the leaders believe that the adaptive capabilities of the nation-state are high, however, the pattern of foreign policy will be radical-revisionist, because the leaders believe such policies can be successful. Where capabilities are low, it is postulated that the pattern of foreign policy will be one of dependence on a stronger nation-state. The essentially cautious policies of the dependent-revisionist nation-state may be partially obscured by a veneer of radical ideology and revisionist pronouncements; however, the basic pattern of action is likely to remain dependent-revisionist until such a time as the nation's leaders believe that national capabilities have markedly improved, unless, in relation to limited sectors of the environment, opportunities for radically revisionist actions appear.

The distinction between a radical-revisionist posture and a dependent-revisionist one can be illustrated by the contrast between the pattern of American foreign policy throughout most of the nineteenth century and the pattern characteristic of most of the new nation-states that have gained their independence within the past two or three decades. Many of the leaders of nation-states that have attained independence since World War II have had aspirations no less revisionist than those of the early leaders of the United States. No nation-state in recent times, however, has had opportunities for the fulfillment of revisionist aspirations equal to those enjoyed in nineteenth-century America. Consequently, whereas the pattern of action by the United States in relation to its world environment in the nineteenth century was one of almost uninterrupted revisionism, especially in terms of territorial expansion, the actions of new nation-states in the twentieth century more often than not have been those of conformation to the dictates of more powerful nation-states, although the fortuitous circumstances of a struggle between superpowers for the loyalties of new nations has sometimes enabled the latter to play off one "suitor" against the other, thereby preserving greater independence for itself than would otherwise be the case.

The nonalignment strategy of new nation-states in the era of the Cold War is roughly analogous to the nonentanglement concept of the traditional American foreign-policy posture. In both instances, avoidance of political commitments to more powerful nation-states is a means of preserving freedom of action. In the early American case, nonentanglement in European politics provided greater freedom of action for meeting domestic needs and for expansion on the North American continent. Thus, nonentanglement may be seen as consistent with the description of traditional American foreign policy as radical-revisionist. However, the discussion in Chapter 4, where Hypotheses 1 and 2 were introduced to describe variations in the style of interaction with another nation-state under varying circumstances, usefully supplements the present discussion. Applying Hypothesis 2, we may suggest that in the nineteenth century, the United States generally pursued a confrontation strategy with European powers on the North American continent, where the United States had a strategic advantage. Outside the North American continent, where American capabilities were often inferior to those of the great European powers, the style of interaction pursued by the United States can be described as one of accommodation—achieved through nonentanglement.

The transition that occurred in the foreign-policy posture of the United States as it became a great world power can be suggested by the following hypothesis.

HYPOTHESIS 10   *When the leaders of a nation-state are generally satisfied with the existing environmental structure—*

> HYPOTHESIS 10(a)   *The nation-state will assume a conservative-revisionist posture in relation to the world environment if national leaders estimate that the adaptive capabilities of the nation-state are high.*

> HYPOTHESIS 10(b)   *The nation-state will assume a* status quo *posture in relation to the world environment if national leaders estimate that the adaptive capabilities of the nation-state are low.*

The concept of a conservative-revisionist posture might seem to be a contradiction in terms. In a sense there is a contradiction, but it is one between the desire of the leaders of a nation-state to preserve prerogatives, patterns of authority, and a distribution of resources that benefit their nation-state and the actions of the nation-state that in fact alter the existing environmental structure. Thus, one might say that the pattern is one of policies that are conservative in design but at least partly revisionist operationally. In contrast, a *status quo* posture, as we define it, corresponds to a pattern of foreign policies that in practice as well as in design supports the existing environmental structure. Although twentieth-century American foreign policy has often been described as *status quo* in nature, one might argue that the pattern corresponds more closely to a conservative-revisionist posture. On the one hand, the United States has come to enjoy the benefits of a great power and to be a dominant rule-maker in international politics, thereby gaining a vested interest in the maintenance of existing rules of the game. On the other hand, just as the actions of the General Motors Corporation, in maintaining its competitive position as a giant industry, have the effect of producing profound changes in the economy, so the actions of the United States, in maintaining its interests in the world, are an important stimulus to change in the structure of the geopolitical world environment. In science and technology, as one vitally important example, the investment of the United States in research and innovation far exceeds that of most other nations. The result is an accelerating process of technological change, in turn an important dimension of change of the world environmental structure. Moreover, other dimensions of the environmental structure are affected as well. For instance, technological changes in such fields as atomic energy and space research have had the effect of making the existing rules (for example, international laws and treaties) obsolete, in spite of a commitment on the part of the American government to preserving the existing rules.

Comparison of Hypotheses 9 and 10 provides a partial basis for explaining the difference between the traditional foreign-policy posture of the United States and that developed in the twentieth century. However, the nature and circumstances of the transition cannot be explained by these hypotheses alone. There is an apparent inconsistency that needs to be resolved. The transition was from a radical-revisionist posture to a conservative-revisionist one; as we shall indicate presently, the period of intensive change began in the 1890s. Yet, the changes in foreign policy during this period of imperialistic ventures put the United States in a posture of revisionism toward the world environment that was even more radical than previously. In other words, a transition that eventually proved to be one away from a radical-revisionist posture paradoxically involved challenges to the dominant European powers that were more radical in their immediate effect than many of the previous American policies had been. Thus, categorizing the American foreign-policy posture before (radical-revisionist) and after (conservative-revisionist) the transition from the nineteenth-century tradition to policies of the mid-twentieth century is less difficult than explaining the dynamics of the transition.

Consensus, Dissension, and Change

We may help to explain the paradoxical process of change with the following hypotheses.

> HYPOTHESIS 11   *As long as consensus prevails among national leaders in the images that they maintain of the national identity and the national interest, there will be continuity in the orientation of the nation-state toward its world environment.*

> HYPOTHESIS 12   *Changes in foreign policy sufficient to produce a sustained change in the orientation of the nation-state toward its world environment will occur only after a period of dissension among national leaders in terms of their images of the national identity and the national interest and after the formulation of a new consensus.*

In other words, even in a period of continuing foreign-policy consensus among national leaders, decisions may be made and actions taken in world affairs that represent a temporary deviation from the foreign-policy posture that has been maintained; but an enduring change in foreign-policy posture requires the dissolution of the old images of the national identity and the national interest and the formulation of a new consensus among national leaders. As suggested in Chapter 5, images of the national identity and of the national interest consist of deep-rooted values and beliefs that are not easily changed. Under what circumstances, then, might one expect such changes to occur? The following hypothesis stipulates preconditions for such changes.

HYPOTHESIS 13   *An existing consensus among national leaders regarding the national identity and the national interest will be dissolved by—*

HYPOTHESIS 13(a)   *significant changes in the structure of the geopolitical environment.*

HYPOTHESIS 13(b)   *substantial change in the estimates that national leaders have of the nation-state's adaptive capabilities.*

HYPOTHESIS 13(c)   *substantial alteration of the composition of the national leadership within a short span of time.*

In the discussion that follows, we shall identify a number of changes in the geopolitical world environment and changes in American adaptive capabilities during the latter decades of the nineteenth century that culminated in the 1890s and the turn of the century to undermine the previous consensus among American national leaders in their images of the national identity and the national interest. We shall suggest that, although new policies at the turn of the century of imperialism and political involvement with European powers represented a more intensive revisionism, they also represented a sharp departure from the traditional pattern of American foreign policy. The new course could not be sustained because of sharp cleavages among national leaders in defining the national identity and determining the national interest. These cleavages were attributable not only to differing interpretations of the policy implications of environmental change and of increased capabilities, but also to changes in the composition of the national leadership, especially in the growing urban base of the Democratic party. Only when a new, broad foreign-policy consensus among national leaders was forged during and immediately after World War II, did vacillation in the orientation of the United States toward its world environment give way to a period of stability in the American foreign-policy posture, climaxing a process of change that had begun in the 1890s.

One should note that a rigorous test of Hypotheses 11, 12, and 13 would require a number of steps beyond those that we shall pursue. In Chapter 5, a number of the key terms that have been included in the hypotheses above were generally defined. Further operational criteria for specifying such concepts as national leaders, images of the national identity, and images of the national interest would be desirable if the hypotheses were to be tested. For testing Hypothesis 13, it would be essential to indicate the kinds of environmental change that would be considered significant; the magnitude of change in capability estimates to be treated as substantial; the degree of change of leadership composition to be considered as substantial; and the number of years forming a "short span of time." Moreover, as a prerequisite to testing Hypotheses 11 and 12, an operational definition of consensus and dissension would have to be provided. One might stipulate the minimum degree of agreement (for example, 75 percent) among national leaders to be used as an index of consensus. Assuming that obtaining the views of *all* national leaders on matters of foreign policy would be an insurmountable task, one nevertheless would have to indicate the size and basis of selection of the sample on which one's analysis was based, so that other observers could determine the probability that the data presented were an accurate reflection of the views of the leaders.

We make no pretense of having attained such operational rigor in the discussion that follows, nor in having tested the hypotheses at all. Rather, as previously, reference to specific events provides a basis for illustrating the hypotheses and thereby provoking further thought about the relationships suggested in them.

The 1890s and the Turn of the Century

The Pattern of Continuity

At the risk of some oversimplification, the period from the 1820s to the 1890s may be described as one of remarkable continuity in the broad orientation that the United States maintained toward the world environment. The first key element that defined this orientation was that of avoiding political entanglement with European states. As mentioned earlier, nonentanglement did not imply isolation from the world. Indeed, during this period the United States was in the forefront of diplomatically opening China to the West. Commodore Perry and his "black ships" steamed into Yokohama harbor, and subsequent conversations with the Mikado led to the first treaty between Japan and a Western nation. Diplomatic contacts were established with Korea. Hawaii became an American colony. The islands of Midway, a thousand miles west of Hawaii, were acquired. Filibustering expeditions in the Caribbean extended American interests southward. Commerce was maintained and expanded in Europe. American commercial outposts in Africa were established. In other words, the United States was by no means cut off from the rest of the world; on the contrary, points of contact were numerous. Adherence to the nonentanglement doctrine meant, however, that the foreign policy of the United States should incur no binding political obligations to other nation-states—especially European states—in pursuing her foreign-policy interests.

The second key element in the foreign-policy posture of the United States was that of territorial expansion; the period under consideration was the heyday of expansion. The vast territory of Texas was annexed in 1845, by joint resolution of the United States Congress. The Oregon territorial issue with Great Britain was settled by treaty in 1846. War with Mexico was declared the same year, by a nearly unanimous vote of the Congress; as a result of the Treaty of Guadalupe Hidalgo in 1848, ending the war, the United States acquired an enormous stretch of territory from the western border of Texas to and including California, plus encompassing all or part of the present states of Nevada, Utah, Arizona, Wyoming, Colorado, and New Mexico. In 1853, an additional strip of territory along the southern edge of what are now the states of Arizona and New Mexico was acquired by purchase. In 1867, the territory that was to be the largest state in the union, Alaska, was purchased from Russia.

Although Alaska was the last significant territorial acquisition during the period, the occupation and consolidation of the lands acquired and the development of systems of communication and transportation across the continent greatly consumed the energy of the nation from the end of the Civil War to the 1890s. From the viewpoint of the American government at the time, this was domestic policy. American Indians, however, not American white men, occupied much of the land that was acquired during the period, and they had not been consulted in the negotiations by which the land had been ceded to the United States government. From a different perspective, therefore, the consolidation by the American government of the territory during the post-Civil War era, which involved fighting nearly a thousand separate engagements with Indian tribes, may be regarded as foreign-policy activity designed to secure by force the fruits of expansion.[19]

[19] A recent study cites the number of engagements by the Army with Indians as 943 from 1865 to 1898. Russell F. Weigley, *History of the United States Army* (New York: Crowell-Collier-Macmillan, 1967), p. 267.

Continuity in the orientation of the United States toward the world environment during this period was first promoted by the relative stability of the environmental structure. Especially, the pattern of environmental opportunities and incentives that had been conducive to expansion at the onset of the period continued to prevail. Moreover, it was only toward the end of the period that the politics of compromise among the great European powers, which had been institutionalized at the Congress of Vienna, began to give way to intense imperialistic competition that had important potential consequences for American interests.

Continuity in foreign-policy orientation was also maintained by the perpetuation of a relatively stable consensus among the national leaders in their estimates of adaptive capabilities. These capabilities were dramatically increasing during the period by any set of indexes, but so long as the goal-values of leaders focused largely on territorial expansion on the North American continent, the capabilities of the United States, relative to the barriers to expansion that were encountered, remained roughly constant throughout the period. The growth that was occurring— of American capabilities relative to those of the great powers of Europe —did not become a salient consideration in American foreign policy until late in the century, when the surge of European imperialism threatened America's access to markets and raw materials, and when competition or conflict with European powers began to seem a necessity to many Americans.

Obsolescence of Images of National Identity and National Interest

As suggested in Hypothesis 12, the basic prerequisite for a change of the traditional foreign-policy posture was a dissolution of the consensus among national leaders in their images of the national identity and the national interest. The intense foreign-policy debate that began at the end of the century illustrates Hypothesis 13, identifying the bases for the dissolution of leadership consensus in changes in environmental structure, changes in capabilities, and changes in the composition of national leadership.

Changing Environment   The period after the American Civil War was one of important industrialization and social and political change, both in the United States and in Europe, with effects that were felt throughout the world. The political structures and boundaries in Europe were changed dramatically with the consolidation of Italy and Germany as nation-states. Industrialization of the nation-states of Europe was accompanied by a rapid population growth (the population of Europe increased two and a half times from 1800 to 1900); by urbanization; and by increasing insecurity among the masses of people, foretelling problems that would come to a head in the twentieth century. The nineteenth-century German philosopher Friedrich Nietzsche saw a trend in Europe toward "numerous, talkative, weak-willed, and very handy workmen who *require* a master, a commander, as they require their daily bread. . . ." [20]

As the European nations became industrialized, they turned their attention to the Middle East, to Asia (to which access had been facili-tated by the steamship and by the opening in 1869 of the Suez Canal), and to Africa—for raw materials, markets, and colonies. A rough indica-tion of the frenzied pace of competition that ensued is provided by the fact that prior to 1875 less than one-tenth of the territory in Africa was under European colonial rule; by 1895, all but one-tenth of Africa was under European colonial rule. In the 1880s and the 1890s, European international politics were aggravated not only by imperialistic competi-tion, but also by a growing rigidity of relationships into opposing military alliances and pacts. Alliances included war plans that were to go into effect almost automatically in the case of a triggering incident or provo-cation, since the growing belief was that future wars would be short (like the Franco-Prussian War of 1871) and that the first strike or maneuver probably would be decisive (reflected, for instance, in the development of elaborate plans for surprise attacks, such as the celebrated Schlieffen Plan, developed in 1903 and imperfectly implemented by Germany in 1914 against France).

Increasing American Capabilities For the United States, the post-Civil War decades showed many impressive accomplishments and rapidly developing capabilities. In the 1870s, the United States attained a favor-able balance of trade for the first time in its history.[21] Between 1870 and 1880, American export trade increased more than 200 percent.[22] The same period was also one of rapid industrialization, railroad building, and general growth. The total population of the country increased by roughly 100 percent from 1860 to 1890; the number of those engaged in manufacturing and in mechanical or mining industries increased by over

[20] Friedrich Nietzsche, "Beyond Good and Evil," in *The Works of Friedrich Nietzsche*, ed. Orson Falk (New York: Tudor, 1931), 2:64–66; also excerpted in Baltzly and Salomone, eds., *Readings*, p. 10.

[21] Merle E. Curti, Richard H. Shryock, Thomas C. Cochran, and Fred Harvey Harrington, *An American History*, 2 vols. (New York: Harper & Row, 1950), 2:306–314.

[22] Robert Seager, II, "Ten Years Before Mahan: The Unofficial Case for the New Navy, 1880–1890," *Mississippi Valley Historical Review*, 40 (Dec. 1953), 491–512; reprinted in Williams, 1:338–343.

170 percent.[23] During the nineteenth century as a whole, the population of the United States had increased from 5.3 million to 76.0 million (as compared with an increase in population in Europe by a factor of 2.5).[24]

As historian Thomas A. Bailey has observed, by almost any set of indexes, the capability of the United States compared favorably with that of other major powers as the end of the nineteenth century drew near.

> By 1890 we were the number two white nation in population, still trying to catch up to the Russians. We had bounded into first place in total manufacturing, including top rank in iron and steel—the standard indices of military potential. In addition, we held either first or second place in railroads, telegraphs, telephones, merchant marine, and in the production of cattle, coal, gold, copper, lead, petroleum, cotton, corn, wheat, and rye. The armies and navies were not there, but we had the means of creating them when we needed them—and did.[25]

It is not surprising, then, that most American national leaders in the 1890s drew the conclusion that to Bailey and the rest of us is apparent in retrospect: that the United States had attained capabilities sufficient for the exercise of a role as a great world power.

New Expansionism and its Advocates

With the impetus of such changes as those described above, American foreign policy, for a period beginning in the late 1890s, became more aggressively competitive with the great powers of Europe than previously. To be sure, some of the actions of the United States around the turn of the century might be described as relatively natural extensions of the traditional definitions of the national interest. The intense concern with events in Cuba, for instance, culminating in a war with Spain (1898), was rooted in a long interest in the Caribbean. Likewise, the assertion by the Theodore Roosevelt administration of a right to intervene in Santo Domingo to force the government there to pay debts was

[23] Carroll D. Wright, *The Industrial Evolution of the United States* (New York: Flood and Vincent, 1895), pp. 325–343; excerpts reprinted in Craven, Johnson, and Dunn, pp. 479–483.

[24] U.S. Bureau of the Census, *Historical Statistics of the United States: Colonial Times to 1957* (Washington: Bureau of the Census, 1960), p. 8.

[25] Thomas A. Bailey, "America's Emergence as a World Power: The Myth and the Verity," *Pacific Historical Review*, 30 (1961), 1–16; reprinted in Harry Howe Ransom, ed., *An American Foreign Policy Reader* (New York: Crowell-Collier-Macmillan, 1965), pp. 87–102; the quotation is from p. 101.

explicitly rationalized as a corollary to the Monroe Doctrine. Similarly, the American show of force in support of Panama's independence from Colombia (1903), with the subsequent development of a United States-controlled Panama Canal, reflected long-standing interests in the Western Hemisphere, although the canal also provided convenient new access to trade routes to Asia.

A number of other American actions, however, represented a sharp departure from tradition, especially from the tradition of nonentanglement in world politics. For instance, the United States became a colonial power, with the acquisition of Puerto Rico, Guam, and the Philippines, as a result of war with Spain. The Hawaiian islands, 2400 miles from the California shore, were annexed in 1898. American warships and diplomats worked in conjunction with the British and the Germans to secure the division of Samoa between Germany and the United States (former British territory was relinquished in 1899). In 1899 and 1900, Open Door notes were sent to the major powers with colonial interests in Asia, indicating American interests in preventing the control of China or of Chinese trade by any other power. The United States participated for the first time in an international diplomatic conference with European powers (in the Hague Conference of 1899, to discuss the peaceful settlement of disputes and the laws of war; American delegates also attended the second Hague Conference in 1907). The American government made available its good offices to mediate in a war between Russia and Japan and to provide facilities for a peace conference (at Portsmouth, New Hampshire, in 1905). Likewise, the United States took the initiative in organizing a conference among European powers to resolve a dispute over colonial interests in North Africa (the Algeciras Conference of 1906).[26]

Advocates of the vigorous expansionism of this period were led by a relatively close-knit group of prominent persons, including Theodore Roosevelt, Brooks Adams, Whitelaw Reid, John Hay, Henry Cabot Lodge, and Albert Beveridge.[27] This core group had in common a patrician contempt for the crass materialism of the *nouveau riche* in American society (which partly explains the later identification of Roosevelt and

[26] See Foster Rhea Dulles, *America's Rise to World Power* (New York: Harper & Row, 1954), chaps. 2–4 for details of events of this period.

[27] Evidence of the close personal ties between the core group of expansionists is found in various memoirs and biographies of members of the group. Brooks Adams's brother, Henry, for example, did not actively participate in policy discussions, but has described some of the personal ties in *The Education of Henry Adams* (New York: Random House, Modern Library ed., 1931).

Beveridge, for instance, with the Progressive movement).[28] Members of the group had also in common a belief, articulated in terms that were quite distinct from traditional images of the national identity and the national interest, that the United States stood at a historical watershed. This belief, rooted in a variety of ideas ranging from social Darwinism to analysis of British success as an imperial power, provided the basic rationale for advocating an aggressive new role for the United States in world affairs. Theoretical abstractions were synthesized with practical considerations in their arguments. The newly potent capabilities of the United States meant, they reasoned, that America could compete successfully with the great powers of Europe in virtually any region of the world. Furthermore, the acquisition of new possessions in the Pacific (such as Hawaii, the Philippines, and Guam) could provide coaling stations to support a first-rank navy and convenient access to new markets and sources of raw materials in Asia. Moreover, to fail to engage in imperialistic competition, they warned, would mean that European powers would gain an advantage that in the future would again relegate the United States to a second-class status. A few of the intellectual origins of ideas to which the advocates of vigorous expansionism were committed and some of the central themes that they expressed, will be identified briefly.

Social Darwinism   The first American edition of Charles Darwin's *On the Origin of Species* appeared in 1860. Although the immediate impact of Darwin's work had not been as great in the United States as in England, by the 1870s, Darwin's theory of natural selection was creating a radical transformation not only of theories in the natural sciences, but also in religion and in popular theorizing about the evolution of human beings and of nations. The popularity of theories of social Darwinism was attributable especially to the writings and lectures of two persons. The first of these was an English philosopher, Herbert Spencer, who coined the phrase "survival of the fittest" to describe the application of Darwinian laws to the development of the human species. The second was William Graham Sumner, who had studied the works of Spencer, and who attracted a wide following in his position as a theologian and a professor of political and social sciences at Yale University. Although Sumner was personally unsympathetic to plutocracy, he saw in laissez-

[28] The close relationship between advocacy of imperialism and leadership in the Progressive movement has been described in detail by William E. Leuchtenburg, "Progressivism and Imperialism: The Progressive Movement and American Foreign Policy, 1898–1916," *The Mississippi Valley Historical Review*, 39 (Dec. 1952), 483–504. Also available in the Bobbs-Merrill reprint series, H-125.

faire economics and in the competitive struggle for existence the process of a natural law. The appeal of such ideas in late nineteenth-century America, especially to those who were amassing fortunes in the industrial boom, is understandable. As Richard Hofstadter has noted, "With its rapid expansion, its exploitative methods, its desperate competition, and its peremptory rejection of failure, postbellum America was like a vast human caricature of the Darwinian struggle for existence and survival of the fittest." [29]

Although the direct appeal of social Darwinism had somewhat waned by the 1890s, indirectly social Darwinism had an even greater impact then, because it had become assimilated into the thought and writings of a whole generation of American scholars and public officials. Advocates of a stronger governmental role in the economy and in social welfare, as well as critics of such a role, typically expressed their views in Darwinian or neo-Darwinian form.[30] Likewise, in discussions of the fate of nations and civilizations, adaptations of social Darwinism were common. Theodore Roosevelt, for example, saw in the events at the turn of the century a test of the collective manhood of America; it was a challenge that he welcomed. As he put it,

> The twentieth century looms before us big with the fate of many nations. If we stand idly by, if we seek merely swollen, slothful ease and ignoble peace, if we shrink from the hard contests where men must win at hazard of their lives and at the risk of all they hold dear, then the bolder and stronger peoples will pass us by, and will win for themselves the domination of the world.[31]

Seen in this light, imperial competition with European powers was to be sought, rather than avoided.

Social Darwinism could also be, and was, synthesized with earlier notions that the United States had a Manifest Destiny to fulfill. Senator Albert Beveridge of Indiana was among those who achieved such a synthesis in supporting an imperialistic course in American foreign policy. Much as Woodrow Wilson attempted to reconcile the involvement of the United States in World War I with prior traditions, by arguing that

[29] Richard Hofstadter, *Social Darwinism in American Thought* (Boston: Beacon Press, revised paperback ed., 1955), p. 44. The present discussion of social Darwinism draws heavily from Hofstadter's discerning analysis.

[30] Goldman uses the terms "Reform Darwinism" and "Conservative Darwinism" to describe the competing interpretations that evolved as Darwinism became assimilated into virtually all social thought. Eric F. Goldman, *Rendezvous with Destiny* (New York: Vintage Books, revised, abridged paperback ed., 1958).

[31] Theodore Roosevelt, "The Strenuous Life," in *The Works of Theodore Roosevelt*, 20 vols. (New York: Scribner, 1926), 13:331; also excerpted in Hofstadter, p. 180.

it was America's duty to "make the world safe for democracy," Beveridge defended American imperialism in terms of adapting traditional images of the American destiny to new opportunities and new responsibilities. In 1900, he told his Senate colleagues that God had ". . . marked the American people as His chosen Nation to finally lead in the regeneration of the world. This is the divine mission of America, and it holds for us all the profit, all the glory, all the happiness possible to man." [32]

Interpretations of Historical Experience   Interpretations of historical experience were another important source of the ideas expressed by the advocates of vigorous expansion. The writings of Frederick Jackson Turner, Alfred Thayer Mahan, and Brooks Adams were particularly influential.

Frederick Jackson Turner, professor of history at the University of Wisconsin, set forth what came to be known as "the frontier thesis" in a paper he read at the meeting of the American Historical Association in 1893. Turner observed that the U.S. Census Bureau report of 1890 had indicated that westward migration in the United States had ceased; the frontier, which had been moving steadily west, had reached the coast. Turner argued that the frontier had been of vital importance in American history, stimulating the development of democratic institutions, through the promotion of egalitarian norms, as well as economic development. Such an interpretation of the American past raised the obvious question of what the consequences would be now that the frontier was apparently closed (although in restrospect, we know that westward migration continued for decades).

The frontier thesis expounded by Turner had a profound impact. Historical analyses of the American past were soon infused with Turner's ideas, as such analyses continue to be, in modified form, today. More pertinent to our concern here, however, was the impact on policy makers or on those with direct access to them. Theodore Roosevelt described Turner's ideas as important because they "put into definite shape a good deal of thought which has been floating around rather loosely." [33] Indeed, the concept of a new frontier for the United States crystallized in the minds of many persons a solution that they had been seeking for the mounting social and economic problems from a severe economic depression in 1893. (The idea of a new frontier found appeal again during the

[32] Quoted by Harold A. Larrabee, "The Enemies of Empire," *American Heritage*, 11 (June 1960), 32.

[33] Arthur A. Ekirch, Jr., *Ideas, Ideals, and American Diplomacy* (New York: Appleton, 1966), p. 86, quoting from *The Letters of Theodore Roosevelt*, ed. E. E. Morison (Cambridge, Mass.: Harvard University Press, 1951–1954), 1:363.

Kennedy administration in the early 1960s, but for different reasons and with different content.) The new frontier envisaged by its proponents in the 1890s lay primarily in the vast reaches of Asia, where the lure of new markets and sources of raw materials seemed not only appealing but urgent, in the light of the precarious condition of China, whose seemingly imminent collapse might lead to the carving up of that land and its resources among European imperial powers.

The concern for greater American involvement in the political struggle in Asia was also underlined by the theories of Captain Alfred Thayer Mahan, whose lectures at the Naval War College shaped the thought of a generation of American naval officers, and whose writings had an enduring impact on a far broader audience. Probably his most seminal work was *The Influence of Sea Power on History, 1660–1783*, published in 1890. Drawing primarily upon analysis of the growth of the British empire, Mahan argued that control of land masses could be attained through control of the seas. As imperial competition heightened in the 1890s, Mahan saw the United States at a critical juncture. The Eurasian land mass, he maintained, was the area of which control was crucial for achieving world power.[34] Only a strong navy, coupled with an alliance with Great Britain, the world's strongest naval power, could stave off the expansion of the Russian empire and its eventual domination of the Eurasian land mass. Construction of a canal across the Panama isthmus would provide convenient access from the Atlantic to the Pacific; acquisition of areas such as Hawaii and the Philippines would be useful additional steps to enable the American navy to operate most effectively.[35]

Theodore Roosevelt was among those who followed Mahan's works closely and who regarded his theories as having profound significance. Upon his appointment as assistant secretary of the navy by President McKinley, Roosevelt kept in close touch with Mahan.[36] Less than a year after lecturing officers at the Naval War College that "no triumph of

[34] In this view, Mahan anticipated and influenced the thesis of a British contemporary, H. J. Mackinder, who referred to the Eurasian land mass as the "World Island." Mackinder's notion was that "Who rules the World Island commands the World." A useful discussion of the links between the Mahan and Mackinder theses and an assessment of the influence and the limitations of each is provided by Harold and Margaret Sprout, *Foundations of International Politics* (Princeton, N.J.: Van Nostrand, 1962), chap. 10.

[35] Mahan's life and career are traced in W. D. Puleston, *Mahan* (New Haven, Conn.: Yale University Press, 1939). A reasonably detailed treatment of Mahan's thought and influence in the 1890s and the turn of the century is provided by Robert E. Osgood, *Ideals and Self-Interest in America's Foreign Relations* (Chicago: University of Chicago Press, 1953), chap. 1: "Mahan and Premonitions of World Power."

[36] Beale, chap. 2.

peace is quite so great as the supreme triumphs of war," Roosevelt sent his famous dispatch to Admiral Dewey, stimulating Dewey's attack at Manila Bay, the first battle fought following congressional declaration of war on Spain; the acquisition of the Philippines followed.[37]

The theories of Brooks Adams reinforced the policy implications of Mahan's theories. Brother of Henry Adams and a direct descendant of two presidents of the United States and of the ambassador to Great Britain during the Civil War, Brooks Adams was a serious student of world history, from which he derived a cyclical pattern of the rise and decline of great civilizations.[38] The center of civilization, he thought, had been moving westward. Thus, by the 1890s, he believed, nature had ". . . cast the United States into the vortex of the fiercest struggle which the world has ever known. She has become the heart of the economic system of the age, and she must maintain her supremacy by wit and by force, or share the fate of the discarded." [39] Adams was critical of those of his contemporaries who, in his view, lacked the vision to move from outworn traditions, rooted in a world that Washington and Jefferson had known, to new policies dictated by new realities. The key to future power lay in Asia, Adams contended, especially in China. He saw Germany and Russia as presenting a growing challenge in competition for dominance in that region. Like Mahan, Adams favored entering the competition through an Anglo-American alliance (with the United States as senior partner); failure to compete for an empire, he warned, would place the future of American civilization in jeopardy.

Policies of an expanded American role in Asia, to support the acquisition of new markets and resources, appealed to various groups. Although, as Julius W. Pratt has suggested, many leading American businessmen were initially unsympathetic to the possibility of war with Spain, once the Philippines had fallen into American hands and Hawaiian annexation had been secured, business support for expansionist policies increased markedly.[40] Groups such as the American-China Development Company, founded by leading American industrialists and financiers in 1895, and the American Asiatic Association, organized in 1898 by leading cotton

[37] Roosevelt is quoted in Richard Hofstadter, *The American Political Tradition* (New York: Vintage Books, paperback ed., 1959), p. 213. Chap. 9 of the book is "Theodore Roosevelt: The Conservative as Progressive."

[38] Brooks Adams, *The Law of Civilization and Decay* (New York: Crowell-Collier-Macmillan, 1896).

[39] Adams, *The New Empire* (New York: Crowell-Collier-Macmillan, 1902), p. xxxiv.

[40] Julius W. Pratt, *Expansionists of 1898* (Baltimore: Johns Hopkins Press, 1936), chap. 7: "The Business Point of View."

growers and other businessmen, worked actively to persuade the government to support American interests in Asia and especially to prevent Russia from attaining a dominant sphere of interest in China. The activities of these and other interested groups were rewarded by the notes issued by Secretary of State John Hay to the major imperial powers in 1899 and 1900, calling for the maintenance of Chinese territorial integrity and for the preservation of an "open door" for all interested powers in their relations with China.[41] Hay's own contribution to drafting the first of the Open Door notes appears to have been slight;[42] nevertheless, the policies propounded in the notes, which followed a long-standing British approach to relations with China, and in effect aligned the United States and Great Britain, were consistent with Hay's own views.[43] When his close friend Roosevelt assumed the presidency at the death of McKinley, even closer working ties with the British were forged.[44]

Lingering Tradition

As suggested by the preceding discussion, Theodore Roosevelt was the pivotal figure in a core group of expansionists. The initial successes of the group in influencing the direction of American foreign policy made it appear for a time that a new foreign-policy consensus had emerged, or would emerge, around the ideas propounded by Roosevelt, Mahan, Brooks Adams, and other leading spokesmen of the group. The outbreak of the Spanish-American War, for example, appears to have served as a national catharsis, temporarily unifying disparate elements of the society.[45]

However, with Dewey's victory at Manila and the imminent prospect of an American empire, prominent national leaders began to question

[41] Charles S. Campbell, Jr., "American Business Interests and the Open Door in China," *Far Eastern Quarterly*, 1 (1941), 43–58; reprinted in Daniel M. Smith, ed., *Major Problems in American Diplomatic History: Documents and Readings* (Boston: Heath, 1964), pp. 335–346; also in Williams, 1:414–424.

[42] George F. Kennan, *American Diplomacy 1900–1950* (New York: New American Library, Mentor ed., 1951), pt. 1, chap. 2: "Mr. Hippisley and the Open Door."

[43] Foster Rhea Dulles, "John Hay (1898–1905)," *An Uncertain Tradition: American Secretaries of State in the Twentieth Century*, ed. Norman A. Graebner (New York: McGraw-Hill, 1961), pp. 28–33.

[44] Beale, chap. 3: "Roosevelt and the Cementing of the Anglo-American Entente."

[45] Hofstadter explains the jingoism of the nation at the time as an aggressive outlet from the "psychic crisis" that had developed from complex social and economic origins over a period of years. Richard Hofstadter, "Manifest Destiny and the Philippines," *America in Crisis*, ed. Daniel Aaron (New York: Knopf, 1952), pp. 172–200.

the departure from American foreign-policy tradition. The Anti-Imperialist League, organized in Boston in November 1898, claimed 30,000 members within a year. Leading spokesmen for the anti-imperialist cause formed a heterogeneous group, which included intellectuals and writers, such as Mark Twain, Finlay Peter Dunne, and William James; college presidents, such as David Starr Jordan of Stanford and Henry Wade Rogers of Northwestern; social reformers, such as Jane Addams; political reformers, such as Carl Schurz; and a few business tycoons, such as Andrew Carnegie. William Jennings Bryan made anti-imperialism a major campaign slogan in his unsuccessful bid for the presidency as Democratic candidate in 1900. However, large numbers of those associated with the anti-imperialist cause, including former President Cleveland and a number of his former cabinet members, were identified with the opposition to Bryan because of the "free silver" issue.

The lack of unified leadership and internal frictions among disparate elements diluted the effectiveness of the anti-imperialist movement. Thus, in terms of the hopes of the anti-imperialists to enlist broad public support for their views, it is correct to say that the movement ended in failure.[46]

On the other hand, it would be erroneous to conclude that the advocates of imperialism were completely successful. Rather, as Richard W. Leopold has expressed it, the imperialist movement at the turn of the century withered in a domestic environment that failed to provide it with enduring nourishment.[47] A symbol of the limits of the policy commitment to imperialism was the failure to create a colonial office in the American government. Moreover, growing pacifist sentiments in the nation exerted pressure upon policy makers to tone down the rhetoric of aggressive expansionism and to talk instead of peace. Even Theodore Roosevelt was responsive. As Osgood observed, "It was a sign of the times that the man who had been distinguished for his bellicosity in 1898 was awarded the Nobel Peace Prize in 1906."[48] Roosevelt's successor, Taft, was even more ambivalent in his foreign-policy posture. Both he and his secretary of state, Philander Knox, seem to have been committed in principle, however erratically in practice, to the nineteenth-

[46] Harrington notes that the anti-imperialists "were forced to preach abnegation rather than indulgence, to urge the pride of renunciation as against the pride of glory and possession. Their whole case rested on an abstract principle, the application of which was not altogether clear to the public at large"; from the excerpts in Williams, 1:407.

[47] Richard W. Leopold, "The Emergence of America as a World Power: Some Second Thoughts," *Change and Continuity in Twentieth-Century America* (New York: Harper & Row, Colophon ed., 1966), pp. 3–34.

[48] Osgood, p. 77.

century tradition of avoiding political entanglement with the great powers of the world.[49]

National Leadership in Transition

That no enduring consensus emerged among American national leaders favoring imperialism may be attributed not only to the continuing hold of the traditional values and conceptions of the national identity among important national leaders at the turn of the century, but also to the changing composition of national leadership. It is not possible here to identify precisely the impact upon the composition of national leadership produced by such phenomena as immigration (nine million immigrants entered the United States between 1901 and 1910 alone); the growth of labor unions; the proliferation of socialist, anarchist, and other movements committed to radical change; and the widespread discrediting of politicians and government officials by the "muckrakers" and by the popular cry of the Progressives to "give government back to the people." However, it is possible to suggest with confidence that the impact of such phenomena was cumulatively felt on the composition as well as on the attitudes of national leadership.

Frederick A. Ogg has suggested that the election of 1908 "was the harbinger of a great shift in party power." [50] This shift was occurring not only in the growing strength of grass-roots elements in the Democratic party and in the inroads that Democrats were making in previously secure Republican areas; it was also occurring in the national political structure as a whole. However, the changes that were taking place within the two-party system were of particular significance, since the two major parties in the United States have tended to assimilate or to co-opt the demands, if not the leadership, of third parties and of dissident groups in the society, as such groups become strong enough to pose a political threat to them. Samuel Lubell has shown how the assimilation of immigrants and other socially dispossessed groups in urban areas into the Democratic party produced a shift in national voting patterns that culminated in a long period of Democratic dominance in American politics, beginning in the 1930s.[51] The elections of 1908 may be described as an

---

[49] Walter Scholes, "Philander C. Knox," in Graebner, ed., pp. 59–78.

[50] Frederick A. Ogg, *National Progress 1907–1917*, in A. B. Hart, ed., The American Nation: A History, 28 vols. (New York: Harper & Row, 1904–1918), 27:16–17.

[51] Samuel Lubell, *The Future of American Politics* (New York: Harper & Row, 1952).

early symptom of the process that Lubell has described as continuing into the 1940s and the 1950s. The point that is pertinent in terms of the present discussion is that the restructuring of the composition of national leadership, although begun only slightly in the years between the end of the nineteenth century and World War I, further contributed to the cleavages among national leaders regarding their images of national identity and of the national interest. No enduring foreign-policy consensus among national leaders emerged until a process of domestic policy struggle had allowed previously dissident elements to be more fully assimilated into the political system.

In short, in the American foreign-policy experience beginning in the 1890s and continuing for several decades, we see evidence of the relationships described in Hypotheses 12 and 13. We suggest that dissension among national leaders in regard to the national identity and the national interest contributed to nearly half a century of vacillation in the orientation of the United States toward the world environment. The pattern fluctuated between the active embroilment in world politics in the Spanish-American War and in World War I to the more traditional posture in the period before the war and the even greater efforts to avoid entangling international commitments during the 1930s, as symbolized by the Neutrality Acts. However, the cumulative effect of the imperialistic acquisitions at the turn of the century and of the gains in resources and authority resulting from World Wars I and II left the United States in an unquestionably superior position in world affairs, in which few national leaders could cling to the traditional conceptions of American national interest. A new sustained consensus among American leaders emerged in the post-World War II period; the foreign-policy posture of this consensus might be described loosely as a conservative-revisionist one. In recent years, however, important challenges have been posed to the policy directions to which most American leaders in the postwar period have been committed. Are we entering a new period of important change in American foreign policy? We turn now to an examination, from the perspective of historical dynamics, of American foreign policy in the 1970s.

American Foreign Policy in the 1970s

As we suggested at the outset of the chapter, examination of earlier phases of American foreign policy is of present-day interest not only because some of the past events, decisions, and ideas have had a continuing impact on the orientation of the United States to its world environment, but also because an analysis of patterns of continuity and change in earlier periods provides an informed basis for reflecting on continuity and change in the present and the future. This is not to say that analysis of the past provides an infallible guide to the future; as we observed in Chapter 1, valid explanation is not necessarily a sufficient basis for accurate prediction. The process of change in human events is always complex, and more so today than ever before. As one observer has aptly put it, human experience today is like going over Niagara Falls in a barrel, in comparison with the slow, evolutionary process of change that mankind has known previously.[52]

Nevertheless, the record of human experience suggests that even in more stable, unhurried times, the common failing of Man has not been that of undue brashness in making predictions about the probable course of future events, but rather that of clinging to images of reality long after the images had been outmoded by fundamental change. Thus, para-doxically, one may suggest that what is required of the concerned observer as well as of the practitioner of foreign policy today is *boldness* and imagination in reflecting on the magnitude and direction of changes that may occur, but *caution* in the claims that one makes for his predictions (in the sense of a constant receptivity to evidence that would cause one to revise his predictions).

Our purpose in the book as a whole is to encourage and to provoke the reader to ask a variety of questions about foreign policy, to suggest the kind of questions that are especially meaninful from various analytical perspectives, and to help the reader construct a framework within which at least tentative steps can be taken toward answering the questions. Our purpose for the remainder of the chapter is to encourage the reader to speculate boldly about the changes in the modern world and about the implications of these changes for American foreign policy in the 1970s. A framework for such speculation will be provided by brief allusions to current trends, viewed from the perspective of historical dynamics, and by questions about the foreign-policy implications of these trends. More elaborate and detailed appraisals of current trends, with suggestions of changes to be anticipated in the future, are provided elsewhere.[53] The brief allusions that we shall make here to current trends

---

[52] Barbara Ward (Lady Jackson), *Spaceship Earth* (New York: Columbia University Press, 1966), p. 3.

[53] The ubiquitous Herman Kahn, an important representative of foreign-policy analysis from a strategic perspective, as noted earlier in the book, is here coauthor, with Anthony J. Wiener and associates at the Hudson Institute, of one of the most ambitious and detailed efforts to apply the perspective of historical dynamics to fore-casting future trends. The results are described in *The Year 2000: A Framework for*

identify only a few scattered highlights, but they may be sufficient to trigger further reflections on the events that one has experienced or on the developments to be anticipated in the future.

What patterns of continuity or change in American foreign policy can be anticipated in the 1970s? Has a stable posture of the United States toward its world environment been established, or has the nation crossed the threshold of a new period of foreign-policy vacillation or change? If the foreign-policy orientation of the United States is changing, is it changing rapidly enough to keep abreast of the changes in the world environment? These are some of the questions that we wish the reader to consider about American foreign policy in the 1970s.

Changing World Environment

From the perspective of historical dynamics, foreign policies may be seen as a principal means by which the nation-state attempts to adapt to its geopolitical world environment and to impose a measure of control upon it in order to attain goals formulated within the political system. The environmental structure represents a pattern of both demands upon and opportunities for the national political system. In what respects and to what extent is this pattern changing in the 1970s?

Spatial Relationships   It has become a truism, but an important one, that the world is shrinking as advanced modes of transportation and communication, compounded by accelerating population growth and urbanization, bring the peoples of the world into ever closer contact. However, greater contact among peoples does not necessarily promote greater harmony, as the history of warfare among neighboring tribes or nations shows. Thus, in the nuclear and missile age, the trend has been not only of a world growing smaller, in terms of access from one part of the globe to another, but also of increasing volatility. Access has been facilitated not only for student exchanges and tourism, but also for nuclear-tipped missiles and airborne divisions of armed troops. Indeed, with such trends, some persons would even question whether the concept of a nation-state is any longer meaningful. Traditionally, the claim to sover-

---

Speculation on the Next Thirty-Three Years (New York: Crowell-Collier-Macmillan, 1967). Less inclined toward charts and graphs, but also explicit in identifying radical changes to be expected in the future, is an analysis by Peter F. Drucker, *The Age of Discontinuity* (New York: Harper & Row, 1969). An appraisal that links a review of earlier efforts at forecasting man's future to a consideration of the current impact of technological change on social and political systems is Victor C. Ferkiss, *Technological Man: The Myth and the Reality* (New York: Braziller, 1969).

eignty of a nation-state rested heavily on the inviolability of its territory; now, all nation-states are vulnerable to enormous destruction well within their borders.[54] At the very least, it is clear that traditional principles of war provide little guidance to policy makers anticipating the problems of possible nuclear war.[55] Such traditional principles, which stemmed largely from the writings of Jomini and Clausewitz and rested heavily on a two-dimensional depiction of battle strategy and on utilization of geographic barriers such as oceans and mountains, became largely outmoded by technological advances that enable the full utilization of the third, or vertical, dimension by aircraft and missiles.

At the cultural level, spatial relationships in the world environment are also changing. Marshall McLuhan depicts the current trend as moving us toward a "global village," where social mores and attitudes, as well as facts, become shared throughout the world.[56] Although the cultures and subcultures of the world remain far more heterogeneous than McLuhan's concept of a global village implies, the concept nonetheless gives insights by pointing to radical changes that are occurring in patterns of communication and interaction on a global scale. The transistor radio bringing news of the world to peasants in the rice paddies of southeast Asia or to tribes in the jungles of Africa and the satellite relay of televisions broadcasts across oceans and continents are symbolic of the fantastic developments in technology that have created a worldwide network of communications. For instance, Barbara Ward Jackson reports that she received the news of the assassination of President Kennedy immediately after the event, although she was then visiting Zambia (at that time Northern Rhodesia). A large political gathering that she was attending was halted so that the audience could join in prayer and hymns for the American President; in subsequent hours and days, people throughout the world were able to share, through radio or television, the shock and grief of the American people.[57]

New modes of communication are not only the product of innovation but also important stimulants of change. Daniel Lerner's analysis of the erosion of traditional social structures in the Middle East, for example, revealed that the intrusion of modern communications media into previ-

[54] Implications of the change are examined at length by John H. Hertz, *International Politics in the Atomic Age* (New York: Columbia University Press, 1959).

[55] For an appraisal of some of the classical "principles of war" in the modern era, see Bernard Brodie, *Strategy in the Missile Age* (Princeton, N.J.: Princeton University Press, 1959).

[56] H. Marshall McLuhan and Quentin Fiore, *War and Peace in the Global Village* (New York: Bantam, 1968). See also *The Medium Is the Message* (New York: Random House, 1967), by the same authors.

[57] Ward, p. 5.

ously insulated villages generates "psychic mobility"—a desire to depart from traditionally assigned roles within the social system—as well as physical mobility.[58] More broadly, modern communication and transportation have contributed throughout developing areas to a revolution of rising expectations, by making available goods, services, and opportunities previously unknown or unavailable.

Supply of and Demand for Natural, Material, and Human Resources

The revolution of rising expectations has international, as well as intranational, implications. New markets and new trade patterns emerge in response to new demands. Moreover, governments and entrepreneurs of poor nation-states seek to tap the wealth and the skills of the rich for rapid modernization, thereby helping the rulers of the poor nation-states to cope with the demands and expectations of their people. However, governments in the so-called developing nations have rarely been able to keep abreast of spiraling internal demands. Symbolic substitutes (such as mass rallies, charismatic appeals, and allegations of an external threat) for substantive goods sometimes gain time for the rulers; yet, chronic instability punctuated by the *coup d'état* has been the rule rather than the exception in poor nation-states. Turbulence like that in the Balkans in the period before World War I, but on a broader geographic scale, has served to invite intervention by more powerful nations, thereby exacerbating power rivalry and increasing the risks of general war.

Demands upon resources within developing nation-states, and from these nation-states to the rest of the world, are increasing not only because of rising expectations but also because of population growth. The fact that the world's population has been growing at an exploding rate in recent years is well known.[59] Conservative projections from present trends foresee a doubling of the present world population within half a century; by comparison, nearly seventeen centuries elapsed before the number of persons on earth at the time of Christ had doubled. Less commonly recognized is the fact that the population explosion is occurring with varying intensity in various parts of the world. Specifically, the technologically less developed nation-states are experiencing population growth at a much greater rate than are the technologically advanced nation-states. In Latin America, for instance, where the population is

[58] Daniel Lerner, *The Passing of Traditional Society* (New York: Free Press, 1958).

[59] A brief, provocative, but unemotional discussion of the population problem is provided by Philip M. Hauser, *World Population Problems*, in the Headline Series, no. 174 (New York: Foreign Policy Association, Dec. 1965). Paul R. Ehrlich has written a slightly longer discussion, with a tone of great urgency, in *The Population Bomb* (New York: Ballantine, 1968).

increasing at a rate of about 3 percent per year, the current population will double within twenty-four years if the rate is maintained. In contrast, at the present growth rate of slightly over 1 percent, the population of the United States would take over sixty years to double.

Although the pattern of demand for goods and services reflects a revolutionary upward trend in the developing nations, the pattern of supply —especially of material resources and human skills—reflects vast inadequacies in most developing nation-states, although in a number of instances large reserves of untapped natural resources exist. In contrast, the nations that have already made the most impressive strides technologically possess the capital and the know-how to reach even more impressive technological achievements. Moreover, the more technologically advanced nation-states are entering a post-industrial era.[60] With developments in medicine and surgery, such as the transplantation of human organs, including the heart, daring new ventures in the exploration of outer space or of the suboceanic depths, and the successive generations of computers, new creations and developments are emerging from the world's leading scientific and technological powers (notably the United States, the Soviet Union, and Japan) at a rate that makes even science fiction continually obsolete. Although some of the new knowledge and wealth of the technologically advanced nation-states is shared with others, through bilateral or multilateral assistance programs, UNESCO, and through the other specialized agencies sponsored by the United Nations, the current trend continues to be one in which the rich get richer and the poor, at least in relative terms, get poorer (in many instances in absolute terms as well, if the scattered projections of severe famine are borne out).

International Patterns of Authority and "Rules of the Game"
Change in the structure of the geopolitical world environment is apparent also in patterns of international authority and in the rules of the game of international politics. The relatively simple pattern of bipolarity in the early post-World War II period, with authority concentrated hierarchically around two superpowers, has given way to a more fluid and complex pattern. The United States and the Soviet Union remain superpowers, especially in their military and technological capabilities, but the international system has become multipolar, in that other nation-states have attained widely recognized status as great powers (China, Japan, West Germany, France, and Great Britain), establishing a high degree of

---

[60] The term is Daniel Bell's. See his "Notes on the Post-Industrial Society," *The Public Interest*, 6, 7 (Winter and Spring 1967), 24–35, 102–118. The term has also been adopted by Kahn and Wiener in *The Year 2000*.

autonomy in policy making from the superpowers and exerting influence of their own over the affairs of other nation-states.

China, especially, seems likely to assert increasing authority in world affairs in coming years. It is virtually inescapable that the diplomatic isolation of China from much of the world will be broken in the 1970s through actions that may include admission to the United Nations.[61] Whether an expanded world role for Communist China will have a disruptive or a stabilizing effect on the international environment in the long run is not clear. It is clear, however, that broader recognition of the legitimate status of the Peking regime is likely in international affairs. Especially to peoples of the developing areas, China offers the example of a nation that has made an impressively rapid transition from an underdeveloped economy to one with many of the accouterments of modern technology, and of a maverick state whose denunciation of both of the two superpowers of the world has broad "underdog" appeal.

Quite apart from the growing prominence of China, the pattern of authority in international politics has shifted radically in developing areas in recent decades with the virtual demise of colonialism and the proliferation of newly independent nation-states. Membership in the United Nations, for example, has more than doubled since the organization was founded; most of the new members have come from the developing areas, especially Africa. The mushrooming of new nation-states greatly complicates the structure of the world environment and the process of international politics, but, as in the assessment of an expanded role for China, one's assessment of the probable impact of new nation-states on international politics in general must take into account disintegrative as well as integrative possibilities.

On the one hand, as we have noted above, demands upon the governments of new nation-states often increase at a rate that exceeds their capacities to meet the demands, thereby inducing chronic instability. The proliferation of new nation-states experiencing such a plight is perhaps one indication in world affairs of what Kenneth E. Boulding, borrowing from the natural sciences, has termed "the entropy trap," that is, the growing potential for chaos.[62] The widening economic gap, noted

[61] Since its founding, the United Nations has included representation by the Nationalist faction of Chinese, in spite of protests since 1949 by the Communist regime that they were the rightful representatives of China. Admission to the UN of representatives of the Communist government in Peking, therefore, could be accomplished by acknowledging that regime's claims to the existing China membership slot; alternately, a compromise agreement might be reached for admission of the Peking regime while retaining a seat for the government in Taiwan.

[62] Kenneth E. Boulding, *The Meaning of the 20th Century: The Great Transition* (New York: Harper & Row, 1964), chap. 7.

above, between rich nations and poor nations, seems likely to increase the potential for chaos.

Yet the possibility exists that regional groupings of nation-states, such as the Organization of African Unity (OAU) and the Association of Southeast Asian Nations (ASEAN), may strengthen the economies and political institutions of member nation-states, thereby exerting a stabilizing influence on the world environment in general. It is also possible that international organizations such as the World Health Organization (WHO), the United Nations Conference on Trade and Development (UNCTAD, the permanent organ of which is the Trade and Development Board), or the International Development Association (IDA, an affiliate of the World Bank) may be given expanded authority by their members in the future, thus exerting a counterweight to the disintegrative tendencies in the world community. Moreover, growing demand for international action in areas such as arms control or joint monetary planning and regulation may lead to the creation of new international organizations. In the foreseeable future, however, regional groupings of nation-states seem likely to remain loose coalitions rather than cohesive federations, and international organizations seem likely to remain subject to the severe restrictions imposed by the various self-interests of their members.[63]

Changing Capability Estimates and Changing Goal-Values

Dramatic changes in the world environment represent a rapidly changing pattern of American foreign-policy problems. Significant changes in the structure of the geopolitical environment alter the basis on which leaders estimate the adaptive capabilities of the nation-state; moreover, the images that leaders hold of the national identity and the national interest become subject to revision in relationship to changing patterns of demands and opportunities. Often, however, there is a considerable lag between the emergence of new problems and their recognition. At the present time, among Americans in general, including those in positions of leadership, there is a vast range of foreign-policy attitudes and beliefs. Some persons continue to debate the issues of the day in terms of the reality of a generation or more ago; they show little comprehension of the many dimensions of change or of the probable consequences of the various foreign policies that they espouse.

Differing conceptions of a changing reality are one factor that has stimulated dissension among national leaders. In addition, the composi-

[63] For a detailed assessment of trends, see Ernst B. Haas, *Beyond the Nation-State: Functionalism and International Organization* (Stanford, Calif.: Stanford University Press, 1964).

tion of American national leadership is changing. Sectors of society long underrepresented in the national leadership, such as blacks and youths of college age, are gaining direct or indirect access to leadership positions. However, perhaps more important than the successes of these groups are the tensions generated by their demands. Analogous to the experience in developing nations, there is a gap between the degree of political mobilization of dissident elements of the society in recent years and the degree of assimilation of dissident leaders into the authority structure of the society.[64] The mobilization-assimilation gap represents a challenge to the legitimacy, and thus to the stability, of existing political institutions, thereby serving also to pressure present political leaders to display greater responsiveness to the demands of newly mobilized groups in order to enhance the legitimacy and stability of political institutions.

To a sizable number of Americans, especially among the college population, American technology and military resources have come to symbolize not key elements of world leadership, but perverse symbols of decadence in contemporary American culture. Whereas the traditional images of the American national identity and national interest were founded on a Puritan ethos, identifying a unique destiny for Americans in world affairs, many alienated members of contemporary American society purport to reject everything in the Puritan heritage. Indeed, far from seeing the American national identity as that of a chosen people, many contemporary critics have viewed the United States as a basically corrupt and decadent society, with the traditional values contributing to the corruption.

It appears that not many Americans in positions of national leadership are ready to accept the allegations of national decadence or to indulge the feelings of collective guilt characteristic of some of the most vociferous critics. Nevertheless, among the national leaders as among the society as a whole, there appears to be a widespread sense of doubt and malaise about goal-values that were once widely regarded as inviolable.

The evidence, alluded to above, of profound changes in the 1970s in the structure of the world environment and in estimates by American national leadership of national capabilities and goal-values points to a high probability of important changes in the foreign-policy orientation of the United States in the 1970s. But important normative as well as

---

[64] For a discussion of the "mobilization-assimilation gap," with special reference to the development of nations, see Karl W. Deutsch, *Nationalism and Social Communication* (Cambridge, Mass.: Technology Press, the Massachusetts Institute of Technology, and Wiley, New York, 1953).

empirical questions arise as one attempts to identify the probable direction, magnitude, and decisiveness of change. Can a coherent foreign policy be formulated in an era of domestic turbulence? Will anxieties generated by domestic crises provide a climate conducive to a more belligerent foreign policy by the United States? Alternatively, will the resource and energy demands of domestic crises lead to a withdrawal from American commitments abroad? Will United States and Soviet technological supremacy lead to increased cooperation between the two superpowers in such endeavors as the exploration of outer space, or to increased competition, friction, and danger of nuclear war? Will American policy makers show more sympathy, or less, to the aspirations of peoples in developing areas for revolutionary change? What will be the American response, for instance, to revolutionary *coups d'état*? Will proportionately more, or less, of America's resources be committed to foreign aid and technical assistance? What portion of American economic aid will be devoted to supplementing military security programs? Will American policy makers make a greater effort than in the past to channel American foreign policy through the institutional mechanisms of international organization, or will the American commitment to international organization become weakened? These are but a few of the questions that must be answered if one is to identify the full dimensions of a changing American foreign-policy posture in the years ahead. A country-by-country survey of foreign-policy trends in the 1970s would reveal more completely the complex and turbulent maze of events of which the foreign-policy posture of the 1970s will be composed.

Concluding Observations

The perspective of historical dynamics has the virtue of sensitizing one to broad currents of change, which are often lost in discussions of strategic doctrine and often obscured by details if one focuses on particular foreign-policy decisions or crises. The perspective of historical dynamics is fundamental to an understanding of foreign-policy adaptation to a changing world environment. However, the paradox for policy makers (and thus, for all of us) is that whatever their ability to think in broad terms, relating an understanding of the past to projections of future trends, they must make the thousands of daily decisions of which, in time, new patterns of continuity or change will be composed. Although it is choice rather than fate that points the way to the future, the choices that are made can never be totally geared to a coherent vision of the future; in foreign policy, they are never totally preplanned, not only because of the high degree of unpredictability in the world environment, but also because foreign-policy decision making is not a matter of abstract application of reason to problem-solving situations; rather, decision making is a political process. In the following section of the book, we examine the process of foreign-policy decision making and the structures that are involved in the process. The decision-making perspective for analysis of foreign policy provides an important complement to the perspectives of strategic analysis and of historical dynamics that already have been introduced.

Summary of Hypotheses Developed in Part III

9. When the leaders of a nation-state are generally dissatisfied with the existing environmental structure—
   a. The nation-state will assume a radical-revisionist posture in relation to the world environment if policy makers estimate that the adaptive capabilities of the nation-state are high.
   b. The nation-state will assume a dependent-revisionist posture in relation to world environment if policy makers estimate that the adaptive capabilities of the nation-state are low.
10. When the leaders of a nation-state are generally satisfied with the existing environmental structure—
   a. The nation-state will assume a conservative-revisionist posture in relation to the world environment if national leaders estimate that the adaptive capabilities of the nation-state are high.
   b. The nation-state will assume a *status quo* posture in relation to the world environment if national leaders estimate that the adaptive capabilities of the nation-state are low.
11. As long as consensus prevails among national leaders in the images that they maintain of the national identity and the national interest, there will be continuity in the orientation of the nation-state toward its world environment.
12. Changes in foreign policy sufficient to produce a sustained change in the orientation of the nation-state toward its world environment will occur only after a period of dissension among national leaders in terms of their images of the national identity and the national interest and after the formulation of a new consensus.
13. An existing consensus among national leaders regarding the national identity and the national interest will be dissolved by—
   a. Significant changes in the structure of the geopolitical environment.

b. Substantial change in the estimates that national leaders have of the nation-state's adaptive capabilities.
c. Substantial alteration of the composition of the national leadership within a short span of time.

Part IV

Decision-Making Perspectives

Thus far we have considered two perspectives for analyzing foreign policy: the perspective of strategic analysis and the perspective of historical dynamics. We now turn to a third possibility for viewing foreign policy, the decision-making perspective. In analysis from this perspective, a particular foreign-policy decision or a series of decisions is the primary object of analysis.

Many readers will be familiar with the term "decision-making approach," as applied to the ideas of Richard C. Snyder and a number of his colleagues[1] who have attempted to develop a conceptual framework that would be useful in the identification of key variables and the development and testing of hypotheses in rigorous

[1] Richard C. Snyder et al., Foreign Policy Decision Making (New York: Free Press, 1962). An interesting and thorough application of the decision-making approach to empirical research is Glenn D. Paige, The Korean Decision (New York: Free Press, 1968).

empirical research. Although their writings form an important component of the theoretical foundation on which Part IV of the book draws, it is necessary to note that no attempt is made here to explain the details of Snyder's conceptual framework or to pattern our discussion after it. Instead, the perspective for analysis that we shall describe in Part IV is broadly defined. If we were to identify analyses of American foreign policy that fit into the category of analysis from a decision-making perspective, they would include not only the works of Snyder and his colleagues, but a large number of other works that reflect other bodies of theory, such as the theories of the political process in the Bentley-Truman tradition, systems theory, organization theory, social-psychological theory, and economic theory. In short, a decision-making perspective, as we shall use the term, is not synonymous with a particular decision-making approach, such as that described by Snyder and his colleagues. As we observed much earlier in the book, our purpose is neither to engage in critical analysis of particular works nor to provide a bibliographical essay, but simply to alert the reader to how the application of a particular perspective in analysis of foreign policy can affect the kinds of data one gathers and the kinds of conclusions he derives from his investigation.

Moving from the perspective of historical dynamics to a decision-making perspective means, in a sense, to forsake a view of the whole "forest" in order to study particular "trees," with all the dangers of myopia that such study implies. However, by immersing ourselves in the detail afforded by close scrutiny of the structure and process of foreign policy in relation to particular decisions, we also avoid some of the dangers of misperception or oversimplification associated with the perspective of historical dynamics. For instance, no longer is the nation-state as a whole treated as the primary unit of analysis. Instead, we recognize that policy decisions are made not by nation-states (the idea of a nation-state is an abstraction, after all), but by people, individually or collectively. Thus, much of our attention in Part IV is focused on the behavior of individuals, groups, and organizations.

But in order to help conceptualize how a vast and diverse number of individuals and groups interact with one another to produce foreign-policy decisions, we shall introduce another abstraction into our discussion in Part IV: the concept of a political system. Not all writers whose works might be termed analyses from a decision-making perspective express themselves in the language of systems theory; but the concept of a political system is a useful one to employ in depicting the foreign-policy process, for reasons that we shall indicate in Chapter 7.

7

The Process
of Making
Foreign-Policy
Decisions

Shorthand phrases such as "the machinery of government" or "decision-making machinery" are part of our popular vocabulary for discussing foreign policy. Moreover, computers and other mechanical devices have assumed an important role in foreign-policy operations. Yet, neither semantic shorthand nor technological developments have taken foreign policy out of the hands of man and put it into machines. Foreign policy is made by human beings, as we have emphasized from the first chapter of the book and as we will emphasize further later in the present chapter. However, in order to highlight how and why foreign-policy decisions are actually made, we shall begin this chapter by pushing the metaphor suggested above to an extreme.

207

An Imaginary Ideal Machine for Making Policy

Let us suppose that foreign policy decisions *were* made by machine. Or, let us suppose that we are able to prevail upon some modern-day Rube Goldberg, perhaps a whiz kid, and a few engineers to construct a miraculously sophisticated machine that could make foreign policy decisions independently, performing each requisite task with the maximum efficiency. We might as well also devise an acronym for the machine; let us dub our fanciful creation the Imaginary Ideal Machine for Making Policy—in short, the IIMMP. What tasks would we want the IIMMP to perform, and what performance criteria would we establish for a completely efficient decision-making machine? In other words, what tasks are involved in the process of making foreign-policy decisions, and what is the most efficient performance of such tasks that we can imagine?

Foreign-policy decisions are made in response to events and problems that have occurred or are anticipated in the world environment. The first need, therefore, is for information about what is happening in the world. Consequently, our first request to the designers of the IIMMP would be to construct something analogous to a super-radar, which would be constantly *scanning* the geopolitical environment to observe world events. Because events occur at a rapid pace, simultaneously in distant parts of the globe, the IIMMP would satisfy our demands for perfection only if it could fully detect everything in all parts of the world at all times.

Second, phenomena that are observed in the geopolitical environment need to be identified, classified, and interpreted. Some demands are urgent; others are routine. Some situations affect vital interests; others are remote to policy concerns. Some problems are of such complexity as to require detailed analysis and study; others can be solved simply and quickly. The process of determining the nature of a situation and of classifying it may be described as *coding*. An IIMMP would have a capability of coding data with such reliability that threats to foreign-policy interests would be instantly detected, data relevant to ongoing problems would be identified for processing to appropriate channels in the decision-making structure, and data not immediately relevant would be labeled as such. Moreover, the coding system would be so flexible that classification criteria would change according to changing needs.

When foreign-policy phenomena have been observed and coded, the information needs to be transmitted to the location where it can be analyzed in relationship to other information in weighing alternative courses of action. In order to meet our standards of perfection, we would ask the craftsmen who design the IIMMP to insure that *transmission* of data occurs instantaneously from the time data are gathered and coded, with no loss or distortion of information in transmission. Moreover, transmission should be clear and unambiguous. In the communications idiom, the IIMMP must provide transmission that is free of "noise" and immune to "jamming."

Not all observations of world events have immediate relevance; yet, information that is of no importance at present may be of considerable importance in the future. Moreover, the effective weighing of decision-making alternatives involves a consideration of events and decisions of the past. A system of making foreign-policy decisions, therefore, should have some capacity for *storage* of information for future use and for *recall* of information as needed. Thus, we shall insist that the IIMMP have an unlimited memory storage as well as a capacity for instant and infinite recall whenever a problem arises to which stored data are relevant.

Making decisions involves *weighing alternative courses* of action. The IIMMP would be able to recognize all alternative courses of action that are logically possible in relation to any problem. In weighing various alternatives, our IIMMP would have the ability to handle problems of infinite complexity. That is, unlike a cash register or an ordinary desk calculator, which can perform only a few relatively simple operations involving a small number of variables, our IIMMP would be like the most advanced computer, able to deal with an enormous number of variables at once. Moreover, it would be perfectly rational in the sense that the course of action selected would always be the one for which the estimate of probable gain in terms of the values of society was greatest relative to the estimate of risk of loss, and in the sense that the means selected to carry out the policy would be appropriate to policy objectives.

Foreign-policy decision making involves not only a choice among alternative courses of action, but also a *commitment of resources* for a given course, as well as such pronouncements and communications as are needed to effect *coordination* in the implementation of the decision. Once a choice among alternatives was made by our IIMMP, its remarkable performance would be such that it could instantly generate communications necessary for the implementation of the decision. Resources committed for the decision would be adequate to carrying the task through to completion; they would never be in excess of those required.

Finally, successful foreign policy is more than a matter of making wise choices. It also requires thorough following through. Errors in judgment or in implementation must be corrected, and, as the situation changes, adjustments must be made. Thus, a system of *feedback* must be developed, by which ongoing actions and programs can be monitored. We would insist to the designers of the IIMMP that the machine be instantly self-corrective. That is to say, appraisal of the consequences of every output from the IIMMP would take place continuously. Any corrective actions necessary to improve the solution to the problem at hand or to accommodate new situations would be stimulated immediately.

The attributes of the IIMMP are summarized in Table 2. The IIMMP would provide comprehensive scanning; reliable and flexible coding; instantaneous transmission of data without loss or distortion; infinite memory storage and instant recall; an exhaustive consideration of alternative courses of action; unlimited problem-solving capacity; perfect rationality in the choice among alternatives; instant implementation of the decision, with economy of resources; and an instantaneous system of feedback.

Our flight of fancy in depicting an imaginary ideal machine for making policy has been designed to serve two analytical purposes: first, to indicate the tasks involved in making foreign-policy decisions, and second, to point out the human limitations in the performance of these tasks by stipulating ideal standards that might prevail in an imaginary world. The next two sections of the chapter, in which we discuss the concept of a political system and the foreign-policy decision-making process, are devoted to advancing these two analytical purposes further. Specifically, we shall be concerned with specifying what tasks are performed in the process of making foreign policy in the real world; with describing the structures that are involved in the performance of these various tasks in American foreign-policy making; and with suggesting why and to what

TABLE 2

Capabilities of an Imaginary Ideal Machine for Making Policy

Task	Performance of IIMMP
Scanning	Perfect in detection, comprehensive
Coding	Reliable, flexible
Transmission	Instantaneous, undistorted
Storage and recall	Infinite storage; instant recall
Recognition of courses of action	Exhaustive
Decision making	Unlimited in problem solving, perfectly rational
Implementation	Instantaneous and coordinating; perfectly economical in use of resources
Feedback	Instantaneously self-corrective

extent performance by human beings of the tasks falls short of the standards stipulated for an IIMMP.

The Concept of a Political System

Although human beings do not constitute a machine for making foreign policy, it is fair to describe the collective actions of those who participate in the foreign-policy process as constituting a system. Indeed, it is useful to define the foreign-policy process in terms of a broader political system, in relation to which the foreign-policy process performs certain vital functions. We must preface such a definition with the observation, however, that a number of equally correct definitions of foreign policy might be constructed; to quibble over which of many possible definitions is the truest would be to engage in empty dialogue. A definition is merely an analytical tool.

Although definitions are neither true nor false, clearly definitions of a given term may differ from one another in their usefulness. For example, a definition that employs precise language is usually preferable to a definition shrouded in ambiguity, unless the purpose (for example, in love or diplomacy) is to deceive, to confuse, or to establish a false sense of agreement, rather than to clarify. Moreover, a definition that basically conforms to widespread conventional usage is usually preferable to a definition that ignores conventional usage, but not always (if the purpose is scientific inquiry, for instance, where conventional language is inadequate to technical needs). Thus, definitions are useful depending upon the context in which they are used and upon the purposes for which they are designed. Rather than engage in a meaningless search for the true definition of the term "foreign policy," therefore, we shall attempt to describe the concept in ways that are useful for our present analytical purposes.

It is useful for our present purposes to retain some of the emphasis of the preceding chapter by describing foreign policy in terms of the functions that the foreign-policy process performs for a national political system. Repeating a definition used in Chapter 6, we may say that the foreign-policy process is a mechanism for the adaptation of the political system to its geopolitical environment and for imposing a measure of control upon the environment in order to achieve the goals of the system.

We have alluded to a political system several times in preceding chapters, and the concept will be familiar to many readers. Nevertheless, some further discussion of the concept at this point is essential to develop a picture of the foreign-policy process from a decision-making perspective.

Politics, as an important aspect of American life, reflects the diversity and complexity that characterize America. Is the nature of American politics to be discovered in Washington, D. C., or in Peoria, Illinois? In Gary, Indiana, or in Biloxi, Mississippi? To borrow from Stephen Vincent Benét's invocation in his epic poem, *John Brown's Body*, ". . . all of these you are, and each is partly you, and none is false, and none is wholly true." [1] No single description or analysis can capture all the dimensions of the American political system. To quote from Benét's invocation again, his description of the "American muse" might apply equally to the American political system: ". . . So many men have tried to understand but only made it smaller with their art, because you are as various as your land. . . ." [2]

Although the phenomena that constitute American politics are complex and ever-changing, the concept of a system provides a means to reduce the complex reality to intellectually manageable proportions. By thinking of political activity in terms of a system, we do not capture all its fascinating intricacies and nuances, but we can create a first approximation of reality, an abstract model that suggests what the overall political structure in America looks like and how the various institutions and structures interrelate. A simple diagrammatic representation of the American foreign-policy process is depicted in Figure 3. This conceptualization of the political system will be elaborated below.

The concept of a system has become increasingly prevalent in the social sciences in recent years.[3] In fact, some persons see it as a potential unifying framework for the natural and social sciences, since there is a certain similarity or isomorphism in the relationships observed in the various disciplines that can be categorized as systems.[4] For example,

[1] From *Selected Works of Stephen Vincent Benét,* p. 5. Published by Holt, Rinehart and Wiston, Inc. Copyright 1927, 1928, by Stephen Vincent Benét. Copyright renewed © 1955 by Rosemary Carr Benét. Reprinted by permission of Brandt & Brandt.

[2] Benet, p. 3.

[3] A small sample of works in the social sciences utilizing the systems concept and contributing to its refinement includes the following. David Easton, *The Political System* (New York: Knopf, 1953). Easton, *A Framework for Political Analysis* (Englewood Cliffs, N.J.: Prentice-Hall, 1965). W. C. Mitchell, *The American Polity* (New York: Free Press, 1962). Gabriel A. Almond, "Introduction" to Almond and James S. Coleman, eds., *The Politics of Developing Nations* (Princeton, N.J.: Princeton University Press, 1960). Morton A. Kaplan, *System and Process in International Politics* (New York: Wiley, 1957). Karl W. Deutsch, *The Nerves of Government* (New York: Free Press, 1963).

[4] For example, see Ludwig von Bertalanffy, "General System Theory," *General Systems,* 1 (1965), 1–10; and in J. David Singer, ed., *Human Behavior and International Politics* (Chicago: Rand McNally, 1965), pp. 20–31.

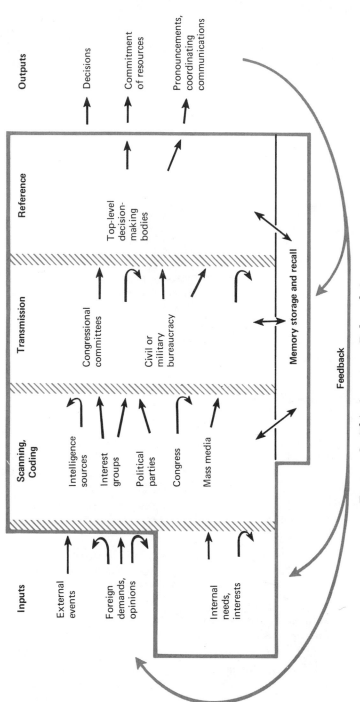

Figure 3 The American Political System

when we talk of solar systems, postal systems, or heating systems, we are using one common organizing analytical concept, that of a system. What does this concept imply?

Purposeful Activity of the Whole System

First, the concept of a system implies a series of component parts that together are capable of performing some kind of purposeful activity. Thus, although Winston Churchill's six volumes on World War II are components of a set, this set is not a system, since the books themselves perform no activity. We would, however, consider the network of pipes, furnace, air vents, and thermostat in a house a system, because the aggregation of components performs the purposeful activity of heating the house.

It is also meaningful to speak of a political system, consisting of an enormous number of parts, the key activity of the system being to make authoritative decisions for a society. Those decisions that identify the goals of the nation-state in its external environment, the instruments and resources to be allocated in pursuit of these goals, and the response of the political system to the demands of the external environment are foreign-policy decisions.

Functional Interrelationships of Parts

Second, the system concept implies a functional interrelationship of the major components of the system. That is, each of the major components performs a function upon which the efficient maintenance of the system as a whole is dependent. For example, keeping an automobile running efficiently requires more than refilling the gas tank; the engine, generator, carburetor, and other major components of the automobile all perform distinct but interrelated functions, upon which the overall performance of the automobile is dependent.

Similarly, within any political system, we find functionally interrelated components. Especially in political systems that have existed over a period of time, we can identify particular institutions that perform functions essential to the system as a whole. Within the American political system, for instance, the institution of Congress exists to perform essential rule-making functions for the system as a whole. The institution of the presidency exists to perform a number of vital functions, including the initiation of legislation, checks on Congress through veto power, supervision of the implementation of rules, and so forth. A vast civil and military bureaucracy exists for the implementation of decisions, for planning, and for coordinating public policy. A judiciary exists for the adjudication of disputes. Interest groups and political parties provide institutionalized means for debating policy issues and for the formulation of policy alternatives, as well as for the recruitment of presidential candidates and members of Congress. An electoral subsystem has been created to provide means for orderly change and succession in government.

Functional interdependence of these major components within a political system means that the effective functioning of the system as a whole is dependent on the effective functioning of the major components. If one of these were destroyed or disabled, it would not necessarily mean the destruction of the system as a whole, but any radical change in a major component of a system will produce a radical change in operation of the system as a whole.

The reason that systems can sometimes survive when a major component ceases to function is that, like organic systems, they have demonstrated a remarkable capacity to create functional equivalents. For example, as President, Woodrow Wilson was incapacitated for months to the point of being unable to perform the functions of the presidency. The American political system survived, but only because functional equivalents for the President were created, such as his wife, his advisers, or others in government. The death of a President in office has not meant the destruction or breakdown of the American political system, but only because the office was not left vacant for more than a few hours and because functional equivalents to the presidency were provided in the meantime.

The System and Its Environment

To relate the third point to be made about systems, we have to introduce the distinction between open and closed systems. Open systems are those in which the operation of the various components is affected by the environment in which the system exists. A closed system is one unaffected by the environment, or one that, at least for theoretical purposes, is considered in isolation from its environment.

In speaking of a political system, and of most organic systems, we are talking about open systems. Therefore, the third implication of political systems is their relationship to the environment. As an open system, it interacts with its environment through the receipt of inputs, in the form of demands and supportive actions from the environment, and through outputs, which represent efforts by the system to adapt to or to control its environment. The process of translating inputs into outputs is a decision-making process. In a heating system in a house, the amount of heat registered on the thermometer is translated into a command to open or close the heating vents, or to keep them in their present position. Analytically, what is happening in such a situation is that information that has been received as input is being interpreted, and a decision is being made by the system on the basis of the interpretation, which, in the case of a heating system, is a prearranged setting of the thermostat.

Once a decision has been made and action taken by a system, that action—that is, the output—becomes part of the environment. The environment has been altered by the output, although in some instances its impact on the environment may be insignificant. Nevertheless, the relationship between a system and its environment is dynamic and reciprocal: the environment influences the system; the system influences the environment; and the changed environment again influences the system. For example, as more heat is generated by a heating system, the house becomes warmer, and the environment has been changed. The mercury in the thermometer now rises in response to the change, and the output has contributed to a new input into the system. This information in turn is interpreted; a new decision is made by the system by closing the vents and stopping the heat flow.

In a political system, the decision-making process is obviously infinitely more complicated, although an analogy clearly exists—inputs are received, interpreted, and translated into outputs. The outputs become part of the environment, which in turn produces subsequent inputs. The component tasks of the process were suggested in our earlier discussion of the IIMMP, and are depicted in simplified form in Figure 3. At this point, by indicating further what is involved in the performance of these tasks in a political system, we may call attention to some of the performance limitations that a political system, as distinguished from an IIMMP, experiences.

The Foreign-Policy Decision-Making Process

Scanning

Hundreds of thousands of events are occurring hourly in the world environment. In contrast to our fictitious IIMMP, no political system in the real world can possibly keep abreast of all these occurrences, much less respond to them all. However, just as in the design of the IIMMP we depicted a radar-like mechanism to perform the task of scanning the geopolitical environment, so we find, on a much spottier basis, a similar scanning function performed in real political systems. The function is performed by diplomatic personnel, intelligence agents, military men, foreign correspondents, and a host of others whose daily responsibilities lead them to scan world events.

To the extent that a political system is alerted to some event, action, or change in its environment, the system receives an input. For example, as soon as representatives of the American government in Korea got the first news early Sunday morning, June 25, 1950, of the North Korean attack, an input had been fed into the American political system. Then, in turn, the news was immediately sent to the American ambassador in Seoul, the State Department in Washington, Secretary of State Acheson, and President Truman. As additional coordinating communications were made at various levels of government and in various locations—Seoul, Tokyo, Washington—the picture quickly became more complicated. Furthermore, concurrently with the transmission of this single input into the political system, thousands of other inputs were being processed, competing with one another for the attention of policy makers.[5]

Thus, if even a fraction of the phenomena that are occurring in the world is detected and fed into the political system, the amount of information passing through its network of communications at any given time is likely to be enormous. This point can be appreciated with the help of another mental image. Supposing that we were able to produce a huge map of the world, large enough to cover the entire wall of an auditorium. Supposing further that on the map we were able to plot the location of every person and installation able to feed information about occurrences in the world environment into the American political system. What we would have, of course, would be thousands of dots reaching to nearly every part of the map. Now let us be more ingenious in our map construction, and for every location of an intelligence source, place a small light bulb, with wires leading from each of the bulbs back to data gathering and processing locations (for example, several of the major capitals of the world, and geographic crossroads such as Honolulu), and to the governmental "nerve center" in Washington. Imagine now that for every impulse received in the form of information about some event by one of the intelligence sources, the bulb at that location would light up.

[5] A classic description of the demands upon the State Department in particular is provided by Charlton Ogburn, Jr., in a report prepared under the auspices of The Brookings Institution for the Senate Committee on Foreign Relations, and reprinted in a number of sources. See U.S. Congress, Senate Committee on Foreign Relations, *United States Foreign Policy: Compilation of Studies*, 86th Cong., 2d sess., 1960, vol. 2, app. C, pp. 970–975. Also, Ogburn, "The Flow of Policy-Making in the Department of State," *Readings in the Making of American Foreign Policy*, eds. Andrew M. Scott and Raymond H. Dawson (New York: Crowell-Collier-Macmillan, 1965), pp. 284–293.

(Readers who have seen the simulation of the battle of Gettysburg or Waterloo on the illuminated map at either location will picture the scene clearly.) Imagine further that every time information was transmitted from a source to data gathering locations and to the nerve center in Washington, the wire between the points would be illuminated. The picture which we would have created would resemble an enormous nervous system; at any given instant, hundreds of bulbs would be flashing, and an intricate web of illuminated wires would define an enormous flow of information to the governmental "nerve center" in Washington. To cite but one tangible index of the information flow, Secretary of State Dean Rusk has indicated that about 1300 cables are received at the Department of State daily.[6] Later in the book, we shall discuss problems such as "system overload," which result from the magnitude of the informational demands that are made upon the political system.

Inputs may be generated from within the system as well as from the external environment. Such endogenous inputs are depicted in Figure 3 by the internal needs and interests shown there by arrows within the dotted line that represents the system's boundaries. An example from Chapter 1 of an endogenous input would be a request from the Ohio County Republican Women's Club in Wheeling, West Virginia, to Senator Joe McCarthy early in 1950 to address the group. Other, more recent examples would include a group of college students demonstrating in protest of college policy permitting the Dow Chemical Company (producers of napalm) to recruit employees on campus. Such a demonstration, like other forms of expression of opinion by individuals and groups within the society about public matters, constitutes an endogenous input into the political system.

Coding

Inputs into a political system are interpreted and classified—that is, coded. However, although we were able to postulate a coding system of perfect reliability and infinite flexibility in our IIMMP, the capability of human beings for accurate and flexible coding is limited. All of us see the world through our own beliefs, attitudes, and biases. Thus, events occurring in the world environment become distorted and sometimes repressed entirely from our consciousness. Moreover, through habit, we

[6] Testimony by Secretary Rusk before the Subcommittee on National Security Staffing and Operations (the so-called Jackson subcommittee, after its chairman, Senator Henry M. Jackson) of the Senate Committee on Government Operations, Dec. 11, 1963. The testimony has been published in Henry M. Jackson, ed., *The Secretary of State and the Ambassador* (New York: Praeger, 1964), pp. 110–129.

sometimes continue to apply the same criteria for interpreting and evaluating phenomena long after they have become outmoded by changing demands and needs.

The distortion or blocking out of information that may occur in the process of coding foreign-policy inputs is depicted in Figure 3 by hatched lines along the boundaries separating the system and its environment, which suggest a filtering process that occurs as inputs are received by the system, and by bent arrows that symbolize the distortion or rejection of incoming information. Misperception can occur at various stages from the original input all the way to the point of decision itself. General Douglas MacArthur apparently remained convinced from a time before his meeting with President Truman at Wake Island until the massive Chinese attack in late November was actually launched that the Chinese would not enter the war in Korea in a major way, in spite of evidence to the contrary flowing into his headquarters from intelligence sources in Korea. In Washington, President Truman and his various top military and civil advisers permitted themselves to believe that MacArthur's prognostication was correct—again, in spite of the evidence to the contrary that was available to them.

Transmission

Information received and coded in the political system is transmitted from one location in it to another, often through a series of stages, at each of which loss or distortion may occur. A retired American diplomat, Charles Thayer, has noted, "An American embassy is in a very real sense a switchboard for messages between Washington and a foreign government. It is duplicated by another switchboard in the host's embassy in Washington." [7] Switchboards, however, may become overloaded, and switchboard operators may get lines crossed or fall behind in processing calls. Faulty communication of information can result from breakdowns in a communications network; from habits of viewing problems or interpreting facts that have become institutionalized within a department, or a bureau, or the government as a whole; or from the personality or idiosyncrasies of a given individual. In Chapters 8 and 9, we shall comment at greater length on problems of communication that result from the characteristics of particular individuals and from attributes of bureaucracy; at this point, we simply note that only in an IIMMP does one find faultless transmission of information. In real political systems, information often becomes lost, garbled, or distorted in transmission from one

---

[7] Charles W. Thayer, *Diplomat* (New York: Harper & Row, 1959), p. 82.

person to another or from one level of bureaucracy to another. The hatched lines in Figure 3 depict a filtering process that occurs at various stages in the flow of information within a political system.

Memory Storage and Recall

All political systems have some capability for storing information for future use. Although this capability is depicted diagrammatically in Figure 3, memory storage in a political system is not embodied in a single location or a given institution. Such storage includes, in the first place, the individual memories of persons who participate in the foreign-policy process—Harry Truman's recollections of his days in the Senate, Douglas MacArthur's memories of his days as a West Point cadet, Joe Martin's thoughts about Franklin Roosevelt and the New Deal, George C. Marshall's reflections on his conversations with Chiang Kai-shek and Mao Tse-tung. The collective memories of groups and whole societies are also part of the memory storage of a political system. These may be transmitted from one generation to the next through customs, traditions, and folklore, but also through more formalized means, such as archives, books, and documents.

Although all political systems maintain some form of memory storage, they vary considerably from each other in the accuracy of stored information and in the agility with which they can recall information relevant to a problem at hand. For instance, individuals suffer lapses of memory; even very recent events are likely to be recalled imperfectly, as any reader will recognize who is familiar with attempted reconstructions of automobile accidents from the accounts of witnesses. Moreover, recall is selective. Some details are called forth, others repressed, according to the compatibility of the details with current desires, fears, and beliefs. Also institutionalized sources of memory are fallible; records may become discarded or misplaced, and procedures for calling upon stored information may prove inadequate to changing requirements.

Decision

A decision is a matter of choice. Alternatives always include, as a minimum, doing something or doing nothing. Characteristically, a major foreign-policy decision is made only after several courses of action have been considered. However, in contrast to the IIMMP, for which we postulated a capability to consider exhaustively all choices logically possible in a situation, decision makers in real political systems rarely, if ever, behave in such a manner. Rather, in a given decision-making situation, they are likely to be predisposed toward consideration of only a few of the many logically possible options, ignoring choices that would force them to reexamine basic goal-values or operational assumptions. Moreover, vital information that would alert decision makers to choices not considered may be missing.

Furthermore, even the most intelligent men and women who participate in the foreign-policy process are limited in the number of variables they are able to cope with at one time in solving problems. Thus, complex problems sometimes become oversimplified, or errors in computation and in judgment are made. Under conditions of stress, fatigue, or illness, foreign-policy decision makers, like all human beings, are subject to a further diminution of their normal capacity for solving problems.

Moreover, although we attributed perfect rationality in decision making to our IIMMP, in real political systems, not only is perfect rationality impossible, but even as an abstract standard it is inappropriate to many decision-making situations. Perfect rationality would assume a set of clearly defined goal-values and a complete set of facts that would enable decision makers to weigh the probable costs and gains of various courses of action in terms of goal-values and would allow them to assess available means in terms of their consonance with particular policy objectives. In practice, however, goal-values may be disputed among decision makers and among others within the society, or at any rate, may not be clearly defined. Moreover, rarely are all the facts relevant to a given decision available; those facts that are available often become so intertwined with values that it is impossible to distinguish a factual appraisal of a given course of action from a value judgment about its relative merits. Choices are based on the relative political influence of those who favor certain ones, not on an abstract calculus in which the best choice is deduced from the facts of the situation. The choice of the means to be employed, far from being a simple problem of finding means that will be consonant with given objectives, often becomes an important value issue in itself; thus, once again considerations of power as well as of logic are determinant.

Given limited information, the costs in time and effort to acquire additional information, the interplay of facts and values, the heated competition among different points of view, the dynamics of ongoing problems, and the fact that many policy decisions are made not by a single set of decision makers assembled in one place, but by a number of scattered individuals and groups, a process that has been termed "disjointed incrementalism" seems to provide a model preferable to that of perfect rationality.[8] In other words, policy decisions, far from representing the systematic application of pure reason to a given set of circumstances, facts, and options, characteristically represent a process of trial and error in which policy changes are made incrementally in response to the exigencies of both domestic and foreign politics.

Implementation and Feedback

The follow-through phase of action in the decision-making process is subject to the same snarls, the same imperfections in coordination, and the same breakdowns or distortions in communication that mark the prior phases. Resource allocation is likely to be based on the relative influence of those who stand to benefit from the commitment of resources, as well as from a consideration of which kinds of programs need which kinds of support. In any event, estimates of needs may be faulty, leading to waste.

Even with the optimum combination of decision and implementation, however, successful performance hinges upon adequate monitoring of actions and of subsequent changes in the situation. The links that are established between outputs from a system and subsequent inputs— including monitoring the environmental effects of the outputs and detecting subsequent environmental changes—are termed "feedback." The concept was introduced earlier, but now merits further discussion because of its importance to the overall effectiveness of a political system.

The term "feedback" has been developed especially in relation to communications systems, but it has application to any kind of open system. A homing torpedo or a ground-to-air missile provides an example of feedback familiar to most readers. The initial decision in the use of such a weapon is made with its launching in a given trajectory; the accuracy of this decision and subsequent changes in the location of the target are detected through radio signals that are sent out continually during the flight of the torpedo or missile, bounced back off the target, and interpreted by the monitoring equipment built into the torpedo or missile, which translates the signals into corrections of the course of flight.

The feedback of foreign-policy decisions to subsequent inputs from the environment is suggested in Figure 3 by an arrow at the bottom of the diagram. The series of decisions made by the American government during the first week of the Korean War illustrates the feedback process vividly. The first news of the attack by the North Korean forces was

---

[8] The decision-making strategy of "disjointed incrementalism" is described by David Braybrooke and Charles E. Lindblom, *A Strategy of Decision* (New York: Free Press, 1963).

received (as input) in Washington on Saturday, June 24, Washington time. The following day, meeting in emergency session at the urgent request (output) of the American government, the United Nations Security Council voted nine to zero (with the Soviet delegate absent) to order the North Korean government to withdraw its forces north of the 38th parallel. United Nations commissioners in Korea were asked to keep the Security Council informed of the situation and to forward recommendations of further action. The same day, Sunday, General MacArthur was authorized (adding to the output) to provide additional ammunition and supplies to the South Korean forces and to use American air and naval units to evacuate American dependents from Korea. In addition, the U.S. Seventh Fleet was ordered (as further output) to the Formosa Strait.

So far, an initial but incomplete reading of the situation in Korea had been made within the American political system. Several rapid responses had been made on the basis of the information available. These responses, in turn, had immediately altered the situation. As Allen Whiting, among others, has noted, the commitment of the United States at this point to defend Formosa from attack represented an abrupt reversal of policy that confronted the Peking government, which had been expected to invade Formosa, with choices that were "few, clear-cut, and dismal." [9] Likewise, the indication that the United States was not going to permit the Communist seizure of South Korea as a *fait accompli* doubtless led to some agonizing reappraisals of policy in Moscow, Peking, and Pyongyang (the North Korean capital). Analytically, in other words, inputs into the American political system had been translated into outputs, which in turn altered the environment. Monitoring the outputs and their impact on a rapidly changing situation would comprise subsequent inputs—a process of feedback.

The situation was changing rapidly; more information about the situation was constantly being transmitted from Korea to General MacArthur's headquarters in Tokyo and to policy makers in Washington. On Monday, General MacArthur was authorized to support the South Koreans with American air and naval forces; American ground forces had not yet been committed. On Tuesday, the UN Security Council passed a resolution, calling upon its members to furnish assistance to the Republic of Korea (South Korea) to repel the attack made upon it. On Thursday, a directive was sent from Washington to MacArthur's headquarters authorizing, in addition to the air and naval units already com-

[9] Allen S. Whiting, *China Crosses the Yalu* (New York: Crowell-Collier-Macmillan, 1960), pp. 48–49.

mitted, the use of American Army Signal Corps and Transportation Corps units in Korea, plus the limited use of combat personnel to protect facilities in the Pusan area. Although these and earlier actions (outputs) in response to the attack (input) had an impact on the situation and affected subsequent inputs (feedback), the situation continued to grow more desperate. Thus on Friday, full authorization was given to General MacArthur to commit American ground troops.

The series of decisions and actions that constituted the outputs of the American political system in response to the first input on Saturday, June 24, when the first news of the North Korean attack was received, is depicted graphically in Figure 4. Although obviously a gross oversimplification of a complex series of actions and events, it suggests the course of policy decisions and actions, like the course of a ground-to-air missile modifying its initial course in response to new signals about the changing location of a moving target. The American political system altered its response to the North Korean attack as information revealed the deterioration of the situation and the failure of the initial actions to check the attack. From an initial appeal to the UN Security Council and a dispatch of emergency supplies to South Korea, the American commitment grew progressively to the commitment of American combat troops.

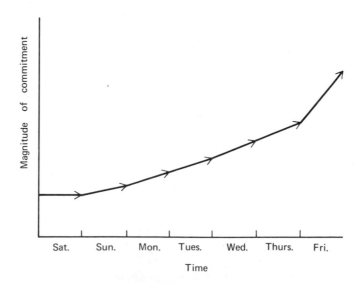

Figure 4 American Response to the North Korean Attack: Increasing Magnitude of Commitment in Response to a Deteriorating Situation

Foreign-Policy Decision Making: The Task of Analysis

The process of making foreign-policy decisions has been described here as one by which a political system attempts to adapt to demands and supportive actions in its geopolitical environment and to impose a measure of control upon it in order to achieve the goals of the system. The process cannot be reduced to a totally logical and orderly sequence of estimates, analyses, and decisions. There is logic in the process, but it is the tumultuous logic of human beings attempting under competing political pressures to cope with a complex and constantly changing environment. There may be frequent frustration and failure. Indeed, perhaps Gunnar Myrdal is correct in his gloomy judgment that "the foolishness of foreign policies may, on balance, be even greater today . . ." than they were three hundred years ago, when the Swedish Chancellor reflected, "My son, my son, if you knew with what little wisdom the world is ruled." [10] In any event, the standards of the IIMMP that we postulated earlier are illusory when one looks closely at real demands and possibilities. The discussion on previous pages has pointed out the limitations that human beings experience in the performance of various tasks in the foreign-policy process.

Limitations in the performance of essential decision-making tasks in real political systems are summarized in Table 3. Scanning is fragmentary and spotty, rather than comprehensive; coding is subject to bias and rigidity, instead of being flexible and reliable. Whereas the IIMMP depicted instant, faultless transmission, in real political systems there is often delay in transmission, and information may be lost or distorted. Human beings suffer lapses of memory; recall is selective, and institutionalized procedures for recall may not be suitable to current needs. Decision makers in real political systems consider only a limited number of the options that are logically possible in a situation. Their capacity for coping with complexity is limited, and irrational behavior may intrude in their choices, which they make under pressures of time and with limited information. Often there is a lag between the time a decision is made and action is implemented. Coordination may be faulty, and resources allocated unwisely. Human systems, unlike the IIMMP, have imperfect mechanisms for detecting error and for correcting it.

[10] Gunnar Myrdal, "With What Little Wisdom the World Is Ruled," *New York Times Magazine*, July 18, 1965, p. 20.

TABLE 3
Human Limitations in Foreign-Policy Decision Making

Task	Human Performance
Scanning	Fragmentary in detection, spotty in coverage
Coding	Subject to bias and rigidity
Transmission	Delayed, distorted, subject to losing information
Storage and recall	Lapsing in memory, distorting in recall
Recognition of courses of action	Limited in options considered
Decision making	Limited in problem-solving capacity; irrational and nonrational
Implementation	Subject to lag; faulty in coordination; wasteful of resources
Feedback	Imperfect in detection and correction of error

Recognition of human fallibility is the beginning of wisdom in the analysis of foreign-policy decisions. It is not the totality of wisdom, however. Political systems vary from one another, as do different individuals, groups, and organizations, in the efficiency of their performance. Moreover, fluctuations in the manner and effectiveness with which decisions are made occur under varying circumstances. Systematic analysis of foreign-policy decision making must move from the rather obvious set of generalizations expounded above to the identification of variables and then to the specification of relationships among variables. We begin these tasks in the following chapter.

8

The Structure of Foreign-Policy Decision Making

In the terms of a phrase coined over three decades ago by Harold Lasswell, the general quest of political science has often been described as an effort to determine "who gets what, when, and how" in politics. Systematic analysis of foreign-policy decision making can be described as a specific example of the quest. From this perspective, a foreign-policy analyst seeks to determine which persons, groups, and institutions participate in the decision-making process; what amount of influence is exerted by various participants; at what stages in the process and under what circumstances such influence is manifested; by what procedures and means influence is wielded; and what the results are.

A number of relevant variables can be identified by means of a paradigm about foreign policy from a decision-making perspective. Decisions, from this view, are made in response to or in anticipation of various kinds of situations and problems (inputs), on the basis of estimates of the tactical capabilities to deal with the situations experienced or anticipated in a given external setting. The decisions are made by policy makers acting individually and in groups, subject to competing political pressures within the American political culture and within the subculture of their organizational environment. The core institution that structures interaction in the foreign-policy process is a vast bureaucracy.

From the paradigm we can identify, in a preliminary way, a number of independent and intervening factors (clusters of variables) to help explain foreign-policy decision-making behavior. For instance, if we wished to explain who exerted how much influence, and by what means and with what effects, in the process of deciding in June 1950 to send American troops to Korea, what factors would we consider? Our preliminary survey suggests some starting points: the nature of the situation, the external setting at the time, American tactical capabilities in 1950, the key officials who were consulted and helped to formulate the response, the political pressures to which they were subjected, and the institutional and ideological framework within which they operated, including especially the bureaucratic structure that prevailed in 1950.[1]

In the following pages, we will examine more fully the relevance of the various factors in a variety of American decision-making situations. In the subsequent chapter, as a further stage in the development of a framework for analysis from a decision-making perspective, we shall incorporate most of the variables discussed below into a series of hypotheses about foreign-policy decision-making behavior.

Key Factors in Decision-Making Analysis

Situation, External Setting, and Tactical Capabilities

The history of American foreign policy in recent decades is filled with reports such as the following. Communist forces attack south of the 38th parallel in Korea; Israeli, British, and French forces attack Egypt; Soviet personnel install intermediate-range ballistic missiles in Cuba; Biafra announces secession from Nigeria, and a bloody civil war ensues; the British government devalues the pound; Prince Sihanouk of Cambodia asks for consultations with the American government about the use of Cambodian territory for sanctuaries by the Viet Cong; the American

---

[1] For a systematic examination of factors similar, although not identical, to these in an analysis of the American decision to commit troops to Korea, see Glenn D. Paige, *The Korean Decision* (New York: Free Press, 1968).

intelligence ship *Pueblo* is seized off the North Korean shore; the American ambassador to Guatemala is assassinated. It is sufficient to cite but a few of the events of recent history to suggest how frustrating, perplexing, and multifaceted the problems that confront American policy makers can be. The analytical point, however, of citing such events is to call attention to the variety of situations with which policy makers may be confronted; an armed attack, an economic crisis, or a diplomatic overture, for instance, each calls for a distinctive pattern of response. Later we shall develop a brief typology of situations, in order to examine the relationship between the type of situation and the foreign-policy response.

Beyond specific aspects of the situation itself, various aspects of the setting in which it arises—terrain, distances, climate, population and resource distributions, the number and kinds of situations that are occurring elsewhere—hinder or facilitate, encourage or discourage various courses of action and limit the possibilities for success in a given undertaking.

However, the extent to which environmental factors impede or advance a particular foreign-policy endeavor depends on the resources at hand. A situation is invariably interpreted in relation to an estimate of the capability of the government to respond to it. Throughout the Korean War, for example, President Truman and his key advisers in Washington hestitated to commit fully the resources of the United States to Korea for fear that to do so would dangerously weaken American and allied defenses in Europe. General MacArthur saw things somewhat differently. However, the fact that the American government had rapidly dismantled its armed forces after World War II and that President Truman had maintained a ceiling of less than $15 billion annually on defense expenditures prior to the Korean War meant that when the war broke out, the military resources of the United States were extremely limited, in turn limiting the policy options realistically available.[2]

Likewise, the nature of the response to installing Soviet missiles in Cuba depended in part on the means available to attempt to remove them. The decision as to what response to make to the North Korean seizure of the *Pueblo* in 1968 depended heavily on an evaluation of what actions could be taken without endangering the lives of the ship's crew. The significance to the American government of British devaluation of the pound depends heavily on the relative health of the American dollar. In short, tactical capabilities are relevant to explaining decision-making behavior.

The variables mentioned thus far—the nature of a situation, the external setting in which it arises, and perceived tactical capabilities for

[2] For an excellent discussion of these points, see Samuel P. Huntington, *The Common Defense* (New York: Columbia University Press, 1961), esp. chap. 4.

dealing with it—may be treated as elements in the coding of a situation. Thus, broadly speaking, we may identify the coding of a situation as an important determinant of the response that is made to it.

Personality Factors

The drama of foreign policy consists not only of complex and challenging situations that must be confronted through the allocation of scarce resources. It is also revealed in the human frailty and courage, stupidity and genius, or conflict and teamwork characteristic of the actors. Therefore, explanation of foreign-policy decisions requires the identification of the particular cast of characters that participated in the decisions, in order to discern the individual weaknesses and strengths, biases and predispositions that helped to determine various responses.

The way in which an individual decision maker conceptualizes a foreign-policy situation is affected by many factors, including his cultural environment, the institutional framework in which he operates, and his policy-making role. For the moment, however, we are concerned only with the influence of personality on individual behavior. Policy makers range in personality from the taciturn, such as Dean Rusk, to the effusive, such as Hubert Humphrey; they range from the bland and nonabrasive, such as William Pierce Rogers, to the rough-hewn and pungent, such as Charles E. ("Engine Charley") Wilson, Eisenhower's secretary of defense, whose offhand statements, such as "What's good for General Motors is good for the country," became quoted widely with delight or derision.[3]

Woodrow Wilson and the League of Nations   The behavior of President Woodrow Wilson is often cited as illustrative of the way that the personality of a key decision maker can fundamentally determine foreign-

---

[3] In the interest of historical accuracy, it should be pointed out that Wilson's exact words differed slightly from the quotation here, although the phrase as cited is ordinarily the one attributed to him. Wilson, the former president of General Motors Corporation, was being questioned by members of a Senate committee pursuant to their consideration of his nomination as secretary of defense. When asked about a hypothetical situation in which he might have to make a decision as secretary of defense that would further the interests of the nation, but would adversely affect General Motors Corporation, in which Wilson continued to hold stock, he replied: "I cannot conceive of one because for years I thought what was good for our country was good for General Motors, and vice versa." U.S. 83d Congress, 1st sess., Senate Committee on Armed Services, *Hearings on the Nomination of C. E. Wilson,* Jan. 15 and 16, 1953, p. 26.

policy outcomes.[4] One pair of authors contends, for instance, that temperamental defects in Wilson's personality, stemming from his early childhood, led him to work for American membership in the League of Nations with such obsession that, ironically, his actions brought about the defeat of the goal that he so devoutly sought.[5] The authors produce evidence to suggest that, as a boy, Wilson had an extremely low sense of self-esteem, especially in relationship to the exacting puritanical standards demanded by his father. They maintain that, perhaps rebelling against his father's domination, while simutaneously seeking the perfection that his father had demanded, Wilson developed a compulsive need to dominate others and to demonstrate his moral worth. Thus, at the time of the drafting of the League Covenant and of negotiations abroad and at home for its ratification by the leading powers, including especially the United States, Wilson was zealous, rigid, and unresponsive to the views of others at the very time that success depended upon a capacity for compromise and sensitivity to the views and desires of allies and of domestic critics.

Numerous actions by Wilson at the time illustrate such behavior. First, he insisted upon attending the Paris Peace Conference personally, against the wishes of the French and British delegations, who pointed out that no other head of state would take part in deliberations, and against the advice of Colonel House and other American advisers, who argued that Wilson's program would have a better chance of success if he left the detailed daily negotiations to his diplomats. Second, in selecting other members of the American commission to attend the Paris Conference, Wilson included no member of Congress, despite the fact that ratification of the peace treaty would depend upon gaining the support of two-

---

[4] The influence upon American foreign policy of the personalities of other key policy makers has also been studied. For example, see Arnold Rogow, *James Forrestal: A Study of Personality, Politics, and Policy* (New York: Crowell-Collier-Macmillan, 1964); Betty Glad, *Charles Evans Hughes and the Illusions of Innocence: A Study in American Diplomacy* (Urbana, Ill.: University of Illinois Press, 1966); Herman Finer, *Dulles over Suez* (Chicago: Quadrangle Books, 1964). At a more general level, see Joseph H. de Rivera, *The Psychological Dimension of Foreign Policy* (Columbus, Ohio: Merrill, 1968). See also L. N. Rieselbach and G. I. Balch, eds., *Psychology and Politics: An Introductory Reader* (New York: Holt, Rinehart and Winston, Inc., 1969).

[5] Alexander L. George and Juliette L. George, *Woodrow Wilson and Colonel House: A Personality Study* (New York: Dover, paperback ed., 1964). Compare Thomas A. Bailey, *Woodrow Wilson and the Great Betrayal* (New York: Crowell-Collier-Macmillan, 1945). See also Sigmund Freud and William C. Bullitt, *Thomas Woodrow Wilson, Twenty-eighth President of the United States: A Psychological Study* (Boston: Houghton Mifflin, 1967).

thirds of the Senate. Third, only one Republican was included in the American commission, although the Republicans had gained control of the Congress in the 1918 elections, and political expediency, at least, seemed to demand some deference to their views. Moreover, the single Republican included in the delegation, Henry White, was not regarded as one of the party leaders or activists. Fourth, even those commissioners who were selected to accompany Wilson to Paris, with the exception for a time of Colonel House, were largely kept in the dark about the proceedings. In short, the negotiations were for Wilson a personal, not a collective, enterprise. The President even refused to take advantage of the expertise that other members of the commission represented in order to consult them on various matters under discussion. Fifth, Wilson rejected and even scorned the efforts of domestic groups such as the League to Enforce Peace, led by former President Taft and supported by thirty-four governors, to promote discussion to arouse public support of a league of nations. Sixth, once the peace treaty (which included the League Covenant) was drafted, Wilson refused to accept such reservations to the treaty that would have ensured Senate support and thus American membership in the League. Instead, Wilson took his case to the American people in a relentless 8000-mile train trip that brought the final strain on his energies and left him paralyzed.

In some respects, as fascinating as the influence of Woodrow Wilson's personality in this tragic historical episode is the influence of the personality of his *bête noire*, Senator Henry Cabot Lodge, who plotted the downfall of treaty ratification with as much zeal as Wilson sought to achieve ratification.

Commander Bucher and the* Pueblo *Affair The attitudes, beliefs, and personalities of individuals occupying positions considerably less prominent than that of President, secretary of state, or secretary of defense can also sometimes have important foreign-policy ramifications. The decision in January 1968 of Commander Lloyd Bucher, captain of the United States intelligence ship *Pueblo*, to surrender his ship, men, and equipment to North Korean seizure created a foreign-policy crisis for the American government. Commander Bucher's decision became the subject of widespread heated discussion and appraisal within the Navy as well as throughout the American society, especially because he had deviated from the traditional naval maxim, "Don't give up the ship," even if confronted with impossible odds. Quite apart from the moral dilemma illustrated so vividly by the difficult and unprecedented situation with which Commander Bucher had to deal, his response raises interesting questions about the attitudes and beliefs that led him to deviate from naval maxims rather than to die and let his men die.[6]

The *Pueblo* case also illustrates the analytical hazards of trying to deal with human motivation, especially when inferences must be derived from sources other than direct, extensive interviewing of the individuals involved. Was there something about Commander Bucher's boyhood training that led him to respond as he did—experience as an orphan in Boys Town, Nebraska, perhaps? Was the fact that he was not an Annapolis graduate relevant to his willingness to depart from the prescribed response?[7] There is a great temptation to indulge in amateur psychoanalytic explanations of foreign-policy decisions, whether made by individuals such as Commander Bucher or by other more prominent figures, such as Richard Nixon, Melvin Laird, Lyndon Johnson, Robert McNamara, or John Foster Dulles. But seldom are data available in sufficient quantity or quality to give one a solid basis for such explanations; moreover, few of us are trained to assess data reliably from a psychoanalytic perspective even when the data are available. This is not to say that the influence of individual behavioral attributes upon foreign-policy decisions is to be ignored, only that inferences about the extent and the origins of such influence must be made with caution.

The perspective of decison making, more so than other analytical perspectives, encourages one to examine individual human behavior in detail. However, in considering foreign policy at the level of human interaction in decision-making situations, two kinds of errors are to be avoided. The first is the error of neglecting the impact that a single individual can have upon a foreign-policy outcome. To put it somewhat differently, the content and quality of foreign-policy decisions can vary considerably according to which persons occupy decision-making positions. The second kind of error to be avoided is interpreting foreign-policy decisions in terms of the personalities of particular policy makers,

[6] As Herman Wouk, author of *The Caine Mutiny*, has observed of the situation in which Commander Bucher found himself, "The skipper was trapped in a queer turn of a queer task, in the queerest of twilight situations. . . . A novelist could never get away with a story based on such a contrived, diagramed case to dramatize a moral dilemma." Wouk, "Topics: The Moral Dilemma of a Not-War Skipper," *New York Times*, Feb. 8, 1969, p. 30.

[7] A detailed, interesting account of the ordeal that Commander Bucher experienced is by Bernard Weinraub, "In the Matter of Lloyd Mark Bucher," *New York Times Magazine*, May 11, 1969, pp. 25 and following. Weinraub probes into aspects of the personality and background of Bucher, highlighting the human dimension of the *Pueblo* affair without purporting to present a complete psychoanalytical explanation of Bucher's behavior.

to the neglect of factors that limit or shape individual behavior quite independently of personality. Each actor in the foreign-policy drama is unique in the sense that each human being is unique, but each policy maker is also the product of his culture and his times. Moreover, each person is also responsive to the demands and expectations associated with his role (for example, as President, senator, or secretary of state), to the public response and potential critics, and to cues from offstage (such as policy directives from higher authority within the hierarchy). The relevance of these factors will be discussed in the sections that follow.

Political Culture

Much of the American foreign-policy process takes place within the context of the American political culture—that is, within distinctively American political norms, beliefs, and an institutional infrastructure. Specifically, the American political culture includes the norms of democracy, as defined and redefined over time, and institutional features such as the two-party system, federalism, and the separation of powers among the three branches of the federal government. An understanding in depth of the workings of the formal and informal institutions of American government and politics and of the prevalent mores and beliefs is essential to an accurate understanding of the American foreign-policy process. We shall refrain, however, from describing American political culture in detail here, on the assumption that, if the reader lacks familiarity with it, descriptive information is readily available in most textbooks on American government. Our present objective is limited to suggesting the relevance of political culture to an explanation of foreign-policy decision making.

The distinctive institutions, traditions, and beliefs of American political culture help to allocate authority and responsibility among the cast of characters in foreign policy, to structure patterns of interaction, and to encourage or inhibit various kinds of behavior. But generalization about the influence of political culture upon individual behavior is hazardous, because the influence is not monolithic, but rather highly differentiated. The cultural milieu of those who grew up during the buoyant period of the pre-World War I decade was considerably different from that of those whose youth and early adulthood spanned the Great Depression and World War II; in turn, those born during and since World War II have experienced a radically different culture in their formative years from that of their parents and grandparents. Moreover, the values and beliefs that characterize the political culture of metropolitan America differ sharply from those characteristic of rural and small-town America. Black Americans have generally known a political culture unlike that experienced by white Americans. In short, political subcultures form a complex political culture in America. Attribution of the behavior of foreign-policy decision makers to particular facets of American culture is therefore hazardous. A particular decision-making group may consist of individuals from a variety of political subcultures; sound analysis requires attention to such differentiation. It is pertinent to examine the sources of recruitment of American foreign-policy makers, to study the process of their early and subsequent socialization, and to investigate the institutional context that, whatever the subculture that policy makers had known in their early years, defines the political subculture within which their decision-making behavior occurs.

Recruitment

Recruitment includes a process of selection and of self-selection. That is, policy makers, using the term as we did in Chapter 5 to refer to persons with formal or informal responsibilities for making policy decisions, are elected or appointed to their posts, but they also make career commitments and choices that make them available for selection or appointment. Thus, we can see some links between recruitment patterns and personality, since those who occupy key policy positions are unlikely to represent a random cross section of the population in terms of personality, but rather, are drawn from the segment of the population with needs and aspirations for responsibility and power.[8]

Moreover, certain kinds of education and training, most notably in the law, have traditionally served to facilitate access to elective office in the United States. Wealth has also enhanced the opportunities of an individual to compete successfully; especially in recent years, with the rising costs of campaigning through television, wealth has become an almost indispensable asset in competition for high office. Protestants traditionally have had greater opportunities than have Catholics or Jews for high elective office, although the religious barriers have been lowered in recent years. However, the competition for high office continues to be confined almost entirely to men and to white Americans. Each of the above generalizations applies with special force to the presidency, the key position in the foreign-policy structure.

The presidency is important not only because of the authority that the President is able to wield in office, but also because he is able to appoint

---

[8] See Harold Lasswell, *Power and Personality* (New York: Norton, 1948).

most of the other key policy makers. Of course, the selections of a secretary of state and a secretary of defense have importance that put these appointments in categories by themselves. These two members of the President's cabinet, above all others, must enjoy the confidence of the President. In some instances, such as Nixon's selection of William Pierce Rogers as his secretary of state, confidence is assured by the appointment of a long-time friend and associate (of more than twenty years, in this case). In other instances, such as Eisenhower's selection of John Foster Dulles, confidence is based primarily on the President's respect for the secretary's long experience and reputation for sound judgment in foreign affairs. In still other instances, such as Kennedy's appointment of Dean Rusk and Johnson's retention of him, confidence is placed in the appointee's training and in his reputation for unswerving loyalty, with the additional consideration that he lacks the national prestige that would compete with the President's own leadership image. Adlai Stevenson, for instance, whose national stature presented serious potential competition to Kennedy's, was not offered the post of secretary of state, which he apparently greatly desired. Instead, Stevenson was appointed ambassador to the United Nations, a position far less prominent in domestic politics.

In the case of the top Defense Department post, managerial experience in industry or experience in defense policy are important credentials for a potential appointee to head the world's largest organization. Charles E. Wilson, who left the presidency of General Motors Corporation to become Eisenhower's secretary of defense, and Robert McNamara, who resigned as president of the Ford Motor Company to accept John Kennedy's invitation to head the Defense Department, are examples of appointees with the former variety of experience. Senator Henry Jackson, who apparently was Richard Nixon's first choice for the top Defense Department post, illustrates a potential appointee with the latter credentials, not only through his experience from the Senate Armed Services Committee and, as chairman, from the Subcommittee on National Security Staffing and Operations of the Senate Committee on Governmental Operations, but also through his close connections with defense industry, most notably Boeing Aircraft Corporation, one of the major defense contractors. Melvin Laird, who received the Nixon appointment as secretary of defense, had been a member of the House Defense Appropriations Committee and had been one of the most prominent critics of the cost-effectiveness approach to defense management that had been utilized by McNamara. However, Laird's credentials at the time of his appointment were not primarily those of a defense or managerial expert, but rather those of a skillful politician and a leader of the Republican party in Congress.

In making other political appointments for foreign policy, even more so than in the case of the selection of the secretaries of state and of defense, the President must rely heavily on the advice and judgment of others. Such reliance is dictated not only by the advantages that the knowledge of others can provide in enlarging the pool of potential manpower from which selections can be made, but also by the political necessity of satisfying a variety of constituencies—or at least of avoiding appointments that would seriously antagonize politically significant groups or leaders. Moreover, cabinet-level appointees are likely to extract at least a veto power over appointment of their subordinates as the price of their own acceptance of office. Domestic political considerations sometimes override considerations of demonstrable competence for the responsibilities that an appointee must assume. However, appointments are largely made from among those who have had prior experience in government, even if not in the specific organization or field to which they are appointed. For instance, a study of the backgrounds of 153 persons appointed to executive positions at the cabinet or subcabinet level in foreign affairs from 1946 to 1962 revealed that half of these had had more than ten years of prior experience in federal government; less than 10 percent of the executive appointees entered office with no prior experience in the federal government.[9]

Although the long tenure of Dulles and of Rusk as secretary of state and of Wilson and of McNamara as secretary of defense are notable, a relatively frequent turnover of political appointees to high-level foreign-policy positions is common. With the rule of thumb that it takes a couple of years for the average occupant of a top-level policy position to attain sufficient familiarity with his responsibilities to make decisions with confidence and sound judgment, frequent turnover in such positions can be an important problem.

With the characteristic turnover in political appointees, continuity is provided by the civil and military professionals in foreign policy and defense; among these, women and blacks are notably underrepresented. In terms of region of birth, however, foreign-policy professionals and military professionals are relatively representative of the American population as a whole. The South is somewhat underrepresented in the Foreign Service, the officers of which constitute the core of foreign-

[9] Derived from figures reported by James L. McCamy, *Conduct of the New Diplomacy* (New York: Harper & Row, 1964), Table 14, p. 237.

policy professionals, but southerners are somewhat overrepresented in the military profession, specifically among Army officers. Virtually all Foreign Service officers and military officers are college graduates, and in increasing numbers both in the Foreign Service and in the military profession, a sizable percentage of officers are receiving postgraduate education in civilian institutions of higher education. Roughly two-thirds of Foreign Service officers have had some formal education beyond the bachelor's degree, and the percentage will doubtless increase in coming years. A similar trend among military professionals is illustrated by the statement of the Superintendent at West Point that three-fourths of recent graduates of the Military Academy can expect to receive postgraduate education.[10]

Aside from demographic statistics about the backgrounds of those who are recruited into careers in foreign and defense policy, it would be analytically useful to be able to identify the attitudes and beliefs that prevail among them. It is clear that variations in career choices occur to some extent according to variations in personality. Thus, those who enter the Foreign Service and those who enter the military service, respectively, by no means represent a random cross section of the population in terms of their personalities and attitudes. On the other hand, the rather sketchy data that are available are sufficient to demonstrate that stereotypic notions of the personality of the American diplomat or of the military mind are grossly inadequate and fail to accommodate the range of personalities that exists within the Foreign Service and the military profession.[11]

Socialization

Recruitment patterns are significant to analysis of foreign-policy decision making because such patterns help to explain why individuals with particular kinds of skills and personalities occupy particular policy-making positions. But these patterns do not provide a complete explana-

[10] For further discussion of recruitment patterns in the Foreign Service, see McCamy. Recruitment patterns in the military profession are discussed and analyzed by Morris Janowitz, *The Professional Soldier: A Social and Political Portrait* (New York: Free Press, 1960), esp. chap. 5.

[11] The McCamy and Janowitz books usefully dispel popular stereotypes of the professional diplomat and the professional soldier, respectively. See also Regis Walther, *Orientations and Behavioral Styles of Foreign Service Officers* (New York: Carnegie Endowment for International Peace, 1965). Although the Walther book reports extensive survey data of interest, comparing the attitudes of Foreign Service officers with those of persons in other occupations, unfortunately Walther does not report statistical data revealing the distribution of views among FSO's.

tion of decision-making patterns. Once recruited (that is, appointed or elected) to a policy-making position, an individual becomes immersed in a process of learning the role that he has selected or that has been assigned to him.

"Socialization" Defined The process of learning a social role may be termed "socialization." Such a simple and rather loose definition will suffice for our purposes. We shall not review here the uses and abuses in the social sciences of the concept of socialization, nor of the concept of role, to which that of socialization is inextricably linked.[12] It is sufficient to observe that a role refers to a pattern of demands and expectations in social relationships; this pattern may be in accord with a formal position —for instance, secretary of state—or an informal one—for instance, confidant. Indeed, although a widely held set of demands and expectations may accord with a given formal role defined in terms of position (for example, senator), a given occupant of a formal position may deviate from conventional expectations in order to assume an informal role of his own choosing (for example, maverick senator).[13]

Moreover, a given individual may redefine his own role in a single position over time. For instance, Dwight D. Eisenhower brought to the presidency a conception of the office that permitted him to delegate vast authority in foreign affairs to his secretary of state, John Foster Dulles. Upon Dulles's death, however, Eisenhower took much more of the initiative for making foreign-policy decisions himself. Franklin Roosevelt is an example of a President with a conception of the office in sharp contrast to that of Eisenhower, acting virtually as his own secretary of state in many important sectors of foreign policy during World War II. However, as Eisenhower's style changed with circumstances and time, so did Roosevelt's. Whereas Roosevelt acted quite independently of Secretary of State Cordell Hull during the war years, prior to that time he had relied on Hull much more heavily, concentrating his own energies on domestic affairs.

In short, the demands and expectations associated with a given role

[12] For more detailed general discussion of the concepts, see extensive bibliographical essays by Theodore R. Sarbin on "Role Theory" and by Irving L. Child on "Socialization" in the *Handbook of Social Psychology*, 2 vols. (Cambridge, Mass.: Addison-Wesley, 1954), 1, chap. 6; and 2, chap. 18, respectively. See also Herbert Hyman, *Political Socialization* (New York: Free Press, paperback ed., 1969); and K. P. Langton, *Political Socialization* (New York: Oxford, 1969).

[13] See Ralph K. Huitt, "The Outsider in the Senate: An Alternative Role," *American Political Science Review*, 55 (Sept. 1961), 566–575; reprinted in Nelson W. Polsby, Robert A. Dentler, and Paul A. Smith, eds., *Politics and Social Life* (Boston: Houghton Mifflin, 1963), pp. 297–308.

range from customs or regulations defining a particular set of duties to personalized conceptions of a given office. Socialization is the process of acquiring and refining attitudes and beliefs in relation to the image one has of the role that he occupies; it is a learning process.

The Improbability of Radical Changes of Attitudes   To describe socialization as a learning process is not to say that individuals come to policy-making positions without any preconceived ideas or values, nor that a radical transformation of attitudes is typically effected in policy-making structures. As noted above, often the process of recruitment or self-selection brings together individuals who already share many basic attitudes. In such instances, common group experience serves to reinforce and to solidify an initial homogeneity of outlook. For example, Theodore Sorensen observed about "the Kennedy team," the men selected to work closely together in top roles in government during the Kennedy administration,

> They were, like him, dedicated but unemotional. . . . There were no crusaders, fanatics or extremists from any camp; all were nearer the center than either left or right. All spoke with the same low-keyed restraint that marked their chief, yet all shared his deep conviction that they could change America's drift. They liked government, they liked politics, they liked Kennedy and they believed implicitly in him. Their own feelings of pride—*our* feelings, for I was proud to be one of them—could be summed up in a favorite Kennedy passage from Shakespeare's *King Henry V* in his speech on the St. Crispin's Day battle: ". . . we . . . shall be remembered—We few, we happy few, we band of brothers . . . And gentlemen . . . now abed Shall think themselves accurs'd they were not here." [14]

The evidence suggests that the experiences of the Kennedy administration served to reinforce the initial homogeneity of outlook, rather than to lead to drastic alterations of the views of the participants. Even in situations where the process of socialization to new roles is highly institutionalized, and where the norms of desired behavior are explicit rather than merely implicit, the magnitude of change of attitude and belief that occurs during the socialization process is sometimes less than one might expect. For instance, empirical investigation of the professional orientations of four classes of West Point cadets and of their attitudes regarding various issues of foreign policy suggests that only slight

[14] Theodore C. Sorensen, *Kennedy* (New York: Bantam Books, paperback ed., 1966), p. 287.

changes in attitude occur during the four-year period in spite of an intensive process of indoctrination through which a young man is to be transformed from a civilian to an apprentice military professional.[15] The process of recruitment and self-selection to West Point (and to the other service academies) appears to result in the admission to the academy almost exclusively of young men whose values and beliefs already are consonant with those sought as end products of the academy socialization process. Findings also bearing out the importance of self-selection and recruitment, relative to socialization, were obtained in a study comparing the political preferences of Foreign Service officers with those of military officers whose assignments in the Defense Department concerned analysis of international political affairs. For most differences of attitudes observed between the two groups, differences in recruitment patterns proved to be a more important explanatory factor than differences in socialization patterns.[16]

The Analytical Relevance of Socialization Nonetheless, although a radical alteration of viewpoints and values is seldom to be anticipated during socialization into various adult roles, the socialization process is of analytical interest especially in terms of the limits of desirable or acceptable behavior that tend to be established by the process; in terms of the pressures for conformity that socialization generates; and in terms of the parochial loyalties and inertia that develop toward the orthodox views within the group. Even in informal groups, such as the "Kennedy team" described by Sorensen above, the sense of comradeship and of team spirit imposes tacit obligations on a group member to behave in accordance with the expectations of his fellows. Group norms serve the individual as guideposts for his behavior and attitudes.

In groups or organizations with a long tradition and highly selective membership, the effect of group norms upon individual behavior is likely to be especially pronounced. For example, nearly 80 percent of 580 members of the U.S. Foreign Service Corps surveyed in a recent study indicated that "winning respect of colleagues in the Corps" was a factor that they considered important or crucial to their success. None of another fifteen factors rated in terms of importance to success in the

---

[15] John P. Lovell, "The Professional Socialization of the West Point Cadet," in Morris Janowitz, ed., *The New Military: Changing Patterns of Organization* (New York: Russell Sage, 1964), pp. 119–157.

[16] Bernard Mennis, "An Empirical Analysis of the Background and Political Preferences of American Foreign Policy Decision-Makers," (unpublished Ph.D. dissertation, University of Michigan, 1967).

Foreign Service received a high rating by such a substantial portion of the FSO sample.[17]

Loyalties to a group or organization may detract from the commitment of members to the purposes of the system of which the group or organization is a part. The inability of leaders of the Army, Navy, Air Force, and Marines to agree on a standardized belt buckle that would be worn by all of the services is a trivial illustration of the impediments to cooperation that can develop, but a symbolic one of a phenomenon that extends to more significant issues and occurs in varying degrees in all organizations. As Sorensen has noted, although "bureaucratic parochialism and rivalry are usually associated in Washington with the armed services . . . they in fact affect the outlook of nearly every agency. They can be observed, to cite only a few examples . . . between State and Treasury on world finance, or State and Commerce on world trade, or State and Defense on world disarmament." [18]

What about the individual whose views or actions differ from those espoused as organizational policy or as informal group orthodoxy? Idiosyncracies and dissent may be tolerated or even encouraged in some groups, but the limits and forms of acceptable eccentricity and dissent are likely to be defined by group mores, if not by organizational regulations (such as the Uniform Code of Military Justice, which sets limits to dissent within the armed forces). Thus, deviance from conventional behavior and attitudes in a group characteristically carries risks, although it is interesting to note that sometimes it may also carry rewards. The latter outcome is illustrated by the finding of Janowitz that the "elite nucleus" in the American military profession consists heavily of those who at various stages in their careers undertook assignments or training that deviated from the conventionally prescribed career path within the profession.[19]

Of course, the findings of Janowitz do not demonstrate that individuals who challenge or deviate from group norms on issues more basic than those of career planning also will be rewarded; nor do the data affirm that those who reach the top in civil and military policy-making posts typically are innovative and creative in outlook. Indeed, Henry Kissinger

---

[17] John E. Harr, *The Professional Diplomat* (Princeton, N.J.: Princeton University Press, 1969), pp. 210–214. Sample selection and survey instrument are discussed in appendices to the book. The Harr study, based upon extensive interviewing and documentary analysis as well as upon survey research, provides a detailed social portrait of the Foreign Service Corps.

[18] Theodore C. Sorensen, *Decision-Making in the White House* (New York: Columbia University Press, paperback ed., 1964), p. 69.

[19] Janowitz, *The Professional Soldier*, chap. 8.

is among those who have argued that an opposite pattern is more typical of those who have had careers in governmental bureaucracy. He has noted that in lower- and middle-level foreign-policy roles, specialization is fostered. Yet successful performance of the responsibilities of top leadership requires breadth of knowledge and the ability to transcend the limited focus of the specialist. Moreover, the routine administrative experience of the civil or military professional in early or mid-career, filled as it is with the preparation of staff papers to be routed through multiple channels and through the working out of policy positions in committees and staff conferences, rewards facility in the expression of orthodox ideas and in the formulation of timely compromises. However, successful response to the demands of foreign policy calls for leadership with the capacity for innovation, for decisiveness, and for a willingness to risk unpopularity with colleagues or subordinates in making decisions. Thus, foreign-policy organizations face the dilemma of appointing to top positions professionals whose training and experience may have reduced rather than enhanced their ability to provide creative and decisive leadership or, on the other hand, of seeking "outsiders" for top positions.[20] The program of Wristonization in the State Department, which began in 1954, had the effect of representing the latter option—that is, of filling a disproportionate number of executive positions with persons who had joined the Foreign Service through lateral entry rather than with persons who had come up "through the ranks." [21] However, the aftermath of Wristonization suggests that there is no simple panacea to the leadership problem. Lateral entrants to the Foreign Service may bring to their new positions perspectives that are novel in the new milieu. Often, however, the perspectives of the lateral entrant are as orthodox as those of the careerist, if not more so, reflecting the effects of a similar pattern of professional socialization in a bureaucratic setting elsewhere in government or in industry.

Especially among civil and military professionals, the institutionalized

[20] Kissinger argues that there are cultural traits and a pervasive bureaucratization of American society which minimize the likelihood that top leaders, however chosen, will have escaped a pattern of socialization that has ingrained in them an insecurity and orthodoxy that preclude creative response to the demands of foreign policy. Henry A. Kissinger, "The Policymaker and the Intellectual," *The Reporter*, 20 (March 5, 1959), 30–35; reprinted in Andrew M. Scott and Raymond H. Dawson, eds., *Readings in the Making of American Foreign Policy* (New York: Crowell-Collier-Macmillan, 1965), pp. 320–333.

[21] Harr, p. 143. The evolution of the Foreign Service Corps has been shaped by various acts of legislation and executive decree, of which implementation of the Wriston Committee report is only one. Harr has described and assessed the pattern of organizational evolution in detail, pp. 11–136.

mechanisms for periodic review of performance (notably the ubiquitous efficiency report), on which promotion and favorable assignments hinge so heavily, pose great risks for those whose attitudes and behavior deviate far from the modal pattern. For a junior- or middle-level professional to challenge basic policy assumptions is to call into question the competence or judgment of those who appraise his performance. Moreover, even among peers, organizational solidarity may be jeopardized by someone whose aggressiveness and candor in discussion violate the mores of the organizational subculture. Thus, adaptation to the organizational subculture requires the Foreign Service officer or the professional military officer to learn to tone down dissident views or to withdraw from interpersonal situations involving potential conflict. Strong emotions are suppressed. Decisions that may shatter group consensus are postponed or watered down to the level of broadly acceptable compromise. As Chris Argyris has noted in an analysis based upon extensive interviews and discussions with Foreign Service officers at various levels, the consequence of the socialization pattern noted, in which the foreign-policy professional's willingness to speak out and to confront sensitive and controversial issues candidly is reduced over time, is often one of growing insecurity and feelings of guilt.[22]

Variations in Socialization Patterns   As noted earlier, the professional socialization process upon which we are focusing here involves not merely adaptation to the subculture of an organization, but also a response to perceived demands and expectations associated with particular roles. Thus, within a given organization, one may find some important differences in socialization patterns.

For instance, Argyris found that those holding substantive policy positions in the State Department and those whose responsibilities in the department were primarily administrative held mutually unflattering views of each other. The substantive officials saw themselves as "humanistic," "reflective," and "qualitative" and as possessing "intercultural sensitivity," in contrast to the administrative officials, whom the substantive officials considered "noncultural," "quantitative," "more interested in form than substance," but "decisive and forceful." The administrative officials agreed with the view of themselves as being "decisive," but their self-images also included being "resourceful," "adaptive," "pragmatic," "dedicated," and "misunderstood." In turn, they saw the substantive

[22] Chris Argyris, *Some Causes of Organizational Ineffectiveness within the Department of State,* Center for International Systems Research Occasional Paper No. 2 (Washington: Dept. of State Pub. 8180, Jan. 1967).

officials as being "dedicated," but also "cautious," "manipulative," "defensive," "isolated," and "surrounded by mystique." [23]

In a study some years earlier, Roger Hilsman, Jr., made a similar comparison of the views of State Department intelligence analysts with officials within the department in operating roles, who were the consumers of intelligence. The intelligence analysts, in contrast to operators, were virtually unanimous in their view that the appropriate role of the intelligence analyst is to identify and interpret emerging policy problems and in their belief that sound policy can be attained once the facts of a problem are determined. The operators, on the other hand, assigned a much narrower role to the intelligence analysts; some operators were willing to acknowledge that intelligence analysts had a "warning" function to perform by alerting operators to impending problems, provided the intelligence analyst did not indulge in policy recommendation. Other operators, however, contended that intelligence analysts should limit themselves to gathering and presenting the facts, leaving all interpretation to the operators.[24]

Hilsman found, however, that the common values and beliefs among intelligence analysts and operating officials outweighed their mutual differences. Attitudes that the two types of official held in common included an antipathy to basic (as distinguished from applied) research, to abstract ideas, and to conceptualization. Neither the intelligence analyst nor the operator saw himself as a scholar or as an intellectual; indeed, Hilsman has described the common outlook as anti-intellectual. Instead, a common faith cultivated in the policy-making milieu was the reliability of impressions derived from firsthand experience in various parts of the world and the intuitive grasp of a situation that was alleged to be the by-product of such firsthand familiarity with an area. Moreover, both the operators and the intelligence analysts attached almost exclusive importance to current intelligence, with a low regard for the importance of long-range or deep historical studies. Anticipation of the future was not disregarded, but the common assumption was that future events could be anticipated best by one immersed in events on a day-to-day basis.

Andrew M. Scott contends that such attitudes still prevail within the State Department. Typically, according to Scott, "when the operator complains that a piece of research is irrelevant, he usually means that

[23] Argyris, pp. 19–21.

[24] Roger Hilsman, Jr., "Intelligence and Policy-Making in Foreign Affairs," *World Politics*, 5 (Oct. 1952), 1–25; reprinted in Davis B. Bobrow, ed., *Components of Defense Policy* (Chicago: Rand McNally, 1965), pp. 349–367.

it is not country- or situation-specific and is not going to help him to-morrow morning." [25] Systematic prediction in foreign affairs is regarded as a chimera; the would-be skillful policy maker therefore sees his task as that of learning to cope with problems as they arise, and of being prepared constantly for the unexpected.

In fairness to foreign-policy practitioners, one should note that if they have neglected discussions or analyses by academic theorists, the failure is not attributable exclusively to the bias of practitioners. Rather, it must also be acknowledged that theory building in the study of foreign policy remains so spotty and often so inadequately supported by empirical verification that claims that can be made for the predictive utility of most academic research are weak. Furthermore, foreign-policy practitioners in fact have established numerous informal contacts, with academic specialists, and do have institutionalized mechanisms for attempting to keep abreast of academic research.[26] These caveats notwithstanding, Scott's critique usefully highlights elements of a distinctive subculture, within which the cliché that foreign policy is "an art, not a science," continues to condition the attitudes of policy makers toward their responsibilities and toward the utilization of intellectual resources available to them.

The Bureaucracy: Core of the Structural Context

The results of professional socialization are reflected indirectly, rather than directly, in foreign-policy decision making. Nevertheless, the socialization process is of considerable analytical significance. Decision-making behavior can scarcely be understood independently of an awareness of the subcultural milieu within which foreign-policy decisions are made, and within which over time the policy maker has developed and adapted his attitudes and beliefs.

The context of decision making is more than a set of customs, values, and beliefs that constitute an organizational or group subculture, however. Rather, there is also an interactional context, defined especially by the structures of authority and communication that largely predetermine who will talk to whom about what kinds of problems and in what kinds of situations. The structure of the political system as a whole is also

[25] Andrew M. Scott, "The Department of State: Formal Organization and Informal Culture," *International Studies Quarterly*, 13 (March 1969), 1–18, 13.

[26] For example, see "The Uses of Academic Research," *FAR Horizons*, 1 (July 1968), 5–6. Also, E. Raymond Platig, "Research and Analysis," *The Annals*, 480 (November 1968), 50–59.

analytically relevant, but it is useful to devote special emphasis to the bureaucracy, which is the core structure of the foreign-policy political system. Subsequent to a discussion of the effects of patterns of authority and communication within the bureaucracy on foreign-policy decision making, a few additional observations will be made about the analytical relevance of the structure of the political system in general.

We have alluded to the bureaucracy in previous discussion. We use the term to refer to the large complex of civil and military departments, agencies, and bureaus within the executive branch of the federal government. Although all the departments with cabinet status perform some activities that relate to foreign policy directly or indirectly, the Departments of State and of Defense, with responsibilities lying almost entirely in the foreign-policy area, are the most frequent objects of comment here.

The immensity of the task of foreign policy and the complexity of patterns of interaction in the foreign-policy process were suggested in Chapter 7. Although no IIMMP is available to perform the task, bureaucratization above all represents an effort to organize the essential activities of foreign policy in a rational manner.[27] Although other sectors of the political system may also contribute to the performance of vital functions in the foreign-policy process, often such functions find their most systematic form of expression within the bureaucracy. It is vital to bear in mind, however, that although bureaucratization of activity is designed to enhance efficiency of performance, in fact the various consequences of bureaucratization often impede efficiency. In short, bureaucratization may be dysfunctional as well as functional in the political system. For example, bureaucratization includes providing for a division of labor among those who participate in the foreign-policy process; but the division of labor provided may lead to the assignment of tasks to individuals without the competence or training to perform them. The bureaucracy participates in the allocation of resources among individuals, groups, and agencies for the performance of various tasks in the foreign-policy process. However, the allocation of resources may be inappropriate to the requirements of a particular situation. Bureaucratization of activity includes the allocation of authority for the performance of essential tasks; but the bureaucracy may misallocate authority, to the

[27] See Max Weber, *The Theory of Social and Economic Organization*, ed., with intro., Talcott Parsons and trans. A. M. Henderson and Talcott Parsons (New York: Oxford, 1947); and Max Weber, *From Max Weber: Essays in Sociology*, trans., ed., and intro., H. H. Gerth and C. Wright Mills (New York: Oxford, Galaxy paperback ed., 1958). Also, Robert K. Merton *et al.*, *Reader in Bureaucracy* (New York: Free Press, 1952); and Anthony Downs, *Inside Bureaucracy* (Boston: Little, Brown, 1967).

detriment of the effective completion of the tasks. The bureaucracy provides institutionalized channels of communication between individuals and groups within the foreign-policy process but the channels that are established may stifle or distort rather than facilitate communication. Bureaucratization includes the development of plans and routines for the systematic processing of problems as they arise; however, the drive to routinize problem solving may reduce the capability of the system to cope with change and the unexpected.

We shall not provide a detailed discussion of the various functions and dysfunctions of bureaucracy here. Our immediate objective is limited to an indication of how the structure of authority and communications within bureaucracy may affect the decision-making process, thereby suggesting more broadly the relevance of analysis of the organizational context of decision-making.

Patterns of Authority and Communication

A glance at organization charts in the civil or military bureaucracy suggests a pattern of authority that is logical and clear. The formal pattern is illustrated by Figure 5, depicting the "chain of command" extending from the President, as commander in chief of the armed forces, in a series of orderly stages down to the infantry soldier in the field in Vietnam. The pattern describes a neat pyramid, with the relationship of each building block in the pyramid to the others clearly identified.

At each level in the hierarchy, except at the top, individuals can identify the person who has been designated as their commander (for example, squad leader, platoon leader, company commander) and a person at the next higher level to whom their commander owes obedience. Within a range of activities prescribed by the operating rules of the system, each commander is able to issue orders to those who are designated as his subordinates with the expectation that such orders will be regarded as legitimate. In short, to the extent that individuals expect those in command positions to issue orders, and to the extent that such orders are regarded as legitimate, the occupants of command positions may be said to possess authority, which is "the expected and legitimate possession of power."[28] The pattern of distribution of authority within those organizations concerned with the making of foreign policy —that is, the authority structure—is relevant to analysis of how and why foreign-policy decisions are made as they are. The set of expecta-

[28] Harold D. Lasswell and Abraham Kaplan, *Power and Society: A Framework for Political Inquiry* (New Haven: Yale University Press, 1950), p. 133.

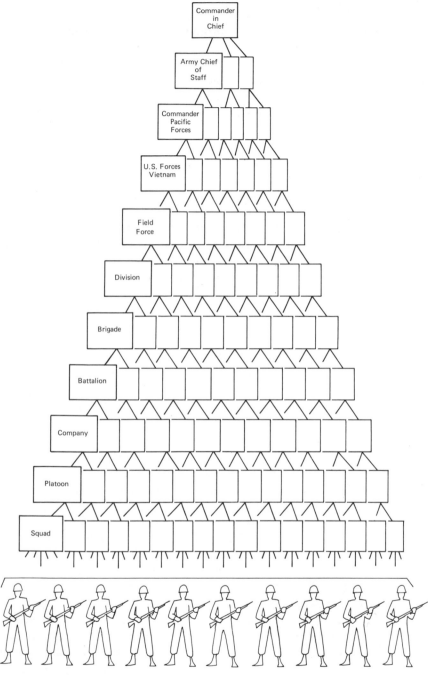

Figure 5   The Chain of Command from the Soldiers in Vietnam
to the Commander in Chief of the Armed Forces

tions within the bureaucracy regarding the kinds of commands and directives that are to be obeyed and the offices entitled to issue various kinds of commands and directives conditions the attitudes and behavior of those within the bureaucracy. When events occur and problems arise, the authority structure helps to determine who will make what kinds of decisions, who will give what kinds of commands, and who will respond to whose direction.

Authority Structure in Practice   However, examination of the actual behavior of those within the civil and military bureaucracy reveals a pattern of distribution of authority that is much less tidy than that depicted on formal organization charts. The actual authority structure within the bureaucracy stems from informal as well as formal sources. The pattern is established through custom and through the informal evolution of working relationships among the members of the bureaucracy, as well as through constitutional precept and practice, through legislation, and through executive orders or directives. To some extent, the pattern is always in flux. Without attempting to generalize about observable patterns of authority, however, the relevance of analysis of authority patterns in particular situations to explanation of decision-making behavior can be suggested through some familiar problems that arise in bureaucracy, stemming from its authority structure.

Perhaps the most familiar problem that organizations experience in allocating authority and responsibility is that of allocating the former in amounts equivalent to the latter. A former member of the State Department has noted that Secretary James Byrnes spent 350 of his 562 days in office outside Washington, mostly in negotiations with the Soviets. Thus, the under secretary of state, Dean Acheson, was forced to assume most of the responsibilities of the secretary's post in Washington. However, to carry out these responsibilities he "had normal authority over neither policy nor operations." [29]

Another form that misallocation of authority may take is undue concentration of authority. Some critics of Defense Department organization under Secretary McNamara contended that he exercised excessive control from the top. For instance, the first man to serve as secretary of the army under McNamara, Elvis Stahr, has been quoted as saying, "Mc-Namara is certainly the ablest man I have ever been closely associated with. But he has a tendency to overreach in exercising control and intrude in small details of administration. The Defense Department is

[29] Joseph M. Jones, *The Fifteen Weeks* (New York: Harcourt, paperback ed., 1964), pp. 105–106.

too big to be run by one man and there are just not enough McNamaras." [30]

The Pattern of Authority in the U-2 Affair Frequently also the opposite problem occurs within bureaucracy—with responsibility unduly diffuse rather than concentrated, and with lines of authority overlapping one another. The consequences of such a pattern for foreign-policy decision-making behavior can be illustrated by the confusion and inconsistencies of the American response to the downing of an American U-2 intelligence plane over Soviet territory in May 1960.

The incident was triggered by the announcement of Nikita Khrushchev to the Supreme Soviet and to a startled world through the mass media that an American "spy plane" had been brought down deep inside Soviet territory. The problem within the Eisenhower administration of formulating an appropriate response to Khrushchev's announcement was made more acute by the fact that the incident had occurred on the eve of a summit conference in Paris, at which Eisenhower was to meet with the leaders of the Soviet Union, Great Britain, and France (Khrushchev, Macmillan, and De Gaulle, respectively).

The coordination of an appropriate response was hampered by the complex pattern of authority under which the flight had been authorized. The U-2 plane had been piloted by Francis Gary Powers, who was nominally on the payroll of Lockheed Aircraft Corporation, which in turn was operating under a contract from the National Aeronautics and Space Administration (NASA). In fact, however, major responsibility for U-2 flights over the Soviet Union rested with the Central Intelligence Agency (CIA), under the authorization of the President, in order to provide intelligence information that would be utilized by the Departments of State and Defense.

In short, a number of offices and agencies had responsibilities for various aspects of Powers's secret flight. Confusion as to which of them should assume responsibility in the event that the secret was uncovered arose on the very first day (May 5) that word was received in the United States of Khrushchev's speech. Responding to questions, Presidential Press Secretary James Hagerty said that Khrushchev's claim was being investigated and that further information on the matter would be provided by NASA and the State Department as it became available.

Shortly thereafter, the State Department, through its spokesman Lincoln White, made the first public statement in response to Khrush-

[30] Quoted in Jack Raymond, *Power at the Pentagon* (New York: Harper & Row, 1964), p. 289. In the same discussion, Raymond noted that in preparing the 1965 budget, McNamara was said to have made more than 500 decisions himself.

chev's allegations. The response was a fabrication, a cover story that, without confirming Khrushchev's claim, nevertheless admitted that an American plane might have "strayed" over Soviet territory. If this had been the case, White indicated, the plane must have been a U-2 weather-reconnaissance plane flying out of Turkey, which had been missing since the pilot on May 1 had experienced difficulties with his oxygen equipment. Shortly after the State Department press conference, reporters obtained from a NASA official a separate statement. The NASA explanation of the incident followed the State Department cover story in most respects, but provided considerably more technical details, including the alleged flight plan of the U-2 and many of its performance characteristics. The NASA statement, which had been cleared with neither the White House, the State Department, nor the CIA, it was later learned, gave enterprising reporters a much more detailed basis for comparing the American government account of the U-2 flight with Khrushchev's account of the flight.

To this point, the fate of Powers was still unknown to American officials. He had been provided with equipment for destruction of the aircraft, in case of difficulty, and for suicide to prevent capture. But a rumor that Powers was alive as a Soviet prisoner reached the American ambassador to the Soviet Union, who cabled the news to Washington early on May 6. The news meant that the Soviets might now be conclusively able to demolish the American cover story. But, uninformed of this news, shortly after noon of May 6, Lincoln White made another press release on behalf of the State Department, reconfirming the original cover story and adding that there had been ". . . absolutely no—N-O—no—deliberate attempt to violate Soviet air space." [31]

It was only a day later that White was forced to begin the process of retracting the cover story. The impetus for the retraction came from a dramatic announcement by Khrushchev that the Soviets were in possession of the wreckage of the U-2, largely intact; that the pilot, Powers, was alive; and that he had admitted that his mission was photographic espionage of Soviet territory. Khrushchev brandished photographs from the U-2 camera as evidence. Shortly after this new announcement by Khrushchev, the State Department, through White, released its latest version of what had occurred. There had been a flight over Soviet territory, White now admitted, but he argued that the Soviet passion for secrecy made such intelligence activity necessary. Furthermore, White

[31] David Wise and Thomas B. Ross, *The U-2 Affair* (New York: Random House, 1962), p. 93. Wise and Ross provide a detailed and fascinating account of the U-2 affair. The analytical point made in the present section of the chapter is explained in greater detail in McCamy, pp. 10–28.

suggested in a vague way, the flight had not been authorized. Two days later, however, he issued still another press release, acknowledging now not only that President Eisenhower had authorized this and earlier flights over Soviet territory, but also implying that such violation of Soviet air space would continue. At the beginning of the summit conference in Paris, President Eisenhower declared that flights over Soviet territory had in fact been discontinued. But it was too late for conciliation. After denouncing the American government for its U-2 flights and deception, Khrushchev walked out, leaving the summit conference, like the U-2 cover story, in shambles.

Patterns of Communication   Just as the pattern of authority that exists within the political system can have a profound effect, for better or worse, upon foreign-policy decision-making behavior, so can the existing network of communication within the political system. An episode a few years ago in *L'il Abner*, the comic strip created by Al Capp, provides a humorous yet suggestive illustration of the importance of communications to the effective functioning of a large complex organization such as a government. In the episode, hundreds of flying anteaters, bred by an ingenious enemy power through crossing anteaters and hawks, had been trained to fly into the United States to communications centers and tie up telephone communications indefinitely by dialing all the key numbers of government with their noses. Capp arranged to have the devilish plot foiled in the nick of time, and thus the United States was spared a fictitious communications disaster. However, as the East Coast power failure of 1965 reveals, near-disaster in communications is not entirely a hypothetical matter. Channels of communication are the nervous system of human organization, which, if clogged or disabled, can paralyze the organization.

Formal channels of communication within bureaucracy correspond in part to the vertical network of communications between various levels of authority, such as those depicted in Figure 5. There are also, however, important horizontal lines of communication among peers within an organization and among agencies. Moreover, informal channels of communication, vertical as well as horizontal, play an important role in shaping patterns of interaction in the foreign-policy process.

Political parties, for example, provide an important channel of communication that has been established by custom to coexist with the formal network of communication. Perhaps an even more important informal channel of communication within the political system is provided by the various mass media. Indeed, the importance of the press, especially, within the political process has led one observer to describe it as "the fourth branch of government" and another to stress the function performed by widely read newspapers such as the *New York Times* in providing congressmen as well as executive officials with a common source of information and comment about foreign-policy problems.[32]

An interesting example of an informal communications channel developed through television was provided by the Cuban missile crisis of 1962. At the height of the crisis, John Scali, a State Department correspondent for the ABC television network, was contacted by a high Soviet official in Washington who apparently had developed considerable trust in Scali through their previous acquaintance. Scali was asked by the Soviet official, as a matter of great urgency, to check with top officials in the American government to see if they would agree to pledge publicly that the United States would not invade Cuba, in return for Soviet agreement to remove the missiles permanently from Cuban soil. Scali contacted Roger Hilsman, director of intelligence and research in the State Department, who in turn put Scali in touch with Secretary of State Rusk. Rusk outlined the American policy position to Scali, for communication back to the Soviets through the official who had contacted Scali. Twice more during the crisis, Scali served as a go-between for the American government and the Soviets. In effect, his contact with a high Soviet official had become an important channel of crisis communications. In the end, the unofficial talks between Scali and the Soviet official established the fundamental basis for negotiations between the American and Soviet governments.[33]

However, even in instances where informal or formal channels of communication remain open, as they did in the Cuban missile crisis, the political system may prove unable to utilize effectively the information that is transmitted through the channels. For example, the fact that the Soviets had been able to proceed as far as they had with the installation of missiles in the weeks before the crisis may be partly attributable to the widespread assumption among policy makers in Washington that the Soviets would not dare to risk such a provocative act; had the policy makers believed such a possibility, some critics contend, intelligence activities would have been pursued more vigorously and with greater attention to details that would have provided clues to missile installation.[34]

---

[32] Cf. Douglass Cater, Jr., *The Fourth Branch of Government* (Boston: Houghton Mifflin, 1959); Bernard C. Cohen, *The Press and Foreign Policy* (Princeton, N.J.: Princeton University Press, 1963).

[33] For further details on the episode, see Roger Hilsman, *To Move a Nation* (New York: Doubleday, 1967), pp. 217–224.

[34] Roberta Wohlstetter, "Cuba and Pearl Harbor: Hindsight and Foresight," *Foreign Affairs*, 43 (July 1965), 691–707. However, Hilsman rejects the Wohlstetter

A more clear-cut case of selective repression of available evidence, however, is the action (and inaction) of American policy makers in the period before Pearl Harbor. In a thorough study of American intelligence activity during the months prior to the Japanese attack, Roberta Wohlstetter found that American unpreparedness for the attack was attributable not to lack of evidence about Japanese intentions, but to the conviction of policy makers that the Japanese would attack elsewhere (Singapore or Hong Kong, for example)—a conviction that led American officials to ignore or dismiss bits of evidence pointing to an attack on Pearl Harbor. "In short, we failed to anticipate Pearl Harbor not for want of the relevant materials, but because of a plethora of irrelevant ones. Much of the appearance of wanton neglect that emerged in various investigations of the disaster resulted from the unconscious suppression of vast congeries of signs pointing in every direction except Pearl Harbor." [35]

Informal Power Structure

Foreign-policy decisions, although made in the name of the nation as a whole, seldom affect all citizens equally. Rather, some persons benefit more than others from a new trade agreement, for instance, or from a cultural-exchange program. Moreover, some persons incur more costs than others from implementing the decision (demands of the draft, for instance, in order to support a war effort) or from its consequences (inflation, for example). The differential impact of foreign-policy decisions is one important reason that the process deviates so greatly in practice from civics-class mythology that policy makers simply study the facts of a situation and then work out the best solutions. Rather, as we noted in Chapter 7 and reemphasize here, foreign-policy making is a process of politics, not of pure reason.

Once we recognize that policy making is a political process, we can no longer concern ourselves only with analysis of the actions of policy makers (those with formal and informal responsibilities in government for foreign policy). By definition, policy makers are those who make foreign-policy decisions; but these decisions are influenced by the opinions and actions of others in the society who stand to benefit or to

---

thesis as applied to the events leading to the Cuban missile crisis. Indeed, on balance, Hilsman deems American intelligence activities in that episode as successful rather than as unsuccessful. See his analysis of the intelligence aspect of the missile crisis in *To Move a Nation*, chap. 14.

[35] Roberta Wohlstetter, *Pearl Harbor: Warning and Decision* (Stanford, Calif.: Stanford University Press, 1962), p. 387.

suffer from them. Thus, we have to distinguish between authority, which is formal power, and informal power—that is, potential for influence derived not necessarily from government position but often from other political resources, such as wealth, prestige, or knowledge. Foreign-policy analysis from a decision-making perspective is concerned not only with the identification of the foreign-policy authority structure, but also with the identification of the distribution of power within the society and with the specification of the weight, scope, and domain of influence of various individuals and groups. We shall not attempt here to describe the power structure of American society as it relates to foreign policy. The structure is a dynamic rather than static one in any event. Rather, we shall simply comment on the problem of locating the power structure with accuracy and on its relevance to foreign-policy analysis from a decision-making perspective.

At the risk of oversimplification, we may divide the problem of identifying the foreign-policy power structure into two tasks: The first is to identify who is expressing what kinds of views and taking what kinds of political actions. The second is to determine the impact of these opinions and actions on the decisions of policy makers.

The first task, although sometimes complex and detailed, is the easier of the two. In a relatively open society such as the American one, most political opinions are expressed in forums accessible to public view, as in the mass media. Thus, one can identify the spectrum of opinion on various issues and can determine the attitude alignments of various sectors of the society. Moreover, although interest groups may lobby through hidden means as well as in public view, the knowledge that such groups attempt to influence particular policies in ways favorable to their own interests is no surprise, nor are such activities often a secret. The patterns of interest-group activity are quite familiar even to the casual observer of the foreign-policy process. It is obvious, for example, that all major aircraft and missile manufacturers are active in lobbying (within the executive branch as well as in Congress) in favor of particular defense programs and policies. Oil corporations attempt to influence American policies in the Middle East, in the Caribbean, and in other parts of the world where they have interests. Sugar manufacturers take an active interest in policies toward Castro's Cuba, whose sugar produc tion can be competitive with American domestic production. Ethnic groups express their views on the policies that the United States ought to pursue toward their former homelands. National Guard and Reserve organizations are active to promote certain force levels within the armed services and to stipulate the kinds of foreign-policy crises that might require reserve call-ups. Labor unions take a public position on immigration laws and on tariffs.

However, if a pattern of political activity by various individuals and groups in relation to foreign-policy issues can be described quite accurately, the second task, determining the impact of the activity, is far more difficult. Let us take the problem of assessing the impact of public opinion on policy, for example. There is little difficulty, in these days of national opinion polling, in finding such opinion, but certain analytical problems must be recognized even in identifying public opinion. For example, it has become axiomatic among political scientists in recent years that there is not one monolithic public but rather various publics, the size and composition of which vary depending on the issue. Moreover, a useful distinction is made between the opinion of the mass public, which does not follow foreign affairs with regularity, and the attentive public, which does. Intensity of opinion, although seldom reported in national polls, is another dimension that is useful in making distinctions among the various viewpoints. These qualifications aside, however, even if one were able to collect public-opinion data in which he had confidence, how would he demonstrate that the opinions had influenced foreign-policy decision making? We may assume as a starting point that foreign-policy decision makers are not totally oblivious to public opinion. But government officials are themselves opinion makers as well as recipients of opinion. The process by which officials attempt to shape opinion and then in turn become attuned to the views that, in part, they have shaped is dynamic and complex.[36] Moreover, it is the "synthetic" public opinion which officials perceive, rather than objective measures of opinion, that are taken into account in policy making.[37]

However, what can we discover about organized political activity consciously designed to influence policy decisions? What happens if an interest group works vigorously to persuade decision makers to pursue a given course of action, and that course of action is adopted? Mere demonstration of a coincidence between the expressed interests of a particular group or sector of society and the course of action selected by foreign-

---

[36] See Gabriel A. Almond, *The American People and Foreign Policy* (New York: Praeger, paperback ed., 1960); James N. Rosenau, *Public Opinion and Foreign Policy* (New York: Random House, 1961); Rosenau, *National Leadership and Foreign Policy: A Case Study in the Mobilization of Public Support* (Princeton, N.J.: Princeton University Press, 1963); Milton J. Rosenberg, "Attitude Change and Foreign Policy in the Cold War Era," in Rosenau, ed., *Domestic Sources of Foreign Policy* (New York: Free Press, 1967), pp. 111–159.

[37] See Cater.

policy decision makers obviously is inadequate as proof that the decision was caused by pressures from the group. Indeed, such a correlation is not necessarily a demonstration of any influence at all. If it can be demonstrated that decision makers were aware of the views of a particular group or a particular set of issues and that they have consistently made decisions in accordance with those views in spite of opposition from other groups, then the inference is strengthened that the group has been influential. Even then, such an inference can be challenged on various grounds, such as the argument that the views of other groups or of the public in general exerted a greater influence on the actions of policy makers, or that policy makers were acting merely in accordance with their own personal beliefs, which happened to coincide consistently with the views of the group in question.

Seldom is a given policy maker or group of policy makers simply the tool or mouthpiece of a particular interest. More often, policy makers seek to reconcile and to satisfy competing interests; the ensuing process has elements of brokerage, of bargaining, of logrolling, and of sheer conflict. Moreover, it is not only the direct demands of individuals and groups on foreign-policy issues that the policy maker must accommodate but also indirect demands that may be unrelated or only peripherally related to foreign affairs. Furthermore, the struggle to influence current policy outcomes and to amass power that can be utilized to influence policy in the future is not peculiar to nongovernmental persons and groups; the struggle goes on among those within government as well. It occurs, for example, between the executive branch and Congress. Policy makers in the executive branch often see congressmen as exerting a perverse effect on the foreign-policy process through their pursuit of narrow political interests to the neglect of objective assessments of national need. The lament of George Kennan regarding congressional failure to respond to his requests as Ambassador to Yugoslavia during 1961–1963 is typical. Kennan observed that "in budgetary and fiscal matters . . . the Ambassador was sadly powerless. In general, he simply took what he got. . . . There were times when a minor area of discretion on the part of the Ambassador would have yielded dividends from the standpoint of national interest, and when the absence of it was frustrating and embarrassing."[38] Although the Congress may frustrate and limit the executive branch, especially through control of appropriations and through investigation, most studies of the role of Congress in foreign affairs suggest that the impact of Congress on most foreign-

[38] U.S. Congress, Senate Committee on Government Operations, Subcommittee on National Security Staffing and Operations, *Hearings, Administration of National Security*, pt. 5, 1st sess., 1963, pp. 358–363.

policy decisions is relatively minor, especially at the stage of initiating new courses of action and new objectives.[39] Nevertheless, the intermittent assertions by members of Congress of claims for recognition and for a voice in policy making contribute to the political pressures to which policy makers in the executive branch are subjected.

The politics of policy making also occurs within the executive branch itself. Departments compete with one another for resources; agencies compete for the largest share of the departmental budget.[40] Presidential assistants vie for his attention. Subject to the clash of competing domestic as well as foreign interests, individual policy makers seek not only to fashion a consensus that will provide a politically workable basis for coping with existing problems, but also to strengthen their own position for influencing subsequent outcomes.

Thus, although an effort to identify the informal power structure is essential to sound analysis of foreign policy from a decision-making perspective, one must recognize the improbability of perfect success in the effort. Demonstration of influence hinges on establishing a link between the actions of those whom one supposes to be influential with the actions of those whom one supposes have been influenced—namely, the foreign-policy decision makers. However, not only the responsiveness of decision makers to interests and demands from domestic politics, but also each of the other factors mentioned earlier in the chapter contributes, in varying degrees in various situations, to an explanation of the behavior of foreign-policy decision makers. Specification of how the various relevant factors are interrelated under various conditions is the next vital step in analysis; in Chapter 9, we shall illustrate how this step may be taken.

[39] See, for example, James A. Robinson, *Congress and Foreign Policy-Making* (Homewood, Ill.: Dorsey, revised ed., 1967); Holbert N. Carroll, *The House of Representatives and Foreign Affairs* (Boston: Little, Brown, revised ed., 1966); David N. Farnsworth, *The Senate Committee on Foreign Relations* (Urbana, Ill.: University of Illinois Press, 1961). Each of the three books cited contains an extensive bibliography of further relevant source materials.

[40] For example, see Aaron Wildavsky, *The Politics of the Budgetary Process* (Boston: Little, Brown, 1964); and James R. Schlesinger, *The Political Economy of National Security* (New York: Praeger, 1960).

9

Decision-Making Perspectives

Some Illustrative Hypotheses

Analytically, our concern with factors such as personality, political culture, role demands, political pressures, and the institutional framework of policy making, focuses on the "who, what, when, and how" questions cited at the outset of Chapter 8. That is, our concern lies in determining the persons, groups, and institutions that participate in the foreign-policy decision-making process in the United States; with specifying the amount of influence that is wielded by various governmental and nongovernmental persons and groups; with indicating the stages in the process and the circumstances under which such influence is manifested; and with explaining the procedures and means that are utilized in the wielding of such influence. This chapter is devoted to suggesting how one might begin to deal with such analytical concerns, through the development of a series of illustrative hypotheses.

261

The format of the hypotheses will be one in which the *type of response* that is made by the political system (or components thereof) to a foreign-policy problem is treated as the *dependent variable*. Types of response are classified according to the extent of reliance upon existing plans and routines, according to the level in the authority structure at which the problem is resolved, or according to the pace of action in dealing with the problem.

The independent variables in the hypotheses that follow correspond to various facets of the way in which the foreign-policy situation was coded or interpreted at various stages in the foreign-policy process. Eight dimensions of the initial coding and subsequent interpretation of foreign-policy problems within a national political system may be broadly identified: (1) the extent to which a situation is anticipated or unanticipated by those who detect the situation; (2) the simplicity or complexity of the situation in terms of the number and kinds of other contemporary problems and issues that have a bearing on it; (3) the salience of the interests at stake, as perceived by policy makers; (4) the extent to which policy makers believe that the situation threatens or supports national interests; (5) estimated tactical capabilities for coping with the situation; (6) the estimated extent to which time will enhance or hinder existing capabilities; (7) the perception that decision makers have of the extent of consensus among national leaders regarding a course of action to be taken in response to the situation; and (8) the perception that decision makers have of the stability of views among national leaders regarding a course of action to be taken.

Many potentially interesting and important interrelationships among variables identified earlier in the chapter are not explored in the hypotheses that are formulated here. For instance, we do not speculate on the conditions under which various interest groups are likely to be successful in their efforts to influence various kinds of foreign-policy decisions. Following the practice of earlier chapters, we endeavor to be suggestive rather than definitive in the scope and form of our hypotheses. Therefore, the reader will want to supplement the relatively small number of hypotheses that follow with others of his own and with hypotheses from other sources about foreign-policy decision making or about organizational behavior in general.[1]

---

[1] As indicated earlier, it is not our intention to develop here an annotated bibliography of the countless works relevant to the study of foreign policy. Nevertheless, a small sample of books can be cited here as suggestions of sources to which the reader might turn for further efforts to hypothesize about the policy-making process or about organizational behavior generally. See Glenn D. Paige, *The Korean Decision* (New York: Free Press, 1968), pts. 4, 5, and 6; Anthony Downs, *Inside Bureaucracy*

The hypotheses formulated here are designed especially to highlight some of the key dilemmas that policy makers face in efforts to structure the activities of policy making to enable the political system to adapt to the incessant and complex demands of the external environment, while responding also to internally expressed needs and goals. The dilemmas are described as the programming-innovating dilemma, the responsibility-reflection dilemma, and the speed-accuracy dilemma. The hypotheses take the form of empirical propositions, although the dilemmas to which they relate are questions that must be resolved partly through normative judgment. The interrelationship between questions of value and questions of fact, although suggested here, will be examined in greater detail in Part V of the book.

The Programming-Innovating Dilemma

One basis for classification of the types of response that a political system, or organizations within a system, make to demands and events is the degree of reliance upon existing plans and routines. A plan may be defined simply as a design for coping with a problem that is expected to occur only once, or infrequently. A routine may be defined as a standardized procedure for dealing with a problem or situation that is expected to occur frequently. Policy papers such as those for the National Security Council or the Joint Chiefs of Staff are examples of plans at high levels of government. The development of such plans is the primary responsibility of the Policy Planning Council (known prior to 1961 as the Policy Planning Staff) within the Department of State and of the Policy Planning Staff within the Office of International Security Affairs of the Department of Defense. But plans and routines exist at all levels of government. Readers with knowledge of military organization will be familiar with the SOP's (standard operating procedures) that are provided for almost every conceivable recurrent problem with which the armed forces deal. SOP's or their counterparts are developed in civil bureaucracy as well. Routines and plans are not necessarily written documents, but may consist of instructions transmitted orally or simply of habits developed from performing a given task repeatedly. Three

(Boston: Little, Brown, 1967); Robert K. Merton *et al.*, eds., *Reader in Bureaucracy* (New York: Free Press, 1952); Theodore Caplow, *Principles of Organization* (New York: Harcourt, 1964); Herbert A. Simon, *Administrative Behavior* (New York: Crowell-Collier-Macmillan, 2d ed., 1957); Sidney Mailick and Edward H. Van Ness, eds., *Concepts and Issues in Administrative Behavior* (Englewood Cliffs, N.J.: Prentice-Hall, 1962); Andrew M. Scott, *The Functioning of the International System* (New York: Crowell-Collier-Macmillan, 1967), chap. 6.

categories of response of a political system or subsystem to a demand or event may be broadly distinguished. A *preprogrammed response* is essentially a reflex action, in which existing routines and plans condition entirely or almost entirely the response that is made. A response in which existing plans or routines are utilized to some extent, but are modified in relation to nuances or peculiarities of the situation, may be termed an *adjustive response*. An *inventive response*, in contrast, involves not only the substantial rejection of existing plans or routines for coping with an existing or anticipated problem, but also a basic reformulation of underlying assumptions on which they are based—a creative leap beyond the rationale on which prior planning had been based.

None of the three types of response is intrinsically superior to any of the others; the question is one of appropriateness to the situation. Successful adaptation of the political system to its geopolitical world environment requires the economical utilization of scarce human energies and skills as well as scarce natural and material resources. To the extent that foreign-policy problems can be anticipated and preprogrammed responses devised, time and creative energies are saved for problems that could not be anticipated. On the other hand, in a complex and rapidly changing world, efforts to respond to situations only on the basis of routines and existing plans are bound to be partially, and perhaps fatally, inadequate.

The programming-innovating dilemma, which is common to all complex organizations as well as to all nation-states, is this: Can the political system increase the predictability of its environment (and thereby deal with a larger share of problems through preprogrammed responses), while maintaining and developing a capacity for innovation and creative growth in the face of complexity and change?

The first set of hypotheses provides a tentative explanation of the type of response that is made to a foreign-policy decision-making situation in terms of the extent to which the situation was anticipated and in terms of its complexity. One must bear in mind that problems that are intrinsically complex sometimes are treated by policy makers as if they were simple, and that basically simple problems are sometimes complicated by the analyses of policy makers. Moreover, often events that should have been anticipated have come as a surprise. Resistance within the policy-making subculture to systematic planning and to analyses that might enhance the predictive capabilities of the government have been noted earlier. The disinclination of policy makers toward long-range forecasting, if combined with a proclivity for amassing detailed facts, can produce an information overload problem that forces policy makers to adjust responses to simple, recurrent events and that induces bewilderment in the face of complex or nonrecurrent problems. For example, an analysis published a few years ago by the Subcommittee on National Security Staffing and Operations, of the Senate Committee on Government Operations, indicated that policy makers in Washington are inadequately informed not only in spite of an enormous volume of information that they receive daily from embassies all over the world, but partly precisely because of this great volume of incoming information. As the analysis indicated, routines had not been adequately established that would provide clear guidelines for the kinds of information to collect and the kinds to report. "No one knows how to issue general instructions on who should be told what and when. As a result the rule seems to be, Report Everything." [2]

Recognizing the fallibility of human coding and interpretation procedures in the foreign-policy process, one may suggest the following three hypotheses, which are depicted graphically in Figure 6.

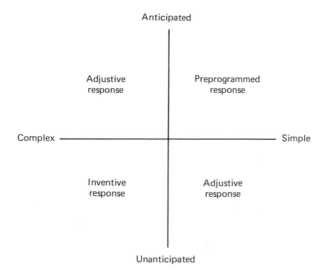

Figure 6   The Extent to Which a Situation Conforms to Expectations and the Degree of Complexity of a Situation as Determinants of the Type of Decision-Making Response (Preprogrammed, Adjustive, or Inventive)

[2] The subcommittee report has been published in paperback, edited by Senator Jackson, chairman of the subcommittee. Henry M. Jackson, *The Secretary of State and the Ambassador* (New York: Praeger, 1964), p. 23.

HYPOTHESIS 14   *Simple, anticipated problems tend to elicit pre-programmed responses.*

Such a routine situation and preprogrammed response may be illustrated by the government's response to the presentation of credentials by a new foreign ambassador. Clear routines exist for dealing with the situation, and little inventive action is required.

HYPOTHESIS 15   *Simple, but unanticipated problems, or complex, but anticipated problems, tend to elicit adjustive responses.*

An example of the former type arose with the release of three American prisoners by the Hanoi regime during the summer of 1968. Working out the arrangements for accepting prisoners released by another government is not characteristically a problem of enormous complexity. Nevertheless, in the context of ongoing peace talks in Paris between representatives of the American and North Vietnamese governments, it seemed possible that the release of prisoners was a gesture on the part of the Hanoi government to influence or to encourage the peace talks. Thus, implications of the release of prisoners made the situation far more than a routine matter, to which a response could not be entirely preprogrammed. Indeed, final procedural details of the American response, such as whether the three released Americans would return to the United States on military or on civil aircraft, were worked out only at the last minute.

An example of a complex, but anticipated problem, on the other hand, arose with the detection in 1964 of a Chinese atom-bomb explosion. It was anticipated that the Communist Chinese would develop nuclear weapons, although the timing of successful testing of such weapons could not be predicted exactly. However, the development of nuclear potential by the Chinese had such far-reaching potential implications for Asian politics, for Sino-Soviet relations, and for American national security that the situation demanded constant study and appraisal. In short, although the ability to anticipate the problem enabled the American government to engage in some contingency planning, the complexity of the situation demanded an adjustive, rather than a preprogrammed response.

HYPOTHESIS 16   *Complex, unanticipated problems tend to elicit inventive responses.*

Sometimes problems arise quite unexpectedly that are multifaceted in their possible ramifications. In such a situation, existing plans and routines provide little or no guidance. A vivid example from the American foreign-policy experience was provided by the announcement, in February 1947, of the British government that, as of the end of March, they would be forced by their own desperate economic situation to terminate economic and military aid to Greece and Turkey. Within fifteen weeks, the American government had formulated two momentous policy statements in response to the situation in Greece and Turkey and related problems in Europe and the Middle East: the Truman Doctrine and the Marshall Plan. These policies were not entirely new, however. As suggested in Chapter 4, the attitudes and beliefs that led to the development of a containment strategy, of which the Truman Doctrine and Marshall Plan were important landmarks, had been evolving since the final months of World War II. Moreover, the momentous American policy decisions of 1947 are not to be explained solely in terms of the facts that the British announcement of February was unanticipated and that the ensuing problems were complex. The point at hand, however, is that the complex, unanticipated nature of the situation rendered existing plans and routines obsolete and challenged policy makers to reappraise existing policies in a fundamental way. As Joseph Jones, who participated in the policy discussions, has put it, the period of fifteen weeks following the British announcement "was one of those rare times in history when shackles fall away from the mind, the spirit, and the will, allowing them to soar free and high for a while and to discover new standards of what is responsible, of what is promising, and of what is possible."[3] Jones's description of the response of American policy makers in 1947 may be a bit extravagant, but there is little doubt that his sense of the challenge and intellectual liberation in the atmosphere of the times was widely shared among his colleagues.

Incentives and Costs for Innovation   There seems to have been another stimulus to creativity at the time of "the fifteen weeks"; Jones also emphasizes the pervasive feeling within the State Department under Secretary Marshall, in contrast to the prevailing atmosphere during the secretaryship of Cordell Hull, that new departures in foreign policy were to be encouraged and that new ideas from all levels in the department would be welcomed.[4] Thus, two additional hypotheses may be suggested.

HYPOTHESIS 17   *The greater the incentives within an organization for suggesting departures from existing policies or for chal-*

[3] Joseph M. Jones, *The Fifteen Weeks* (New York: Harcourt, paperback ed., 1964), p. 259.
[4] Jones, pp. 100–118.

lenging existing policy assumptions, the greater the probability that the organization will respond inventively to unanticipated problems.

The converse of Hypothesis 17 may be stated as Hypothesis 18:

HYPOTHESIS 18   *The fewer the incentives and the higher the probable costs to personnel within an organization for challenging basic assumptions upon which ongoing policies are based, the lower the probability that the organization will respond inventively to unanticipated problems.*

Reference may be made not only to the sense of stagnation that Jones sensed within the State Department under Cordell Hull, but also to the later McCarthy era of the 1950s. In the early years of John Foster Dulles's tenure as secretary of state, a purge of the State Department, conducted on the basis of extensive security checks into past as well as present associations, actions, and attitudes of departmental personnel, created an atmosphere in which deviation or dissent from established policies and their rationale carried great risks. As five former State Department officials noted at the time in a letter to the *New York Times* protesting Dulles's policies, "a premium . . . has been put upon reporting and upon recommendations which are ambiguously stated or so cautiously set forth as to be deceiving. When any such tendency begins its insidious work it is not long before accuracy and initiative have been sacrificed to acceptability and conformity." [5] Some critics have contended that the stifling effects of the McCarthy era upon creativity within the State Department—most notably within the Bureau of East Asian Affairs—could still be detected a decade later in the form of policy rigidity in Vietnam. [6]

Additional Determinants of Response: Turnover and Job Mastery

Hypotheses 14, 15, and 16 may be viewed as tentative descriptions of typical patterns of response of the bureaucracy to foreign-policy problems. Hypotheses 17 and 18 essentially represent corollaries to the previous three hypotheses, suggesting conditions under which one can

[5] Letter published January 17, 1954, cited with comment by Hans J. Morgenthau, "John Foster Dulles," in Norman A. Graebner, ed., *An Uncertain Tradition: American Secretaries of State in the Twentieth Century* (New York: McGraw-Hill, 1961), pp. 289–308, 299.

[6] For example, see James C. Thomson, Jr., "How Could Vietnam Happen? An Autopsy," *Atlantic Monthly*, 221 (April 1968), 47–53. Thomson's views were formulated on the basis of observations as an East Asian specialist working in government on the White House staff and in the Department of State during 1961–1966.

expect deviations from typical patterns of response. Two additional hypotheses suggest further conditions under which the bureaucracy or its various component organizations may, on the one hand, increase reliance on preprogrammed responses to problems or, on the other hand, response inventively to a greater extent to problems.

> HYPOTHESIS 19 *During periods of high turnover of key personnel, but relatively low turnover of middle-level and lower-level personnel, an organization will increase its reliance on routine procedures for coping with problems.*

During such periods, an extra burden for decision making falls to those persons at middle and lower levels who provide the major element of continuity in bureaucracy. Such individuals, however, are likely to feel restrained from making new policy departures during a period of turnover at the top by their doubt whether such departures would receive the endorsement and support of the new leadership. It has often been noted, for example, that in the transition period from the election of a new administration to its assumption of office, such as the period in late 1968 prior to the transfer of authority from President Johnson to President Nixon, innovative activity in foreign policy (and in domestic policy for that matter) is at a minimum. Those key officials of the outgoing administration who have not already departed are likely to spend much of their time during the transitional period either seeking new positions for themselves or briefing their successors on ongoing policy problems and on organizational procedures. Meanwhile, subordinate officials hesitate to promote new ideas or new programs, for fear that innovation begun in the old administration may be rejected by the new administration.

Closely related to the previous hypothesis is another, Hypothesis 20.

> HYPOTHESIS 20 *The greater the sense of security and mastery of their responsibilities that top-level decision makers possess, the greater the probability that an organization will respond inventively to the problems it confronts.*

The contrast between President Kennedy's troubled acceptance during the first months of his administration of plans initiated by the previous administration for an invasion of Cuba by exiles, leading to the Bay of Pigs fiasco, and Kennedy's subsequent active control of the decision-making process during the Cuban missile crisis of 1962, producing a response to the problem that has been generally acclaimed as creative and successful, suggests support for the hypothesis. The respective accounts of Sorensen, Schlesinger, and Hilsman, for instance, all attribute Kennedy's hesitancy to challenge the views of the established experts who had designed and organized the Bay of Pigs invasion to the newness of the President to his office and his unfamiliarity with the strengths and weaknesses of various advisers.[7] In contrast, from the start of the Cuban missile crisis, as Elie Abel has observed in one of the most detailed accounts of the decision-making process during the crisis, "Kennedy meant to control events, not to be swept along by them. The political initiative was to be his alone." [8]

The Responsibility-Reflection Dilemma

Another dilemma that plagues the structures involved in the making of American foreign policy, as it plagues most complex organizations, may be termed the responsibility-reflection dilemma. It is desirable that those persons in positions of highest authority within an organization assume responsibility for making the decisions of greatest importance. This means that problems originated or detected at lower levels within the organization should be fed upward through channels to the top, if major decisions of policy are required. On the other hand, it is also desirable that those in key executive positions have time for reflection and for creative consideration of their responsibilities. If they are to have this time, they must delegate a considerable amount of responsibility for problem solving and decision making to subordinates at lower levels. The dilemma, as it applies to foreign-policy decisions, is this: Can the political system ensure that the big problems that arise will be sent to top levels for decisions, without so overburdening top policy makers that they have no time for the reflection essential to sound judgment and broad vision?

A number of hypotheses may be formulated about the levels at which foreign-policy decisions are made. Key variables here include the salience of the interests at stake, the extent to which the situation supports or threatens national interest, the degree of complexity of the situation, and the extent to which key policy makers probe in detail into the concerns of their subordinates.

The salience of a situation and the extent to which it seems to support or threaten existing interests are relevant to a determination of the level

---

[7] Cf. Theodore C. Sorensen, *Kennedy* (New York: Bantam Books, 1966), pp. 340–341; Arthur Schlesinger, Jr., *A Thousand Days* (Boston: Houghton Mifflin, 1965), p. 258; Roger Hilsman, *To Move a Nation* (New York: Doubleday, 1967), pp. 217–224.

[8] Elie Abel, *The Missile Crisis* (New York: Bantam Books, paperback ed., 1966), p. 36.

within the hierarchy of authority at which a decision will be made. The general relationship postulated is that the higher the salience of the situation, and the greater the threat, the more likely it is that the final decisions will be made at top levels of government. The relationship is frequently noted in accounts of foreign-policy decision making; it has received further empirical support in a study by Dean G. Pruitt based upon extensive interviewing of State Department officials about how they handle various kinds of problems.[9] The following hypotheses, illustrated graphically in Figure 7 make the relationship between variables explicit.

HYPOTHESIS 21   *Decisions regarding situations of low salience that are classified as supportive or neutral tend to be made at low levels.*

An example would be a situation in which two small nations, with which the United States had little diplomatic contact or commerce, signed a mutual trade agreement. Such a situation would be relatively neutral in its implications for American interest and of low salience;

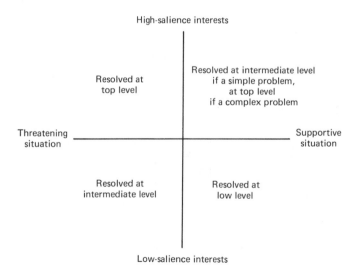

Figure 7   Degree of Salience of Interests at Stake and Extent to Which a Situation Supports or Threatens Interests, in Relation to the Level at Which a Decision-Making Situation Is Resolved

[9]Dean G. Pruitt, *Problem Solving in the Department of State*, in Monograph Series in World Affairs, no. 2 (Denver: University of Denver, 1964–1965).

there would be no occasion for referring the situation to high levels of government.

HYPOTHESIS 22   *Decisions regarding situations of middle salience that are neutral or supportive, or those of low salience that are threatening, tend to be made at intermediate levels.*

An example of the former type is the situation in which the regime of Ahmed Ben Bella, President of Algeria, was overthrown in June 1965 in a revolt led by Algerian Army Colonel Houari Boumedienne. The even was important in the context of North African politics, but difficult to assess for its future significance to American foreign policy. Ben Bella had been somewhat a thorn in the side of the United States, with his expressions of praise for Castro, for instance, and his support of insurgents in the Congo, where the United States was seeking to bolster the efforts of the United Nations to stabilize the political situation. On the other hand, upon taking power, Boumedienne stated that there would be no change in Algerian foreign policy. In such a context, foreign-policy response is typically left at the level of the State Department desk officer, who has detailed expertise in the area, in consultation with his immediate superiors.

A hypothetical example of a low-salience, but threatening, situation would be one in which an anti-American demonstration occurred among students in an area rather peripheral to American interests, such as Ceylon. The former situation would be referred to intermediate levels because interests of middle salience were involved, the latter, because of the threat involved.

HYPOTHESIS 23   *Decisions regarding situations of high salience that are threatening tend to be made at top levels.*

Most of the major crisis decisions of foreign policy have arisen from situations of this sort. The Cuban missile crisis is one example. High-salience American interests were severely threatened; thus the American response was formulated at the highest levels of government.

HYPOTHESIS 24   *Problems of middle salience that are threatening tend to be resolved at intermediate levels if they are simple, at top levels if they are complex.*

The former problem is illustrated by the assassination in 1967 of two American military officers in Guatemala. Such a situation could be handled primarily at the level of the ambassador and of the assistant secretary, without deeply involving the secretaries of state and defense or the President. On the other hand, a *coup* in Iraq in 1958, although posing an immediate threat to interests perhaps no more salient than those in Central America, occurred in a context of such tension throughout the Middle East and under such circumstances as to make it uncertain in the United States whether the *coup* was an isolated event or part of a widespread conspiracy, perhaps inspired by Cairo or Moscow, to overthrow pro-American governments in the Middle East. Consequently, the problem was referred to top levels of the American government for decision.

> HYPOTHESIS 25 *Problems of high salience that are supportive or neutral tend to be resolved at intermediate levels if they are simple, at top levels if they are complex.*

The defections of various Soviet scientists to the West, for instance, which have occurred infrequently, have represented problems generally supportive of American interests, relative to the Cold War conflict with the Soviet Union, which is a situation of high salience. Nevertheless, the issues surrounding such defections can be described as simple, relative to other problems to be dealt with in areas of high salience. On the other hand, the defection of Stalin's daughter, Svetlana Alliluyeva, in 1967, involved a person of such world renown that the possible international implications of her defection were extremely complex.[10] The latter problem required the persistent attention of policy makers at top levels, therefore, whereas the defection of less important or lesser known persons usually can be analyzed at intermediate levels of government.

Hypotheses 21–25 depict decision-making strategy within organizations involved in the foreign-policy process that assigns the major problems to the top levels for decision, but lets lower levels handle the less important problems. Such a strategy is designed to promote efficiency. It is interesting to consider, however, conditions under which the government, or its component organizations and agencies, might deviate from this strategy. Hypotheses 26 and 27 suggest some conditions that might produce such a deviant response; Hypotheses 26 and 27 might be viewed as corollaries to Hypotheses 21–25.

> HYPOTHESIS 26 *The greater the reluctance of those at top levels in an organization to concern themselves with details of policy problems, and the greater their insistence that only questions of paramount importance be presented to them for decision, the*

[10] Details of her escape to the West are contained in Svetlana Alliluyeva, *Only One Year* (New York: Harper & Row, 1969).

higher will be the proportion of decisions made at lower and middle levels.

President Eisenhower's dislike of detail and his preference to have problems presented to him in digested form, after they had been thoroughly "staffed," led numerous critics to assert that matters that properly should have been handled by the President were in fact being decided by his subordinates.[11]

The opposite problem is postulated in Hypothesis 27:

HYPOTHESIS 27   *The greater the tendency of policy makers at top levels to call into question matters of detail in the operation and activities of those at lower levels, the higher will be the proportion of problems submitted to top levels for decision.*

Just as the Eisenhower presidency tends to illustrate Hypothesis 26, so the presidency of John F. Kennedy tends to illustrate Hypothesis 27. Whereas Eisenhower eschewed detail, Kennedy immersed himself in it, often bypassing channels to communicate directly with those at lower echelons who could provide him with the information he sought about a particular matter. As one associate put it, "President Kennedy is a desk officer at the highest level." [12] An advantage of such an approach is that if bureaucratic channels have become bogged down, top leaders can sometimes energize the bureaucracy by probing directly into affairs at lower levels, thereby also getting an idea of the key points at which communications within the bureaucracy are being clogged. As the hypothesis suggests, however, and as others have observed of the Kennedy presidency, the effect of such an approach is likely to be that of funneling proportionately more problems to the top for decision. As one observer has put it, "The great risk of the Kennedy method is that no single mind, even a Presidential mind, can absorb the information or muster the wisdom necessary for sound judgment of many intricate issues pouring upon the President." [13]

[11] Critics who have made this allegation are too numerous to list completely. An example of one of the strongest condemnations of the Eisenhower reliance on his staff is found in Richard E. Neustadt, *Presidential Power* (New York: New American Library, Signet paperback ed., 1964), pp. 146–170. An assessment that points out advantages as well as disadvantages of the Eisenhower approach, although on balance critical of it, is presented in Louis W. Koenig, *The Chief Executive* (New York: Harcourt, paperback revised ed., 1968), pp. 167–171. The former President himself contended that his reliance on his staff was not excessive. See Dwight D. Eisenhower, "Some Thoughts on the Presidency," *Reader's Digest* (Nov. 1968), pp. 49–55.

[12] Cited in Joseph Kraft, "Kennedy's Working Staff," *Harper's*, 225 (Dec. 1962), p. 33.

[13] Koenig, p. 176.

The Speed-Accuracy Dilemma

Organizations characteristically strive both for speed in processing the demands made upon them and for accuracy in estimating the nature of the problems and the tactics to be employed in coping with them. However, just as even the most skilled typist finds, above a certain threshold increases in speed can be attained only through a reduction in accuracy; thus, organizations too must sometimes sacrifice accuracy in the estimates they make about a problem in order to respond to it quickly, or they must sacrifice speed of response for accuracy. For those persons and organizations involved in the making of American foreign policy, the dilemma is particularly acute, because time is an especially scarce resource, and delay may increase the probability of failure in a given situation; on the other hand, the costs of misjudgment in responding to critical problems of foreign affairs may be monumental.

In considering the criteria to be employed in assessing the costs of misjudgment, we may suggest the following hypothesis.

> HYPOTHESIS 28 *The more unanticipated the problem, the greater its complexity, the higher the salience of interests at stake, or the greater the threat to interests, the greater will be the tendency of decision makers to delay action.*

The factors cited increase the probability or the costs of error from hasty judgment. However, this probability must be weighed against the costs anticipated from delay in acting to solve a problem. Especially pertinent questions are whether delay is likely to reduce or to increase the capabilities available to policy makers to deal with the problem (tactical capabilities) and whether delay is likely to be advantageous or detrimental to maintaining or securing a consensus among national leaders regarding a course of action to be taken. The term "decision makers" is used here to refer to those among the group of policy makers (those with formal responsibility for making policy decisions) who actually participate in the process of making the decision in question. The term "national leaders" is used as it was defined by Rosenau, and as used by us in Chapter 5, to refer to "those members of the society who *occupy positions which enable them to transmit, with some regularity, opinions about foreign policy issues to unknown persons.*" [14]

Pace of Decision Making and Tactical Capabilities The relationship postulated between tactical capabilities for dealing with a situation and

---

[14] James N. Rosenau, *National Leadership and Foreign Policy* (Princeton, N.J.: Princeton University Press, 1963), p. 6. Italics in original text.

the speed or delay with which decision makers will move toward action is depicted graphically in Figure 8. It is depicted verbally in Hypotheses 29 and 30, each of which consists of two components.

> HYPOTHESIS 29   *When tactical capabilities for dealing with a problem are perceived as high—*
>
>> HYPOTHESIS 29(a)   *Decision makers will act quickly to deal with the problem if capabilities are deteriorating.*

The rationale is "striking while the iron is hot."

>> HYPOTHESIS 29(b)   *Decision makers will move at a moderate pace toward dealing with the problem if capabilities are stable or improving.*

Given high capabilities that will remain high or improve, there is no reason to delay action; on the other hand, neither is there an urgency to act and increase the risks of judgment error.

> HYPOTHESIS 30   *When tactical capabilities for dealing with a problem are perceived as low—*
>
>> HYPOTHESIS 30(a)   *Decision makers will delay in taking action if capabilities are improving.*

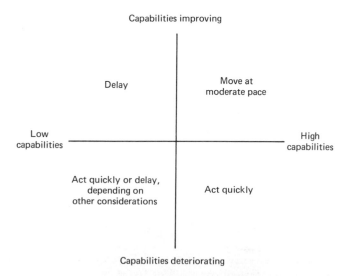

Figure 8   Relationships between Tactical Capabilities for Dealing with a Problem and the Speed or Delay with Which Decision Makers Move toward Action Designed To Solve the Problem

The rationale for waiting until the probability of success is improved is self-evident.

> HYPOTHESIS 30(b) *If capabilities are stable or deteriorating, the speed with which decision makers act will depend exclusively on their assessment of other costs of delay or of judgment error.*

Under such grim circumstances, decision makers may be inclined to put off action even though the prospects for success in the future are no better than they are at present. On the other hand, factors other than those identified here may persuade decision makers to act quickly, even though the probability of success is small.

The Bay of Pigs Decision The relationship between the pace of action by decision makers and their estimates of tactical capabilities can be illustrated by the actions of the Kennedy administration during the early months of 1961 in pushing through, to ultimately disastrous consequences, plans for an invasion of Cuba by a force of Cuban exiles trained and supported by Americans. Specifically, the Kennedy go-ahead for the Bay of Pigs invasion illustrates Hypothesis 29(a).

The worsening relations between the United States and Cuba after Castro came to power on New Year's Day in 1959 led President Eisenhower to order the CIA to begin a program of organizing and training volunteers from among the thousands of exiles who had fled Cuba, for the purpose of invading the island and hopefully bringing about the overthrow of the Castro regime. Thus, by the time Kennedy took office in January 1961, invasion plans were well under way. Kennedy had the authority, of course, to call off the invasion (although one account suggests that so much momentum had developed by that time that, if Kennedy had canceled invasion plans, the CIA operatives who worked directly with the Cuban exile force would have arranged for the invasion to be launched anyway).[15] However, the military and in-

---

[15] A meeting is described between Frank, a United States Army colonel working for the CIA as commander of one of the principal training bases for the invasion, and Pepe and Oliva, Cuban exile leaders: "There were forces in the administration trying to block the invasion, and Frank might be ordered to stop it. If he received such an order, he said he would secretly inform Pepe and Oliva. Pepe remembers Frank's next words this way: 'If this happens you come here and make some kind of show, as if you were putting us, the advisors, in prison, and you go ahead with the program as we have talked about it, and we will give you the whole plan, even if we are your prisoners.'" Haynes Johnson, with Manuel Artime, Jose Perez San Roman, Erneido Oliva, and Enrique Ruiz Williams, *The Bay of Pigs* (New York: Norton, 1964), p. 75. The book is the most detailed account of the invasion episode from the perspective of the Cuban exiles.

telligence experts who had been working with the operation since its inception argued that the prospects for success were high, at least for the limited objective of establishing a sizable guerrilla force in Cuba, which in turn could serve as a rallying point for dissident elements, thereby eventually bringing the downfall of Castro. A more optimistic view was that spontaneous uprisings throughout the island in response to the invasion would lead Castro to capitulate almost immediately.

Yet President Kennedy was warned that the favorable conditions for the operation would last only for a very limited period of time. Castro's air force, for instance, which in the first few months of 1961 seemed to present no serious threat to an invasion, would shortly be markedly strengthened by the return from Czechoslovakia of Cuban pilots who had received training there in jet aircraft. According to intelligence reports, jet aircraft in crates were already in Cuba and would soon be assembled for use by the newly trained pilots. Moreover, a rainy season was due in Cuba in late spring that would hamper operations; CIA officials argued that the invasion should take place prior to the onset of the heavy rains. Furthermore, although some 1500 Cuban exiles were purportedly eager for the opportunity to return to liberate their homeland, unless the invasion was made soon, existing serious frictions among various factions of the exiles might grow to the point that the entire operation would be jeopardized. In addition, the President of Guatemala, who had made sites available for training the invasion force, was urging that the invasion be implemented quickly, so that he could rid himself of a potentially politically embarrassing situation. A related consideration was what Washington officials referred to as "the disposal problem." Unless the exile force was put into action soon on the mission for which they had been trained, the United States government might be faced with having to find something to do with 1500 discontented Cuban refugees. Finally, by April, the invasion plan was an open secret; various enterprising reporters had uncovered facets of the operation. Unless the invasion was launched quickly, such minimal element of surprise as could still be mustered would be lost.[16]

When put to the test for three agonizing days beginning April 17, 1961, the plan for the invasion of Cuba at the Bay of Pigs proved to have been constructed on a series of tragic miscalculations. When the failure was

---

[16] A highly readable account of the invasion and of the events leading up to and including the disastrous invasion is provided by two reporters who followed the events closely from an early stage. Tad Szulc and Karl E. Meyer, *The Cuban Invasion: The Chronicle of a Disaster* (New York: Ballantine, 1962). The fiasco is analyzed in retrospect from the vantage point of one involved in the policy-making process of the Kennedy administration by Schlesinger; Sorensen, *Kennedy*; and Hilsman, *A Thousand Days*, respectively.

complete, the invasion force decimated, and the prestige of the United States badly marred, President Kennedy lamented to an adviser, "How could I have been so far off base? . . . All my life I've known better than to depend on the experts. How could I have been so stupid, to let them go ahead?" [17] Part of the explanation for the blunder was that the President, new to his responsibilities, felt under great pressure to act quickly in response to a plan that, with more deliberate consideration, he might have rejected.

Pace of Decision Making and Leadership Consensus The relationship postulated between the perceived possibilities of eliciting a consensus among national leaders regarding a course of action to be taken and the speed or delay with which decision makers will move toward action is depicted graphically in Figure 9; it is depicted verbally in Hypotheses 31 and 32, each of which consists of two components.

HYPOTHESIS 31 *When decision makers perceive that a given decision is likely to elicit a high degree of consensus among national leaders in support of the decision—*

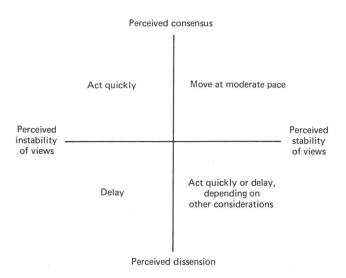

Figure 9 Relationships between the Perceptions that Decision Makers Have of the Extent and Stability of Consensus among National Leaders Regarding a Course of Action To Be Taken, and Speed or Delay with Which Decision Makers Will Move toward Action.

[17] Sorensen, *Kennedy*, p. 346.

HYPOTHESIS 31(a)   *Decision makers will move at a moderate pace toward action if the consensus appears to be a stable one.*

If a consensus is stable, there is no reason to delay; however, neither is there a need to risk judgment error through hasty decision.

HYPOTHESIS 31(b)   *Decision makers will act quickly if the consensus appears to be an unstable one.*

A decision must be made rapidly, or the advantages of consensus will be lost.

HYPOTHESIS 32   *When decision makers perceive that a given decision is likely to elicit a high degree of dissension among national leaders—*

HYPOTHESIS 32(a)   *If the dissension appears to be stable, the speed with which decision makers act will depend exclusively on their assessment of other costs of delay or of judgment error.*

That is, if decision makers are confronted with a situation in which they will be faced with divided views among national leadership, regardless of whether they act now or later, under some circumstances they will be inclined to "get it over with," whereas under other circumstances, they will avoid risking the displeasure of certain sectors of national leadership by avoiding a decision as long as possible.

HYPOTHESIS 32(b)   *If the dissension appears unstable, decision makers will seek to delay action.*

In this situation, the instability of views holds out the hope that additional time will enable decision makers to build a consensus.

Truman and the H-Bomb, Nixon and the Anti–Ballistic-Missile System

In an analysis of the decision of the Truman administration to develop a hydrogen bomb, Warner R. Schilling has noted the "minimal" character of Truman's initial commitment in January 1950. He suggests that the course of action selected by Truman was one that seemed to the President to close off the fewest number of choices in the future. It was a decision that left unresolved most of the key policy issues stemming from the implications of the development of a superbomb. Schilling explains Truman's desire to delay a firm and final commitment to the H-bomb largely in terms of his desire to avoid an open split among key leaders in the administration. The most ominous was the split between officials of the Defense Department, who generally favored developing an H-bomb, and officials of the Atomic Energy Commission, who opposed it. Delay by the President of a final commitment to the project might provide time for the development of a consensus.[18]

The more recent approach by President Nixon to the controversial anti–ballistic-missile (ABM) issue suggests a similar political strategy of delay, in order to retain the maximum number of options for the future and try to forge a future consensus.

Shortly after the Nixon administration took office, Nixon's secretary of defense, Melvin Laird, indicated that plans begun under the Johnson administration to develop Sentinel ABM systems in some fifteen sites throughout the United States would probably be continued.[19] However, amidst mounting opposition to the ABM program in the Senate and in local communities around many of the sites selected for the installation of the Sentinel systems, Laird announced in February a temporary halt to the acquisition and construction of missile sites, pending a review of the program.[20] In March, President Nixon made a major policy statement regarding the ABM system. However, the decision was one that committed the administration immediately only to two missile sites, rather than fifteen. Moreover, the two sites selected were in areas that could protect American intercontinental ballistic missile (ICBM) sites and were relatively distant from metropolitan areas, in contrast to the major emphasis on protection of cities envisaged in the original planning. The so-called Safeguard system proposed by Nixon left open the possibility for expansion of the system in the future. However, the President also announced that the Foreign Intelligence Advisory Board, "a nonpartisan group of distinguished private citizens," would review the program annually to make sure that the defense system was adequate to needs but not excessive.[21] Faced by critics entirely opposed to an ABM system, as well as by others, who argued the need for a system even thicker in its coverage than that proposed by the Johnson administration, Nixon had pursued a course of action that seemed designed to convince both groups that he was still receptive to their views. Like Truman nineteen

[18] Warner R. Schilling, "The H-Bomb Decision: How to Decide Without Actually Choosing," *Political Science Quarterly*, 76 (March 1961), 24–46; reprinted in Davis B. Bobrow, ed., *Components of Defense Policy* (Skokie, Ill.: Rand McNally, 1965), pp. 390–409.

[19] William Beecher, "Laird Supports Antimissile Net," *New York Times*, Jan. 31, 1969, p. 1.

[20] "Halt of Sentinel is Traced to a 10-Month-Old Memo," *New York Times*, Feb. 9, 1969, sec. 1, p. 1.

[21] "Text of President Nixon's Announcement on Revised Proposals for Sentinel Antiballistic Missile Program," *New York Times*, March 15, 1969, p. 17.

years earlier, Nixon had found a minimal decision to be a way of buying time in the hope of building a future consensus.[22]

Summary of Hypotheses Developed in Part IV

14. Simple, anticipated problems tend to elicit preprogrammed responses.
15. Simple, but unanticipated problems, or complex, but anticipated problems, tend to elicit adjustive responses.
16. Complex, unanticipated problems tend to elicit inventive responses.
17. The greater the incentives within an organization for suggesting departures from existing policies or for challenging existing policy assumptions, the greater the probability that the organization will respond inventively to unanticipated problems.
18. The fewer the incentives and the higher the probable costs to personnel within an organization for challenging basic assumptions upon which ongoing policies are based, the lower the probability that the organization will respond inventively to unanticipated problems.
19. During periods of high turnover of key personnel, but relatively low turnover of middle-level and lower-level personnel, an organization will increase its reliance on routine procedures for coping with problems.
20. The greater the sense of security and mastery of their responsibilities that top-level decision makers possess, the greater the probability that an organization will respond inventively to the problems it confronts.
21. Decisions regarding situations of low salience that are classified as supportive or neutral tend to be made at low levels.
22. Decisions regarding situations of middle salience that are neutral or supportive, or those of low salience that are threatening, tend to be made at intermediate levels.
23. Decisions regarding situations of high salience that are threatening tend to be made at top levels.
24. Problems of middle salience that are threatening tend to be resolved at intermediate levels if they are simple, at top levels if they are complex.
25. Problems of high salience that are supportive or neutral tend to be

---

[22] For further elaboration of the Nixon approach, see Max Frankel, "Nixon Takes Middle Ground in First Difficult Decision," *New York Times*, March 15, 1969, p. 18.

resolved at intermediate levels if they are simple; at top levels if they are complex.

26. The greater the reluctance of those at top levels in an organization to concern themselves with details of policy problems, and the greater their insistence that only questions of paramount importance be presented to them for decision, the higher will be the proportion of decisions made at lower and middle levels.

27. The greater the tendency of policy makers at top levels to call into question matters of detail in the operation and activities of those at lower levels, the higher will be the proportion of problems submitted to top levels for decision.

28. The more unanticipated the problem, the greater its complexity, the higher the salience of interests at stake, or the greater the threat to interests, the greater will be the tendency of decision makers to delay action.

29. When tactical capabilities for dealing with a problem are perceived as high—
   a. Decision makers will act quickly to deal with the problem if capabilities are deteriorating.
   b. Decision makers will move at a moderate pace toward dealing with the problem if capabilities are stable or improving.

30. When tactical capabilities for dealing with a problem are perceived as low—
   a. Decision makers will delay in taking action if capabilities are improving.
   b. If capabilities are stable or deteriorating, the speed with which decision makers act will depend exclusively on their assessment of other costs of delay or of judgment error.

31. When decision makers perceive that a given decision is likely to elicit a high degree of consensus among national leaders in support of the decision—
   a. Decision makers will move at a moderate pace toward action if the consensus appears to be a stable one.
   b. Decision makers will act quickly if the consensus appears to be an unstable one.

32. When decision makers perceive that a given decision is likely to elicit a high degree of dissension among national leaders—
   a. If the dissension appears to be stable, the speed with which decision makers act will depend exclusively on their assessment of other costs of delay or of judgment error.
   b. If the dissension appears unstable, decision makers will seek to delay action.

Part V

Normative Analysis of Foreign Policy

In Chapter 1, we identified four interrelated tasks for foreign-policy analysis: explanation, evaluation, prediction, and prescription. Thus far, our discussion has been limited almost exclusively to explanation, although most of the analytical framework that has been developed could be applied to prediction as well. (The reader might wish to review the discussion in Chapter 1 for similarities and differences between explanation and prediction.) We now turn our attention to foreign-policy evaluation.

Like earlier parts of the book, this section is designed to contribute to the construction of a framework that the reader can usefully employ in his own analysis of foreign policy and in his assessment of others' analyses. Thus, the point is to raise pertinent questions and to develop guidelines for answering the questions—not to provide answers.

In our discussion of value questions about

foreign policy, we shall no longer make explicit distinctions between the perspectives of strategic analysis, historical dynamics, and decision making, respectively; the value questions raised in Chapters 10 and 11 might be approached from any of the three analytical perspectives. It is therefore appropriate to comment briefly on the relative significance of each perspective to one's normative concerns.

No doubt the most fundamental perspective for dealing with important value questions is the perspective of historical dynamics, since patterns of adaptation and goal attainment visible from this perspective can reveal the "batting average" of a political system across an entire season or series of seasons, whereas the success or failure of a given strategy or a given decision amounts to little more than the record of the system in a limited and perhaps unrepresentative series of "games." Moreover, the perspective of historical dynamics, more than other perspectives, alerts one to the primacy of adaptation in foreign policy.

Especially now, in the latter half of the twentieth century, the task of adaptation by a political system to the demands of a rapidly changing and volatile world environment is enormous. Goal attainment requires a measure of control of the environment, but goals must be readjusted to conform to the possibilities in an environment that can be manipulated only to a limited extent. Even in a great power like the United States, policy makers cannot fully predict, much less fully control, the turn of events in world affairs. One is reminded of the instructive observation of John F. Kennedy, in a memorable radio-television interview after two years in office as President, that one of the most striking differences between his current assessment of the responsibilities of President and his assessment prior to assuming the office was his increased recognition of how limited the United States is in solving problems in world affairs.[1]

The perspective of historical dynamics, more than the other two analytical perspectives, is likely to alert one to the limited range of choices available to policy makers at any important juncture in world affairs. Yet, it is the very existence of options that raises the central normative issues of foreign policy. The "roads not taken" in history, rather than fate, circumstances, or accident, define the meaningful occasions for making value judgments about foreign policy. It is because man does have choices that a basis is provided for foreign-policy evaluation.

Emphasis on choice leads one to supplement evaluation from the perspective of historical dynamics with evaluation from a strategic and a decision-making perspective for at least two reasons. First, the patterns

---

[1] "After Two Years—A Conversation with the President," television and radio interview on all major networks, Dec. 17, 1962.

of continuity and change apparent in analysis of foreign policy from the perspective of historical dynamics are composed, in the final analysis, of choices that were made among different strategies at key decision-making junctures. Second, the concept of a political system and description of foreign policy as a means of adaptation to the environment and of imposing control on it direct our attention to the fact that severe changes in the environment may require not merely imaginative foreign policies, but also structural changes within the political system. Although a historical-dynamics perspective does not preclude a consideration of structural change within the political system, it is especially from a decision-making perspective that the structure, as well as the process from which foreign policies are shaped is emphasized. Moreover, in a political system committed to values of democracy, such as the American system, both structural and policy adjustments to severe external changes and threats are likely to be fraught with agonizing issues, because the norms for successful adjustment to change can never be established merely in terms of efficiency, but must include democratic values and practices. A decision-making perspective is especially useful in coping with such issues because of its emphasis on the structure and process of foreign-policy decision making.

We shall focus first on the goals that are pursued in foreign policy and on the means that are utilized in their pursuit. We ask, in essence, by what criteria we can distinguish good goals from bad ones, and desirable means from undesirable ones. In the final chapter, we shall turn to the performance of the political system in translating inputs into outputs. Emphasis is placed on the problems of reconciling the quest for efficiency in foreign policy with a commitment to the maintenance of democratic practice and values.

10

The Goals
and Means
of Foreign Policy

Norms for Evaluation
and Prescription

The Search for Universal Norms

Few of the readers of this book are likely to be so timorous or apathetic as to refrain from voicing some strong opinions about the desirability or undesirability of various foreign-policy goals being pursued by the United States and about the means utilized in pursuing them. Indeed, the current social climate impels us as it rarely has in the past to take a stand on the key issues of the day. Leaders of student protests, political candidates, government officials, television commentators, editorial writers, college professors, and others implore us to accept or reject this view or that.

The questions to which the chapter is directed are the following. Are there any objective, or universally acceptable, criteria by which one may measure the goodness or badness, the desirability or undesirability of foreign-policy goals and means? Or are the norms of evaluation to be selected or rejected merely on the basis of personal preference? For example, is the question whether or not a détente between the United States and the Soviet Union should serve as a goal of American foreign policy a matter that each of us can decide only subjectively, or could we establish objective criteria for evaluating such a goal? Is the question whether or not napalm ought to be employed as an instrument of warfare merely a matter of opinion, or could we agree upon a set of norms that would enable us to term napalm an acceptable or unacceptable instrument of policy? Few of us would like to believe that such questions are merely matters of taste. Before accepting the opposite conclusion, however, that objective and universal norms for evaluating foreign policy can be formulated, one ought to give rather detailed consideration to the problem of describing precisely the content of such norms.

The Analytical Relevance of Intermediate Goals and Means

The difficulty of constructing criteria that are likely to be both universally acceptable and operationally meaningful, in the sense of providing guidelines for a policy maker, can be emphasized at the outset by distinguishing the broad, general value commitments of the members of a society from the instrumental choices that are often made in the name of the general value commitments.

On the one hand, for example, we might have little difficulty agreeing upon the desirability of such general foreign-policy goals as the promotion of world peace, the maintenance of justice among all nations, the advancement of liberty for all peoples, and the development of general human welfare. On the other hand, the vague, abstract quality in which such goals are cast offers policy makers little guidance in making meaningful choices in reality and offers us little guidance in evaluating the choices that are made. However much lofty concepts such as peace, justice, and liberty may embody the basic ideals of a nation, the policy maker is seldom confronted with a clear-cut choice between such ideals and their opposites. Rather, he is much more likely to be confronted with the sticky questions of which intermediate objectives are most likely to be instrumental to the attainment of long-range, general goals, and which means are appropriate to their attainment.

For example, when the forces of North Korea crossed the 38th parallel in June 1950, invading South Korea, the meaningful issue confronting American policy makers was not whether peace was preferable to war. Rather, the meaningful issues included the question whether a forcible response by the United States to the North Korean attack would serve the cause of future maintenance of peace and the related question whether the failure of the United States and other United Nations powers to respond to the North Korean attack would permanently jeopardize the effectiveness of the United Nations to maintain world peace. Subsequent to the commitment of American troops to South Korea, other questions arose regarding the intermediate objectives to be pursued— should the United Nations objective be to restore the *status quo* ante-bellum in Korea or rather, to take advantage of probable victory over the forces of North Korea to bring about the unification of all Korea? Questions of means arose as well. Should atomic weapons be employed? Should targets in Manchuria be bombed? For the same reasons that meaningful choices of policy makers are likely to relate to questions of intermediate objectives and means, rather than to questions of general foreign-policy goals, meaningful evaluation of foreign policy by the layman will deal largely with the question of which choices among intermediate objectives and means were made by policy makers, rather than the question of which general goals the foreign-policy process is pursuing.

Limiting our focus, then, to foreign-policy outputs defined in terms of selecting intermediate objectives and means, can any universally acceptable criteria be established that could serve policy makers as guideposts in choosing among various intermediate policy objectives and among policy means and tactics, or that could serve the student of foreign policy in evaluating the choices made by policy makers?

Among the criteria that have been proposed in the past and continue to be proposed in the present, three sets of criteria deserve special consideration: criteria of legality, morality, and realism.

Legal Norms

The appeal of legal norms to policy makers as guideposts for action, as well as to the public as criteria for evaluating policy, has a strong tradition in American culture. As former Ambassador George F. Kennan, among others, has noted, much of American conduct of foreign affairs in the twentieth century has been guided by "the belief that it should be possible to suppress the chaotic and dangerous aspirations of governments in the international field by the acceptance of some system of legal rules and restraints."[1]

After all, law is an essential concomitant of every society, and respect for law a part of the heritage that all societies must endeavor to cultivate

---

[1] George F. Kennan, *American Diplomacy 1900–1950* (New York: Mentor, 1951), p. 83.

if they are to avoid anarchy. Unless the international community is to have continual disorder and perpetual "war of all against all," like the condition of primitive man suggested by the philosopher Thomas Hobbes, the cultivation of law is essential at the international, as well as at the national and local level. The United States, as a leader in world affairs, would seem to bear a prime obligation to further this process, both by respecting existing international law and by seeking to develop it further. Would not legality, therefore, serve as a useful criterion in evaluating choices of objectives, means, and tactics in the foreign-policy process? Applying legal norms as criteria of evaluation, the basis for deciding whether a given foreign-policy objective was good or bad would be whether or not it was consistent with established international law; the basis for approving or disapproving the means used to implement policy would be whether or not these means were sanctioned by international law.

The problems in practice in applying such seemingly reasonable criteria to the evaluation of foreign policy are many, only a few of which need be cited here. First is the problem of the primitive state of development of international law. Vast areas of conduct among nations remain uncovered by international law. For instance, acts generally regarded as among the most heinous in history, committed by the Nazis against the Jews in the 1930s and 1940s, were criminal according to no generally accepted international law. Consequently, in order to convict those responsible for the acts by duly instituted legal proceedings, law had to be created and applied ex post facto. This was done at the famous postwar trials at Nuremberg; but whether law thus created now constitutes a well-established precedent for future application is widely doubted among international lawyers.

A second problem, related to the first, is the ambiguity of existing law. For instance, a term of central importance in the efforts to establish a legal order in international affairs is the concept of aggression. What is aggression, and how does one tell if a nation is guilty of aggression? This term, so fundamental if an idea such as collective security, first embodied in the League of Nations and subsequently in the United Nations, is to be meaningful, has occupied literally thousands of man-hours of time in discussions both in the League and the United Nations. But to this day, delegates have been unable to agree upon a definition of aggression that all members have found satisfactory. To define aggression narrowly, to refer only to the armed attack by one nation upon another, when the latter had not provoked the former, would mean to exclude most of the complex acts that have led to conflict and have disturbed international peace in the twentieth century. However, to try to include in the definition of aggression every conceivable act by one nation that another could find unwarranted would mean that invoking collective-security sanctions against a nation would be so dependent upon subjective judgments that few statesmen would want to risk relying upon the definition. Thus, aggression remains ambiguous both as a technical term and as a term in everyday parlance.

One might cite numerous other examples of ambiguous terminology, but to do so would serve little purpose here. The point is that even those principles or documents of international law that would seem, to the impartial observer, to be clear and free of ambiguity attain various shadings and nuances when applied to particular cases. All law is interpreted by human beings, often in the heat of political controversy. Consequently, whether a particular foreign-policy decision is consistent with the United Nations Charter or not, for example, or whether the means used to carry out a decision is acceptable or not from the standpoint of international law, is likely to be a function not only of the wording of the Charter and of other sources of international law, but also of the configuration of power in international affairs. The result is that major powers, such as the United States, while not altogether immune from the restraints of international law, are able to bend the law or bypass it in cases where strict legal interpretation of their actions might prove embarrassing.

The susceptibility of legal norms to distortion, in response to changing distributions of power and changing dictates of the powerful, points to a third, and particularly debilitating, limitation of legal norms as criteria for the evaluation of foreign policy. It is patently obvious that international law, far from exclusively embodying a set of norms the validity of which is established by their universal quality, is comprised of an imperfect mixture of the results of a noble search for universal norms with the results of pragmatic political bargaining and the particularistic values of those bargaining from positions of strength. It is interesting and significant that the most cynical interpretations of international law, attributing to it an arbitrary and political character, have tended to come in recent years from the poor nations, that is, the politically and economically weak nations, which are sensitive to the disadvantage in shaping the rules of international politics to their own ends. The rich nations, in contrast, have tended to stress the idealistic, universal quality of international law.[2] Without subscribing to an unduly cynical view that international law is merely a demonstration that might makes right,

[2] An interesting description and analysis of the conflicting views with which rich and poor nations describe international law is provided in a case study of two United Nations conferences on the Law of the Sea held in Geneva in 1958 and 1960, by Robert L. Friedheim, "The 'Satisfied' and 'Dissatisfied' States Negotiate International Law," *World Politics*, 18 (Oct. 1965), 20–41.

but avoiding the naïve illusion that international law is characteristically above politics rather than a reflection of them, one can recognize the hazards of relying exclusively upon norms of legality in assessing foreign-policy objectives and means.

Moral Principles

If the norms of international law fail to provide a universally acceptable set of criteria for evaluation of foreign policy, some would search instead for some higher law, or a set of moral principles, according to which policy decisions and acts could be assessed. Indeed, in reviewing public discourse over the past several years dealing with United States policies in Vietnam, one finds countless examples of implicit or explicit moral judgments. "It is our moral duty to stop communism in Vietnam!" says one person. "The use of napalm in Vietnam is immoral!" charges the next. "We are morally bound to honor our commitments to the government of South Vietnam!" contends another. "Our bombing of North Vietnam, which has resulted in the death of innocent women and children, is clearly immoral!" argues still another.

In the abstract, it is possible to devise rules of conduct that would at least be likely to be accepted by most students of foreign policy as humane and reasonable. One such rule, for example, might be, "It is immoral to use unnecessary violence in the conduct of foreign policy." Such a rule is implicit in both the criticism of the use of napalm and the expression of horror over the death of innocent women and children. Difficulties arise, however, over the applicability of the abstract rule to concrete situations. Unnecessary violence is immoral, but when is violence necessary and therefore morally justified? President Truman and his advisers concluded reluctantly that the use of an atom bomb to kill thousands of Japanese men, women, and children in the cities of Hiroshima and Nagasaki was necessary in order to bring the war to an early conclusion, thereby saving thousands of other lives. Earlier in the war, the British government had debated a strategic policy in their struggle against Germany and had concluded that it was necessary to launch an air offensive against residential areas in German cities and that it was necessary to concentrate the attacks on working-class areas, where the greater concentration of houses would lead to a greater number of dwellings destroyed per bomb load.[3] Illustrations such as these reveal

[3] The strategic bombing policy of the British, adopted also by the American government, is critically reviewed by an eminent British physicist and novelist, C. P. Snow, in a brief and provocative book, *Science and Government* (New York: Mentor, 1962), esp. pp. 46–50 and 104–112.

not the total irrelevance of moral principles to foreign-policy decisions, but rather the difficulty of determining the circumstances under which, and the way in which, moral principles are to be applied. As Professor Hans Morgenthau has wisely observed, "To know that nations are subject to the moral law is one thing, while to pretend to know with certainty what is good and evil in the relations among nations is quite another." [4]

The difficulties of trying to apply moral norms to the evaluation of foreign policy are compounded by the differences between standards of ethics applicable to an individual and standards that most persons would recognize as applicable at the nation-state level. For example, for an individual to enter another's house secretly for the purpose of stealing information to be used to advance the housebreaker's personal interests, at the expense of the interest of the person whose home was entered, would generally be regarded as unethical. Yet, for nations to employ spies to carry on analogous activity for the interests of the nation-state they represent, at the expense of the interests of the nation-state in which they intrude, is generally regarded as justified. For individuals to tell deliberate falsehoods or to deceive others for the purpose of their own selfish advantage would be regarded as unethical, but for a statesman of one nation to lie to the statesman of another or otherwise intentionally deceive him, in order to advance the selfish interests of the nation is, under many circumstances, judged to be not only proper but dutiful. Furthermore, although self-sacrifice may be regarded as a virtue in an individual, few would find an act virtuous in which a policy maker sacrificed the interests of his nation, even if he attempted to justify the sacrifice in terms of some higher good. Conversely, defense of the vital interests of the nation is almost always an acceptable rationale for the behavior of an individual policy maker, even though the same behavior for his private interests might be regarded as unethical.

As Professor E. H. Carr has noted—in a remarkable and important treatise on international politics written as the precarious peace in the period between the two world wars was collapsing—because there is no supreme authority above the nation-state to impose conformity to moral standards and no well-developed international community to develop conventions of moral conduct, we must expect less of the state than of the individual.[5] In other words, as we noted in Chapter 3, the nature of the system of nation-states, each of which regards itself as sovereign, is such that survival and a struggle for power become controlling con-

[4] Hans J. Morgenthau, *Politics among Nations* (New York: Alfred A. Knopf, 4th ed., 1967), p. 10.

[5] A paperback edition of this book is now available. E. H. Carr, *The Twenty Years' Crisis, 1919–1939* (New York: Harper & Row, 1964), esp. chap. 9.

cerns of all nation-states. In this context, as the noted German historian Friedrich Meinecke put it, "It seems that the state must sin." [6]

Perhaps the grossest error of all, however, in trying to deal with the slippery concept of morality as applied to the nation-state is to confuse the justification of national necessity with a justification of moral right. Unfortunately, throughout history, in the arguments of nations, rulers, and peoples for their parochial interests and claims, one finds a recurrent pattern of hypocrisy and self-delusion in the theme of a higher calling, which is alleged to provide moral justification for acts largely compelled or motivated by self-interest. A search for the Holy Grail, carrying religion to the heathen, working to achieve a world of classless societies, or making the world safe for democracy, each in its own way, may serve the individual committed to such a calling as a dream to be realized. Ironically, however, such dreams can bring as much havoc to mankind as pure lust for power. "Men are dangerous not only because they have unlimited appetites and unlimited yearning for power," Reinhold Niebuhr reminds us, "but because they are creatures with dreams; and their extravagant dreams turn into nightmares if they seek to realize them in history." [7]

Realism

So..e persons contend that if foreign-policy goals or means cannot be assessed reliably in terms of their legality or their morality, a preferable yardstick for evaluation is the realism of the goals and means. If policy makers are realistic, according to proponents of this set of criteria, they will make choices among goals and means based upon an accurate assessment of the demands and opportunities of the times or of the given situation, and upon the way that various courses of action would affect the interests of the nation-state. Realistic goals and means would be those

[6] Friedrich Meinecke, *Machiavellism: The Doctrine of Raison d'État in Modern History* (New Haven, Conn.: Yale University Press, 1957), as cited in Richard W. Sterling, "Political Necessity and Moral Principle in the Thought of Friedrich Meinecke," in Roger Hilsman and Robert C. Good, eds., *Foreign Policy in the Sixties* (Baltimore: The Johns Hopkins Press, 1965), p. 263.

[7] Reinhold Niebuhr, *The Structure of Nations and Empires* (New York: Scribner, 1959), p. 293. Dr. Niebuhr is a theologian whose extensive writings on religion and politics, and the relationship between the two realms, have had a profound impact on intellectual activity in America over the past several decades. Particularly compelling and relevant to our present discussion is his concept of the moral ambiguity inherent in political order. On this point, in addition to the work cited, see his *Moral Man and Immoral Society* (New York: Scribner, 1941, first ed., 1932).

that, in the existing pattern of demands and opportunities, would best maintain or promote the national interest.

In considering legality, morality, and now realism, our quest is for a standard of evaluation that can be applied objectively rather than subjectively. That is, we are searching for a standard by which each of us, in appraising the same set of foreign-policy goals and means, would arrive at the same conclusions as to which goals and means were good and which were bad. The question whether realism provides such an objective standard hinges upon the objectifiability of the national interest, which realistic goals and means should be designed to protect or to promote.

Subjectivity of the Concept of National Interest   The "discovery" of the national interest of the United States is a recurring phenomenon. Indeed, justification of particular policies on grounds that they are in the national interest or criticism of other decisions and actions, which are found to be deviations from the national interest, are themes with a long tradition in American governmental practice and oratory. Like the public eulogy and other long traditions, however, the perennial rediscovery of the national interest and its utilization as a norm for explaining or evaluating foreign policy indicates the durable appeal of ambiguous phrases in situations where precision is emotionally as well as intellectually costly. It is comforting to be told that a given decision or action is in the national interest; it is emotionally disquieting to be told that the national interest has been ignored or compromised. But the fact is that there is no definitive, objectively discoverable national interest. Rather, as we suggested in Chapter 5, there are various competing images of the national interest, which exist in the minds of policy makers and each of us.

Political systems, we indicated in Chapter 7, must meet certain functional requisites in order to survive and to develop within an environment that is constantly bombarding the system with new demands. The foreign-policy process is a mechanism by which the system attempts to adapt to the environment and to impose a measure of control upon it. In a sense, then, the system has interests (functional requisites), and foreign policies are in part directed to the attempt to satisfy these interests.

Ambiguity arises, however, when we try to define more precisely, in operational terms, just what the interests or functional requisites of a national political system in relation to its environment are and what kinds of actions contribute to the fulfillment of these needs. As we noted earlier, at the level of broad abstraction, consensus about foreign-policy goals is relatively easy to reach, but it is also relatively meaningless. Likewise, we might agree that survival is the basic need of every nation-state. But to agree that survival is the central imperative that defines the national interest is really to say little that is translatable into terms that are useful for the evaluation of specific choices of intermediate objectives and means in the foreign-policy process. Similarly, other general statements, suggesting that "America has traditional interests in the Caribbean," or that "the partnership with Great Britain is of prime importance to the American national interest," or that "the national interest now extends to Asia," become of dubious analytical or evaluative utility when the complex ordering of values involved in concrete policy decisions is considered. Only when choices are posed in terms of such bald dichotomies that to all reasonable men the choice will appear to be between survival and extinction, or between victory in war or defeat, and so on, is the concept of national interest likely to provide a guide to action and a standard for evaluating the choice that is made. Rarely, however, are foreign-policy choices posed in such bald terms. Instead, the choice most of the time is among possibilities on which reasonable men, each committed in principle to the national interest, *may disagree.* In such instances, the criterion of realism is clearly more hindrance than help.

The essential analytical point is that the needs of a political system are not self-interpreting. Determination of which foreign-policy goals must be sought and which means must be utilized is a subjective process. National leaders and all of us formulate ideas about what the needs of the nation are in relation to our own experience and our own values. Moreover, virtually every policy decision has a differential impact upon members of the polity. Some members benefit more than others; some pay more than others. The struggle to influence the allocation of benefits and costs is what politics is all about, and none of us can wholly disentangle private motives and interests from our perception of the interests of the nation as a whole.

Realism as Narrow Chauvinism   In addition to the ambiguity of the national interest as a set of criteria for evaluating foreign-policy decisions and actions, the criterion of realism suffers from the potential danger of myopia, of so restricting one's vision as to obscure other important values. Such a danger is best illustrated by the actual behavior and attitudes that persons employing realism as a sole frame of reference have manifested.

Many sophisticated defenses of the use of realism as a primary frame of reference in the conduct of foreign policy have been made. Advocates of realism have observed that legalists and moralists are dangerously naïve about the kinds of political action that are possible given the exist-ing nature of the system of sovereign nation-states, and that they are pretentious about their ability to prescribe norms of conduct that have universal validity.

In contrast, those who view themselves as realists claim that by recognizing and avoiding foreign-policy objectives that are utopian under present conditions, they are able to support actions that will bring the substance of progress, rather than the illusion of it. Moreover, their modest claim for "enlightened self-interest" is seen as definitely prefer-able to the exaggerated claims of those who say that their interests and values are valid for all mankind.

The humility and pragmatism of sophisticated proponents of realism in foreign policy are attractive qualities. Ironically, however, in practice, politicians, newspaper editorialists, government officials, college pro-fessors, and others who use realism as a rallying cry often display pre-cisely the sort of pretentiousness and shortsightedness that, according to their theoretical formulations, the criterion of realism would help them avoid.

In a review of the writings of several of the leading figures of the so-called realist school of foreign-policy thought, Robert C. Good has made the penetrating observation that, unless one accepts some criteria "for directing or judging state behavior *other than those derived from state necessity*, the realist must end up the cynic." [8] This is so because, if no values were taken into account other than the self-interest of the state, only a crass success ethos in world politics would remain to guide foreign policy. No distinctions could be made among various foreign-policy ob-jectives and means other than that of enhancing national power, at whatever cost to the interests, dignity, or welfare of other nation-states and other human beings. But as Good emphasizes, the leading theorists of the realist school have been anything but cynical in their own analyses of foreign policy and their prescriptions for future action. Rather, they have invariably displayed in their writings a sensitivity to a whole range of norms by which national interest might be defined as the *enlightened* self-interest of the state. In other words, implicit in most of their writings, and explicit in some of them, such as those of Reinhold Niebuhr, are criteria for evaluation of foreign-policy actions and decisions other than the sole criterion of national interest.

Unfortunately, however, not all of those who find national interest attractive as a general frame of reference for evaluating foreign-policy

[8] Robert C. Good, "National Interest and Moral Theory: The 'Debate' among Contemporary Political Realists," in Hilsman and Good, p. 281. Italics added.

outputs make their judgments with the same prudence and sensitivity to other values as the leading theorists of the realist school ordinarily have done. Ironically, in cynically rejecting legal or moral norms in favor of realism as a criterion for making foreign-policy assessments, chauvinistic adherents of the concept have imputed to the nation itself a godlike quality. Most of us, however, would attempt to take a less myopic view of foreign affairs. However strong a sense of loyalty and obligation we may feel to our own nation-state, most of us would not regard our nation-state as the final or the only point of reference in our efforts to understand and to evaluate various facets of human endeavor, including our national foreign policy. And with whatever pride we identify ourselves with the traditional ideals and accomplishments of our nation-state, most of us would regard as also important our identification as members of a world community and of the human race.

Problems of Devising Criteria for Evaluation of Foreign-Policy Goals and Means: Summation

Our discussion thus far in the chapter has been concerned with some basic questions that confront us in an effort to make value judgments about the goals of American foreign policy and about the means utilized in their pursuit: Are there any objective, or universally acceptable, criteria by which one may measure the goodness or badness, the desirability or undesirability, of foreign-policy goals and means?

Our discussion has led us to the following conclusions. At the level of broad, abstract, general formulations of foreign-policy goals, one might identify a set of values that, if not universally acceptable, at any rate would command such broad acceptance as to transcend purely personal preferences—values such as peace, justice, the self-determination of peoples, and the promotion of human welfare. The vague, abstract quality of such general goals, however, renders them virtually meaningless at the operational level. When we search for universally acceptable criteria, applicable to meaningful operational choices, various kinds of criteria come to mind: legal norms, moral principles, conceptions of the national interest. Upon careful scrutiny, however, we find that none of these sets of criteria fully meets standards of objectivity and universal acceptability.

This is not to say that notions of legality, morality, and the national interest are irrelevant or meaningless in the evaluation of foreign-policy decisions and actions. On the contrary, each of us is likely to find such notions indispensable in making value judgments about foreign-policy outcomes. However, our conclusion must be that at the level of choices among intermediate objectives and means in foreign policy, reasonable men can and do disagree about what is legal, moral, and in the national interest, and under what conditions various norms are applicable. Indeed, we may conclude that politics is a struggle not only to influence particular policy outcomes or to influence the allocation of costs and benefits that accrue from the policy process; politics is also a struggle to influence the structuring of norms by which various policy choices are judged to be legitimate and broadly acceptable.

Goals and Means: The Cuban Missile Crisis

The struggle to legitimate policy choices by norms of legality, morality, or national interest occurs at the international as well as at the intra-national level. It is useful to conclude our discussion of evaluation of foreign-policy goals and means with reference to a case that illustrates this, as well as other points made earlier in the chapter—the Cuban missile crisis of 1962.

The crisis arose from analysis of photographs in the CIA from a U-2 flight over Cuba the previous day, revealing the beginnings of installation on the island of a number of Soviet medium-range missiles capable of delivering nuclear warheads on targets deep within the United States or throughout much of Latin America. It is instructive to review the case, and especially the American decision-making process at the time, in terms of norms of legality, morality, and national interest.

It is interesting to note, in the first place, that Soviet installation of the missiles on Cuban soil, however provocative, was perfectly legal. Indeed, actions of the United States in placing missiles on foreign territory, such as Turkey, close to the Soviet Union, provided a precedent that the Kennedy administration feared the Soviets might exploit for bargaining purposes during the Cuban missile crisis (agreeing to remove missiles in Cuba only in exchange for the removal of American missiles in Turkey, for instance). It is also rather interesting, in the light of legal arguments used by the American government to justify its actions, that the means utilized to detect the missiles in the first place and used subsequently for continuing surveillance were, strictly speaking, illegal. That is, by generally accepted standards of international law, the American U-2 flights represented a violation of Cuban airspace. Moreover, the means selected by the American government to bring about a removal of Soviet missiles, a partial blockade of Cuba, constituted an act of war according to international law. Indeed, recognition of the latter fact led American policy makers to term their action a "quarantine" of Cuba rather than a blockade, in an effort to avoid the full legal implications of the act. The various points made here suggest that, from a strictly legal standpoint, it is difficult to applaud the American position in the missile crisis.[9]

However, it would be erroneous to conclude that American policy makers during the Cuban missile crisis were oblivious to considerations of legality. Nor would it be correct to imagine that significantly large numbers of persons in the United States or elsewhere regarded the Soviet Union rather than the United States as the more law-abiding adversary in the conflict. Rather, it appears that the Kennedy administration quite successfully mobilized legal arguments (as well as others to be discussed below) for the legitimacy of American actions. Especially important was the solicitation from twenty members of the Organization of American States (OAS) of a resolution describing Soviet missiles in Cuba as a threat to the hemisphere and unanimously endorsing the American blockade. It was deemed important by American policy makers to convince not only the American people and other allies that the law was on the side of the United States, but also to present a formidable legal case to the Soviets, who were believed to attach importance to such factors in bargaining situations.[10]

Even more than in respect to legal questions, issues of morality occupied the attention of American policy makers during much of the crisis. Indeed, according to an account by Robert Kennedy, who as brother and confidant to the President played a major role in discussions at the time, the moral issue in the question whether or not to launch a surprise air attack to wipe out the missile bases in Cuba was the topic of discussion to which policy makers devoted the most time during the first five days of the crisis.[11] Yet the question of where morality lies in this, as in most foreign-policy decisions, was and is an elusive one. For instance, former Secretary of State Dean Acheson, who was included in the small group discussing the possibilities for bringing about the removal of Soviet missiles, argued that it was the President's "responsibility" and "obligation" to use force to destroy the missiles. Rejecting this interpretation of the President's moral obligation, Robert Kennedy suggested that he did

---

[9] A detailed critique of the American legal position at the time is presented by Quincy Wright, "The Cuban Quarantine of 1962," in John G. Stoessinger and Alan F. Westin, eds., *Power and Order* (New York: Harcourt, 1964), pp. 179–213.

[10] In discussions within the American government at the time, Llewellyn Thompson, expert on Soviet affairs, especially stressed the Soviet sensitivity to legalities. Elie Abel, *The Missile Crisis* (New York: Bantam, 1966), p. 73.

[11] Robert F. Kennedy, *Thirteen Days* (New York: New American Library, Signet paperback ed., 1969), p. 39.

not want to see his brother become the Tojo of the 1960s (an allusion to the Japanese surprise attack on Pearl Harbor), and that a surprise attack on Cuba would be contrary to the traditions of the American people.

Although the argument of Robert Kennedy (made in similar form also by Secretary of Defense McNamara and Secretary of State Rusk) eventually prevailed, it is not certain that the persuasiveness of the argument lay in its appeal to the consciences of policy makers, nor is it clear that the argument was intended merely to raise matters of conscience. "The strongest argument against the all-out military attack . . ." Robert Kennedy recalled, "was that a surprise attack would erode if not destroy the moral position of the United States throughout the world." [12] It is not unduly cynical to suggest that concern for the moral position of the United States in the world is not identical to concern for the moral rightness or wrongness of the action being considered. No doubt such concerns are often parallel, as they probably were in this instance. But what seems most clearly articulated in the quotation is a concern for legitimizing American actions in moral terms.

The cornerstone of American governmental efforts to justify actions taken to secure the removal of Soviet missiles from Cuba was neither a legalistic nor a moralistic argument, however. Rather, the case for legitimizing American governmental actions was built largely on the argument that the actions were a justifiable response in protection of vital national interests that were threatened by the Soviet installation of missiles. As President Kennedy emphasized in the radio-television address of October 22 that alerted the nation and the world to the missile crisis, the "secret, swift and extraordinary buildup of Communist missiles" constituted ". . . a deliberately provocative and unjustified change in the *status quo*. . . ." A change in the *status quo* "in an area well-known to have a special and historical relationship to the United States . . ." was one which "cannot be accepted by this country. . . ." [13] In short, justification of the American position was based on an appeal to political realism, with all the ambiguities of such a criterion noted in earlier discussion. Yet, such a criterion was adequate justification for policy makers because there was a consensus among them on the belief that vital national interests were at stake in the crisis; moreover, expression of opinion at home and abroad suggests that the criterion was sufficient to provide broad legitimization of American actions.

[12] Kennedy, pp. 31–49.

[13] Longer excerpts from the speech are contained in the following works: Theodore C. Sorensen, *Kennedy* (New York: Harper & Row, 1965); Arthur M. Schlesinger, Jr., *A Thousand Days* (Boston: Houghton Mifflin, 1965); Roger Hilsman, *To Move a Nation* (New York: Doubleday, 1967).

With rare exception, accounts of the Cuban missile crisis have produced highly favorable judgments about the American foreign-policy goal formulated (removal of Soviet missiles) and about the means selected (a blockade of Cuba) to implement the goal. Yet, it is clear that the criteria—norms of legality, morality, or realism—on which such judgments have been made are not totally objective ones, and cannot be. On the other hand, whatever the subjective content of such criteria, it is clear that policy makers themselves attach some importance to them in at least two closely related respects. First, the choice among the possible courses of action is influenced in varying degrees by the perceptions that policy makers have of the legality, morality, or political realism of the various options. Second, once the choice is made, issues of legality, morality, and the national interest become mobilized by policy makers to support the course of action selected, in an effort to legitimize their decision.

Given the proclivity of policy makers for seeking to legitimate their actions, the concerned observer of foreign policy is well advised to regard with a measure of skepticism sweeping claims by policy makers that various decisions have been justified on the grounds of legality, morality, or realism. On the other hand, unless he is to be reduced to total cynicism in the face of imperfect normative criteria, he must be willing to make partially subjective judgments of his own about the goals pursued and the means utilized in foreign policy, while recognizing his own susceptibility to error.

11

The Problem
of Reconciling
Demands for Efficiency
with the Maintenance
of Democratic Values

Assessment of the Performance of the System

When making judgments about goals pursued, or means utilized, in the conduct of foreign policy, we are essentially focusing on outputs of the political system. An alternative, or additional, focus for evaluative inquiry is that of the performance of the political system in translating inputs into outputs. The latter focus is distinct from the former in the sense that one can evaluate the process by which the political system arrives at particular goals or means independently of one's judgments about the decisions that are made. For instance, one could find that the political system had been operating clumsily in pursuit of admirable goals or that foreign-policy goals that were despicable had been formulated and executed brilliantly or at least democratically.

305

In Chapter 11, the concluding chapter, we shall focus on the crucial matter of the performance of the political system in the formulation and execution of foreign-policy decisions. A focus on systemic performance returns us to many of the topics that concerned us during Part IV of the book, when we considered foreign-policy analysis from a decision-making perspective. Indeed, our normative concern in the present chapter with whether the foreign-policy process is functioning well or badly can be satisfied only in relationship to the empirical question of *how* the system is functioning. The close relationship between normative and empirical questions makes it appropriate to structure the remainder of the discussion in Part V in terms that emphasize the links between evaluation and explanation. A series of hypotheses, stemming from important normative issues, but empirically testable and applying many of the variables introduced in Part IV, will provide such a structure.

Problems of Defining "Efficiency"

Efficiency is perhaps the most obvious criterion for the evaluation of the performance of the political system in making foreign policy. However, the criterion is a slippery one to apply. As used in evaluation of the performance of systems generally, efficiency is usually measured in one of two ways: as the ratio of the output of a system to its inputs, or as the ratio of the actual performance of a system to ideal performance.

Taking first the concept of efficiency as the ratio of outputs to inputs, one must ask what criteria to employ to measure foreign-policy outputs and inputs. Is the number of problems solved in a given day in the State Department a measure of the output of the department for that day? The number of cables dispatched to various embassies? The number of high-level conferences held? And what are inputs? The number of student demonstrations in front of the White House? The number of telephone calls from corporation executives? The number of men enlisting or inducted into the Army on a given day? Clearly, there is some utility in trying to formulate notions of gains made or losses incurred in relationship to resources and energies invested in pursuing a given policy, but measurement is invariably elusive and imprecise. Many of the important accomplishments in foreign policy are intangible, and gains and losses in world affairs are often felt in scarcely distinguishable increments—a foreign leader persuaded to be slightly more sympathetic to American interests, an ally tacitly agreeing not to raise certain controversial issues at a forthcoming conference, an antagonist reducing the intensity of propaganda attacks. Furthermore, one can seldom be confident that his vision has the depth and the breadth to make meaningful judgments about efficiency. A foreign-policy action that promotes value *A* in respect to area *X* may impose losses of value *A* in respect to area *Y*. A foreign policy with favorable consequences in the short run may impose severe costs in the long run.

Looking next at efficiency as the ratio of actual performance to ideal performance, one must ask how the ideal performance of the foreign-policy system is to be estimated. In Chapter 7, the IIMMP, an imaginary ideal machine for making foreign policy, was postulated as a way of illustrating, by contrast, the sources of inefficiency in human organization. But the problem of measuring the degree of inefficiency (and conversely, therefore, the efficiency) in the foreign-policy process remains one that cannot be neatly reduced to percentages. Thus, if the notion of an automobile engine that is 60 percent efficient is meaningful to the student of mechanics, for the student of foreign policy, comparable percentages for the performance of the foreign-policy system would be meaningless. What is possible is to make rather gross comparisons between organizations operating within the foreign-policy process that serve as indexes of their efficiency relative to one another. For example, one might find that the Navy is able to feed and equip personnel at lower cost per man than the Army. Or one might make comparisons over time that reveal an increase or decrease in efficiency within a given organization in the performance of certain tasks. For example, one might find that overhead costs for the processing of foreign aid in Thailand have been reduced over a period of years.

Keeping in mind the difficulties of devising rigorous indexes for the measurement of efficiency, it is nonetheless useful to make distinctions, however crude, among relative degrees of efficiency in the formulation and execution of foreign-policy decisions and to attempt to account for the differences between relatively efficient performance and relatively inefficient performance. Some key normative issues that arise from consideration of the problems of efficiency have already been raised in Chapter 9. The issues were ones that pertain generally to the activities of any large, complex organization. However, in the present chapter we shall raise issues that are peculiar to political systems such as the American one, where the quest for efficiency must be weighed against a commitment to democratic values.

The problem of attaining efficiency in the conduct of American foreign policy is of particular moment in the light of the commitment of the United States to democratic values. One of the most perceptive observers ever to comment on American government and politics, Alexis de Tocqueville, viewed the problem of efficiency in just such a light a century and a half ago. It was his view that democracy was a hindrance to the attainment of efficiency in foreign-policy performance. Indeed, he asserted that in the conduct of foreign affairs, democracies were "decidedly inferior to governments carried on upon different principles."[1] His reasoning, in part, was as follows.

> Foreign politics demand scarcely any of those qualities which a democracy possesses; and they require, on the contrary, the perfect use of almost all of those faculties in which it is deficient. . . . A democracy is unable to regulate the details of an important undertaking, to persevere in a design, and to work out its execution in the presence of serious obstacles. It cannot combine its measures with secrecy, and it will not await their consequences with patience. These are qualities which more especially belong to an individual or to an aristocracy. . . .[2]

Tocqueville's view that undemocratic systems are likely to be more efficient than democratic ones in the conduct of foreign policy may be disputed. A comparison of the Soviet foreign-policy process with that of the United States, for instance, does not offer impressive substantiation of the proposition that undemocratic systems are more efficient.[3] On the other hand, whether or not one contends that the United States has been efficient in the conduct of foreign affairs relative to other political systems, Tocqueville's argument still raises the provocative and important question of the extent to which a commitment to efficiency and a commitment to democracy are compatible. For example, to reverse the emphasis in Tocqueville's thesis from a concern for efficiency to a concern for democracy, one might ask: To the extent that a political system is able to maintain efficiency in the conduct of foreign policy, must it do so at some cost to democratic values? The question takes on added significance when one considers the complex and multitudinous demands of the environment in the modern world, which make the problems of efficient performance far more complicated today than they were in

[1] Alexis de Tocqueville, *Democracy in America*, trans. Henry Reeves, 2 vols. (New York: J. and H. G. Langley, 1841), 1:254.

[2] Tocqueville, 1:254.

[3] For example, see Zbigniew Brzezinski and Samuel P. Huntington, *Political Power: USA/USSR* (New York: Viking, 1964). The authors find strengths and weaknesses in each system. Another scholar disputes Tocqueville's hypothesis even more strongly, in these terms: "It was long believed that America's democratic institutions would prevent her from behaving effectively and responsibly in the world. The judgment should be reversed. American institutions facilitate rather than discourage the quick identification of problems, the pragmatic quest for solutions, the ready confrontation of dangers, the willing expenditure of energies, and the open criticism of policies." Kenneth N. Waltz, *Foreign Policy and Democratic Politics* (Boston: Little, Brown, 1967), pp. 307–308.

Tocqueville's time—indeed, more complicated than they were three or four decades ago.

In Part III of the book, we discussed in some dtail a number of characteristics of the structure of the geopolitical environment and the changes that are occurring in environmental structure. Here we may note simply that the environment has become increasingly complex (there are more nation-states, more complex patterns of interaction and diffusion of authority, and greater technological complexity), and its rapidly changing demands are difficult to predict. The time available to policy makers for responding to events has been progressively reduced at the same time that the risks of error or misjudgment have increased astronomically. Finally, the growth of American power, both relative to that of other nation-states and in absolute terms, has led to unprecedented involvement of the United States in the affairs of other parts of the world; hence, a higher proportion than ever before of what is happening, or what will happen, in the world environment is of concern to American policy makers.

In short, during the present age, the American political system has been subjected to stresses of increasing variety and magnitude. Thus, the problem of maintaining efficiency in the foreign-policy process has progressively increased. However, efficient performance of foreign-policy making in the face of current environmental stresses requires adaptation in structure as well as policy. A crucial issue is this: Can the American political system make the structural adjustments necessary to the maintenance of efficiency in the conduct of foreign policy, without compromising or reducing democratic practices? In short, can a political system enjoy both efficiency and democracy in the present age, or must one be sought at the expense of the other?

Problems of Defining "Democracy"

The kind of answer that one would give to these questions would depend upon how he defined "efficiency" and "democracy," as well as upon his prognostication of present and future trends. The concept of democracy is even more elusive than that of efficiency.

What is democracy? We shall exclude at the outset interpretations that would treat democracy and anarchy as synonymous and interpretations that would envisage direct democracy, in the sense of a system of policy making in which the views of the masses of people are solicited on every matter. In other words, in the following discussion of democracy the need for a government is assumed. Moreover, it is assumed that the term "democracy" is used in reference to a reasonably complex political system, in which a clear distinction can be made between those who have authority to make decisions that have the binding effect of law and the vast majority of the society who do not have such authority. It is perhaps unnecessary to add that the following discussion of democracy also excludes from consideration Orwellian distortions of the term, as used by regimes or rulers to describe practices that are clearly authoritarian in nature.

Although the above qualifications allow some limits, a variety of interpretations of democracy remains. The writings of Plato and Aristotle, later figures such as Locke, Jefferson, and John Stuart Mill, and current political philosophers and political activists provide a multitude of interpretations of democracy and its essential requisites. We do not propose here to review the body of democratic theory that has accumulated over the centuries or to defend any particular school of thought.

Although the extant body of democratic theory includes important disagreements among various theorists, there does seem to be a core area of agreement at a rather high level of abstraction. Most of the established theories of democracy focus, with varying degrees of emphasis, upon three broad goal-values that must be attained if a political system is to be described as democratic. The first of these is *accountability* of policy makers to the people. The second is *political equality* among the people who participate in the political system. The third is *individual liberty* against oppression by the state.

Disagreement among political theorists exists about which institutions and procedures best promote or guarantee the values identified above. Disagreement also exists about how fully the values must be satisfied before it is appropriate to describe a political system or its component practices as democratic. However, because broad agreement does exist among theorists that the above values comprise the core of the democratic ethos, it is possible and useful to organize subsequent discussion around them.

Broadly, the remainder of the chapter is concerned with the problem of reconciling the demands of efficiency in the formulation and execution of American foreign policy with a commitment to democratic values. The overall problem is examined in terms of three component dilemmas: the dilemma of reconciling efficiency and accountability; the dilemma of reconciling efficiency and political equality; and the dilemma of reconciling efficiency and individual liberty.

The investigation has empirical as well as normative dimensions. Based upon analysis of current trends in environmental demands upon the American political system, and of trends in response to the demands, a series of hypotheses, empirically testable, is presented that relate to each of the three dilemmas. Normative dimensions of investigation lie in comparing one's hypotheses about the relationship that does prevail between efficiency and accountability, political equality, or individual liberty with one's notions about what weights ought to be assigned to efficiency in comparison with the respective democratic values under various conditions. The key terms and the dilemmas will be clarified further as we proceed.

Accountability and Efficiency

Accountability refers to the relationship between government officials and the rest of the society. What mechanisms exist within the political system by which the people may determine who within the government is responsible for various actions and decisions, and by which the people may hold policy makers responsible for their actions? How effective are the mechanisms in providing accountability of those who govern to those who are governed?

Political theorists differ in the criteria that they would establish as to the specific mechanisms that are essential to ensure accountability and as to the standards of accountability that must be met to satisfy the norms of democratic practice. It is true that virtually all theorists include a system of regular, free, and competitive elections as one mechanism essential to accountability in a political system. However, as vital as elections may be, they provide only intermittent opportunities for the people to call policy makers to account for their actions. The outcome of an election is often ambiguous in terms of the preferences of the electorate on specific issues. Thus, the candidate who wins the most votes may formulate important policies that reflect the desires of only a minority of the electorate.

Moreover, even in instances where a candidate seems to have committed himself clearly to a given position on an important policy issue, and where he seems to have won broad popular support for his stand, once he is in office, he may greatly alter his position on the grounds that the situation has changed. For example, President Lyndon Johnson won broad support in the 1964 election partly through depicting his policies in Vietnam as exhibiting great restraint in contrast to the views of his opponent, Senator Barry Goldwater, who, it was alleged, would probably pursue "trigger-happy" policies that would lead to a considerable expansion of the war. Having won the election, President Johnson initiated policies almost immediately that led to the beginning of bombing of North Vietnam and to utilization of American forces in a role of direct combat. Many persons who had voted for Johnson decried the escalation of the war and claimed that they had been deceived. The President replied, however, that the situation in Vietnam had deteriorated so rapidly since the election that he was forced to reassess his previous position and to become an advocate of more forceful measures. President Johnson's alteration of his policies illustrates the point that, however free and meaningful elections may be in a political system, they are at best an imperfect mechanism for assuring that policy makers will respond to popular preferences in the interim between elections. What other mechanisms must therefore be provided to ensure accountability? Knowledgeable students of democracy differ on this question.

Some theorists stress the importance of various mechanisms for articulating and aggregating public opinion in the interim between elections. For example, one might argue that Lyndon Johnson's announcement in March 1968 that he would not run again for the presidency and that he was ordering a partial bombing halt in North Vietnam, coming as the announcement did soon after mounting popular protests of American policies in Vietnam, was evidence that the President had finally been held to account by public opinion for his policies in Vietnam. The role of the mass media in shaping public opinion and in highlighting, supporting, or criticizing government policies is a closely related object of concern to many theorists interested in mechanisms of accountability. The role of political parties, and especially of the party in opposition to the administration in power, is of similar interest. Likewise, some theorists stress the importance of the separation of powers among the three branches of the national government for maintaining accountability, by providing constitutional incentives for each of the branches to check the authority of the others.

We cannot pursue in detail these various topics. Moreover, we shall not attempt to provide a definitive assessment of the relative importance of various mechanisms such as those cited. Instead, we shall focus on one key institution in the foreign-policy process, the presidency. By advancing a number of hypotheses about the extent to which the President may wield discretionary authority in the formulation and execution of foreign policy, we shall illustrate how empirical inquiry might proceed in this problem, as well as showing selective aspects of the normative issues that stem from the trends observed.

Authority of the President in Foreign Affairs

We might begin by noting that in the conduct of foreign affairs, authority has always been concentrated heavily in the executive branch of the American government (as in the governments of virtually all nation-states). It is important to our analysis that the rationale for such distribution of authority in foreign affairs be made clear. The statement that has come to be regarded as the classic one in distinguishing the demands of foreign affairs from those of domestic affairs, and in providing a rationale for the concentration of vast discretionary authority in the presidency, is the opinion of the Supreme Court in the case of *United States* v. *Curtiss-Wright Export Corporation*.[4] The decision is particularly interesting because it supported the exercise by the President of vast discretionary authority in foreign affairs at a time when the Court was cutting broadly through various pieces of domestic New Deal legislation, on the grounds that they represented unconstitutional delegation of authority to the President.

The Curtiss-Wright Case   The key constitutional issue in the Curtiss-Wright case was whether Congress, vested in Article I, Section 1, with "all legislative Powers" in the American federal government, could delegate legislative authority to the President. To place the focus differently, could the President exercise authority, essentially legislative, not enumerated as presidential power in the Constitution?

In 1935, the Court had ruled on the constitutionality of a major piece of New Deal legislation, the National Industrial Recovery Act. This act had been designed to promote economic recovery from the depression through the creation of a large administrative apparatus in the executive branch to supervise "codes of fair competition." The codes, regulating prices, wages, and working conditions, were to be drawn up by the industries themselves, with the approval of the President, or by the President in cases where industries were unable to agree upon an acceptable proposal. To the dismay and indignation of the President, the Court had declared the act unconstitutional, on the grounds that it represented congressional delegation of legislative authority to the President.

In the Curtiss-Wright case, the Court was faced with an institutional arrangement similar to the one it had declared unconstitutional in the cases involving the National Industrial Recovery Act (*Schechter* v. *United States* and *Panama Refining Company* v. *Ryan*). In an atmosphere of growing public concern over the stimulation of international conflict by munitions manufacturers (symbolized by the Nye Munitions Hearings, to be discussed below, which began in the Senate in 1934), the Congress passed a joint resolution in 1934 authorizing the President to prohibit the sale of arms and munitions to certain countries in South America if, in his judgment, such sale would stimulate conflict in the countries concerned. The resolution left it to the discretion of the Presi-

---

[4] 299 U.S. 304 (1936).

dent to issue an order prohibiting such sale; moreover, having issued the order, he could subsequently revoke it. Pursuant to the congressional resolution, President Roosevelt did in fact issue an order setting up an embargo of arms shipments to countries at war in the Chaco (Bolivia and Paraguay). The Curtiss-Wright Export Corporation was convicted of violating the order through the sale of guns to Bolivia; the corporation appealed, in turn, on the grounds that the congressional delegation of authority to the President was unconstitutional.

Mr. Justice Sutherland, one of the "nine old men" whom President Roosevelt denounced for "obstruction" of the New Deal, rendered the opinion for the Court in the Curtiss-Wright case, upholding the constitutionality of the congressional delegation of authority to the President. The fact that the President was not granted such authority in enumerated form in the Constitution was, in the opinion of the Court, not a barrier to the exercise of such authority in foreign affairs. The Court decision said in part,

> The broad statement that the federal government can exercise no powers except those specifically enumerated in the Constitution, and such implied powers as are necessary and proper to carry into effect the enumerated powers, is categorically true only in respect of our internal affairs. . . . The powers to declare and wage war, to conclude peace, to make treaties, to maintain diplomatic relations with other sovereignties, *if they had never been mentioned in the Constitution*, would have vested in the government as necessary concomitants of nationality. . . .
>
> Not only, as we have shown, is the federal power over external affairs in origin and essential character different from that over internal affairs, but participation in the exercise of the power is significantly limited. In this vast external realm, with its important, complicated, delicate and manifold problems, *the President alone* has the power to speak or listen as a representative of the nation. . . .[5]

In spite of the persuasiveness of the Court's opinion in the Curtiss-Wright decision, and in spite of the legitimation that the Court support in the case provided for subsequent exercise of vast discretionary authority by the President in foreign affairs, some troublesome questions remain. First, how much concentration of authority in the presidency is needed to enhance the efficiency of the process of making and executing foreign policy? Or, to phrase the question differently, to what extent do checks or restraints on presidential authority by other branches detract from efficiency in the foreign-policy process? Second, at what point and

[5] *U.S.* v. *Curtiss-Wright.* Italics are added. Justice McReynold dissented. Justice Stone took no part in the proceedings.

to what extent does concentration of authority in the presidency in the conduct of foreign affairs reduce the accountability of the government to the people? In other words, what distribution of authority in the making and executing of foreign policy among the various branches and institutions of government best contributes to the maintenance of accountability of policy makers to the people?

Thoughtful observers differ considerably about how the questions should be answered. It is also clear that each of us might find different answers appropriate, depending upon the circumstances of foreign affairs at the time and upon our perception of the needs of the polity in such circumstances. It is useful therefore to hypothesize about how varying circumstances affect the behavior of policy makers in various branches, in seeking or relinquishing authority for the making and executing of foreign policy.

Congress is by no means the only institutional device for providing a check on presidential authority in the conduct of foreign affairs; moreover, there are considerable differences of viewpoint among concerned observers as to the relative effectiveness and the relative desirability of the checks that Congress does impose on the President. Nevertheless, it is convenient to use the relationship of the Congress to the President as a focal point for advancing a series of propositions.

Expansion of Presidential Authority: The Rationale   In the years since the Curtiss-Wright decision—which had served to legitimize considerable concentration of discretionary authority in the presidency on the grounds that efficiency in the conduct of foreign policy demanded such concentration—the problems of American foreign policy have grown more fearsome and complex than ever before. The level and forms of involvement of the United States in world affairs have dramatically increased. War or the threat of war have become an incessant concern. How have such trends affected the distribution of authority between the President and Congress in foreign affairs? Both the President and Congress have become more deeply involved in issues of foreign policy in recent decades than ever before, but it would appear that the President's discretionary authority, relative to the authority of Congress, has increased. The relationship between environmental trends and the distribution of authority between the President and Congress may be suggested as follows.

> HYPOTHESIS 33   *The higher the proportion of events in the world environment that bear directly on high-salience interests of the United States and the more widespread the belief among Ameri-*

can national leaders that present or future events pose significant threats to these interests—

> HYPOTHESIS 33(a)   *the greater will be the tendency of the President to seek or to assert authority to respond to the threats without being obliged to gain prior approval of the response from Congress.*

> HYPOTHESIS 33(b)   *the greater will be the tendency of the Congress to yield to the President authority to respond to the threats without being obliged to gain prior approval of the response from Congress.*

In more specific terms, the hypotheses suggest that, as the United States has become more deeply involved in world affairs in recent decades, with the result that proportionately more of what is happening in the world bears directly upon American interests, and as threats to these interests have arisen, first in the form of Nazism and Japanese militarism, later in the form of communism and the threat of nuclear war, the President has sought greater authority and thus greater flexibility to deal with the threats. Congress, by and large, has found the rationale persuasive.

The vast amount of discretionary authority that President Roosevelt sought and acquired during World War II and the acquiescence of the majority of Congress in seeing presidential authority expanded illustrate the hypotheses. President Roosevelt presented an argument for expanded discretionary authority in his message to Congress in January 1941, almost a year before the formal entry of the United States into the war.

> No one can tell the exact character of the emergency situations that we may be called upon to meet. The Nation's hands must not be tied when the Nation's life is in danger. We must all prepare to make the sacrifices that the emergency—as serious as war itself— demands. *Whatever stands in the way of speed and efficiency in defense preparations must give way to the national need.*[6]

Congress responded to the President's plea by granting him broad sanction to exercise emergency powers, extending his discretionary authority to a number of areas. For example, he was able to regulate wages, prices, and hours in accord with his estimates of national need; to issue rules rationing food, gasoline, and other goods critical to the war effort; to control the activities of aliens and of citizens of German, Italian, and Japanese descent; to order government control of mines and factories if

[6] U.S., *Peace and War: United States Foreign Policy, 1931–1941* (Washington: Government Printing Office, 1943), pp. 608–611. Italics are added.

strikes or other disturbances threatened, in his judgment, the interruption of war production. In the Lend-Lease Act, passed early in 1941, Congress empowered the President to loan American goods and services to those nation-states whose defense he deemed vital to the preservation of American security.

Moreover, many important and far-reaching foreign-policy decisions were made by the President during, or on the eve of, the war without prior congressional sanction. The most notable of these include the agreement in 1940 to loan fifty American destroyers to Great Britain, in return for a ninety-nine-year lease of air and naval bases on British territory in Newfoundland and the Caribbean, and the secret agreements negotiated by President Roosevelt with other heads of state at Casablanca, Cairo, Tehran, and Yalta.

Congressional Efforts to Regain or to Assert Authority When Congress grants discretionary authority to the President to cope with a specific emergency, such as World War II, it characteristically reserves the right to terminate such authority with a declaration that the emergency has ended. Thus, presidential authority in such areas as price and wage control, and rationing, was ended by congressional action at the end of World War II. If, however, without specific congressional authorization, the President simply assumes expanded authority for engaging in various kinds of activities in the foreign-policy process, on the grounds that conditions of stress require this expansion, the following hypotheses may be suggested as to the subsequent behavior of Congress and the President.

> HYPOTHESIS 34 *Once Congress has condoned, although never formally sanctioned, a reduction in its authority relative to that of the President for engaging in various kinds of activities in the foreign-policy process, members of Congress will attempt to reassert or to expand their authority if—*
>
> > HYPOTHESIS 34(a) *they believe that the particular actions in which the President acted without congressional advice or consent are regarded by the members' constituents with broad disapproval.*
> >
> > HYPOTHESIS 34(b) *they believe that a congressional attempt to reduce presidential authority in general would be a popular one among their constituents.*
> >
> > HYPOTHESIS 34(c) *particular current or pending foreign-policy commitments are of such repugnance to the members or their constituents that they believe congressional*

authority must be asserted in order to reverse or prevent the commitments by the President.

HYPOTHESIS 35 *Once Congress has condoned, although never formally sanctioned, a reduction of its authority relative to that of the President for engaging in various kinds of activities in the foreign-policy process, the President will resist relinquishing authority to Congress even if the rationale under which the authority was originally asserted has become outmoded by changing circumstances.*

The general rationale for these hypotheses stems from the observation that often in times of national emergency or severe stress, the President will simply take action to cope with a problem even though no specific congressional or constitutional sanction of his authority exists. If Congress condones the action, through passive or active support, the authority of the President in this area of activity tends to be legitimized. Even if circumstances change and the original rationale for presidential action becomes outmoded, the President (perhaps a successor to the President who originally asserted the authority) will seek to maintain his authority against congressional efforts to check or withdraw it. Some factors that might provoke congressional action in attempting to reduce or limit presidential authority, however, are suggested in the hypotheses. Congressional-presidential interaction during the debate over the Bricker Amendment provides a specific illustration of the hypotheses.

The Bricker Amendment   On the first day that Congress convened in January 1953, an amendment to the Constitution was introduced into the Senate by Republican John W. Bricker of Ohio, cosponsored by sixty-two other Senators. The amendment was generally designed to increase congressional authority in foreign affairs relative to the authority of the President. Various specific problems and general grievances, of the type suggested in the above hypotheses, had prompted the senators to take such action.

One key target of the Bricker Amendment was the authority of the President to commit the nation to agreements with other nation-states that were as binding as treaties, without obtaining the consent of two-thirds of the Senate. Such executive agreements had been used, for instance, in the destroyer-for-bases deal in 1940 and in the controversial agreements signed among the heads of government of the Big Three powers at Yalta and Potsdam. More recent concern stemmed from the fear of some members of Congress that, through American membership in the United Nations, the President might commit the United States to international agreements, such as the Universal Declaration of Human Rights, that would permit the United Nations to interfere in American civil-rights problems—areas of concern reserved by the United States Constitution to the several states or to the federal government. Thus, the Bricker Amendment provided (in Section 3) that "Congress shall have power to regulate all executive and other agreements with any foreign power or international organization. All such agreements shall be subject to the limitations imposed on treaties by this article." [7]

A related source of concern to proponents of the Bricker Amendment was the ability of the President to make international commitments that had the force of law within states, even in respect to matters of legislation reserved constitutionally to the states. For instance, although the courts had declared unconstitutional an act of Congress providing for the protection of migratory birds, on the grounds that this was an area of concern reserved to the states, the Supreme Court had subsequently sustained the constitutionality of congressional legislation to the same effect, made in the implementation of a treaty between the United States and Canada. Mr. Justice Holmes, speaking for the Court majority in the case, contended that "no doubt the great body of private relations usually fall within the control of the state, but a treaty may override its power. . . ." [8] The Bricker Amendment would have eliminated the distinction that the Court had made between the constitutionality of legislation passed in support of a treaty or executive agreement and legislation passed independently of such international commitments. The proposed amendment would have prevented any treaty or other international agreement from having validity as internal law, except as supplemented by legislation, the constitutionality of which was supportable independently of the international commitment.

Proponents of the Bricker Amendment also wished to eliminate the distinction that the Court had made, in the Curtiss-Wright case, between strict interpretation of the Constitution in domestic affairs but loose interpretation, with broad recognition of presidential discretionary authority, in foreign affairs. In somewhat vague or even tautological terms, the Bricker Amendment provided that, if any provision of a treaty or executive agreement violated the Constitution, then the provision was invalid.

Aside from the specific grievances of the proponents of the Bricker Amendment, they shared a general feeling that the authority of the President in foreign affairs had grown to excessive proportions and that

---

[7] U.S., 83d Cong. 1st sess., S J Res. 1, reproduced with commentary in *Congressional Quarterly Almanac, 1953* (Washington: Congressional Quarterly News Features, 1954), pp. 233–237.

[8] Missouri v. Holland, 252 U.S. 415 (1920).

public opinion was favorable for the imposition of congressional restraints on the President. It is an interesting commentary on the low level
of general public awareness regarding most matters of foreign affairs
that, in October 1953, during the peak months of congressional debate
of the Bricker Amendment, 81 percent of those polled in a nationwide
sample had neither heard of nor read of the Bricker Amendment. But, as
V. O. Key points out, the remaining fifteen million who were more or less
knowledgeable about the amendment comprised a sizable number of
people in absolute terms.[9] Moreover, the salient point for present discussion is that proponents of the Bricker Amendment in Congress perceived a popular receptivity to the kinds of measures provided for in the
amendment. For example, Senator Lyndon Johnson indicated that he
would support the amendment "because all my people in Texas want
it." [10] Of course, it is difficult or perhaps impossible analytically to
distinguish a situation in which a member of Congress acts in accordance
with his actual perception of the wishes of his constituents from one in
which he acts for other reasons and then claims that his constituents
demanded the course of action that he followed. Without claiming an
ability to make such distinctions categorically, we can contend that, in
spite of the relatively small portion of the public who had knowledge
of the Bricker Amendment, evidence suggests that members of Congress were responsive to a synthetic public that existed at least in their
own minds.[11]

It had been the presidency of Franklin Roosevelt that had served as
the primary stimulus to which the Bricker Amendment had been a response, although Truman's unpopularity in the aftermath of his dismissal
of General MacArthur increased the vulnerability of the presidency to
criticism. However, it fell to the popular Dwight Eisenhower to cope
with the specific problem of the Bricker Amendment. President Eisenhower's reaction is particularly interesting and instructive, lending cre-
dence to Hypothesis 35 above. Although Eisenhower himself had often
expressed agreement with other Republicans that President Roosevelt
had usurped power from Congress, Eisenhower came to resist congressional efforts to restrict presidential authority in foreign affairs once the
threat was to his own prerogatives. After a few months of trying to con-

[9] Key, *Public Opinion and American Democracy* (New York: Knopf, 1961), pp.
82–85.
[10] Quoted by Richard M. Nixon, then Vice-President, in Emmet John Hughes,
The Ordeal of Power (New York: Dell, paperback ed., 1964), p. 126.
[11] For further discussion of the useful distinction between "synthetic" and "objective" public opinion, see Douglas Cater, *The Fourth Branch of Government* (Boston:
Houghton Mifflin, 1959).

ciliate Senator Bricker and his supporters, President Eisenhower came to regard the Bricker Amendment as "a damn thorn in our side" that would reduce needed flexibility in the government's capacity to meet the demands of foreign affairs.[12] Thus, the President began to work vigorously to defeat the amendment. After more than a year of intense discussion between the President, augmented by his advisers, and key senators, which was supplemented by heated debate on the floor of the Senate, the amendment was brought to a vote. When the votes were tallied, the Bricker Amendment had fallen one vote short of the two-thirds majority essential to its passage in the Senate.[13]

Eliciting Congressional Cooperation: The Tonkin Resolution Controversy Congressional efforts to impose formal checks on the President in his conduct of foreign affairs subsided with the defeat of the Bricker Amendment in 1954. However, in spite of the fact that President Eisenhower resisted congressional restraints on his foreign-policy authority, as no doubt his successors would resist similar threats of congressionally imposed restraints, neither President Eisenhower nor his successors could prudently ignore the sizable body of support that the Bricker Amendment had enjoyed even in defeat. That Presidents do in fact accommodate themselves to the need for enlisting congressional support, at least for major foreign-policy undertakings, even if congressionally imposed restraints on presidential authority are resisted, may be suggested by the following hypothesis.

> HYPOTHESIS 36 *If a foreign-policy course of action favored by the President requires the commitment of a substantial number of American troops in its implementation, the President will seek advance endorsement of the decision by Congress.*

In 1954, in consideration of a French request for American air and naval support of the beleaguered French outpost, Dienbienphu, President Eisenhower sought the advice of congressional leaders from both houses and both major parties. Congressional unwillingness to endorse the use of American armed force at Dienbienphu, unless multilateral support for the venture could be attained, eventually led to presidential rejection of the plan.

---

[12] President Eisenhower's attitudes toward Congress in general and toward the Bricker Amendment in particular are described colorfully in Hughes, pp. 107–116, 125–128.

[13] Even if a two-thirds majority had been attained, two subsequent hurdles would have remained. The House would have had to approve the amendment by a two-thirds majority, and three-fourths of the state legislatures would have had to ratify it before the amendment was effective.

Slightly more than ten years later, in August 1964, another American President again sought congressional approval for the commitment of American armed force in Vietnam. This time Congress approved. In August 1964, following an alleged attack on United States destroyers in the Gulf of Tonkin by four North Vietnamese patrol boats, President Johnson sought and obtained from Congress a joint resolution (S J Res. 189) assuring the President of congressional approval and support of "all necessary measures" that the President, as Commander in Chief of United States forces, might take to protect American forces in Southeast Asia. The resolution gave prior sanction to "all necessary steps, including the use of armed forces" to assist any state within the SEATO area. Thus, the resolution provided an aura of congressional legitimation to the major escalation, in the form of American bombing of targets in North Vietnam and of employment of United States troops in South Vietnam in direct combat, that followed beginning in 1965.

Ironically, although on the one hand the Tonkin Resolution provides an example of the felt presidential need to enlist congressional support for major foreign-policy ventures, on the other hand, it provides an example of the limits and frustrations of Congress in attempting to contribute to the formulation of policy. As American troop commitments mushroomed in the months and years after the Gulf of Tonkin incident, as casualties mounted, and as the war escalated in other respects, a number of senators, especially, came to regard the Tonkin Resolution not as presidential collaboration with Congress in key policy matters, but rather as presidential trickery and manipulation, which provided the form of congressional participation in the shaping of policy without the substance. Senator Fulbright, for example, chairman of the Senate Committee on Foreign Relations, who had spoken on the floor of the Senate in support of the Tonkin Resolution, subsequently expressed regret that the resolution had been cast in such broad terms that the administration could claim congressional sanction for major escalation of the war. As Senator Albert Gore of Tennessee, another member of Congress who came to regret the Tonkin Resolution, explained, "I interpreted that resolution as approving the specific and appropriate response to this attack [by the North Vietnamese patrol boats], and the chairman of this Committee, in presenting such a resolution, stated to the Senate that this was his interpretation." [14]

The reply of President Johnson, Secretary of State Rusk, and other leading policy makers in the administration to the complaints by mem-

---

[14] U.S. Congress, Senate Committee on Foreign Relations, *Hearings on Supplemental Foreign Assistance for Fiscal Year 1966, Vietnam*, 89th Cong., 2d sess., 1966, p. 53.

bers of Congress was that, if sufficient members of Congress felt that way, another resolution could be passed repudiating the broad language of the Tonkin Resolution. To most congressional critics of the Johnson administration on this matter, however, such a reply evaded the central problem confronting the members of Congress who wanted to make a genuine contribution to the formulation of foreign policy without detracting from its effective implementation. From the point of view of congressional critics, major policy decisions had already been made. Members of Congress could speak out now, in an effort to modify or to clarify American policy in Vietnam, but with substantial numbers of American troops committed, few members of Congress could feel justified in withholding support or otherwise undermining the policies, however unwise, that had produced the requirement for troops. As one critic of the policies of the Johnson administration, Senator Frank Church of Idaho, put it, "I do not think that in the face of the actuality of war Congress is going to repeal the law [that is, the Tonkin Resolution], and there is very little to do but support the American boys who are committed there with such funds as may be required." [15]

Summary: The Problem of Presidential Authority

The normative issue that has just been discussed is complex and easily subject to distortion. It is important that the issue not be misrepresented. The trend over the past several decades has not been one of unmitigated centralization of authority in the conduct of foreign affairs. Within the context of a burgeoning bureaucracy, considerable delegation of authority from the presidency to lower levels has occurred in many areas of policy making. Nor is it the case that the involvement of Congress in foreign affairs has been on the decline; the opposite is true. More members of Congress spend proportionately more of their time on matters of foreign policy today than ever before.

What is true, however, is that the United States has attained new heights of influence in world affairs in recent decades and that the President of the United States, more than any other person or group in the nation, symbolizes and commands that influence. Moreover, both in relative and in absolute terms, the foreign-policy responsibilities and the authority of the President have risen since the 1930s even more sharply than those of Congress. Furthermore, although the authority of the President is delegated on many matters, authority for making major

[15] *Hearings on Supplemental Foreign Assistance for Fiscal Year 1966, Vietnam,* p. 73.

policy decisions, especially in time of crisis, tends to be concentrated in the office of the President.

Only a few dimensions of the problem have been suggested in the discussion above. Emphasis has been placed on the Supreme Court and on Congress as potential checks on the exercise of authority in foreign affairs, and upon Congress especially as an institutional mechanism for the expression of popular will in the shaping of foreign policy. But many checks upon presidential authority other than the Supreme Court or Congress exist within the political system, and many instruments of popular expression and participation exist in addition to Congress. However, the preceding discussion should at least have been sufficient to illustrate and to underscore the key dilemma, of which the problem of presidential authority in foreign affairs is but one example. This dilemma is that of reconciling the desire to optimize efficiency in the conduct of foreign policy, especially in response to major threats from the external environment, with the desire to retain accountability to the people of those who wield authority in the conduct of foreign policy.

The efforts to define appropriate limits of presidential authority in the conduct of foreign affairs reveal that no simple formula for the reconciliation of commitments to efficiency and to accountability has been devised. Some have looked to a strengthened role of Congress in foreign affairs as desirable in providing an institutional check on presidential authority without unduly hampering efficiency. Others contend that Congress provides, at best, a clumsy instrument of accountability and, at worst, a serious impediment to needed efficiency in foreign-policy performance. No doubt policy makers in various branches of government will continue to develop their own *ad hoc* guidelines as to the kind of reconciliation between efficiency and accountability that is possible in the light of existing circumstances and as to the kind that is desirable in the light of the interests and claims associated with their respective roles. In the final analysis, each of us must compare such guidelines with his own independent assessment of what is possible, and with his own judgment as to what is desirable.

Political Equality and Efficiency

A second dilemma that concerns us in the present chapter is that of reconciling the demands for efficiency in the conduct of American foreign policy with the democratic commitment to political equality. That some persons wield more influence than others in decisions of public policy is a basic fact in all political systems. In that sense, political inequality exists in all of them. Yet, systems differ from one another considerably in the degree of political inequality that exists and in the extent to which particular individuals and groups within the society are systematically excluded from political participation or are accorded inferior status. Thus, although theorists of politics vary widely in their estimates of the extent of political equality that is possible, necessary, or desirable, most agree, as a minimum, that systematic (that is, legalized or institutionalized) discrimination among adults in their opportunities to participate in the political process is undemocratic; conversely, the lower the amount of systematic discrimination, the more democratic the system.

Over the years, since the founding of the Republic, the United States has clearly become more democratic, at least in the sense of experiencing a gradual elimination of blatant and highly visible forms of political discrimination. Legislation and constitutional amendments bringing an end to property requirements for voting and extending suffrage to the Negro, and later to women, are examples of the broadening of the egalitarian base of American democracy. On the other hand, more subtle or more obscure forms of political discrimination often have been more difficult to combat. Many such forms persist today—for instance, in the mechanisms by which state and local parties select candidates for office or in the allocation of committee chairmanships in the Congress (overrepresenting those from "safe," generally southern and rural, districts).

This is not the place to recount the history of the struggle for political equality in the United States or to comment on the full spectrum of current issues, ranging from the rights of blacks to the sorry plight of migrant workers, that might be included in a comprehensive discussion of political equality. Rather, we shall focus only on the extent of equality or inequality in gaining access to and influence upon the American foreign-policy process. We are especially interested in examining the consequences, in terms of political equality or inequality, of the demands for efficiency in foreign-policy making and execution.

As indicated much earlier in the chapter, in our discussion of the key values of democracy we assume a reasonably complex political system, in which a clear distinction can be made between those who have authority to make decisions that have the binding effect of law and the vast majority of the society, which lacks such authority. Thus, we assume that those occupying formal positions, with responsibilities for making and executing foreign policy, will be limited in number. Although authority for making foreign-policy decisions is assumed to be hierarchically structured, the matters that concern us here are the opportunities available to various individuals and groups within the political system to make their views on foreign policy known to decision makers and the relative weight assigned to various views in the formulation of foreign policy. In the sense of opportunities for access, and of relative weight accorded to views, to what extent does equality characterize the American foreign-policy process? How does the desire for efficiency in response to contemporary demands of foreign affairs affect the degree of equality attained?

The Concept of a Power Elite

The picture of a relative handful of powerful men, making deals in the citadels of power in the United States, while the masses of the population remain politically impotent, has been one that many persons in the past and the present have taken as an accurate representation of reality. Groups that can be loosely described as populist in political orientation, for instance, have characteristically rallied to the cry that the voice of the people was being ignored, while a band of powerful men ruled the nation. The verbal attacks of William Jennings Bryan on the "organized wealth" of the industrialists of the East Coast, of Huey Long on the "moguls" of business, of Joseph McCarthy on "commies and fellow-travelers" and of George Wallace on the Supreme Court and on "pseudointellectuals and agitators" all have in common the attribution to a small minority of persons a dominant and perverse influence over the political fortunes of the nation.

Among the theories of elite dominance that have focused specifically on the American foreign-policy process, those advanced during the period of the Senate munitions investigation of the early 1930s are a prominent and instructive illustration. The investigation was a direct outgrowth of disillusionment with American involvement in World War I, which at the time had been justified in such idealistic terms as helping "to make the world safe for democracy" and as participating in a "war to end wars." In the postwar atmosphere of disillusionment, critics of the decision to involve the United States in the war unearthed evidence that to many persons seemed to explain the decision in crassly materialistic and sinister, rather than idealistic, terms. Among such revisionist theories of the reasons that the Wilson administration committed the nation to enter the war on behalf of England and France was one that attributed a dominant influence to the manufacturers of arms, munitions, and ships. Such manufacturers had promoted American participation in the war, according to the theory, in order to advance their own profits. In the spring of 1934, an article presenting such a thesis was published in *Fortune* magazine. The article was inserted into the *Congressional Record* at the request of Senator Gerald Nye; a condensed version was published in the *Reader's Digest*. A book by other authors, entitled *Merchants of Death: A Study of the International Armament Industry*, became a best seller and a Book-of-the-Month Club selection in the spring. A number of groups, notably the Women's International League for Peace and Freedom, sought to arouse public opinion and to enlist government support to investigate the alleged responsibility of arms manufacturers for American involvement in World War I. It was in this atmosphere of mounting popular concern that the Senate instructed a special committee, headed by Gerald P. Nye, a young (aged forty-two) republican Senator from North Dakota, to investigate the manufacture and sale of munitions.[16]

The investigation was able to unearth evidence to show that various manufacturers of arms and ships had reaped enormous profits during World War I and that bribery of foreign governments and blatant violations of American arms embargoes had been among the devices used to expand the markets for their goods. However, after two years of committee hearings, it became abundantly clear that the broader thesis that had provoked the investigation in the first place, namely that American involvement in World War I had been *caused* by profit-hungry manufacturers, was unsubstantiated by the facts. Indeed, the author of the most thorough study of the Nye committee investigation suggests that, of the committee's achievements, "perhaps the most notable one was debunking—inadvertently to be sure—the merchants-of-death thesis." [17]

As a result of the gap between the highly publicized rationale for the munitions investigations and the facts actually produced by the Nye committee, the investigation is often cited in history texts and in other writings on American foreign policy as symbolic of the naïveté of those who view foreign-policy making in terms of the sordid manipulations of an elite. Likewise, modern behavioral analysis has revealed that theories of elite dominance of policy, as simplistic models of reality, tend to be particularly attractive to persons socially or psychologically insecure. Individuals anxious about their social or political status—for example, those experiencing rapid upward or downward social or political mobility —seem more inclined than other individuals to participate in political movements protesting alleged elite dominance of policy. Individuals with paranoid or authoritarian personalities also seem characteristically attracted to explanations of policy making that blame the alleged defects of policy on a wicked group of conspirators.

[16] The only detailed account and analysis of the activities of the Nye committee is that by John Edward Wiltz, *In Search of Peace* (Baton Rouge: Louisiana State University Press, 1963).

[17] Wiltz, p. 231.

Although it is important to recognize that theories of elite dominance would appeal to some persons irrespective of facts, it is equally important to avoid the fallacy that the invalidity of particular theories can be established by finding that exaggerated claims have been made for them or by finding that intellectually naïve or emotionally insecure persons have found the theories attractive. The validity or invalidity of a theory is to be determined through investigation of empirical data relevant to the theory, not by inference from observation of the kinds of individuals or groups that accept or reject the theory.

Moreover, fallacies or inadequacies of a theory as a whole do not necessarily invalidate the particular propositions that constitute a theory. Theories that depict the policies of the American government during a particular period of history as having been controlled by an elite, for example, may be invalid as sweeping generalizations, but accurate as applied to particular areas of policy making. In the current era, the massive commitment of the nation's resources and energies to matters of national security makes it particularly appropriate to determine the extent of political equality or inequality in influencing this area of public policy. Although defense commitments constitute only a part of foreign policy, throughout the remainder of this section of the chapter they will be used to illustrate the general problem of reconciling demands for efficiency with those of political equality.

Patterns of Influence on Defense Policy

The magnitude of the modern national security commitment of the United States can be suggested by some historical comparisons. In mid-1938, at a time when worldwide concern was mounting over the possibility of another world war, the total active-duty strength of the United States Army, including the Air Corps (forerunner to the Air Force), was approximately 180,000 personnel. By 1968 there were 634,000 American military personnel in Southeast Asia alone, and 2,793,000 elsewhere. In 1938, expenditures for defense totaled slightly less than one billion dollars, roughly 12 percent of total government expenditure. By 1968, annual defense expenditures had passed $80 billion, roughly half of the total government expenditures.[18]

Given the magnitude of the American defense commitment, the question whether a power elite dominates defense policy making, irrespective

---

[18] Cf. *The World Almanac* (1939 ed.; New York: *World-Telegram*), pp. 173, 947; U.S. Bureau of the Budget, *The Budget in Brief: Fiscal Year 1970*, pp. 21–25.

of the validity or invalidity of the broader thesis of power elite domination of American politics, merits serious investigation. Indeed, it is in this area of policy that power-elite theories, such as that of C. Wright Mills, are particularly provocative.[19] In this regard, it is instructive to note that some of the harshest critics of Mills's general theory that a power elite controls American politics have expressed at least limited agreement with the proposition that vast differences exist in the amount of access that various individuals and groups within the United States have to defense policy-making bodies and in influence upon defense policy decisions.[20]

President Eisenhower, certainly no subscriber to the full dimensions of Mills's thesis, nonetheless warned in a famous passage in his farewell message that "in the councils of government, we must guard against the acquisition of unwarranted influence, whether sought or unsought, by the military-industrial complex."[21] According to a close associate of the President, it was his own prior military experience, coupled with the resistance that he had encountered as President to his efforts to cut the defense budget, that had convinced him that he understood the problem of a military-industrial complex in a way that successors to the presidency might lack. Therefore, it seemed important to him to help his successors withstand the pressures that he had experienced by making his warning public.[22]

Mills's argument, Eisenhower's warning, and other writings about the politics of defense policy suggest that two empirical questions are of particular importance in an effort to trace patterns of influence on this area of policy. First, to what extent are matters of defense policy disproportionately influenced by individuals, groups, or organizations with income or status heavily dependent upon defense expenditures? Second, to what extent are matters of defense policy disproportionately influenced by individuals, groups, or organizations that supply the expertise and material resources upon which the defense establishment is dependent?

[19] See Mills, *The Power Elite* (New York: Oxford, Galaxy paperback ed., 1959).

[20] Cf. Robert A. Dahl, "A Critique of the Ruling Elite Model," *American Political Science Review*, 52 (June 1958), 463–469; Talcott Parsons, "The Distribution of Power in American Society," *World Politics*, 10 (Oct. 1957), 123–143; Arnold Rose, *The Power Structure* (New York: Oxford, Galaxy paperback ed., 1967), esp. pt. 1.

[21] Dwight D. Eisenhower, farewell radio-television address to the American people from Washington, D.C., Jan. 17, 1961; reprinted in U.S. Office of the Federal Register, National Archives and Record Service, *Public Papers of the Presidents of the United States: Dwight D. Eisenhower 1960–61* (Washington, 1961), pp. 1035–1040.

[22] "Pressures from 'Military-Industrial Complex' Focus on New Secretary of Defense," *Congressional Quarterly Weekly Report*, 81 (May 24, 1968), pt. 1:1155–1156.

We may help the reader to explore these questions by formulating a series of hypotheses. It will be obvious that the handful of hypotheses that follows constitutes but a small sample of relevant hypotheses.

First, one of the bases for the links that establish a military-industrial complex might be suggested.

> HYPOTHESIS 37   *The greater the dependence of an industrial firm on defense contracts or on the sale of war materials—*
>
> > HYPOTHESIS 37(a)   *The greater will be the tendency of key stockholders and managers of the firm to become advocates of particular defense policies.*
> >
> > HYPOTHESIS 37(b)   *The greater will be the tendency of key stockholders and managers of the firm to seek alliances with leaders of arms or branches of the armed forces that rely heavily on materials produced by the firm.*

The rationale for these interrelated hypotheses is that stockholders and corporation managers whose investments or positions are tied closely to particular defense policies or programs can secure these investments or positions only by gaining sufficient influence over the policies to ensure that no change is implemented that will jeopardize the defense profits of their firm.

Some support for the hypotheses can be suggested by the activities of General Dynamics Corporation, which has been among the top two or three recipients of defense contracts for a number of years. Often it has led the field, with the annual gross income from defense characteristically exceeding a billion dollars. Corporation profits are heavily, if not totally, dependent upon defense contracts.[23] Over the years, the corporation, as producer of such major weapons systems as the Polaris submarine and the controversial F-111 (formerly TFX), has established important contacts with each of the three services. A prime means of access has been through the employment of key military personnel upon their retirement from the service. By the early 1960s, the corporation led all others in the numbers of retired military officers employed, with nearly 200 on their

---

[23] During the period 1961–1967, General Dynamics Corporation received $8,824,000,000 in defense contracts; 67 percent of their sales during these years were to the government in the form of defense contracts. Ralph E. Lapp, *The Weapons Culture* (New York: Norton, 1968), pp. 186–187. In an earlier year, 1959, examination of the corporation's annual report revealed that the corporation had suffered a net loss in its civilian ventures, whereas enormous profits were reaped from defense contracts. Victor Perlo, *Militarism and Industry* (New York: International Publishers, 1963), app. II, p. 190.

payroll. Frank Pace, former secretary of the army, had been named president of the corporation. While serving in this capacity, Pace was named by President Eisenhower to serve on a Commission on National Goals. Pace wrote a supplement to the regular commission report, in which he advocated "the encouragement of revolutionary new ideas in weapons systems."[24]

It is, of course, difficult to distinguish between ideological appeals made by representatives of a corporation or of the military, stemming from personal conviction, which coincidentally serve the interests of the corporation or one of the branches of service, and appeals deliberately designed to promote corporation or branch interests. However, efforts to shape the direction or magnitude of policy commitments in ways that will benefit the interests of one's corporation or one's arm of the service sometimes become quite evident when a particular contract is at stake. For example, after suffering a cut in appropriations in the House of Representatives for the development of a mobile medium-range ballistic missile (MMRBM), representatives of the Air Force are reported to have communicated with key corporations whose contracts would be adversely affected by such a cut. In turn, representatives of Hughes Aircraft, with an assembly plant for the MMRBM in Tucson, and of Goodyear Aircraft, with a plant in Phoenix for the manufacture of trailers for the missiles, contacted Arizona's two senators, Carl Hayden and Barry Goldwater, in an effort to persuade them to try to increase appropriations for the MMRBM as the bill came through the Senate. The lobbyists made, as one senator recalls the meeting, "a glowing statement of the importance of this amazing new weapon to the defense of the Free World," also reminding the senator of contributions made to his election campaign.[25]

The apparent indirect lobbying efforts by the Air Force in the MMRBM episode and more obvious instances such as, earlier, Air Force lobbying for bombers, suggest the following hypotheses.[26]

HYPOTHESIS 38 *The greater the anxiety of the leaders of an arm or branch of the armed forces that appropriations for their arm or branch will be lower than they desire—*

> HYPOTHESIS 38(a) *the broader will be the rationale and the more intensive will be the efforts of the leaders to promote*

[24] *New York Times*, Nov. 28, 1960, p. 23.

[25] Julius Duscha, "Arms and the Big Money Men," *Harper's Magazine* (March, April, May 1964), pt. I, p. 43.

[26] See Paul Y. Hammond, "Super Carriers and B–36 Bombers: Appropriations, Strategy and Politics," in Harold Stein, ed., *American Civil-Military Decisions* (Birmingham: University of Alabama Press, 1963), pp. 465–564.

> *the rationale for the defense programs in which their arm or branch of service participates.*

> HYPOTHESIS 38(b)   *the greater will be their efforts to seek political alliances with the producers of arms, munitions, or delivery systems whose interests also are at stake.*

The hypotheses postulate circumstances under which politicizing of the activities of military leaders (or civilian leaders working for a particular military arm or branch) is most likely.

Although many of the efforts of defense contractors or of military officers to lobby for particular policies or programs escape public notice, the task of arriving at an empirical approximation of the extent to which such efforts characterize particular firms and arms of service under varying conditions (and thereby testing hypotheses 37 and 38) is not insurmountable. Much more elusive, however, is the question whether such efforts have been effective in influencing the direction or magnitude of policy commitments. Mere demonstration that a corporation received a contract that it sought or that appropriations for a particular arm of service were of the amount that leaders of the arm desired is, of course, insufficient evidence to demonstrate a causal relationship between the efforts of the corporation or the arm of service and the policy results. Much of the popular writing in recent years attributing a perverse policy influence to the military-industrial complex has been weak precisely because a causal link between the objectives of military-industrial leadership and the policy outcomes has been assumed or inferred from insufficient evidence rather than demonstrated empirically.

An example of a work more attentive than usual to the difficulties of demonstrating such cause and effect relationships is a recent study of the process leading to the awarding of a contract in 1962 for development of the TFX (tactical fighter, experimental) aircraft. The $439 million contract for the design of an aircraft for the Navy and the Air Force went to General Dynamics Corporation. As indicated above, this corporation is one of the top defense contractors, with numerous links to all three armed services. Critics of the decision also noted that the area to receive the most financial benefit from the contract was Texas, President Johnson's home state, and more specifically Fort Worth, the site of the plant that General Dynamics planned to use for the development of the TFX, where Secretary of the Navy Fred Korth had been a bank president. In spite of these and other facts suggesting the possibility of bias in the decision and in spite of abundant evidence demonstrating that political pressures were brought to bear on those making the TFX decision, the author was scrupulous in his conclusion about the limits of the inferences that could be drawn: "It is not possible to conclude either that political pressures influenced the awarding of the contract or that they did not. In short, the charge of political or personal bias is unanswerable." [27]

On the other hand, although it is important to be sensitive to the difficulties of establishing conclusively that particular policy decisions were caused by the pressures of particular industries or military elites, it is also important to note that the arguments of sophisticated critics of the military-industrial complex, such as Mills, do not rest on the conclusiveness with which influence on particular decisions can be demonstrated. The argument of such critics is not that particular corporations or particular arms of service are consistently successful in their efforts to influence policy decisions. Rather, the argument is that policy debate takes place within the limited confines of a power elite, of which the military-industrial complex is the core. Consequently, although one major corporation may fail in competition for a particular major defense contract, another in the cluster of the largest corporations will succeed. For example, although one of the largest defense contractors, Boeing Aircraft, failed to get the TFX contract, General Dynamics Corporation succeeded.

Moreover, sophisticated critics of the military-industrial complex argue that the general thrust of pressure from all defense contractors and from the various arms of service is toward the maintenance of a sizable enough budget so that each of the participants in the limited competition realizes benefits. Support for the maintenance of a large defense budget seems to come most consistently from the members of Congress in whose districts major defense industries or sizable military posts are located. For example, in October 1968, Secretary of Defense Clark Clifford announced that Fort Polk, Louisiana, had been designated as a permanent military installation. Had Fort Polk not been so designated, with the end of the war in Vietnam it might have been closed, thereby terminating the employment of some 35,000 persons at the base and ending the flow in federal funds of some one billion dollars annually for maintenance and construction at the base. An aide to Senator Russell B. Long, Democratic Whip from Louisiana, told a reporter from the *Congressional Quarterly* that "the decision wasn't nailed down until after Russell Long talked to Clifford. The decision really was a rather direct result of pressure from us and the rest of the state's delegation." [28] The *Congressional Quarterly* also quoted a Pentagon official as observing of Senator Long, "It goes without saying that you'll never see him voting to cut defense appropria-

---

[27] Robert J. Art, *The TFX Decision* (Boston: Little, Brown, 1968), p. 3.
[28] "Military Bases Lobbying," *Congressional Quarterly Weekly Report*, 26 (Oct. 25, 1968), 3031, 3038.

tions. It's really quite a neat little system, with really subtle mutual understandings." [29]

Various critics have contended that the interests of major industrial firms and of leaders of the armed forces have become dependent upon the maintenance of a climate of concern, with sufficient external threat to legitimatize major defense expenditures.[30] Whether or not industrial and military leaders consciously seek to maintain tension, one may advance the following hypothesis relating to the extent of their influence under conditions of tension.

> HYPOTHESIS 39   *The greater the tension within the society stemming from concern about an external threat to the nation, the greater will be the influence on defense policies of military leaders and of defense contractors whose resources and skills are salient to coping with the threat.*

The substantial influence of military leaders on defense policies during World War II, for example, was readily apparent. Leading industrialists participated in a subordinate role, characteristically, and exerted a less pronounced effect on policy. Although the influence of the military on foreign policy was not universally applauded at the time, the legitimacy of such influence was widely accepted in the light of the broad popular acceptance of what were considered the imperatives of a just war.

Thus, we see that normative judgments about how the demands for efficiency in the conduct of national security affairs are to be reconciled with the desire for political equality are likely to vary relative to the perceived legitimacy and urgency of the national security effort. Concern with President Eisenhower's warning about "the acquisition of unwarranted influence . . . by the military-industrial complex," for example, will vary according to one's notions about how much influence is warranted, given existing demands. In the present era, the issue has become a matter of heightened debate because, although the national investment in national security has reached unprecedented heights, no longer does a consensus, as in World War II, for instance, prevail regarding the urgency of national security matters, the intentions of potential adversaries, and the policies that are most appropriate to our relations with potential adversaries. On matters of normative judgment, disagreement is to be expected. However, because the matter of national-security policy is so complex, it is important to root normative judgments in a solid foundation of empirical analysis.

---

[29] "Military Bases Lobbying," 3038.
[30] For example, see the argument by John Kenneth Galbraith, "The Cold War and the Corporations," *The Progressive* (July 1967), pp. 14–18.

Individual Liberty and Foreign-Policy Efficiency

The final dimension of democratic values with which we shall be concerned in the chapter is that of individual liberty. As in the previous section, we shall focus on national-security affairs to illustrate the general problem of reconciling efficiency in the conduct of foreign policy with democratic values.

Few ideas have had such a powerful grip on the imaginations of individuals or on the destinies of nations as that of liberty. Clearly, no political system can fairly claim to be democratic without maintaining a large measure of liberty for the individuals within it; conversely, the suppression of individual liberty is a mark of undemocratic regimes.

On the other hand, it is obvious that political systems differ from one another not in the presence or absence of individual liberty, in absolute terms, but rather in the extent to which individuals within the system enjoy liberties of various kinds; like efficiency, liberty is a matter of degree. Just as no political system can be totally efficient in performance, neither can it provide complete freedom for individuals. All governments must impose certain demands or restrictions on members of the polity in order to ensure the survival of the political system, as a minimum, and in order to carry out policies efficiently.

The Sedition Act of 1798

Early government practice in the United States reflects a dual concern for individual liberty on the one hand, and for national security on the other, that continues to the present day. Insistence on the inclusion in the Constitution of a Bill of Rights reflects the determination of Jefferson, Madison, and others that American citizens should be protected from government absolutism, a practice characteristic at the time in Europe. Advocates of the Bill of Rights were sensitive also to the danger that a particular region or faction might become politically dominant in the United States and utilize its position to intimidate or suppress opposition. On the other hand, the precarious position of the new nation-state relative to a number of potential adversaries caused anxieties in the minds of many persons, lest undue permissiveness on the part of government bring about its collapse and the end of independence. The Sedition Act of 1798 reflected, in part, such anxieties.

Critics of the Washington and Adams administrations focused especially on measures such as the Jay Treaty, which to the critics suggested a dangerous drift toward resumption of close ties with England. Many Federalists, in turn, attributed criticisms of the government to the work of French agents or sympathizers. The Sedition Act was one of several measures passed through Congress by the Federalists to combat the allegedly subversive tendency of such criticisms. The most controversial section of the act made it a crime to write, print, utter, or publish any false, scandalous, or malicious statement against the government of the United States or to assist in drafting or circulating such a statement. The section also made it a crime to "excite the people" against the government or to excite them to oppose any law or any act of the President.

Advocates of the Sedition Act defended their position in terms echoed more recently in the assertions of those who would restrict the activities of communists, on the grounds that the latter are allegedly agents of a foreign power. The records of the proceedings of the House of Representatives during the debate of the Sedition Act, for instance, contain the following description of the views of a proponent of the act.

> He did most firmly believe that France had a party in this country, small indeed, and sure to be disgraced and destroyed as soon as its designs should become generally known, but active, artful, and determined, and capable, if it could remain concealed, of effecting infinite mischief.[31]

Arguments in defense of the Sedition Act also reveal the appeal then, as now, of law and order as a condition that, in the eyes of many, is threatened unless the activities and expressions of dissident elements in the society are restricted. For example, the proponent of the Sedition Act whose views were cited above continued his argument by observing that freedom of speech and of the press, although important, were subject to abuse. He asked, rhetorically,

> . . . Did this liberty of the press include sedition and licentiousness? Did it authorize persons to throw, with impunity, the most violent abuse upon the President and both Houses of Congress? . . . As well might it be said that the liberty of action implied the liberty of assault, trespass, or assassination.[32]

One of the leading opponents of the Sedition Act, Thomas Jefferson, was elected President in 1800. In his inaugural address, he sharply distinguished his own views from the proponents of the Sedition Act.

[31] Robert Goodloe Harper of South Carolina, speech in U.S. House of Representatives, July 10, 1798, in U.S. Congress *Annals*, 5th Cong., 2d sess., p. 2165; quoted in Charles S. Hyneman and George W. Carey, *A Second Federalist: Congress Creates a Government* (New York: Appleton, 1967), p. 295.

[32] Harper, *Annals*, p. 2167, in Hyneman and Carey, p. 296.

Jefferson was by no means oblivious to the risk that those whose freedom is respected by a government may utilize it to oppose or undermine the government. He argued, however, that the risk ought to be accepted. "If there be any among us who would wish to dissolve this Union or to change its republican form," he said, "let them stand undisturbed as monuments of the safety with which error of opinion may be tolerated where reason is left free to combat it." [33]

Subsequent historical experience reveals even more vividly the complexity of the issue of how much individual liberty should be guaranteed or permitted within a political system. Even those of us who share with Jefferson a belief in the vital importance of individual liberty are likely to recognize as appropriate the reduction of our freedom under some circumstances. In time of war, for instance, or when we believe that the nation-state is facing a serious external or internal threat, we are likely to be willing to accept government restrictions designed to strengthen the nation's war effort or to enhance the capacity of the government to cope with the threat. The increase of probable costs to the society (measured in terms of lives as well as dollars and other costs) for inefficient performance of the government in time of danger serves to justify increased restrictions that are aimed at improving the nation's security.

On the other hand, not all restrictions will be deemed acceptable. For example, if we believe that the war to which the government has committed or seeks to commit the nation is unjust, then we are unlikely to regard as justified those restrictions on our liberties designed to make it easier for the government to fight the war. Likewise, if we believe that restrictions of individual liberty are being used to cover up government stupidity or bad judgment, rather than being essential to national security, we are likely to resent them. Or if we believe that the burden of the restrictions is being borne inequitably, for reasons that are unwarranted, we are unlikely to find the restrictions legitimate. Finally, if we see in the restrictions a pattern of erosion of constitutional government, then we are likely to view the restrictions with alarm, whatever our concern with a threat to national security.

It is impossible, of course, to devise a totally acceptable formula for reconciling the quest for national security (which may be viewed as a dimension of the demand for efficiency in the foreign-policy process) with the maintenance of individual liberty. Restrictions that will seem

[33] Thomas Jefferson, first inaugural address, Washington, D.C., Mar. 4, 1801; reprinted in U.S. Congress, House of Representatives, *Inaugural Addresses of the Presidents of the United States*, 89th Cong., 1st sess., House Doc. no. 51, pp. 13–16.

appropriate to some persons will seem intolerable to others; expressions of individual liberty, such as strikes or demonstrations, that to some will seem a vital expression of the right to dissent will, under some circumstances, seem to others a form of disorder that the government may legitimately forbid or halt. We not only differ with one another on the relative importance that we attach to different values, such as order or individual liberty, but also we are bound to differ about the probable consequences of events and actions. Each of us can only form educated guesses, rather than infallible predictions, about the extent to which particular measures restricting individual liberty will in fact enhance national security, for example, or about the extent to which particular actions justified in the name of liberty will, in the long run, actually advance it.

Restrictions of Liberty: Some Hypotheses

Although no magic formula for resolving the national security-individual liberty dilemma exists, and although our judgments must be based in part on hunches rather than on infallible predictions, educated guesses are preferable to uneducated ones as a guide for making value judgments. The hypotheses that follow are designed to suggest how one might formulate such educated guesses. The reader may wish to modify, reject, or supplement the following hypotheses by his own independent empirical analysis. In any event, the hypotheses can be tested against the historical and current experience of the United States, some of which is described below in order to suggest the empirical framework within which the hypotheses were derived.

> HYPOTHESIS 40   *The greater the tension within the society stemming from concern about a threat to the nation—*
>
>> HYPOTHESIS 40(a)   *the lower will be the level of tolerance by the general public of individuals and groups whose words, deeds, or ethnic origins seem alien to established national-policy objectives.*
>>
>> HYPOTHESIS 40(b)   *the greater will be the tendency of politicians to seek to suppress dissent from policies which purport to cope with the threat.*
>>
>> HYPOTHESIS 40(c)   *the more limited will be the range of individual action and expression regarded as constitutionally protected by the courts.*

Some support for the hypotheses is provided by the experience of dissidents and those whose ethnic origins were identified with the enemy during World War I, World War II, and the Korean War, respectively. The experience of analogous individuals and groups during the war in Vietnam has been somewhat more ambiguous, as we shall indicate.

World War I   On the eve of asking Congress to declare war against Germany, President Woodrow Wilson was apprehensive about what the consequences might be. "Once lead this people into war," he said, "and they'll forget there ever was such a thing as tolerance. To fight you must be brutal and ruthless, and the spirit of ruthless brutality will enter into the very fiber of our national life, infecting Congress, the courts, the policeman on the beat, the man in the street." [34]

Indeed, it is clear that one of the first victims of American entry into the war was tolerance within the society. A variety of patriotic and vigilante groups moved into action, reporting suspicious actions and utterances to government officials and in many instances taking action on their own initiative to punish persons deemed disloyal. Among the key targets of suspicion were Socialists, members of the IWW (Industrial Workers of the World, a radical labor organization), aliens, German-Americans, sympathizers with the Irish fight for independence, the Nonpartisan League (an agrarian-based organization active largely in the Dakotas and Minnesota), and Negroes. [35]

Government at the national, state, and local levels moved swiftly to mobilize the nation for war and to impose stiff penalties on those who would impede the war effort. A bill providing for the conscription of young men into the Army became law in May 1917. The following month, an Espionage Act was enacted, providing severe punishment for persons obstructing the war effort or the recruitment of men into the armed forces. Various states and municipalities passed similar legislation, coupled with additional provisions such as the banning of the German language in schools.

[34] From a conversation between Wilson and his friend, Frank Cobb, editor of *The World*, the New York newspaper of Joseph Pulitzer. The conversation, as recalled by Maxwell Anderson, to whom Cobb later described it, is quoted in John L. Heaton, *Cobb of "The World"* (New York: Dutton, 1924), pp. 268–270.

[35] A scholarly and detailed account of dissident groups and of measures employed against them during the war is provided by H. C. Peterson and Gilbert C. Fite, *Opponents of War 1917–1918* (Madison: University of Wisconsin Press, 1957). Much of the subsequent discussion of the World War I period draws heavily from their account.

Although many young Americans rushed to enlist in the Army, seeing the war as a great crusade, a small but intense minority of persons in the country regarded conscription as an unconstitutional infringement on individual liberty. Speeches and pamphlets throughout the nation denounced the draft. Most of those who opposed the draft also opposed the war. Some were pacifists; others viewed American entry into the war as a design by wealthy bankers and industrialists to save their investments.

Retribution for dissent was swift. The second-class mailing privileges of approximately sixty Socialist newspapers throughout the country were suspended. Offices and meeting halls of Socialists, the IWW, and other supposedly suspect groups were raided, and thousands of arrests were made. In many cases, heavy fines and jail sentences followed. For example, a Socialist candidate for governor in New Jersey was arrested after a street-corner speech in which he said that he didn't see how the government could compel troops to go to France, and if it were up to him, he'd tell them "to go to hell." [36] He was charged with a willful attempt to cause insubordination and disloyalty in the armed forces, was fined one thousand dollars, and was sentenced to five years in prison. An organizer of the Nonpartisan League was arrested for a speech in North Dakota, in which he denounced the "rich man's war" and described the draft as "an injustice, unconstitutional, and wrong." [37] He was sentenced to two years in the penitentiary at Fort Leavenworth. Conversely, in Indiana, a jury acquitted a man who had killed an alien; the alien had provoked him by shouting, "To hell with the United States." [38]

The Bolshevik Revolution in Russia in the autumn of 1917, while World War I was still in progress, generated further tensions in the United States. The widely publicized claims of Bolshevik leaders that this was but the first of a wave of revolutions that would bring an end to capitalism throughout the world, coupled with overt enthusiasm for the revolution by various radical elements in the United States, contributed to a wave of sentiment among those fearful of revolution in support of further suppression of dissident elements in the American society. The Vice-President of the United States, Thomas Marshall, for example, recommended that the citizenship be annulled and the property confiscated of every American who was not "heartily in support of the Government in this crisis." [39] Various newspapers, patriotic groups, and politicians at

[36] Peterson and Fite, p. 47.

[37] Peterson and Fite, pp. 65–66.

[38] Frederick Lewis Allen, *Only Yesterday* (New York: Bantam Books, paperback ed., 1959), p. 32. Allen says the jury deliberated for two minutes in deciding to acquit.

[39] Peterson and Fite, p. 209.

every level began to call for legislation that would allow the government to deal more severely with disloyal elements in the society than was possible under existing legislation. Congress responded in April 1918 with a Sedition Act, analogous to the Sedition Act of 1798. Nominally an amendment to the Espionage Act, the Sedition Act of 1918 made it illegal to speak or to write anything that would be "abusive" about the American form of government and anything that was intended to bring the Constitution, the flag, or the armed forces of the United States into disrepute.

Legal and extralegal action against dissidents in the war effort continued with great vehemence and frequency for the remaining months of the war. The vast majority of attempts by those convicted of having violated federal or state sedition acts or other wartime legislation to appeal their convictions failed. However, a few cases reached the United States Supreme Court, pitting the claim of those arrested that constitutionally guaranteed rights of individual expression had been violated against the contention of the government that it was merely carrying out legislation that had been enacted with the legitimate intention to protect itself from foreign and domestic threats.

Six prominent cases involving convictions under the Espionage and Sedition Acts reached the Supreme Court. The first (*Schenck* v. *United States*) involved the conviction of a number of Socialists on the grounds of circulating material that would obstruct the draft and recruitment into the armed forces. The second (*Frohwerk* v. *United States*) involved the conviction of persons accused of obstructing the war effort through articles in a German-language newspaper denouncing the war and criticizing conscription. The third (*Debs* v. *United States*) resulted from the arrest of Eugene V. Debs, a prominent Socialist leader and former presidential candidate, for statements made at a Socialist party convention that were critical of the war and of the draft. The fourth case (*Abrams* v. *United States*) involved the arrest of a group of young immigrants from Russia, who protested the armed intervention by the United States that had taken place in Russia in the aftermath of the Bolshevik Revolution. The young radicals had distributed leaflets denouncing "the hypocrisy of the plutocratic gang in Washington" and calling on workers to "Awake! Rise! Put down your enemy and mine." In the fifth case (*Schaefer* v. *United States*), the defendants were charged with aiding the cause of the enemy and with obstructing recruitment into the United States armed forces, through publication of false news reports in a German-language newspaper. In the sixth case (*Pierce* v. *United States*), the defendants were charged with conspiring to cause insubordination and with refusal of duty in the armed services, through speeches and the distribution of pamphlets of the Socialist party denouncing American participation in the war and the conscription of troops.[40]

In the first three cases, the Court decided unanimously in favor of the government, against the contention of those arrested that rights of free expression guaranteed by the First Amendment had been violated. It was in the Schenck case that Justice Oliver Wendell Holmes formulated the famous doctrine to decide at what point the expression of an individual ceased to enjoy constitutional protection. The government was justified in suppressing individual expression, according to the Holmes doctrine, if a particular speech or writing constituted a "clear and present danger" to society. The compelling factor for Holmes in the first three cases was the fact that the nation was at war; therefore, if there was doubt about whether or not the utterances of an individual constituted a "clear and present danger" to society, doubt had to be resolved in favor of society's right to protect itself and against the individual's right to free expression. As Holmes put it in his opinion in the Schenck case, "When a nation is at war many things that might be said in time of peace are such a hindrance to its effort that their utterance will not be endured so long as men fight and . . . no court could regard them as protected by any constitutional right." Even though a particular act of expression by an individual was not demonstrably disruptive of the war effort, the possibility that the act might, under some circumstances, present a danger was legitimate reason for the government to stop the act, Holmes argued. For instance, in regard to the question whether articles critical of the war in a German-language newspaper really endangered the society, Holmes said, "It is impossible to say that it might not have been found that the circulation of the paper was in quarters where a little breath would be enough to kindle a flame and that the fact was known and relied upon by those who sent the paper out."

Finally, however, in the Abrams case, Holmes, along with Justice Brandeis, became convinced that the ideas expressed by those arrested really presented no "clear and present danger" to the society. He recognized that the ideas were ones that many persons regarded with great hostility and anxiety. However, it is precisely when unpopular ideas are voiced, he observed, that the constitutional guarantee of freedom of expression attains its significance. As he put it, "We should be eternally vigilant against attempts to check the expression of opinions that we

---

[40] Full citations for the cases are as follows. Schenck v. United States, 249 U.S. 47 (1919); Frohwerk v. United States, 249 U.S. 204 (1919); Debs v. United States, 249 U.S. 211 (1919); Abrams et al. v. United States, 250 U.S. 616 (1919); Schaefer v. United States, 251 U.S. 466 (1920); Pierce et al. v. United States, 252 U.S. 239 (1920).

loathe and believe to be fraught with death, unless they so imminently threaten immediate interference with the lawful and pressing purposes of the law that an immediate check is required to save the country." [41]

Holmes's defense of dissident expression, in which Brandeis joined, was itself a dissenting opinion in this and in the succeeding Schaefer and Pierce cases. The majority of the court in these, as in earlier cases arising from convictions under the Espionage and Sedition Acts, upheld the convictions and the constitutionality of the acts.

World War II The experience of Japanese-Americans during World War II provides a further illustration of Hypotheses 40(a), 40(b), and 40(c).

Following the Japanese attack of December 7, 1941, on Pearl Harbor, various groups, especially along the west coast of the American mainland, began planning reprisals and demanding government action against alleged treasonous activities of citizens and aliens of Japanese descent. Within weeks, many hundreds of persons of Japanese descent had felt the wrath of angry and suspicious Caucasian Americans. Raids at night on the homes of Japanese-Americans and aliens were reported, homes were burned, graves of Japanese were desecrated, licenses for the operation of businesses were canceled, and persons of Japanese descent were discharged from their jobs. [42]

Illustrative of the general receptivity of Caucasian Americans to rumors about allegedly subversive activity being conducted by Japanese-Americans or Japanese aliens was the attitude of the American military commander for the West Coast area. Recommending to his superiors in Washington that persons of Japanese descent be evacuated from the West Coast, he reasoned ingeniously that the absence of any sabotage attempts along the West Coast during a period of two months after Pearl Harbor was an even more compelling argument for evacuating those of Japanese descent than actual sabotage. "The fact that nothing has happened so far is more or less . . . ominous," he warned, "in that I feel that in view of the fact that we have had no sporadic attempts at sabotage that there is a control being exercised and when we have it it will be on a mass basis." [43]

[41] Abrams et al. v. United States, 250 U.S. 616, 630.

[42] U.S. Department of the Army, Office of the Chief of Military History, "Japanese Evacuation from the West Coast," in Stetson Conn, Rose C. Engelman, and Byron Fairchild, eds., *Guarding the United States and its Outposts* (Washington, 1964), p. 127. See also Eugene V. Rostow, "The Japanese American Cases—A Disaster," *Yale Law Journal*, 54 (June 1945), 489–533.

[43] *Guarding the United States*, p. 121.

About the time that the military commander was forwarding this grim observation, a plea was made to President Roosevelt, signed by every member of Congress from the West Coast states, recommending the "immediate evacuation of all persons of Japanese lineage and all others, aliens or citizens alike, whose presence shall be deemed dangerous or inimical to the defense of the United States from all strategic areas." [44]

The movement to oust those of Japanese descent from the West Coast encountered brief resistance from officials of inland regions, who objected to having such "undesirables" settled in their areas. However, in February 1942, President Roosevelt signed into effect an executive order authorizing the secretary of war to remove citizens and aliens from strategic areas. By voice vote in both houses, Congress in March provided legislative authorization for the compulsory eviction plan. Consequently, beginning the same month, more than 110,000 persons of Japanese descent, American citizens as well as aliens, were forcibly evicted from their homes. Those evicted were moved to so-called relocation centers, a term that Supreme Court Justice Roberts, in a dissenting opinion, later described as "a euphemism for concentration camps." [45] Some of the Japanese-Americans or aliens were released from the relocation centers after a few months, when investigations of their loyalty had been completed; others were detained during most of the war. Those released, however, were excluded from the West Coast and were subject to a special curfew.

Many of those evicted from their homes attempted to seek legal protection from the action being taken against them. As a counter to the claim of government officials that the evictions were dictated by military necessity, those evicted and forcibly detained against their will protested that their constitutional rights were being denied. A few of the cases reached the Supreme Court, which, in every case, sustained the constitutionality of the relocation program against the protests of Japanese-Americans and aliens. [46]

The first of these cases will suffice to illustrate the issues with which the Court was faced and its reasoning. Gordon Hirabayashi was a citizen of the United States and a senior at the University of Washington. He was arrested and sentenced to three months in prison for each of two counts: failing to report to a military control station for evacuation from his home in Seattle and violating the curfew, by staying out after 8:00 P.M. The Court held simply that the curfew, imposed selectively against

---

[44] *Guarding the United States*, p. 133.

[45] Korematsu v. United States, 323 U.S. 214, 230.

[46] Hirabayashi v. United States, 320 U.S. 81 (1943); Yasui v. United States, 320 U.S. 115 (1943); Korematsu v. United States, 323 U.S. 214 (1944); Ex parte Mitsuye Endo, 323 U.S. 283 (1944).

those of Japanese descent, was a reasonable measure for the government to take in time of war. Having sustained the conviction for violation of the curfew, the Court found it unnecessary to deal with the other count, since the sentences ran concurrently. The constitutionality of the order excluding those of Japanese descent from the West Coast was sustained by the Court in the Korematsu case.

The Korean War The atmosphere of "McCarthyism" that arose beginning in 1950 has been described in Chapter 2 and alluded to at various points in subsequent chapters. Even a year after an armistice in Korea had been reached, a survey based on a probability sample of a cross section of the American public revealed that more than 40 percent of those sampled believed that "American Communists" were a "great danger" to the nation.[47]

The attempt to employ government action at various levels to deal with the alleged Communist menace can be illustrated briefly. At the federal level, in addition to the congressional investigations of possible Communist infiltration of government, noted in Chapter 2, in 1950 Congress passed an Internal Security Act (McCarran Act), creating a Subversive Activities Control Board with the authority to determine which organizations in the nation were "Communist-action" or "Communist-front" groups. Such groups were required by the law to register, indicating the names of members, sources of funds, and activities of the organizations. Anticipating court review of the act, Congress declared that the Communist movement constituted "a clear and present danger to the security of the United States."

The Internal Security Act of 1950 represented a modification of bills sponsored by Karl Mundt and Richard M. Nixon, introduced in 1948 when both were members of the House of Representatives. In 1950, President Truman vetoed the Internal Security Act, questioning both the constitutionality of the registration requirement and its practicality. To expect Communists to register, he observed, was "about as practical as requiring thieves to register with the Sheriff." [48] Undeterred by the President's argument, Congress passed the bill over his veto.

At state and local levels too, governments moved to enact laws to cope

[47] Samuel A. Stouffer, *Communism, Conformity, and Civil Liberties* (New York: Doubleday, 1955), pp. 75–76. Of the sample of 4933 cases, 19 percent thought American Communists presented "a very great danger," 24 percent "a great danger," 38 percent "some danger," 9 percent "hardly any danger," 2 percent "no danger," and 8 percent "don't know." The survey was conducted during the summer of 1954.

[48] Quoted in Milton R. Konvitz, *Expanding Liberties* (New York: Viking, paperback ed., 1967), p. 141.

with an alleged Communist threat. The requirement of loyalty oaths for public employees, including schoolteachers, became commonplace at state, local, and federal levels.[49] Some states and municipalities carried the oath requirement even further. The Texas legislature enacted a statute in 1952 requiring applicants for pharmacists' licenses to swear that they neither belonged to nor believed in the doctrine of any group that advocated the overthrow of the American government by illegal means. In the state of Washington, a similar oath was required of those wishing to practice veterinary medicine.[50] The Indiana legislature declared in 1953 that it was the policy of the state "to exterminate Communism and Communists, and any or all teachings of the same." [51]

In a five-to-four decision in 1961, the Court upheld the constitutionality of the key provisions of the Internal Security Act of 1950.[52] However, subsequent court decisions have, in effect, sustained the view of dissenting justices in the 1961 case that compulsory registration amounts to self-incrimination and is therefore unconstitutional.[53]

More relevant to Hypothesis 40(c), however, are decisions the Court reached during the McCarthy era. Illustrative of the Court's views at that time is the Dennis decision, in which the Court upheld the conviction of a number of the leaders of the Communist party of the United States under the Smith Act of 1940, against the claim of those arrested that the act was unconstitutional.[54] Against the claim of attorneys for those arrested that their litigants had done nothing that presented a clear and present danger to the United States, the Court majority adopted a modification of this doctrine, which Judge Learned Hand had formulated when the case was in the Court of Appeals. The fact that the number of Communists in the United States was small was deemed unimportant; the salient point was that the government had a right to protect itself against any effort, however futile it might seem, to bring about its forcible overthrow. The spreading of the doctrine of Marxist-Leninism, although a form of individual expression, could not be regarded as protected by the First Amendment, since the possible consequences of the spread of such doctrine were too threatening to the

[49] See Ralph S. Brown, Jr., *Loyalty and Security* (New Haven, Conn.: Yale University Press, 1958).

[50] Walter Gellhorn, *American Rights, The Constitution in Action* (New York: Crowell-Collier-Macmillan, 1960), pp. 105–106. See also Gellhorn, ed., *The States and Subversion* (Ithaca, N.Y.: Cornell University Press, 1952).

[51] Cited in Konvitz, pp. 141–142.

[52] Communist Party v. Subversive Activities Control Board, 367 U.S. 1 (1961).

[53] Albertson and Proctor v. Subversive Activities Control Board, 86 S. Ct. 194 (1965).

[54] Dennis v. United States, 341 U.S. 494 (1951).

society. The test of whether or not the government could suppress the expression by individuals was "whether the gravity of the 'evil,' discounted by its improbability, justifies such invasion of free speech as is necessary to avoid the danger." [55]

The War in Vietnam: Limits of Dissent Reexamined

Dissent over American involvement in Vietnam became fused by the mid-1960s into a chorus of social protest over a variety of other grievances, especially grievances about the plight of the urban ghetto. In response to such broad social protests, attempts to stifle dissent have also had diverse motivations. Racial prejudice, protection of economic interests, and emotional attachment to the *status quo* are among the factors that seem to have provoked suppression of dissent, when suppression has occurred. Thus, it is especially difficult to test Hypotheses 40(a), 40(b), and 40(c) against the American experience with the war in Vietnam. The difficulty is compounded by conflicting evidence whether the recent period has been one in which individual liberty has been threatened or expanded.

Supporting the contention that individual liberties became increasingly jeopardized as the United States became more deeply involved in Vietnam, one might cite evidence such as the following. A number of students who participated in demonstrations against American policy in Vietnam were reclassified 1-A by their draft boards. Julian Bond, an outspoken critic of American policy in Vietnam, was refused his seat in the Georgia legislature, even though he was duly elected. Muhammad Ali was stripped of his boxing title because of his refusal, on grounds of conscience, to submit to conscription into the armed forces. Various members of Congress and of the executive branch, including the commanding general of American forces in Vietnam, publicly denounced critics of American policies in Vietnam, on the grounds that such criticism gave comfort to the enemy and prolonged the war by holding out the hope to the enemy that the American society would become so divided as to be unable to continue the war.

In June 1967, officials of the American Civil Liberties Union, an organization that has championed individual liberties since 1920, felt obliged to warn in a press release that

> There are signs, ominous signs, that a storm is brewing, that we may indeed be in the eye of a hurricane. . . . As the war escalates, and citizens continue to demand more bombing—or the end of bomb-

[55] *Dennis v. United States.*

ing, or negotiation or outright withdrawal of American troops—clear and discernible pressures are rising for restraints on and punishment of those who oppose the war. . . . Just as dissent is produced by people, it can be destroyed by people, caught in the ground swell of emotion which squeezes tighter and tighter, until dissent is crushed. It is not a big step from official statements saying that dissent injures the war effort to official and unofficial efforts to punish those who refuse to keep silent, by economic coercion, public condemnation, or criminal penalties. . . .[56]

On the other hand, the contention that individual liberties were expanding, or in any event were enjoying greater protection than in previous wartime periods, could be supported by the following evidence.[57] A district court ordered a draft board to restore the former classifications of students from the University of Michigan who had been reclassified 1-A because of engaging in antiwar demonstrations. Julian Bond eventually was seated in the Georgia legislature. Although some members of Congress and the executive branch denounced critics of American policies, others spoke out strongly in defense of the right to criticize the war. At a time in mid-1967, when a majority of the general public still favored the Johnson administration's policies in Vietnam, 61 percent of a nationwide sample expressed their belief in the right of persons to demonstrate in opposition to the war, as compared to 30 percent who expressed the contrary belief (9 percent not sure).[58]

Thus, judgments about the extent to which individual liberties have been jeopardized or protected during the war in Vietnam are hazardous. Many of the conflicting claims of the individual for the freedom of expression and of the state for an efficient national-security process during the recent period are ones that have been voiced in earlier conflicts, dating back not simply to World War I, but to the War of 1812 and the Revolutionary War. The conviction (later reversed on appeal) of Dr. Benjamin Spock, Reverend William Sloane Coffin, Jr., and three others for "counseling, aiding, and abetting" young men to resist the draft, for instance, had its precedent in earlier wars. But conflicting claims have been expressed in some new forms during the war in Vietnam, and some of the old issues have recurred with new intensity.

For instance, although the question of the constitutional rights of the

---

[56] "Dissent in Wartime, ACLU Sees Gathering Storm, Calls for Vigil," *Civil Liberties*, no. 247 (July 1967), 6.

[57] For a detailed exposition of evidence of a post-World War II trend toward enlargement of the sphere of individual liberty, see Konvitz.

[58] Poll conducted by Louis Harris for *Newsweek*, reported in a special issue, "The Vietnam War and American Life," *Newsweek*, 70 (July 10, 1967), 22.

expression of the individual who is in the armed forces is not new, it has attained new prominence during the war in Vietnam. The complaint that unrestrained expression of individuals may hamper efficiency is particularly compelling when applied to the possible human and material costs of the inefficiency of a military unit in battle. Moreover, because military units need discipline in battle, they must cultivate it also while troops are serving garrison duty. However, does one abandon the guarantees of individual freedom cited in the Bill of Rights when one enters the military service? Should not a soldier at least have the right to express his opinions freely when he is off base and out of uniform? In fact, if soldiers are to become the instruments of foreign policy, should they not be entitled to debate foreign-policy issues on base? What about a soldier who decides after entering the service that he is a conscientious objector to serving in a combat role? Should an individual be exempt from combat duty in a particular war, if he claims conscientious objection to that war, even though he professes no absolute objection to serving in all wars? These are among the questions that were raised in the middle and late 1960s from the American experience in Vietnam.[59]

The issue of the range of free expression to be accorded persons in military service is complicated further by the tradition of civilian supremacy, a tenet of which is that military men are to take no active part in politics. Many persons who regard themselves as libertarians no doubt would want to demand of unit commanders that they permit their men, at least off duty, to criticize American policies in Vietnam, but would be appalled if the commanders themselves made speeches during off-duty hours recruiting for the John Birch Society, for instance, or advocating nuclear war with China. Indeed, whatever the content of political opinions expressed by military men, their active expression of political views would raise serious questions of the compromising of the traditional norm of an apolitical military establishment.

The position of the courts thus far on the complex issues regarding the constitutional rights of men in the armed forces has been to retain a distinction between persons in civilian life and those in military service. For instance, Lieutenant Henry H. Howe, Jr., who participated in an antiwar demonstration during his off-duty hours in civilian clothes, carrying a sign reading, "Let's have more than a choice between petty ignorant Facists in 1968," and "End Johnson's Fascist aggression in Viet

[59] For a number of differing points of view on these questions see the following articles in the Oct. 1968 issue of *Civil Liberties*, no. 258. Michael Tigar, "The Case for Free Speech"; Jacquard H. Rothschild, "The Case for Discipline"; Robert E. Jordan, III, "The Balancing Test"; Edward J. Ennis, "The Clear & Present Danger Test."

Nam," was sentenced to one year in a military prison. Another officer, Captain Howard B. Levy, was sentenced to three years' imprisonment at hard labor for a conviction stemming from his refusal to teach medics in the Special Forces and for his outspoken criticism of the war in Vietnam. These cases and others, however, have been appealed; thus, the legal doctrine that will emerge regarding the rights of men in uniform has not yet been fully defined.

Another problem area that has attained new prominence during the American involvement in Vietnam is that of symbolic expression. Does the First Amendment guarantee an individual the right to burn the nation's flag as a form of protest to foreign policies? Does it guarantee high-school students the right to wear black arm bands as a symbol of mourning for war deaths in Vietnam, in spite of school regulations to the contrary? Does it guarantee the right of college students to demonstrate against recruitment on campus by representatives of Dow Chemical Company, as a protest against the use of napalm by the United States in Vietnam? Does it guarantee the right of a deceased veteran of the United States Army, who also happened to be a leader of the American Nazi party, to be buried wearing the Nazi swastika, if he otherwise had the right as a veteran to be buried in a national cemetery? Each of these questions has arisen in recent years. Especially with the composition of the Supreme Court in a state of flux as a result of vacancies that have occurred recently or are pending, it is too early to determine the precise guidelines the Court will establish for dealing with such issues.

The more fundamental question, however, is not what guidelines the Supreme Court will establish, but how the society as a whole will cope with conflicting demands of national security and individual liberty. Tension has been increased in recent years by the increased militancy of protests and by the frequency with which individuals and groups have turned to confrontation tactics in seeking to satisfy their objectives. A description of confrontation tactics that many frustrated observers would find apt was made by a New York city official following a year of nearly endless strikes, sit-ins, slowdowns, and threats by groups including students at Columbia University, schoolteachers, policemen, and garbage collectors. The official described confrontation as the "politics of selfishness—grab everything you can get and the hell with everybody else." [60] Because the politics of confrontation and other forms of expression may stem from selfish as well as from idealistic motives, the degree of freedom to be accorded such expression becomes a particularly agonizing one for

[60] Quoted by Richard Reeves, "Confrontation, It Threatens the Fabric of a Democratic Society," *New York Times*, Dec. 8, 1968, sec. 4, p. 1.

the society. Moreover, there is the ironic possibility that over the long run, unrestrained protest may result, through a backlash effect, in less individual liberty rather than more. Thus, the dilemma of how conflicting claims of national security and individual freedom are to be reconciled has become more profound than ever before. John Stuart Mill made one of the strongest arguments for individual liberty guaranteeing free expression in his nineteenth-century essay, *On Liberty*, when he wrote, "If all mankind minus one were of one opinion, and only one person were of the contrary opinion, mankind would be no more justified in silencing that one person, than he, if he had the power, would be justified in silencing mankind." [61] But Mill also recognized the complexity of the problem. In words that highlight the dilemma of modern Americans, he wrote, "It is not even impossible that men, by their ill-directed efforts after unbounded freedom, may destroy those very features of our social life which tend to enlarge their freedom, and may thus bring themselves under a more degrading and oppressive bondage than that which they have cast off." [62]

Some Concluding Observations

The attainment of efficiency in the performance of various key tasks in formulating and executing foreign-policy decisions has become increasingly complex in the modern age. Whether efficiency can be attained, or maintained, without seriously compromising the democratic values of accountability, of political equality, and of individual liberty, is a question that we have raised but have not answered here. However, we have generated a number of hypotheses, supported by illustrative data, designed to increase the reader's sensitivity to this problem and to provoke further consideration of the complex empirical and normative issues involved.

Some persons may regard it as curious that so much attention has been devoted in this final chapter to topics sometimes treated in studies of civil liberties or democratic theory, or alluded to in popular journals but seldom accorded serious treatment in books on foreign policy. It has become increasingly obvious to many serious students of foreign policy, however, that foreign-policy decisions and domestic political activities

---

[61] Mill, *On Liberty and Consideration on Representative Government* (Oxford: Blackwell, 1946), p. 14.

[62] Mill, *On Social Freedom* (New York: Columbia University Press, 1941, reprinted from the *Oxford and Cambridge Review* of June 1907, with an introduction by Dorothy Fosdick), p. 35.

are interdependent.[63] To focus on one area to the neglect of the other can provide at best only a partial analysis. The concluding chapter of the book has been designed to emphasize especially the point that the demands of foreign policy may have important structural as well as policy consequences domestically and may directly affect the lives of each of us.

To the perceptive observer, the demands of foreign policy are a call to participate in the process by which his own life and the lives of others may be profoundly altered. Happily, more Americans than ever before—especially in the college generation—show a determination to get involved in the policy processes by which vital social and political issues are resolved. However, involvement is not enough. The quality of life that all of us experience in the years ahead will depend not only upon the extent of participation in the foreign-policy process, but also upon the quality of judgment by which values are ordered and upon the rigor of thought and analysis that serve as guideposts for action.

Summary of Hypotheses Developed in Part V

33. The higher the proportion of events in the world environment that bear directly on high-salience interests of the United States and the more widespread the belief among American national leaders that present or future events pose significant threats to these interests—
   a. The greater will be the tendency of the President to seek or to assert authority to respond to the threats without being obliged to gain prior approval of the response from Congress.
   b. The greater will be the tendency of the Congress to yield to the President authority to respond to the threats without being obliged to gain prior approval of the response from Congress.
34. Once Congress has condoned, although never formally sanctioned, a reduction in its authority relative to that of the President for engaging in various kinds of activities in the foreign-policy process, members of Congress will attempt to reassert or to expand their authority if—
   a. They believe that the particular actions in which the President acted without congressional advice or consent are regarded by the members' constituents with broad disapproval.
   b. They believe that a congressional attempt to reduce presidential

---

[63] For example, see the series of articles in James N. Rosenau, ed., *Domestic Sources of Foreign Policy* (New York: Free Press, 1967).

authority in general would be a popular one among their constituents.

   c. Particular current or pending foreign-policy commitments are of
such repugnance to the members or their constituents that they
believe congressional authority must be asserted in order to
reverse or prevent the commitments by the President.

35. Once Congress has condoned, although never formally sanctioned, a
reduction of its authority relative to that of the President for engaging in various kinds of activities in the foreign-policy process, the
President will resist relinquishing authority to Congress even if the
rationale under which the authority was originally asserted has become outmoded by changing circumstances.

36. If a foreign-policy course of action favored by the President requires
the commitment of a substantial number of American troops in its
implementation, the President will seek advance endorsement of the
decision by Congress.

37. The greater the dependence of an industrial firm on defense contracts or on the sale of war materials—

   a. The greater will be the tendency of key stockholders and managers of the firm to become advocates of particular defense
policies.

   b. The greater will be the tendency of key stockholders and managers of the firm to seek alliances with leaders of arms or branches
of the armed forces that rely heavily on materials produced by
the firm.

38. The greater the anxiety of the leaders of an arm or branch of the
armed forces that appropriations for their arm or branch will be
lower than they desire—

   a. The broader will be the rationale and the more intensive will be
the efforts of the leaders to promote the rationale for the defense
programs in which their arm or branch of service participates.

   b. The greater will be their efforts to seek political alliances with
the producers of arms, munitions, or delivery systems whose
interests also are at stake.

39. The greater the tension within the society stemming from concern
about an external threat to the nation, the greater will·be the influence on defense policies of military leaders and of defense contractors whose resources and skills are salient to coping with the
threat.

40. The greater the tension within the society stemming from concern
about a threat to the nation—

    a. The lower will be the level of tolerance by the general public of individuals and groups whose words, deeds, or ethnic origins seem alien to established national-policy objectives.

    b. The greater will be the tendency of politicians to seek to suppress dissent from policies which purport to cope with the threat.

    c. The more limited will be the range of individual action and expression regarded as constitutionally protected by the courts.

A Selective
Bibliography

In the footnotes of preceding chapters, numerous suggestions for further reading on particular topics have been provided. No attempt is made here to provide a cumulative list of those works cited. Rather, the bibliography is designed as a handy reference to some of the many useful sources of information and insight that are available (including many not cited in footnotes) about foreign-policy events, institutions, and decision makers.

The three parts into which the bibliography is divided correspond roughly to the three analytical perspectives discussed in the book. Only books published within the past decade have been considered for inclusion; indeed, the majority of the books listed below have been published within the past five years. Because the bibliography is limited to books, the concerned reader will wish to turn elsewhere for a listing of documents, periodicals, theses, and research monographs of interest. Some general suggestions are provided by J. K. Zawodny, *Guide to the Study of International Relations* (San Francisco: Chandler, 1966).

In his efforts to locate articles on particular topics, the reader should consult the *Social Sciences and Humanities Index* (formerly entitled *International Index to Periodicals*) as well as the more familiar *Readers' Guide to Periodical Literature*. Each issue of the journal *Foreign Affairs*, published quarterly by the Council on Foreign Relations, contains a list of current foreign-policy documents and pamphlets, as well as a list of recent books in the field. In addition, the reader may wish to consult *Foreign Policy Information Materials and Services*, U.S. Department of State, Publication 8382, revised April 1969.

Foreign-Policy Strategy and Tactics

Bobrow, Davis B., ed. *Components of Defense Policy.* Chicago: Rand McNally, 1965.

Chayes, Abram, and Jerome B. Wiesner. *ABM: An Evaluation of the Decision to Deploy an Anti-ballistic Missile System.* New York: Harper & Row, 1969.

Dulles, Eleanor Lansing, and Robert Dickson Crane, eds. *Détente: Cold War Strategies in Transition.* New York: Praeger, 1965.

Etzioni, Amitai. *Winning without War.* New York: Doubleday, 1964.

Green, Philip. *Deadly Logic: The Theory of Nuclear Deterrence.* Columbus, Ohio: Ohio State University Press, 1966.

Hahn, Walter F., and John C. Neff, eds. *American Strategy for the Nuclear Age.* New York: Doubleday, 1960.

Halperin, Morton H. *Contemporary Military Strategy.* Boston: Little, Brown, 1967.

————. *Limited War in the Nuclear Age.* New York: Wiley, 1963.

Holst, Johan, and William Schneider, Jr., eds. *Why ABM? Policy Issues in the Missile Defense Controversy.* New York: Pergamon, 1969.

Jordan, Amos A., Jr. *Foreign Aid and the Defense of Southeast Asia.* New York: Praeger, 1962.

Kahn, Herman. *On Thermonuclear War,* 2d ed. New York: Free Press, 1969.

Kaufman, William W. *The McNamara Strategy.* New York: Harper & Row, 1964.

Kintner, William R. *Peace and the Strategy Conflict.* New York: Praeger, 1967.

Knorr, Klauss, and Thorton Read, eds. *Limited Strategic War.* New York: Praeger, 1962.

McNamara, Robert S. *The Essence of Security: Reflections in Office.* New York: Harper & Row, 1968.

Marshall, Charles Burton. *The Exercise of Sovereignty: Papers on Foreign Policy.* Baltimore, Md.: The Johns Hopkins Press, 1965.

Millis, Walter, ed. *American Military Thought*. Indianapolis, Ind.: Bobbs-Merrill, 1966.

Nelson, Joan M. *Aid, Influence, and Foreign Policy*. New York: Crowell-Collier-Macmillan, 1968.

Osgood, Charles E. *An Alternative to War or Surrender*. Urbana, Ill.: University of Illinois Press, 1962.

Osgood, Robert. *Alliances and American Foreign Policy*. Baltimore, Md.: The Johns Hopkins Press, 1968.

Posvar, Wesley W. *et al.*, eds. *American Defense Policy*. Baltimore, Md.: The Johns Hopkins Press, 1965.

Rapoport, Anatol. *Strategy and Conscience*. New York: Harper & Row, 1964.

Schelling, Thomas C. *Arms and Influence*. New Haven, Conn.: Yale University Press, 1966.

————. *The Strategy of Conflict*. New York: Oxford, 1960.

Schurmann, Franz, Peter Dale Scott, and Reginald Zelnik. *The Politics of Escalation in Vietnam*. New York: Fawcett, 1966.

Schwarz, Urs. *American Strategy: A New Perspective*. New York: Doubleday, 1966.

Smith, Mark E., and Claude J. Johns, Jr., eds. *American Defense Policy*. Baltimore, Md.: The Johns Hopkins Press, 1968.

Tarr, David W. *American Strategy in the Nuclear Age*. New York: Crowell-Collier-Macmillan, 1966.

Turner, Gordon B., and Richard D. Challener, eds. *National Security in the Nuclear Age: Basic Facts and Theories*. New York: Praeger, 1960.

Wolf, Charles, Jr. *United States Policy and the Third World*. Boston: Little, Brown, 1967.

Young, Oran R. *The Politics of Force: Bargaining during International Crises*. Princeton, N.J.: Princeton University Press, 1968.

Broad Patterns of American Foreign-Policy Experience

Bailey, Thomas A. *The Art of Diplomacy: The American Experience*. New York: Meredith, 1968.

Ball, George W. *The Discipline of Power: Essentials of a Modern World Structure*. Boston: Atlantic Monthly Press, 1968.

Brandon, Donald. *American Foreign Policy: Beyond Utopianism and Realism*. New York: Meredith, 1966.

Brown, Seyom. *The Faces of Power: Constancy and Change in United States Foreign Policy from Truman to Johnson*. New York: Columbia University Press, 1968.

Carleton, William G. *The Revolution in American Foreign Policy: Its Global Range*, 2d ed. New York: Random House, 1967.

Divine, Robert A., ed. *American Foreign Policy since 1945*. Chicago: Quadrangle Books, for *The New York Times*, 1969.

Ekirch, Arthur A., Jr. *Ideas, Ideals, and American Diplomacy: A History of Their Growth and Interaction.* New York: Meredith, 1966.

Haas, Ernst B. *Tangle of Hopes: American Commitments and World Order.* Englewood Cliffs, N.J.: Prentice-Hall, 1969.

Halle, Louis. *The Cold War as History.* New York: Harper & Row, 1967.

Hoffmann, Stanley. *Gulliver's Troubles, Or the Setting of American Foreign Policy.* New York: McGraw-Hill, 1968.

Houghton, N. D., ed. *Struggle against History: United States Foreign Policy in an Age of Revolution.* New York: Washington Square Press, 1968.

Kolko, Gabriel. *The Roots of American Foreign Policy: An Analysis of Power and Purpose.* Boston: Beacon, 1969.

LaFeber, Walter. *America, Russia, and the Cold War: 1945–1966.* New York: Wiley, 1967.

Lerche, Charles O., Jr. *The Cold War . . . and After.* Englewood Cliffs, N.J.: Prentice-Hall, 1965.

Liska, George. *Imperial America: The International Politics of Primacy.* Baltimore, Md.: The Johns Hopkins Press, 1967.

McCarthy, Eugene J. *The Limits of Power: America's Role in the World.* New York: Holt, Rinehart and Winston, Inc., 1967.

McLellan, David S. *The Cold War in Transition.* New York: Crowell-Collier-Macmillan, 1966.

Morris, Bernard S. *International Communism and American Policy.* New York: Atherton, 1966.

Oglesby, Carl, and Richard Shaull. *Containment and Change.* New York: Crowell-Collier-Macmillan, 1967.

Pfeffer, Richard M., ed. *No More Vietnams? The War and the Future of American Foreign Policy.* New York: Harper & Row, 1968.

Seabury, Paul. *The Rise and Decline of the Cold War.* New York: Basic Books, 1967.

————, and Aaron Wildavsky, eds. *U.S. Foreign Policy: Perspectives and Proposals for the 1970s.* New York: McGraw-Hill, 1969.

Spanier, John. *American Foreign Policy since World War II,* 3d ed., rev. New York: Praeger, 1968.

Steel, Ronald. *Pax Americana.* New York: Viking, 1967.

Williams, William Appleman. *The Roots of the Modern American Empire.* New York: Random House, 1969.

The Structure and Process of Foreign-Policy Decision Making

Abel, Elie. *The Missile Crisis.* Philadelphia: Lippincott, 1966.

Acheson, Dean. *Present at the Creation: My Years in the State Department.* New York: Norton, 1969.

Armacost, Michael. *The Politics of Weapons Innovation.* New York: Columbia University Press, 1969.

Art, Robert J. *The TFX Decision: McNamara and the Military.* Boston: Little, Brown, 1968.

Baldwin, William L. *The Structure of the Defense Market, 1955–1964.* Durham, N.C.: Duke University Press, 1967.

Barnet, Richard J. *Intervention and Revolution: The United States and the Third World.* New York: World Publishing, 1968.

Bauer, Raymond A., Ithiel de Sola Pool, and Lewis A. Dexter. *American Business and Public Policy: The Politics of Foreign Trade.* New York: Atherton, 1963.

Beichman, Arnold. *The "Other" State Department.* New York: Basic Books, 1968.

Bohlen, Charles E. *The Transformation of American Foreign Policy.* New York: Norton, 1969.

Briggs, Ellis. *Anatomy of Diplomacy: The Origin and Execution of American Foreign Policy.* New York: McKay, 1968.

Carroll, Holbert N. *The House of Representatives and Foreign Affairs,* rev. ed. Boston: Little, Brown, 1966.

Chase, Harold W., and Allen H. Lerman, eds. *Kennedy and the Press: The News Conferences, Edited and Annotated.* New York: Crowell, 1965.

Chomsky, Noam. *American Power and the New Mandarins.* New York: Pantheon, 1969.

Clark, Keith C., and Laurence J. Legers, eds. *The President and the Management of National Security: A Report by the Institute for Defense Analyses.* New York: Praeger, 1969.

Cohen, Bernard C. *The Press and Foreign Policy.* Princeton, N.J.: Princeton University Press, 1963.

Conlin, Joseph R., ed. *American Anti-War Movements.* New York: Free Press, 1968.

Davis, Vincent. *The Admirals Lobby.* Chapel Hill, N.C.: University of North Carolina Press, 1967.

Derthick, Martha. *The National Guard in Politics.* Cambridge, Mass.: Harvard University Press, 1965.

Draper, Theodore. *The Dominican Revolt: A Case Study in American Policy.* New York: Commentary, 1968.

Dulles, Eleanor Lansing. *American Foreign Policy in the Making.* New York: Harper & Row, 1968.

Einstein, Lewis. *A Diplomat Looks Back,* Lawrence E. Gelfand, ed. New Haven, Conn.: Yale University Press, 1968.

Elder, Robert E. *The Information Machine.* Syracuse, N.Y.: Syracuse University Press, 1968.

———. *The Policy Machine: The Department of State and American Foreign Policy.* Syracuse, N.Y.: Syracuse University Press, 1960.

Ferguson, Ernest B. *Westmoreland: The Inevitable General.* Boston: Little, Brown, 1968.

Finletter, Thomas K. *Interim Report.* New York: Norton, 1968.

Fox, William T. R., and Annette Baker Fox. *NATO and the Range of American Choice.* New York: Columbia University Press, 1967.

Frankel, Joseph. *The Making of Foreign Policy: An Analysis of Decision Making.* New York: Oxford, 1963.

Fuchs, Lawrence H. *"Those Peculiar Americans": The Peace Corps and American National Character.* New York: Meredith, 1967.

Galbraith, John K. *Ambassador's Journal.* Boston: Houghton Mifflin, 1969.

————. *How to Control the Military.* New York: Doubleday, 1969.

Gerson, Lewis L. *John Foster Dulles.* New York: Cooper Square Publishers, Inc., 1968.

Graber, Doris A. *Public Opinion, the President, and Foreign Policy: Four Case Studies from the Formative Years.* New York: Holt, Rinehart and Winston, Inc., 1968.

Gurtov, Melvin. *The First Vietnam Crisis: Chinese Communist Strategy and United States Involvement, 1953–1954.* New York: Columbia University Press, 1967.

Hammond, Paul Y. *Organizing for Defense: The American Military Establishment in the Twentieth Century.* Princeton, N.J.: Princeton University Press, 1961.

Hapgood, David, and Meridan Bennett. *Agents of Change: A Close Look at the Peace Corps.* Boston: Little, Brown, 1968.

Harr, John Ensor. *The Professional Diplomat.* Princeton, N.J.: Princeton University Press, 1969.

Hero, Alfred. *The Southerner and World Affairs.* Baton Rouge, La.: Louisiana State University Press, 1965.

Hilsman, Roger. *To Move a Nation: The Politics of Foreign Policy in the Administration of John F. Kennedy.* New York: Doubleday, 1967.

Hoopes, Townsend. *The Limits of Intervention: An Inside Account of How the Johnson Policy of Escalation in Vietnam Was Reversed.* New York: McKay, 1969.

Huntington, Samuel P. *The Common Defense: Strategic Programs in National Politics.* New York: Columbia University Press, 1961.

Hutchins, Lavern C. *The John Birch Society and United States Foreign Policy.* New York: Pageant, 1968.

Jackson, Henry A., ed. *The National Security Council: Jackson Subcommittee Papers on Policy-Making at the Presidential Level.* New York: Praeger, 1965.

————. *The Secretary of State and the Ambassador: Jackson Subcommittee Papers on the Conduct of American Foreign Policy.* New York: Praeger, 1964.

Janeway, Eliot. *The Economics of Crisis: War, Politics, and the Dollar.* New York: Weybright and Talley, 1968.

Janowitz, Morris. *The Professional Soldier: A Social and Political Portrait.* New York: Free Press, 1960.

Jewell, Malcolm. *Senatorial Politics and Foreign Policy.* Lexington, Ky.: University of Kentucky Press, 1962.

Kennan, George F. *Memoirs: 1925–1950*. Boston: Little, Brown, 1967.

Kennedy, Robert. *Thirteen Days: A Memoir of the Cuban Missile Crisis*. New York: Norton, 1969.

Kirkpatrick, Lyman B., Jr. *The Real CIA*. New York: Crowell-Collier-Macmillan, 1968.

Kissinger, Henry A. *American Foreign Policy: Three Essays*. New York: Norton, 1969.

Knoll, Erwin, and Judith Nies McFadden, eds. *American Militarism, 1970: A Dialogue on the Distortion of Our National Priorities and the Need to Reassert Control over the Defense Establishment*. New York: Viking, 1969.

Landecker, Manfred. *The President and Public Opinion: Leadership in Foreign Affairs*. Washington, D.C.: Public Affairs Press, 1968.

Lapp, Ralph E. *The Weapons Culture*. New York: Norton, 1968.

Leacocos, John P. *Fires in the In-Basket: The ABC's of the State Department*. Cleveland, Ohio: World, 1968.

Levantrosser, William F. *Congress and the Citizen Soldier*. Columbus, Ohio: Ohio State University Press, 1969.

Lyons, Gene M., and Louis Morton. *Schools for Strategy: Education and Research in National Security Affairs*. New York: Praeger, 1965.

Moss, Norman. *Men Who Play God*. New York: Harper & Row, 1969.

Murphy, Robert. *Diplomat among Warriors*. New York: Doubleday, 1964.

Paige, Glenn D. *The Korean Decision: June 24–30, 1950*. New York: Free Press, 1968.

Raskin, Marcus G., and Bernard B. Fall, eds. *The Viet-Nam Reader: Articles and Documents on American Foreign Policy and the Viet-Nam Crisis*. New York: Random House, 1965.

Raymond, Jack. *Power at the Pentagon*. New York: Harper & Row, 1964.

Reston, James. *The Artillery of the Press: Its Influence on American Foreign Policy*. New York: Harper & Row, 1966.

Rieselbach, Leroy N. *The Roots of Isolationism: Congressional Voting and Presidential Leadership in Foreign Policy*. Indianapolis, Ind.: Bobbs-Merrill, 1966.

de Rivera, Joseph H. *The Psychological Dimension of Foreign Policy*. Columbus, Ohio: Merrill, 1968.

Robinson, James M. *Congress and Foreign Policy-Making*, rev. ed. Homewood, Ill.: Dorsey Press, 1967.

Rogow, Arnold A. *James Forrestal: A Study of Personality, Politics and Policy*. New York: Crowell-Collier-Macmillan, 1963.

Rosenau, James N. *National Leadership and Foreign Policy: A Case Study in the Mobilization of Public Support*. Princeton, N.J.: Princeton University Press, 1963.

————, ed. *Domestic Sources of Foreign Policy*. New York: Free Press, 1967.

Sapin, Burton M. *The Making of United States Foreign Policy*. Washington, D.C.: Brookings, 1966.

Schilling, Warner R., Paul Y. Hammond, and Glenn H. Snyder. *Strategy, Politics, and Defense Budgets*. New York: Columbia University Press, 1962.

Schlesinger, Arthur F., Jr. *A Thousand Days: John F. Kennedy in the White House*. Boston: Houghton Mifflin, 1965.

Scott, Andrew M., and Raymond H. Dawson, eds. *Readings in the Making of American Foreign Policy*. New York: Crowell-Collier-Macmillan, 1965.

Simpson, Smith. *Anatomy of the State Department*. Boston: Beacon, 1968.

Skolnikoff, Eugene B. *Science, Technology, and American Foreign Policy*. Cambridge, Mass.: M.I.T. Press, 1967.

Smith, Bruce L. R. *The RAND Corporation: Case Study of a Nonprofit Advisory Corporation*. Cambridge, Mass.: Harvard University Press, 1966.

Snyder, Richard C., H. W. Bruck, and Burton Sapin. *Foreign Policy Decision-Making: An Approach to the Study of International Politics*. New York: Free Press, 1962.

Sorensen, Theodore C. *Kennedy*. New York: Harper & Row, 1965.

Stein, Harold, ed. *American Civil-Military Decisions: A Book of Case Studies*. University, Ala.: University of Alabama Press, 1963.

Szulc, Tad. *Dominican Diary*. New York: Dell, 1966.

———, and Karl E. Meyer. *The Cuban Invasion: Chronicle of a Disaster*. New York: Ballantine, 1962.

Thayer, George. *The War Business*. New York: Simon and Schuster, 1969.

Vagts, Alfred. *The Military Attaché*. Princeton, N.J.: Princeton University Press, 1967.

Van Dyke, Vernon. *Pride and Power: The Rationale of the Space Program*. Urbana, Ill.: University of Illinois Press, 1964.

Walton, Richard J. *The Remnants of Power: The Tragic Last Years of Adlai Stevenson*. New York: Coward-McCann, 1968.

Waltz, Kenneth N. *Foreign Policy and Democratic Politics: The American and British Experience*. Boston: Little, Brown, 1967.

Wise, David, and Thomas B. Ross. *The Invisible Government*. New York: Random House, 1964.

Wohlstetter, Roberta. *Pearl Harbor: Warning and Decision*. Stanford, Calif.: Stanford University Press, 1962.

Indexes

Name Index

Subject Index